DRAWING NEAR

John F. MacArthur, Jr.

CROSSWAY BOOKS

WHEATON, ILLINOIS

Drawing Near.

Copyright © 1993 by John F. MacArthur, Jr.

Published by Crossway Books
   a publishing ministry of Good News Publishers
   1300 Crescent Street
   Wheaton, Illinois 60187.

Cover photo: Dick Dietrich

Case design: Jennifer Kok

Art Direction / Design: Mark Schramm

First printing, 1993

First trade paperback edition, 2002

Printed in the United States of America

All Scripture quotations in this book, except those noted otherwise, are from the *New American Standard Bible*, © 1960, 1962, 1963, 1968, 1971, 1972, 1973, 1975, and 1977 by The Lockman Foundation, and are used by permission.

Library of Congress Cataloging-in-Publication Data
MacArthur, John, 1939
  Drawing near / John F. MacArthur, Jr..
   p. cm.
  1. Devotional calendars. 2. Christian life—1960- I. Title.
ISBN 13: 978-1-58134-413-4
ISBN 10: 1-58134-413-9
BV4811.M23 1993   242'.2—dc20   93-5469

VP		18	17	16	15	14	13	12	11	10	09	08
20	19	18	17	16	15	14	13	12	11	10	9	

DRAWING NEAR

For Jonathan
Merry Christmas
2009!

I am praying that
the Lord will strengthen
your heart and faith
as you faithfully draw
near to Him. I hope this
book will be an encouragement to you in being
reminded about our Great
God and His great Truth.
I care about your heart.

I love you!
Mom

To Dick Mayhue—
his friendship, loyalty, and ongoing leadership of
The Master's Seminary have been a tool of the Lord
to do exceeding abundantly above
all I could ask or think

Contents

Introduction

Throughout the years of my ministry, I can't count the number of times people have asked me about Bible study. How to do it, when to do it, and why to do it are a few of the basic questions. While those are important, you can't get past the simple fact that you must do it. Your life as a Christian depends on it.

Real growth in your spiritual life takes place only by daily exposure to God's Word. The Apostle Peter put it this way: "Like newborn babes, long for the pure milk of the word, that by it you may grow in respect to salvation" (1 Peter 2:2). I find that the longer, the more intensely, and the more devotedly I look into the glory of Jesus Christ through the pages of Scripture, the more the Spirit of God changes my life into the image of Christ. But there are no shortcuts. If you and I are to grow, to mature, and to finally be transformed, we must feed on the Word!

Unfortunately, our entertainment-conscious, quick-fix, fast-food society does everything it can to divert us from setting aside time to study God's Word. As you well know from your own efforts, Bible study is not often entertaining—it's hard work. It takes discipline to set aside time each day to reap the benefits such study has to offer.

If you reach an impasse when it's time to sit down, open your Bible, and try to decide what to do, you're not alone. Without some plan to follow, it's easy to become frustrated and eventually give up after only one or two days. That's where this book comes in.

For many years I've had the desire to produce a book that could be used as a daily devotional guide, yet offer significantly more than the typical thematic or topical anecdotes that make up the majority of devotionals. It would also need to reflect what I am committed to: an in-depth approach to Bible exposition. And this book does just that, drawing from the main passages I have taught over the years.

This devotional is designed to be used 365 days a year. Each month will lead you through an entire chapter or portion of Scripture, usually a verse or two at a time each day. By the time you have spent a year studying this material, you will have gained a firm grasp of many of the great texts of the Bible.

But this is not simply an intellectual exercise. The real benefit of studying God's Word is the practical applications you draw from it. So while you are studying verse by verse through a passage, you'll find that each day stands on its own and makes direct application to your life.

To achieve these benefits, you need to be willing to make the sacrifice necessary to be what God wants you to be. I've always believed that the first step in becoming self-disciplined is to start small. Setting an attainable goal allows you to accomplish one thing, however small, and encourages you to forge ahead to greater things. Thus as you begin your study, have limited goals. Each day's plan is short enough to allow you to read the Scripture passage and lesson, and take time to pray.

The first few days and weeks are critical as you begin to cultivate the daily habit of Bible study. As you become more consistent, you'll want to expand your time to include the suggestions for further study. You'll probably find yourself discovering other related passages to pursue. Don't let the format restrict you— follow the Lord's prompting.

As you use this book daily, you will learn how to approach Scripture on your own, developing the study skills you need to open up the Bible and discover its rich and marvelous truths for yourself. Such repeated exposure to God's Word trains you to think Biblically, and that's what ultimately makes a difference in your spiritual life. The added Bible reading schedule will take you through the entire Bible in a year's time.

It is my prayer that you will be "one who looks intently at the perfect law, the law of liberty and abides by it, not having become a forgetful hearer but an effectual doer" (James 1:25). May this devotional be a wonderful encouragement in that pursuit!

Daily Readings

"Paul, an apostle of Christ Jesus by the will of God, to the saints who are at Ephesus, and who are faithful in Christ Jesus" (Eph. 1:1).

❖❖❖

God is more interested in your faithfulness than
He is in your accomplishments.

Our society is success-oriented. We love success stories. We even have television programs that exalt the lifestyles of the rich and famous. But God's standard for success is quite different. Unimpressed by our status or wealth, He looks instead for faithfulness to His will.

Paul understood that principle and diligently pursued his calling as an apostle—one of those unique men who were foundational to the church and who were recipients, teachers, and writers of the New Testament.

That was a high calling, and yet, judging from Paul's lifestyle, most people would hardly call him successful—having suffered imprisonments, beatings, death threats, shipwrecks, robberies, hatred from his theological enemies, sleepless nights, hunger, thirst, and exposure to the elements (2 Cor. 11:23-27). But none of those things deterred him from obeying God's will. His final testimony was, "I have fought the good fight, I have finished the course, I have kept the faith" (2 Tim. 4:7). That's true success!

Although we're not apostles, we're to follow Paul's example of faithfulness (1 Cor. 11:1). That's possible because, like the Ephesian believers, we are "saints [holy ones] . . . who are faithful in Christ Jesus" (Eph. 1:1). By God's grace we've trusted in Christ as our Lord and Savior (Eph. 2:8-9) and have received His righteousness (Phil. 3:9) and His Spirit (Eph. 3:16) and every spiritual resource necessary for faithful, victorious Christian living (Eph. 1:3).

What remains is to cultivate greater love for Christ and more consistent obedience to His Word. Those are the hallmarks of a true disciple and God's measure of success. Make it your goal that your life today warrants the Lord's commendation: "Well done, good and faithful [servant]" (Matt. 25:21).

❖❖❖

Suggestions for Prayer: Praise God for His wonderful grace, by which He granted you salvation and all the spiritual resources you need. ❖ Thank Him for His Word, through which you learn the principles of godly living. ❖ Ask Him for opportunities today to encourage the faithfulness of others.

For Further Study: Read Ephesians 1:3-4; 2:10; Titus 2:11-12. ❖ What is the goal of your salvation? ❖ Are you living each day in light of that goal?

"Grace to you and peace from God our Father and the Lord Jesus Christ" (Eph. 1:2).

❖❖❖

True peace is God's gift to those who love and obey Him.

Throughout history mankind has sought peace through military alliances, balances of power, and leagues of nations. Yet lasting peace still remains an elusive dream. Even during times of relative peace, nations struggle with internal strife and crime.

The Bible says that man on his own cannot know peace because he is alienated from its source. But we need not despair. True peace is immediately available from God our Father ("the God of peace," Rom. 15:33) and from the Lord Jesus Christ (the "Prince of Peace," Isa. 9:6). It's a gift of God's grace to those who love and obey Jesus Christ.

The New Testament so clearly teaches the inextricable link between God's grace and peace that "Grace to you and peace" became a common greeting in the early church. Grace is God's great kindness toward those who are undeserving of His favor but who have placed their faith in Jesus Christ. It is the fountain, and peace is the stream. As recipients of His grace, we have "peace with God" (Rom. 5:1); we are reconciled to Him through faith in His Son, and we will never experience His wrath. We also have the "peace *of* God" (Phil. 4:7, emphasis added)—the Spirit's way of assuring us that God is in control even in the midst of difficult circumstances. That's why Paul calls it the peace that "surpasses all comprehension" (Phil. 4:7).

The world's peace is relative and fleeting because it is grounded in circumstances. God's peace is absolute and eternal because it is grounded in His grace.

Does God's peace reign in your heart, or have you allowed sin or difficult circumstances to diminish your devotion to Christ?

❖❖❖

Suggestions for Prayer: Thank God that you have peace with Him through faith in Jesus Christ. ❖ Ask the Spirit to reveal any sin that might be hindering God's peace from ruling in your heart. Be prepared to respond in confession and repentance. ❖ Ask for opportunities to demonstrate God's peace to others today.

For Further Study: Read Philippians 4:6-7. ❖ What is God's antidote for anxiety? ❖ How does God's peace affect a believer's heart and mind?

"Blessed be the God and Father of our Lord Jesus Christ, who has blessed us . . ." (Eph. 1:3).

✧✧✧

When we bless God, it is with words of praise; when He blesses us, it is with deeds of kindness.

Paul's brief doxology identifies God the Father as the ultimate recipient and source of blessing—the One to whom blessing is ascribed and the One who bestows blessings on those who love Him.

"Blessed" translates the Greek word *eulogeō*, from which we get *eulogy*. To bless or eulogize God is to praise Him for His mighty works and holy character.

That should be the response of your heart and mine, just as it has been the response of believers throughout the ages. The psalmist said, "Blessed be God, who has not turned away my prayer" (Ps. 66:20); and "Blessed be the Lord God, the God of Israel, who alone works wonders" (Ps. 72:18). Peter said, "Blessed be the God and Father of our Lord Jesus Christ, who according to His great mercy has caused us to be born again to a living hope through the resurrection of Jesus Christ from the dead" (1 Peter 1:3).

When the situation is reversed and God blesses us, it isn't with praise, for apart from Him there is nothing praiseworthy about us. Instead, He gives us undeserved benefits through His many deeds of kindness. Scripture identifies Him as the source of every good thing (James 1:17), who works all things together for our good and His glory (Rom. 8:28).

That is but a sampling of the many blessings He lavishes on us in His Son, Jesus Christ. It's a marvelous cycle: God blesses us with deeds of kindness; we bless Him with words of praise.

Beware of the sin of thanklessness. Recognize God's blessings in your life, and let them fill your heart and lips with humble, sincere praise.

✧✧✧

Suggestions for Prayer: Identify ten specific blessings God has granted to you in recent days, and praise Him for each one. ✧ Ask Him to make you more aware of and thankful for His goodness in your life. ✧ Always be ready to seek forgiveness when you take His blessings for granted.

For Further Study: Read Psalm 103. ✧ What blessings does David mention? ✧ How do they apply to your life?

"God . . . has blessed us with every spiritual blessing" (Eph. 1:3, emphasis added).

❖❖❖

**As a Christian, you possess every spiritual resource
you need to fulfill God's will for your life.**

The story is told of a wealthy London businessman who searched many years for his runaway son. One afternoon he was preparing to board a train to London when he spotted a man in ragged, dirty clothing begging for money from passengers along the station platform. His first impulse was to avoid the beggar, but there was something strangely familiar about him.

When the beggar approached and asked if the man could spare a few shillings, the businessman realized he had found his long-lost son. With tears in his eyes and joy in his voice he embraced his son, crying, "A few shillings? You are my son—everything I have is yours!"

That pictures many Christians who are ignorant or negligent of their spiritual resources. They are children of the King, yet live like spiritual paupers.

Paul repeatedly emphasized our sufficiency as believers. In Colossians 2:10 he declares that in Christ "you have been made complete." In Philippians 4:13, 19 he says, "I can do all things through Him who strengthens me . . . my God shall supply all your needs according to His riches in glory in Christ Jesus." Peter adds that God's "divine power has granted to us everything pertaining to life and godliness" (2 Peter 1:3).

The word translated "spiritual" in Ephesians 1:3 speaks of the work of the Holy Spirit. Every blessing you receive, whether material or immaterial, has God as its source.

As a Christian, you possess every spiritual resource you need to fulfill God's will for your life. You need not pray for more love, for example, because His love is already poured out in your heart through the Holy Spirit (Rom. 5:5). The same is true of joy (John 15:11), peace (John 14:27), strength (Phil. 4:13), and every other resource you need.

The key to spiritual progress and victory is learning to apply what you already have, not seeking more.

❖❖❖

Suggestions for Prayer: Praise God for His abundant spiritual resources. ❖ Ask Him to help you apply them with wisdom and consistency.

For Further Study: Read Matthew 6:25-34 and Philippians 4:6-8. ❖ What specific promises does God make in those passages? ❖ What does He require of you?

"God . . . has blessed us with every spiritual blessing in the heavenly places" (Eph. 1:3, emphasis added).

❖❖❖

Christians hold a dual citizenship. We are citizens of earth, but, more importantly, we are also citizens of Heaven.

It's been said that some Christians are so heavenly-minded, they're no earthly good. But usually the opposite is true. Many Christians are so enamored with this present world that they no longer look forward to Heaven. They have everything they want right here. The health, wealth, and prosperity doctrine has convinced them that Christians can have it all, so they pursue "the good life" with a vengeance.

Despite the prevalence of such thinking, the old Negro spiritual says well, "This world is not my home, I'm just a passin' through."

Paul reminds us of that truth in Philippians 3:20: "Our citizenship is in heaven, from which also we eagerly wait for a Savior, the Lord Jesus Christ." That's why we must set our minds on heavenly, not on earthly, things (Col. 3:1-2). Our deepest affections and highest aspirations should center there. Our actions and decisions should reflect heavenly priorities, not earthly indulgences.

Even though we live in a sin-stained world and must constantly fight against its corrupting influences, God hasn't left us stranded. He extends to us all the rights and privileges of our heavenly citizenship. Let that assurance encourage you today to live to His glory and to rely on His heavenly provisions. Take care not to let impure aspirations or trivial pursuits distract you from your heavenly priorities.

❖❖❖

Suggestions for Prayer: Tell Jesus how thankful and full of praise you are because of the place He is preparing for you in Heaven (John 14:1-3). ❖ Pray for a greater awareness of the fleeting value of this world and the surpassing value of the world to come (1 John 2:17).

For Further Study: Read Revelation 4, 5, 21. ❖ What primary activity are the inhabitants of Heaven engaged in? ❖ List some of Heaven's blessings.

> *"God . . . has blessed us with every spiritual blessing in the heavenly places* in Christ" *(Eph. 1:3, emphasis added).*

✧✧✧

Christianity isn't simply a belief system—it's a whole new identity.

Many people mistakenly believe that one's religious preference is irrelevant because all religions eventually lead to the same spiritual destination.

Such thinking is sheer folly, however, because Scripture declares that no one comes to God apart from Jesus (John 14:6). He is the only source of salvation (Acts 4:12) and the only One powerful enough to redeem us and hold us secure forever (John 10:28).

Every Christian shares a common supernatural union with Christ. Paul said, "The one who joins himself to the Lord is one spirit with Him" (1 Cor. 6:17). We are in Him, and He is in us. His life flows through us by His Spirit, who indwells us (Rom. 8:9).

As a non-Christian, you were in bondage to evil (Rom. 3:10-12), enslaved to the will of Satan (1 John 5:19), under divine wrath (Rom. 1:18), spiritually dead (Eph. 2:1; 4:17-18), and without hope (Eph. 2:12). But at the moment of your salvation a dramatic change took place. You became a new creation in Christ (2 Cor. 5:17), alive in Him (Eph. 2:5), enslaved to God (Rom. 6:22), and a recipient of divine grace (Eph. 2:8). When you came to Christ, you were "delivered . . . from the domain of darkness, and transferred . . . to the kingdom of [God's] beloved Son" (Col. 1:13). You now possess His righteousness (2 Cor. 5:21) and share in His eternal inheritance (Rom. 8:16-17).

All those blessings—and many more—are yours because you are in Christ. What a staggering reality! In a sense, what He is, you are. What He has, you have. Where He is, you are.

When the Father sees you, He sees you in Christ and blesses you accordingly. When others see you, do they see Christ in you? "Let your light shine before men in such a way that they may see your good works, and glorify your Father who is in heaven" (Matt. 5:16).

✧✧✧

Suggestions for Prayer: Thank God for His marvelous grace in taking you from spiritual death to spiritual life in Christ. ✧ Ask Him for wisdom and discernment to live this day for His good pleasure.

For Further Study: Read the book of Ephesians, noting every occurrence of the phrase "in Christ." ✧ What has God accomplished in Christ? ✧ What blessings are yours in Christ?

*God "chose us in [Christ] before the foundation of the world"
(Eph. 1:4).*

❖❖❖

**A true sense of identity comes from knowing that God Himself
personally selected you to be His child.**

Many people in our society are on a seemingly endless and often frantic quest for personal identity and self-worth. Identity crises are common at almost every age level. Superficial love and fractured relationships are but symptoms of our failure to resolve the fundamental issues of who we are, why we exist, and where we're going. Sadly, most people will live and die without ever understanding God's purpose for their lives.

That is tragic, yet understandable. God created man to bear His image and enjoy His fellowship forever. But when Adam and Eve disobeyed God, they violated that purpose and plunged the human race into sin. That created within man a spiritual void and an identity crisis of unimaginable proportions. Throughout the ages ungodly people have tried to fill that void with a myriad of substitutes, but ultimately all is lost to death and despair.

Despite that bleak picture, a true sense of identity is available to every Christian. It comes from knowing that God Himself personally selected you to be His child. Before the world began, God set His love upon you; it was according to His plan that Christ died for you (1 Peter 1:20). That's why you responded in faith to the gospel (2 Thess. 2:13). Also, that's why you can never lose your salvation. The same God who drew you to Himself will hold you there securely (John 10:29).

Don't allow sin, Satan, or circumstances to rob you of your sense of identity in Christ. Make it the focus of everything you do. Remember who you are—God's child; why you are here—to serve and glorify Him; and where you are going—Heaven, where you will spend eternity in His presence.

❖❖❖

Suggestions for Prayer: Thank God for choosing you to be His child and for drawing you to Himself in saving faith. ❖ Praise Him for His promise never to let you go.

For Further Study: Read John 6:35-44; 10:27-30; Romans 8:31-39. ❖ According to Jesus, how many believers will lose their salvation? What was His reasoning? ❖ What did Paul base his certainty on?

"[God] chose us . . . that we should be holy and blameless before Him" (Eph. 1:4).

❖❖❖

**The challenge of Christian living is to increasingly
match your practice to your position.**

God chose you in Christ to make you "holy and blameless" in His sight. To be "holy" is to be separated from sin and devoted to righteousness. To be "blameless" is to be pure, without spot or blemish—like Jesus, the Lamb of God (1 Peter 1:19).

Ephesians 1:4 is a positional statement. That is, Paul describes how God views us "in Him [Christ]." God sees us as "holy and blameless" because Christ our Savior is holy and blameless. His purity is credited to our spiritual bank account. That's because God made Christ "who knew no sin to be sin on our behalf, that we might become the righteousness of God in Him" (2 Cor. 5:21).

Despite our exalted position in God's sight, our practice often falls far short of His holy standard. Therefore, the challenge of Christian living is to increasingly match our practice to our position, realizing that sinless perfection won't come until we are fully glorified in Heaven (Rom. 8:23).

How do you meet that challenge? By prayer, Bible study, and yielding your life to the Spirit's control. Commit yourself to those priorities today as you seek to fulfill the great purpose to which you've been called—the "good works, which God prepared beforehand, that we should walk in them" (Eph. 2:10).

❖❖❖

Suggestions for Prayer: Thank God that He does not expect you to earn your own righteousness but has provided it in His Son. ❖ Ask His Spirit to search your heart and reveal any sin that might hinder your growth in holiness. Confess that sin, and take any steps necessary to eliminate it from your life.

For Further Study: Read Philippians 1:9-11. ❖ What ingredients must be added to Christian love to produce sincerity and blamelessness? ❖ What is the primary source of those ingredients (see Ps. 119:97-105)? ❖ What specific steps are you going to take to add or increase those ingredients in your life?

"In love [God] predestined us to adoption as sons through Jesus Christ to Himself, according to the kind intention of His will" (Eph. 1:4-5).

❖❖❖

Because God loves you, He adopted you as His child and grants you all the rights and privileges of family membership.

Moses told Israel that God didn't choose them because of their great numbers or any inherent goodness on their part, but as an expression of God's sovereign will and sacrificial love (Deut. 7:7-8). That's true of you as well if you're a Christian.

The Greek word translated "love" in Ephesians 1:4 speaks not of emotional or sentimental love but of love that seeks God's best for others at any cost. It is marked by sacrifice rather than selfishness—giving rather than receiving. It seeks to forgive rather than condemn—to dismiss offenses rather than count them.

Such love is epitomized in God Himself, who loved you so much that He sacrificed His Son on your behalf as He willingly laid down His own life for you (John 3:16; 15:13).

While false gods are worshiped out of fear and ignorance, the true God—your Heavenly Father—has eliminated all fear so that you can confidently enter into His presence (Heb. 10:19; 1 John 4:18). You have "received a spirit of adoption" and can address Him as "Abba! Father!" (Rom. 8:15), *Abba* being the Aramaic equivalent of "Daddy" or "Papa."

Your Heavenly Father delights in your praise and glories in your obedience. Be a faithful child. Make this day count for Him. Live out your royal heritage. Seek His wisdom in all you do. Go to His Word, and follow its counsel. Demonstrate His love to others in practical ways.

❖❖❖

Suggestions for Prayer: Thank God for granting you the privilege of being a member of His family. ❖ Thank Him for the many manifestations of His love that you enjoy each day. ❖ Ask Him to lead you to someone to whom you can demonstrate His love in a practical and sacrificial way.

For Further Study: Read 1 Corinthians 13. ❖ List the characteristics of godly love. ❖ How does the quality of your love for others compare to God's standard? What steps can you take today to bring your love into greater conformity to His?

*God chose us "to the praise of the glory of His grace, which He
freely bestowed on us in [His beloved Son]" (Eph. 1:6).*

❖❖❖

You were created to glorify God.

Henry Martyn, an Englishman, served as a missionary in India and
Persia in the late eighteenth and early nineteenth centuries. Upon his
arrival in Calcutta he cried out, "Let me burn out for God." As he watched the
people prostrating themselves before their pagan idols and heard blasphemy
uttered against Christ, he wrote, "This excited more horror in me than I can
well express. . . . I could not endure existence if Jesus was not glorified; it
would be hell to me, if He were to be always thus dishonored" (John Stott,
Our Guilty Silence [Downers Grove, Ill: InterVarsity Press, 1967], pp. 21, 22).

Martyn had a passion for God's glory—and he was in good company.
Angels glorify God (Luke 2:14), as do the heavens (Ps. 19:1) and even animals (Isa. 43:20). But as a believer, you glorify God in a unique way because
you are a testimony to His redeeming grace.

You were created for the purpose of glorifying God—even in the most
mundane activities of life, such as eating and drinking (1 Cor. 10:31). You are
to flee immorality so you can glorify God in your body (1 Cor. 6:18-20). You
are to walk worthy of your calling, so "that the name of our Lord Jesus may
be glorified" (2 Thess. 1:12).

Glorifying God is an enormous privilege and an awesome responsibility.
When others see His character on display in your life, it reminds them of His
power, goodness, and grace. But when they don't, God is dishonored, and His
character is called into question.

Aim your life at God's glory; make it the standard by which you evaluate
everything you do.

❖❖❖

Suggestions for Prayer: Thank the Lord for the privilege of glorifying Him.
❖ Ask Him to show you any areas of your life that do not honor Him. ❖ Find
a trusted Christian friend who will pray with you and hold you accountable
for the areas in which you know you need to change.

For Further Study: Read Exodus 33:12–34:9. ❖ What did Moses request? ❖
What was God's response, and what does this teach us about His glory?

"In [Christ] we have redemption" (Eph. 1:7).

❖❖❖

Slavery to sin is bondage; slavery to God is freedom.

Freedom is a precious thing. People throughout history have prayed, fought, and even died for it. Our Declaration of Independence upholds it as one of our inalienable rights.

But the truth is, no matter what one's political situation might be, everyone is a slave—either to sin or to God. Jesus said that "everyone who commits sin is the slave of sin" (John 8:34). Paul added that all of creation is in slavery to corruption (Rom. 8:21). However, believers have "been freed from sin and enslaved to God" (Rom. 6:22).

The Roman Empire had as many as twenty million slaves; slave trade was a major industry. For a slave to gain his or her freedom, a redemption price had to be paid. The Greek word for such a transaction is *lutroō*, which Paul uses in Ephesians 1:7 to speak of our "redemption" from sin's bondage.

Slavery to sin is bondage; slavery to God is freedom. That sounds paradoxical, but God is the Sovereign King, and true freedom means having the ability to bend your will to His and thereby become all He created you to be. Even though you will fail at times, your greatest desire and highest pursuit as a believer is to be like Christ (1 John 2:5-6). Those enslaved to sin cannot do that, nor do they want to.

Today you will have many opportunities to demonstrate your submission to Christ. Let your attitudes and actions speak clearly of your love for the Master.

❖❖❖

Suggestions for Prayer: Thank the Lord that He is a faithful and just Master who always does what is best for His servants. ❖ A self-seeking slave is a contradiction in terms. Ask the Lord to guard you from thoughts and actions that are contrary to His will.

For Further Study: According to 1 Corinthians 4:1-2 what key characteristic is required of a servant of Christ? ❖ Read Matthew 24:42-51. How does Jesus describe a wise servant? ❖ Read Philippians 2:5-11. How did Jesus demonstrate the heart of a servant? What implications does His example have for your life?

"In [Christ] we have redemption through His blood" (Eph. 1:7, emphasis added).

❖❖❖

Redeeming grace is free to us, but its cost to God is inestimable.

Sin is not a serious issue to most people. Our culture flaunts and peddles it in countless forms. Even Christians who would never think of committing certain sins will often allow themselves to be entertained by those same sins through television, movies, music, and other media.

We sometimes flirt with sin, but God hates it. The price He paid to redeem us from it speaks of the seriousness with which He views it. After all, we "were not redeemed with perishable things like silver or gold . . . but with precious blood, as of a lamb unblemished and spotless, the blood of Christ" (1 Peter 1:18-19).

In Scripture the shedding of blood refers to violent physical death—whether of a sacrificial animal or of Christ Himself. Sin is so serious that without bloodshed, there is no forgiveness of sin in God's sight (Heb. 9:22).

The sacrificial animals in the Old Testament pictured Christ's sacrifice on the cross. That's why John the Baptist called Jesus "the Lamb of God who takes away the sin of the world" (John 1:29).

The Old Testament sacrifices were necessary but incomplete. Christ's sacrifice was perfect, complete, and once for all (Heb. 10:10). No further sacrifices are needed other than the "sacrifice of praise to God" for what He has done (Heb. 13:15) and our very lives in service to Him as "a living and holy sacrifice" (Rom. 12:1).

By His sacrifice Christ demonstrated not only God's hatred for sin, but also His great love for sinners. You could never redeem yourself, but Christ willingly paid the price with His own precious blood. He "gave Himself up for [you], an offering and a sacrifice to God as a fragrant aroma" (Eph. 5:2). His sacrifice was acceptable to the Father; so your redemption was paid in full.

❖❖❖

Suggestions for Prayer: Worship God for His wonderful plan of salvation. ❖ Worship Christ for the enormous sacrifice He made on your behalf. ❖ Worship the Holy Spirit for applying Christ's sacrifice to your life and for drawing you to Christ in saving faith. ❖ Ask God to help you guard your heart from flirting with sin.

For Further Study: Read 2 Samuel 11. ❖ What circumstances led to David's sin with Bathsheba? ❖ How did David attempt to cover his sin? ❖ How did David finally deal with his sin (see Ps. 51)?

"In Christ we have . . . the forgiveness of our trespasses, according to the riches of [God's] grace, which He lavished upon us" (Eph. 1:7-8).

✧✧✧

In Christ we have infinite forgiveness for every sin— past, present, and future.

On Israel's Day of Atonement (Yom Kippur), the high priest selected two goats. One was sacrificed, the other set free. Before releasing the second goat, the high priest symbolically placed the sins of the people on it by laying his hands on its head. This "scapegoat" was then taken a great distance from camp and released—never to return again (Lev. 16:7-10).

The Greek word translated "forgiveness" in Ephesians 1:7 means "to send away." It speaks of canceling a debt or granting a pardon. Like the scapegoat, Christ carried away our sins on the cross.

In Christ, God canceled your debt and pardoned your transgressions, and He did so "according to the riches of His grace, which He lavished upon [you]" (v. 8). That means you have infinite forgiveness, because God's grace is infinite. You cannot sin beyond God's grace, because where sin abounds, grace super-abounds (Rom. 5:20).

God delights in lavishing His grace upon you. Such grace is overflowing and cannot be contained. You are forgiven for every sin—past, present, and future. You will never be condemned by God or separated from Him (Rom. 8:1-2, 31-39). Even when you fail, God doesn't hold your sins against you. Christ bore them all so that you might know the joy and peace that freedom from sin and guilt brings.

Let the reality of God's grace fill your heart with joy and assurance. Let the responsibility of glorifying Him fill you with awe and reverence. Let this day be a sacrifice of praise and service to Him.

✧✧✧

Suggestions for Prayer: Thank God for His infinite grace and forgiveness. ✧ Look for opportunities to extend forgiveness to others.

For Further Study: Read Matthew 18:21-35. ✧ What characteristic marked the wicked slave? ✧ What was the king's response to the wicked slave's actions? ✧ What point was Jesus making? How does it apply to you?

"In all wisdom and insight [God] made known to us the mystery of His will" (Eph. 1:8-9).

❖❖❖

***Even if you haven't obtained academic degrees,
you have wisdom that far surpasses the most educated unbeliever.***

When God redeemed you, He not only forgave your trespasses and removed the guilt and penalty of sin, but He also gave you spiritual wisdom and insight—two essential elements for godly living. Together they speak of the ability to understand God's will and to apply it to your life in practical ways.

As a believer, you understand the most sublime truths of all. For example, you know that God created the world and controls the course of history. You know that mankind's reason for existence is to know and glorify Him. You have goals and priorities that transcend earthly circumstances and limitations.

Such wisdom and insight escapes unbelievers because they tend to view the things of God with disdain (1 Cor. 2:14). But you "have the mind of Christ" (v. 16). His Word reveals His will, and His Spirit gives you the desire and ability to understand and obey it.

Today is another opportunity to cultivate that desire through diligent prayer and Bible study. Let the psalmist's commitment be yours: "O how I love Thy law! It is my meditation all the day. Thy commandments make me wiser than my enemies. . . . I have more insight than all my teachers. . . . I understand more than the aged. . . . I have restrained my feet from every evil way, that I may keep Thy word" (Ps. 119:97-101).

❖❖❖

Suggestions for Prayer: Thank God for the wisdom and insight He gives you through His Word. ❖ If you have neglected the Word, ask His forgiveness, and begin once again to refresh your spirit with its truths. ❖ Ask for wisdom to respond Biblically to every situation you face today.

For Further Study: Many Christians think God's will is vague or hidden from them. But Scripture mentions several specific aspects of His will. Once you align yourself with those specifics, the Spirit will direct you in the other areas of your life. ❖ List six elements of God's will from these passages: Ephesians 5:17-18; 1 Thessalonians 4:3; 1 Thessalonians 5:18; 1 Peter 2:13-15; 1 Peter 3:17; 2 Peter 3:9. ❖ Are you following God's will in those areas? If not, what steps can you take today to do so?

"[God] made known to us the mystery of His will, according to His kind intention which He purposed in [Christ] with a view to an administration suitable to the fulness of the times, that is, the summing up of all things in Christ, things in the heavens and things upon the earth" (Eph. 1:9-10).

❖❖❖

God is intimately involved in the flow of human history and is directing its course toward a specific, predetermined climax.

For centuries men of various philosophical schools have debated the cause, course, and climax of human history. Some deny God and therefore deny any divine involvement in history. Others believe that God set everything in motion, then withdrew to let it progress on its own. Still others believe that God is intimately involved in the flow of human history and is directing its course toward a specific, predetermined climax.

In Ephesians 1:9-10 Paul settles that debate by reminding us that Jesus Himself is the goal of human history. In Him all things will be summed up; all human history will be resolved and united to the Father through the work of the Son.

As Paul said elsewhere, "It was the Father's good pleasure for all the fulness [of deity] to dwell in [Christ], and through Him to reconcile all things to Himself, having made peace through the blood of His cross" (Col. 1:19-20). The culmination of Christ's reconciling work will come during His millennial Kingdom (Rev. 20). Following that, He will usher in the eternal state with a new heaven and new earth (Rev. 21).

Despite the political uncertainty and military unrest in the world today, be assured that God is in control. He governs the world (Isa. 40:22-24), the nations (Isa. 40:15-17), and individuals as well (Prov. 16:9). God's timetable is right on schedule. Nothing takes Him by surprise, and nothing thwarts His purposes. Ultimately He will vanquish evil and will make everything right in Christ.

❖❖❖

Suggestions for Prayer: Thank God for the wisdom and insight He gives you to see beyond your temporal circumstances to His eternal purposes. ❖ Live today with that perspective in mind.

For Further Study: Read Revelation 20. ❖ What happens to Satan prior to the millennial Kingdom? ❖ How does Satan meet his final doom? ❖ What happens at the Great White Throne Judgment?

"In [Christ] also we have obtained an inheritance" (Eph. 1:10-11).

❖❖❖

***As a member of God's family, you have obtained a future inheritance
that has many present benefits.***

An inheritance is something received by an heir as the result of a will or a legal process. It's a legacy one receives from family connections.

As a member of God's family, you are an heir of God and a fellow-heir with Christ (Rom. 8:17). As such you have obtained an inheritance that Peter called "imperishable and undefiled . . . reserved in heaven for you" (1 Peter 1:4). It cannot perish, fade away, or be defiled because Heaven is timeless and sinless. It is a secure inheritance.

In Ephesians 1:11 Paul refers to it in the past tense ("have obtained"). That's significant, because the fullness of your inheritance won't be revealed until you are glorified in God's presence (1 John 3:2). But your inheritance is so sure that Paul refers to it as if it is already in hand.

Although its fullness lies in the future, your inheritance has present benefits. In addition to inheriting Christ and the Holy Spirit, you also inherit peace, love, grace, wisdom, joy, victory, strength, guidance, mercy, forgiveness, righteousness, discernment, and every other possible spiritual benefit. Paul sums it all up in 1 Corinthians 3:22-23: "All things belong to you . . . and you belong to Christ; and Christ belongs to God."

Nowadays many Christians are so preoccupied with acquiring material goods that they miss many of the present benefits of their spiritual inheritance and the joy of anticipating its future fulfillment. Don't fall into that trap!

Looking forward to your eternal inheritance will help you maintain a proper perspective on temporal things and will motivate you to praise and adore God.

❖❖❖

Suggestions for Prayer: Praise the Lord for the incredible inheritance that awaits you in Heaven. ❖ Thank Him for the present benefits of your inheritance, which are yours to enjoy daily.

For Further Study: One precious aspect of your eternal inheritance is God's mercy. Psalm 136 reflects on the lovingkindness God demonstrated toward Israel. Read that psalm, noting the manifestations of God's love that relate to your life.

"Having been predestined according to [God's] purpose who works all things after the counsel of His will" (Eph. 1:11).

❖❖❖

God took the initiative in salvation by choosing you and granting you saving faith.

In Ephesians 1:4 Paul says that God "chose us in [Christ] before the foundation of the world, that we should be holy and blameless before Him." In verse 11 he reiterates that marvelous truth by affirming that believers have been predestined to salvation according to God's own purpose and will.

Many reject the teaching that God chose ("predestined") believers to salvation. They think believers chose God. In one sense they're right. Salvation involves an act of the will in turning from sin to embrace Christ. But the issue in predestination goes deeper than that. It's a question of initiative. Did God choose you on the basis of your faith in Him, or did He, by choosing you, enable you to respond in faith?

The answer is clear in Scripture. Romans 3:11 says that no one seeks for God on his own. Unregenerate people have no capacity to understand spiritual truth; it's all foolishness to them (1 Cor. 2:14). They are spiritually dead (Eph. 2:1), blind (2 Cor. 4:4), and ignorant (Eph. 4:18).

How can people in that condition initiate saving faith? They can't! That's why Jesus said, "No one can come to Me, unless the Father who sent Me draws him. . . . All that the Father gives Me shall come to Me; and the one who comes to Me I will certainly not cast out" (John 6:44, 37). Paul added, "God . . . has saved us, and called us with a holy calling, not according to our works, but according to His own purpose and grace which was granted us in Christ Jesus from all eternity" (2 Tim. 1:8-9).

God took the initiative. He chose you and gave you saving faith (Eph. 2:8-9). Rejoice in that truth. Rest in His power to conform all things to His will. Draw strength and assurance from His promise never to let you go (John 10:27-29). Then live each day as God's elected one by shunning sin and following after holiness.

❖❖❖

Suggestions for Prayer: Praise God for placing His love upon you and for granting you salvation. ❖ Pray for the salvation of others, and seek opportunities to share Christ with them today.

For Further Study: Read Ezekiel 36:22-32. ❖ Why will God one day redeem Israel? ❖ What does that passage teach you about God's initiative in salvation?

*We were predestined "to the end that we who were the first to hope
in Christ should be to the praise of His glory" (Eph. 1:12).*

❖❖❖

**In salvation, as in everything else, God is preeminent.
He deserves all the credit.**

The word *preeminence* implies supreme standing, picturing one who
excels over all others in a particular quality or achievement. Only God
is truly preeminent, worthily so.

Ephesians 1:12 underscores that truth. You were redeemed and were
granted an eternal inheritance so that God might be glorified. Certainly you
benefit greatly from salvation, but God's glory is the primary issue.

Our man-centered culture doesn't share that perspective. Sadly, its self-
seeking and self-glorifying mentality has crept into the church, and even the
gospel itself has been subjected to its influence. For example, sin is often
defined by how it affects man, not by how it dishonors God. Salvation is often
presented as a means of receiving what Christ offers, not as a mandate to obey
what He commands. Many modern-day evangelists have reduced the gospel
to little more than a formula by which people can live a happy and more fulfilling life. The focus has shifted from God's glory to man's benefit.

Such a convoluted gospel fuels the fire of self-love and self-exaltation.

As believers we know better than that. We know that the purpose of life is
to glorify God. In other words, living to His glory is to govern everything we
do.

What higher or more noble purpose could life afford? "Forgetting what lies
behind and reaching forward to what lies ahead," Paul said, "I press on toward
the goal for the prize of the upward call of God in Christ Jesus" (Phil. 3:13-
14). Keep that goal clearly in mind in all you do today. By doing so, your day
will be "to the praise of [God's] glory."

❖❖❖

Suggestions for Prayer: Praise God for His preeminence in all things. ❖ Pray
for opportunities to speak of His preeminence to others, remembering that
they will see Him in your actions as well as in your words.

For Further Study: Read Job 38:1–42:6. ❖ How did God convince Job of His
surpassing knowledge and power? ❖ What was Job's response?

"In Him, you also, after listening to the message of truth, the gospel of your salvation—having also believed . . ." (Eph. 1:13).

❖❖❖

The gospel is true because Jesus is true, not simply because Christians believe in Him.

After stating salvation from God's perspective in verse 12, Paul here states it from man's perspective. Faith in Christ is your response to God's elective purpose in your life. Those two truths—God's initiative and man's response—coexist throughout Scripture.

Paul rightly called the gospel "the message of truth" because truth is its predominant characteristic. Salvation was conceived by the God of truth (Ps. 31:5) and purchased by the Son, who is the truth (John 14:6) and is applied by the Spirit of truth (John 16:13). To know it is to know the truth that sets men free (John 8:32). Believers are people of the truth (John 18:37), and they worship God in spirit and in truth (John 4:24) and obey the Word of truth (John 17:17).

Yet, as profound and powerful as God's truth is, people have rejected, neglected, redefined, and opposed it for centuries. Some, like Pilate, cynically deny that truth even exists or that it can be known by men (John 18:38). Others foolishly think that denying truth will somehow make it go away.

Perhaps you've heard someone say, "Jesus may be true for you, but that doesn't mean He has to be true for me." That view assumes that belief somehow determines truth. But just the opposite is the case. Truth determines the validity of one's belief. Believing a lie doesn't make it true. Conversely, failing to believe the truth doesn't make it a lie.

The gospel is true because Jesus is true, not simply because Christians believe in Him. His resurrection proved the truth of His claims and constitutes the objective basis of our faith (Rom. 1:4; 1 Peter 1:3).

You will face today armed with the message of truth and empowered by the Spirit of truth. Truth is your protection and strength (Eph. 6:14). Lost souls desperately need to hear that truth. Represent it well, and proclaim it with boldness.

❖❖❖

Suggestions for Prayer: Thank the Lord that by His Spirit He has enabled you to understand His truth (1 Cor. 2:14-16). ❖ Ask for wisdom and boldness to speak His truth in love (Eph. 4:15).

For Further Study: Read 1 Corinthians 15:1-11 and Acts 17:30-31. ❖ What key elements of the gospel does Paul list? ❖ What is the relationship between Christ's resurrection and God's judgment on sinners?

"You were sealed in Him with the Holy Spirit of promise, who is given as a pledge of our inheritance" (Eph. 1:13-14).

❖❖❖

The Holy Spirit is God's first installment on your eternal inheritance.

The Holy Spirit's ministry in your life is multifaceted and profound. Among other things, He brings salvation, conviction, guidance, and strength. He indwells and equips you for spiritual service and gives assurance of your salvation. He is your Helper and Advocate. He is the Spirit of promise who seals you until the day when your redemption will be fully realized (Eph. 4:30).

Sealing speaks of security, authenticity, ownership, and authority. Ancient kings, princes, and nobles placed their official seal on documents or other items to guarantee their inviolability. To break the seal was to incur the wrath of the sovereign whom it represented (cf. Dan. 6:17; Matt. 27:62-66).

A seal on a letter authenticated it as being from the hand of the one whose seal it bore. Legal documents such as property deeds and wills were often finalized with an official seal. Those who possessed the sealed decree of a king had the king's delegated authority to act on that decree.

Each of those aspects of sealing is a picture of the Spirit's ministry. He is God's guarantee that your salvation is inviolable and that you are an authentic member of God's Kingdom and family. You are His possession, having been purchased with His Son's precious blood (1 Cor. 6:20). You are His ambassador and so have delegated authority to proclaim His message to a lost world (2 Cor. 5:20).

The Spirit is the "pledge" of your eternal inheritance (Eph. 1:14). The Greek word translated "pledge" in that verse (*arrabōn*) was used for a down payment or earnest money given to secure a purchase. Rejoice in the assurance that God, who cannot lie (Titus 1:2), has given you His Spirit as a guarantee that He will keep His promises.

❖❖❖

Suggestions for Prayer: Praise God for the security of your eternal inheritance. ❖ Praise the Spirit for His many ministries in your life. Be sensitive to His leading today, so that your ministry to others will be powerful and consistent with His will.

For Further Study: Read Esther 3, 8. What role did the king's signet ring play in the decree of Haman (chapter 3)? The decree of Ahasuerus and Mordecai (chapter 8)?

You were sealed with the Holy Spirit "with a view to the redemption of God's own possession, to the praise of His glory" (Eph. 1:14).

❖❖❖

Someday God will take full possession of all that is rightfully His.

Yesterday we saw that God seals us with the Holy Spirit as a pledge of our eternal inheritance. Here Paul says He does so "with a view to the redemption of [His] own possession." That refers to the day when God will take full possession of all that is rightfully His.

Satan, to a certain degree, usurped God's rulership to become the "god of this world" (2 Cor. 4:4), and the whole world currently lies under his power (1 John 5:19). Consequently, all creation is in bondage to decay and "groaning as in the pains of childbirth right up to the present time" (Rom. 8:22, NIV). It eagerly awaits the time when the curse of Genesis 3 will be reversed, all Christians will be fully glorified, and sin will be eternally vanquished. What a glorious time that will be!

You are God's special possession because you are His by redemption as well as by creation. In Revelation 5:9 the four living creatures and the twenty-four elders sing to the Lord, "Worthy art Thou . . . for Thou wast slain, and didst purchase for God with Thy blood men from every tribe and tongue and people and nation." In Acts 20:28 Paul charged the Ephesian elders to guard carefully "the church of God which He purchased with His own blood."

That makes you a priceless commodity to God—part of "a chosen race, a royal priesthood, a holy nation, a people for God's own possession, that you may proclaim the excellencies of Him who has called you out of darkness into His marvelous light; for you once were not a people, but now you are the people of God" (1 Peter 2:9-10).

As God's special possession, you should reflect His ownership and sovereign rule in everything you do. Remember, "you are not your own . . . for you have been bought with a price: therefore glorify God in your body" (1 Cor. 6:19-20).

❖❖❖

Suggestions for Prayer: Thank God that you are His treasured possession. ❖ Seek His Spirit's leading in proclaiming His excellencies to others through your words and deeds. ❖ Ask Him to teach you to esteem other believers as highly as He does.

For Further Study: Read Ephesians 2:1-13, noting the spiritual privileges and responsibilities that are yours in Christ.

"For this reason I too, having heard of the faith in the Lord Jesus which exists among you, and your love for all the saints, do not cease giving thanks for you, while making mention of you in my prayers" (Eph. 1:15-16).

❖❖❖

**Your love for other Christians is as much a
mark of true faith as your love for God.**

The Ephesian Christians demonstrated two important characteristics of genuine Christian faith: faith in the Lord Jesus and love for fellow believers.

"Faith in the Lord Jesus" implies both an affirmation of Christ's deity and submission to His sovereignty. Because He is God, He is the Sovereign Lord, and therefore we must obey what He commands (John 14:15; 1 John 2:3-6).

Your "love for all the saints" is as much a mark of true faith as your love for God. John said, "The one who says he is in the light and yet hates his brother is in the darkness until now" (1 John 2:9). In that passage "light" is a metaphor for righteousness and truth, and "darkness" is a metaphor for sin and error. It is sinful and erroneous to claim you love God if you have no love for other believers. Those who love God will love fellow-believers as well.

If you love others, you will pray for them and will praise God for their spiritual progress—as Paul did for the Ephesians; and they will do the same for you. That's a wonderful dynamic within the Body of Christ, one you must diligently pursue.

❖❖❖

Suggestions for Prayer: If you haven't done so already, start a prayer list of individuals for whom you will pray each day. List their names and some specific requests. Record answers to your prayers as you see God moving in their lives. ❖ Remember to thank God for their spiritual progress as well as praying for their needs. Let them know you are praying for them. That could be a source of great encouragement for them. ❖ If you are at odds with another believer, seek to reconcile immediately (Matt. 5:23-24), so your witness will be strong and the Lord's name won't suffer reproach.

For Further Study: Read Philippians 1:9-11 and Colossians 1:9-14. ❖ What requests and concerns did Paul express in his prayers? ❖ Do your prayers reflect Paul's priorities? If not, what adjustments must you make to have a more Biblical pattern of prayer?

> *"[I pray] that the God of our Lord Jesus Christ, the Father of glory, may give you a spirit of wisdom and of revelation in the knowledge of Him" (Eph. 1:17).*

❖❖❖

Your inheritance in Christ is so vast and profound that you cannot comprehend it apart from God's enabling.

The late newspaper publisher William Randolph Hearst invested a fortune in collecting great works of art. One day he read of an extremely valuable work that he determined to add to his collection. His agent searched the galleries of the world but to no avail. Finally, after many months of effort and at great expense, the agent found the prized artwork. It had been stored in one of Hearst's own warehouses all along!

That story parallels Christians who are constantly searching for something more because they don't understand what they already have in Christ. Since Paul knew that was a potential problem, he prayed for God to enable us to comprehend our spiritual riches.

"Spirit" in verse 17 refers to a disposition or attitude of humility, as in, "Blessed are the poor in spirit" (Matt. 5:3). "Revelation" means knowledge that God imparts through His Word. "Wisdom" is the application of that knowledge to daily living. The combined effect is a humble attitude toward God's Word that compels you to learn it and to integrate it into every aspect of your life.

On the human level, the fullness of your inheritance in Christ is incomprehensible. God's Word reveals many of its benefits, and the Holy Spirit empowers you as you learn to live according to its principles, but much of it will remain a mystery in this life (1 John 3:2). Paul's prayer is that you will understand as much as possible so that godly wisdom and revelation will govern all your attitudes and actions. Let that be your goal today.

❖❖❖

Suggestions for Prayer: Thank God for the incomprehensible riches that are yours in Christ. ❖ Pray that you might always approach His Word with a submissive and teachable heart.

For Further Study: Reviewing God's promises motivates praise and reminds us of His gracious provisions. Read the following passages, noting the promises they contain: Psalm 29:11; Isaiah 26:3; 41:10; Matthew 6:25-34; John 14:2-3, 13-14; 1 Corinthians 10:13; 2 Corinthians 1:3-4; Philippians 4:6-7; 1 John 1:9; 5:11-12; Revelation 21:3-4. ❖ Study your life. Does it demonstrate confidence in God's promises?

"I pray that the eyes of your heart may be enlightened"
(Eph. 1:18).

❖❖❖

Spiritual enlightenment doesn't come through self-effort or
introspective meditation but through God's Holy Spirit.

Our society has been enamored with the pursuit of spiritual enlightenment, especially since the influx of Eastern thought into the West during the 1960s. Now we are drowning in a sea of false religions and New Age philosophies.

True enlightenment continues to elude many because they have denied its source and have turned to gurus and teachers who have no light to give. They propagate self-effort and introspective meditation, but spiritual enlightenment doesn't come through such means. It comes only through the Holy Spirit (1 Cor. 2:14-16). That's why Paul prayed that God Himself would enlighten the hearts of the Ephesian believers (Eph. 1:18).

We might expect Paul to pray for enlightened minds rather than hearts, but that's because we associate the word *heart* with emotions rather than with thought. But in Hebrew and Greek thinking, the heart was considered the seat of knowledge, thinking, and understanding. For example, Jesus said that evil thoughts come out of the heart (Matt. 15:19). Emotions are important, but they must be guided and controlled by an enlightened mind.

How does the Spirit enlighten you? As you pray and study God's Word, He transforms and renews your mind (Rom. 12:2) by filling you with "the knowledge of [God's] will in all spiritual wisdom and understanding" (Col. 1:9). He teaches you to recognize and uphold what is excellent so that you will be "sincere and blameless" before God (Phil. 1:10). He implants Biblical truth into your thinking so that your responses become more and more like Christ's.

How wonderful to know that each moment of the day God is working within you in such a way. Be diligent to pray and spend time in the Word so that your spiritual progress will be evident to all (1 Tim. 4:15).

❖❖❖

Suggestions for Prayer: Thank God for the Spirit's transforming work within you. ❖ Reaffirm your love for Him, and express your willingness to be changed by His Spirit in any way He sees fit. ❖ Be alert for attitudes or actions that need to be changed. Rely on His grace and strength in doing so.

For Further Study: Read Genesis 27–33, noting how God used the events of Jacob's life to transform his weak spiritual commitment to one that was strong and unconditional (see especially Gen. 28:20-22; 32:9-12).

"I pray that . . . you may know what is the hope of [God's] calling" (Eph. 1:18).

❖❖❖

The hope of your calling is grounded in God's promises and in Christ's accomplishments.

In Ephesians 1:3-14 Paul proclaims the blessings of our salvation. In verse 18 he prays that we will comprehend those great truths, which he summarizes in the phrase, "the hope of His calling."

"Calling" here refers to God's effectual calling—the calling that redeems the soul. Scripture speaks of two kinds of callings: the gospel or general call, and the effectual or specific call. The gospel call is given by men and is a universal call to repent and trust Christ for salvation (see, e.g., Matt. 28:19; Acts 17:30-31). It goes out to all sinners, but not all who hear it respond in faith.

The effectual call is given by God only to the elect. By it He speaks to the soul, grants saving faith, and ushers elect sinners into salvation (John 6:37-44, 65; Acts 2:39). All who receive it respond in faith.

The hope that your effectual calling instills is grounded in God's promises and in Christ's accomplishments (1 Peter 1:3), and is characterized by confidently expecting and yet patiently waiting for those promises to be fulfilled. It is your hope of final glorification and of sharing God's glory when Christ returns (Col. 3:4). It is a source of strength and stability amid the trials of life (1 Peter 3:14-15). Consequently it should fill you with joy (Rom. 5:2) and motivate you to godly living (1 John 3:3).

As you face this new day, do so with the confidence that you are one of God's elect. He called you to Himself and will hold you there, no matter what circumstances you face. Nothing can separate you from His love (Rom. 8:38-39)!

❖❖❖

Suggestions for Prayer: Thank God for the security of your salvation. ❖ Ask Him to impress on your heart the blessings and responsibilities of your calling. ❖ Live today in anticipation of Christ's imminent return.

For Further Study: Joshua's call to lead Israel was not a call to salvation, but it illustrates some important principles for spiritual leadership. You might not see yourself as a spiritual leader, but you are important to those who look to you as an example of Christian character.

Read Joshua 1:1-9 and then answer these questions: ❖ What were the circumstances of Joshua's call (vv. 1-2)? ❖ What promises did God make to him (vv. 3-6)? ❖ What did God require of him (vv. 7-9)?

"I pray that . . . you may know . . . what are the riches of the glory of His inheritance in the saints" (Eph. 1:18).

❖❖❖

How you perceive your spiritual resources dictates how you live.

Throughout Ephesians 1 Paul is clearly struck with the magnificence of our inheritance in Christ. Here he prays that we will know the riches of its glory.

Some commentators see "His inheritance" as a reference to believers, who are God's inheritance or special possession (v. 14). That view stresses the value God places on us as believers, as demonstrated in Christ's death, the forgiveness of our sins, and the abundant grace that He lavishes on us (vv. 7-8).

Others see it as referring to the believer's inheritance, which Paul calls "His inheritance" because God is its source. Just as "His calling" (v. 18) issued from Him and was received by believers, so His inheritance issues from Him.

Both views are theologically sound, but the second seems more consistent with Paul's emphasis in verses 11 and 14. In either case Paul's point is clear: redemption and its accompanying blessings are so profound that we must have supernatural help to understand them. That's why he prayed for our enlightenment (v. 18).

Such enlightenment is crucial because how you perceive your spiritual resources dictates how you live. If, for example, you realize you have every resource for godly living (Eph. 1:3), you are less likely to succumb to temptation. Knowing God has given you His very best in Christ (Rom. 8:32) assures you that He won't withhold lesser things, and consequently you'll not tend to worry about earthly needs. Understanding that you have already received "grace upon grace" (John 1:16), abundant life (John 10:10), and "everything pertaining to life and godliness" (2 Peter 1:3) gives you confidence that God's future grace and resources will be more than sufficient (2 Cor. 12:9).

Let that motivate you to praise your rich and glorious God for His rich and glorious inheritance!

❖❖❖

Suggestions for Prayer: Thank God for the privilege of being His child. ❖ Memorize Ephesians 1:3 and 2 Peter 1:3 and recite them often as anthems of praise for the Lord's abundant grace.

For Further Study: Read 2 Corinthians 11–12. ❖ What kinds of trials did Paul face? ❖ How did God respond to Paul's prayer to remove his "thorn in the flesh"? ❖ How might Paul's response influence you when you face difficulties?

"I pray that . . . you may know . . . the surpassing greatness of [God's] power toward us who believe" (Eph. 1:18-19).

❖❖❖

The same divine power that created, sustains, and controls the universe secures your salvation.

God's power is awesome! David wrote, "Thine, O Lord, is the greatness and the power and the glory and the victory and the majesty, indeed everything that is in the heavens and the earth; Thine is the dominion, O Lord, and Thou dost exalt Thyself as head over all. Both riches and honor come from Thee, and Thou dost rule over all, and in Thy hand is power and might; and it lies in Thy hand to make great, and to strengthen everyone. Now therefore, our God, we thank Thee, and praise Thy glorious name" (1 Chron. 29:11-13).

In Ephesians 1:19 Paul focuses on one key feature of God's power: His ability to secure the salvation of His people. And he prays for you to understand the surpassing greatness of that truth.

The Greek word translated "power" is *dunamis*, from which we get *dynamite* and *dynamo*. This power is active, dynamic, and compelling—and it is mightily at work on your behalf. You might not always sense it, but it's there nonetheless.

Peter expresses the same thought in 1 Peter 1:5, where he says you are "protected by the power of God through faith" in Christ. In that verse "protected" means "to keep or guard" and reflects Peter's confidence that salvation is inviolable.

The same limitless power that created, sustains, and controls the universe saved you and keeps you saved. That's why Jesus said no one can snatch you out of the Father's hand (John 10:29). Not even Satan has the power to do that. Paul confidently added that nothing therefore can separate you from God's love (Rom. 8:38-39). That's the confidence you should have as you live each day.

❖❖❖

Suggestions for Prayer: Pray for greater spiritual enlightenment and a clearer understanding of your security in Christ. ❖ Nothing will rob you of your assurance quicker than unconfessed sin. If that has happened to you, confess it immediately and turn from it. Then ask God to restore to you the joy of your salvation.

For Further Study: Read 1 Chronicles 29:11-13. ❖ What prerogatives did David attribute to God (vv. 11-12)? ❖ What was David's response to God's power (v. 13)?

"These are in accordance with the working of the strength of [God's] might which He brought about in Christ, when He raised Him from the dead" (Eph. 1:19-20).

✧✧✧

In Christ you have all the power you will ever need.

The resurrection of Jesus Christ is the great hope of believers. Because He lives, we will live also (John 14:19). Peter said that we have been "born again to a living hope through the resurrection of Jesus Christ from the dead, to obtain an inheritance which is imperishable and undefiled and will not fade away" (1 Peter 1:3-4). We and what we have are protected by God's power (v. 5).

In Ephesians 1:19-20 Paul draws two comparisons. The first is between the power God demonstrated in the resurrection and ascension of Christ and the power He demonstrates on behalf of every believer. That power is described as God's "working," "strength," and "might." Together those synonyms emphasize the greatness of God's power, which not only secures our salvation but also enables us to live godly lives.

The second comparison is between our Lord's resurrection and ascension and ours. The grave couldn't hold Him, nor can it hold us (1 Cor. 15:54-57). Satan himself couldn't prevent Christ's exaltation, nor can he prevent us from gaining our eternal inheritance.

In Christ you have all the power you will ever need. For evangelism you have the gospel itself, which "is the power of God for salvation to every one who believes" (Rom. 1:16). For difficult times you have the assurance that the surpassing greatness of God's power is at work in you (2 Cor. 4:7). For holy living you have God Himself at work in you "both to will and to work for His good pleasure" (Phil. 2:13).

No matter how weak or ill-equipped you may at times feel, realize that God "is able to do exceeding abundantly beyond all that [you] ask or think, according to the power that works within [you]" (Eph. 3:20). So keep striving according to that power (Col. 1:29), but do so with the confidence that ultimately God will accomplish His good in your life.

✧✧✧

Suggestions for Prayer: Thank God that He can and will accomplish His purposes in your life (Phil. 1:6; 1 Thess. 5:24). ✧ Pray for wisdom in how you might best serve Him today.

For Further Study: Read Psalm 145, noting every mention of God's power David makes. Allow those examples to fill your heart with confidence and praise.

"[God] seated [Christ] at His right hand in the heavenly places"
(Eph. 1:20).

❖❖❖

Christ occupies the highest place of power, prominence, authority, and honor.

To exalt someone is to elevate that person in status, dignity, power, and honor. As God, Jesus possesses all power and authority and is deserving of all honor and glory. But when He was on earth, most people refused to give Him the glory He deserved. Instead they mocked and eventually murdered Him.

Just prior to His death, Jesus prayed to the Father, "Glorify Thou Me together with Thyself, Father, with the glory which I ever had with Thee before the world was" (John 17:5). The Father answered that prayer by giving Him an exalted name and an exalted position.

Paul wrote, "God highly exalted [Christ], and bestowed on Him the name which is above every name, that at the name of Jesus every knee should bow, of those who are in heaven, and on earth, and under the earth, and that every tongue should confess that Jesus Christ is Lord, to the glory of God the Father" (Phil. 2:9-11).

Hebrews 1:3 adds that when Christ had made purification of sins, He sat down at the right hand of the Majesty on high. Old Testament priests didn't sit down while on duty because their work was never finished. Repeated sacrifices were necessary because of the priest's own sins and the sins of the people. Christ, on the other hand, made one all-sufficient sacrifice, then sat down. His atoning work was completed.

The "right hand" of God is a metaphor for the highest place of power, prominence, authority, and honor. From that exalted position Christ reigns as the Sovereign Lord of the universe.

There's one aspect of Christ's exaltation that we as believers can participate in right now. David said, "O magnify the Lord with me, and let us exalt His name together" (Ps. 34:3). Psalm 99:5 adds, "Exalt the Lord our God, and worship at His footstool." Be generous in praising Him today, for He is worthy!

❖❖❖

Suggestions for Prayer: Read Psalm 34 and exalt the Lord for all the benefits He demonstrates on behalf of His people.

For Further Study: Read Colossians 3:1-4. ❖ Describe your position in Christ (vv. 1, 3). ❖ What should be the focus of your life (v. 2)? ❖ When ultimately will God vindicate your faith in Christ (v. 4)? ❖ What must you do to be exalted by God (see James 4:10; 1 Peter 5:6)?

God exalted Christ "far above all rule and authority and power and dominion, and every name that is named, not only in this age, but also in the one to come. And He put all things in subjection under His feet" (Eph. 1:21-22).

❖❖❖

Now and forever Christ is the Supreme One!

Yesterday we saw that Christ has both an exalted name and an exalted, authoritative position. In verses 21-22 Paul elaborates on the extent of Christ's authority, which is "far above all rule and authority and power and dominion."

"Rule," "authority," "power," and "dominion" are designations for angelic beings, whether good or evil (cf. Eph. 6:12; Col. 1:16). In His incarnation Christ was made lower in rank than the angels, that He might suffer death on our behalf (Heb. 2:9). Now He has "become . . . much better than the angels, as He has inherited a more excellent name than they" (Heb. 1:4), and the Father commands all the angels to worship the Son (v. 6).

But Christ's rule extends far beyond angelic beings. In Ephesians 1:21 the phrase "every name that is named" is a general reference to any form of authority—whether angelic or human, eternal or temporal. Now and forever Christ is the Supreme One! Ultimately every knee will bow before Him, and every tongue will confess that He is Lord (Phil. 2:10-11).

The implications of that truth are staggering. For example, Christ precedes the Great Commission of Matthew 28:19-20, the heart of Christian evangelism and discipleship, with this significant statement: "All authority has been given to Me in heaven and on earth."

Ultimately your evangelism and discipleship efforts will bear fruit because they are backed by the authority of Christ Himself. Does that encourage you to seize every opportunity to share Christ and His Word with others? It should!

Be faithful today, realizing that you represent the One in whom lies all authority. Nothing can thwart His purposes.

❖❖❖

Suggestions for Prayer: Ask the Holy Spirit to direct you to a lost soul or anyone else you can encourage from the Word. Be sensitive to His leading.

For Further Study: Read Colossians 1:15-23. ❖ What was Christ's role in creation (vv. 15-17)? ❖ What is His role in the church (v. 18)? In salvation (v. 22)? ❖ What place have you given Him in your life?

> *God exalted Christ "and gave Him as head over all things to the church, which is His body, the fulness of Him who fills all in all" (Eph. 1:22-23).*

❖❖❖

The church was designed to complement Christ.

Here Paul uses a graphic analogy to illustrate the relationship of Christ to the church: He is the head; believers are His Body. Paul elaborates that we're to hold "fast to the head [Christ], from whom the entire body, being supplied and held together by the joints and ligaments, grows with a growth which is from God" (Col. 2:19; cf. Eph. 4:15-16).

Just as the head controls the human body, so Christ governs His Body, the church (cf. 1 Cor. 12:12-31). By His Spirit and His Word He supplies all the resources the church needs to function to His glory. In that way He guarantees that His purposes will be fulfilled.

The church is in fact "the fulness of Him who fills all in all" (Eph. 1:23). The implication is that the incomprehensible, all-sufficient, all-powerful, and utterly supreme Christ is in a sense incomplete—not in His nature, but in the degree to which His glory is seen in the world.

A synonym for "fulness" is "complement." The church was designed to complement Christ. He is the One who "fills all in all"—the fullness of deity in bodily form (Col. 2:9) and the giver of truth and grace (John 1:14). Yet He chooses to reveal His glory in and through the church. Therefore, until the church is fully glorified, Christ will not be fully complemented.

Does your life complement Christ? Do you "adorn the doctrine of God our Savior in every respect" (Titus 2:10)? Do you "let your light shine before men in such a way that they may see your good works, and glorify your Father who is in heaven" (Matt. 5:16)? You have every spiritual resource to do so, so don't let anything hold you back (Heb. 12:1-2).

❖❖❖

Suggestions for Prayer: Read Psalm 139:23-24 and pray with David that God will search your heart and reveal any sin that might hinder you from complementing Christ today.

For Further Study: Read 1 Corinthians 12:1-30. ❖ What spiritual gifts are mentioned in this passage? ❖ How does Paul deal with the misconception that some gifts are more important than others (see vv. 14-30)? ❖ As a member of Christ's Body, you are gifted by the Spirit to minister to others. Are you doing so?

"I rejoice and share my joy with you all" (Phil. 2:17).

❖❖❖

True joy is directly related to godly living.

Philippians is often called the epistle of joy, and rightly so because the believer's joy is its major theme. Paul loved the Philippian Christians, and they loved him. When they learned that he had been imprisoned for preaching the gospel, they were deeply concerned.

Paul wrote to alleviate their fears and to encourage their joy. Of his own circumstances he said, "Even if I am being poured out as a drink offering upon the sacrifice and service of your faith, I rejoice and share my joy with you all. And you too, I urge you, rejoice in the same way and share your joy with me" (Phil. 2:17-18).

Often a Jewish animal sacrifice was accompanied by a libation or drink offering (see, e.g., Num. 15:1-10). The animal was the greater sacrifice, the libation the lesser. Drawing from that picture, Paul placed greater significance on the faith and spiritual well-being of his readers than on his own life. To suffer for Christ's sake brought him joy, and he wanted the Philippians to understand that perspective and to rejoice with him.

He also wanted them to understand that joy doesn't operate in a vacuum. It's directly related to godly living. Christ is its source, obedience its sustenance. We see this in David's cry of repentance: "Restore to me the joy of Thy salvation" (Ps. 51:12). Paul knew the joy of the Lord because he trusted Christ and obeyed His will.

The scarcity of joy and godliness in the world today makes it imperative that Christians manifest those characteristics. As we do, others will see our good works and will glorify our Father in heaven (Matt. 5:16).

This month we will highlight various aspects of joy and godliness from Philippians 1:1-11 and Colossians 1:9-12. I pray that you will be eager to learn from God's Word and will willingly obey what you learn, for therein is "joy inexpressible and full of glory" (1 Peter 1:8).

❖❖❖

Suggestions for Prayer: Ask the Holy Spirit to use our daily studies to strengthen your joy and to increase your godliness. ❖ Seek to emulate Paul's attitude of preferring others to yourself—a key element in joyful living.

For Further Study: Read the book of Philippians, noting each reference to joy. ❖ What brought joy to Paul? ❖ On what or whom do you rely for joy?

"Rejoice in the Lord" (Phil. 3:1).

❖❖❖

Happiness is related to circumstances; joy is a gift from God.

Not long ago it was common to see bumper stickers proclaiming every conceivable source for happiness. One said, "Happiness is being married." Another countered, "Happiness is being single." One cynical sticker read, "Happiness is impossible!"

For most people happiness is possible, but it's also fickle, shallow, and fleeting. As the word itself implies, happiness is associated with happenings, happenstance, luck, and fortune. If circumstances are favorable, you're happy; if not, you're unhappy.

Christian joy, however, is directly related to God and is the firm confidence that all is well, regardless of your circumstances.

In Philippians 3:1 Paul says, "Rejoice *in the Lord*" (emphasis added). The Lord is both the source and object of Christian joy. Knowing Him brings joy that transcends temporal circumstances. Obeying Him brings peace and assurance.

Joy is God's gift to every believer. It is the fruit that His Spirit produces within you (Gal. 5:22) from the moment you receive the gospel (John 15:11). This joy increases as you study and obey God's Word (1 John 1:4).

Even severe trials needn't rob you of your joy. James 1:2 says you should be joyful when you encounter various trials because trials produce spiritual endurance and maturity. They also prove that your faith is genuine, and a proven faith is the source of great joy (1 Peter 1:6-8).

You live in a world corrupted by sin. But your hope is in a living God, not in a dying world. He is "able to keep you from stumbling and to make you stand in the presence of His glory blameless with great joy" (Jude 24). That's your assurance of future glory and eternal joy! Until that time, don't neglect His Word, despise trials, or lose sight of your eternal reward. These are key ingredients of your present joy.

❖❖❖

Suggestions for Prayer: Thank the Lord for any difficult circumstances you might be facing. Ask Him for continued grace to see them through His perspective and to not lose heart (Gal. 6:9). ❖ Be aware of any sinful attitudes or actions on your part that might diminish your joy. Confess them immediately.

For Further Study: Read Acts 16:11-40. ❖ What difficulties did Paul and Silas face in founding the Philippian church? ❖ How did God use their difficulties for His glory?

"Paul and Timothy, bond-servants of Christ Jesus . . ." (Phil. 1:1).

❖❖❖

If exalting Christ is your goal,
anything that furthers the gospel will bring you joy.

Next to the Lord Himself, Paul is perhaps the greatest illustration that joy is not necessarily related to one's circumstances.

Paul wrote to the Philippians from a prison cell, and yet he spoke of joy and contentment. His life was a series of difficulties and life-threatening situations (see 2 Cor. 11:23-33). In fact the Lord, shortly after confronting him on the road to Damascus, said, "[Paul] is a chosen instrument of Mine, to bear My name before the Gentiles and kings and the sons of Israel; for I will show him how much he must suffer for My name's sake" (Acts 9:15-16). Yet, in every situation Paul found cause for rejoicing.

His compelling desire to exalt Christ drove him to endure trial after trial. When Christ was exalted, Paul rejoiced. That was evident in Philippi where, after a brief ministry in which God redeemed a businesswoman named Lydia and expelled demons from a slave girl, Paul and Silas were falsely accused, unjustly beaten, and thrown into prison. Even that didn't stifle their joy, for "about midnight Paul and Silas were praying and singing hymns of praise to God, and the prisoners were listening to them" (Acts 16:25).

That was such a powerful testimony to the joy of the Lord that soon afterward the jailer and his entire family believed the gospel and were saved.

Even when imprisonment prevented Paul from ministering as effectively as he desired, and when others usurped his apostleship and preached Christ out of envy and strife, he remained undaunted (Phil. 1:18). His circumstances were secondary to the priority of exalting Christ.

Is that your perspective? It can be! If your priority is to exalt Christ in every circumstance, whatever furthers that purpose will bring you joy.

❖❖❖

Suggestions for Prayer: Ask the Lord to help you maintain the priority of exalting Christ in every area of your life. ❖ If you feel envy or resentment toward others who proclaim the gospel (Phil. 1:15-17), confess that, and learn to rejoice whenever Christ is exalted.

For Further Study: Read Exodus 15:1-21 and Psalm 99. How did Moses, Miriam, and the psalmist exalt the Lord?

"Paul and Timothy, bond-servants of Christ Jesus . . ." (Phil. 1:1).

❖❖❖

**Despite their shortcomings, people of kindred spirit are
precious gifts from the Lord.**

Timothy was Paul's trusted companion in the gospel. In Philippians 2:20 Paul describes him as a man "of kindred spirit." That is, they were like-minded, sharing the same love for Christ and His church.

Elsewhere Paul described Timothy as his "beloved and faithful child in the Lord" (1 Cor. 4:17) and as a "fellow-worker in the gospel of Christ" (Rom. 16:21; 1 Thess. 3:2). Those are significant compliments coming from Paul, whose standard of ministry and personal integrity was very high.

However, as godly and useful as Timothy was, he apparently struggled with many of the same weaknesses we face. For example, 2 Timothy implies he might have been intimidated by the false teachers who challenged his leadership (1:7). He perhaps was somewhat ashamed of Christ (1:8) and was tempted to alter his theology to avoid offending those who disagreed with sound doctrine (1:13-14). He might have been neglecting his studies in the Word (2:15) and succumbing to ungodly opinions (2:16-17). Other struggles are implied as well.

Paul wrote to strengthen Timothy's spiritual character and to encourage him to persevere in the face of severe trials.

Despite those apparent weaknesses, Paul valued Timothy highly and entrusted enormous ministerial responsibilities to him. In addition, Timothy's friendship and ministry were sources of great joy and strength to Paul.

I pray that you have people of kindred spirit in your life—brothers and sisters in Christ who encourage you, pray for you, and hold you accountable to God's truth. Like Timothy, they may not be all you want them to be, but they are precious gifts from God. Esteem them highly, and pray for them often. Do everything you can to reciprocate their ministry in your life.

If perhaps you lack such friends, seek the fellowship of a local church where Christ is exalted, His Word is taught, and holy living is encouraged. Build relationships with mature Christians who will stimulate you to love and good deeds (Heb. 10:24).

❖❖❖

Suggestions for Prayer: Identify three people who are of kindred spirit with you. Pray for them. Tell them how much you appreciate their examples and ministries.

For Further Study: Read 2 Timothy 1:1-14. ❖ What were Paul's admonitions to Timothy? ❖ How might they apply to you?

"Paul and Timothy, bond-servants of Christ Jesus . . ." (Phil. 1:1).

❖❖❖

A faithful slave fulfills the will of his master.

The metaphor of Christians as slaves to Christ is common in Paul's writings. It is one his readers would have readily understood because of the prevalence of slavery in the Roman Empire.

Peter, James, John, and Jude used the same metaphor of their own ministries, as did Jesus in Mark 10:45—"The Son of Man did not come to be served, but to serve, and to give His life a ransom for many." In Philippians 2:7 Paul refers to Christ as a bond-servant who set aside the glory He was due and humbled Himself to the point of death.

The Greek word translated "bond-servant" in Philippians 1:1 was commonly used of those who, out of devotion to their masters, chose to remain as slaves though having the opportunity to be released. They were also known as love slaves because they served out of love, not compulsion.

That is a beautiful picture of the believer. We are God's "bond-servants" (Rev. 1:1), "having been freed from sin and enslaved to God" (Rom. 6:22).

While slavery brings to mind deprivation and inhumane treatment of one's fellowman, slaves in the Roman Empire usually were treated with dignity and respect. Although most had no personal possessions, their masters supplied everything they needed for life and health. Additionally, many were entrusted with significant responsibilities in their master's home.

A disobedient or self-willed slave was of no use to his master, but faithful slaves who set aside their personal interests to accomplish their master's will were valued highly.

Jesus said, "My food is to do the will of Him who sent Me, and to accomplish His work" (John 4:34). As God's bond-servant, that should be *your* goal as well. Be faithful, so God can use you mightily.

❖❖❖

Suggestions for Prayer: Thank God for the privilege of serving Him. ❖ Seek wisdom to appropriate your spiritual resources as you perform the tasks God has entrusted to you.

For Further Study: The book of Philemon is a letter Paul wrote to accompany Onesimus, a runaway slave whom Paul had led to the Lord and was now returning to his master, Philemon. ❖ Read Philemon. ❖ What was Paul's desire for Onesimus? ❖ What does this letter reveal about Philemon's character?

". . . to all the saints in Christ Jesus" (Phil. 1:1).

❖❖❖

Every Christian is a saint.

Many people think of saints as men and women who are or were especially holy or who have been canonized by an official church body. Usually only those who have been long dead and have extraordinary religious accomplishments to their credit qualify.

God, however, has a different perspective on sainthood. Paul called the Corinthian believers "saints" (1 Cor. 1:2), then went on for many chapters correcting their sinful practices. He called the Roman, Ephesian, and Colossian believers "saints" too, but they weren't perfect either.

What, then, qualifies someone as a saint? The answer is in Philippians 1:1—"to all the saints *in Christ Jesus*" (emphasis added). That's the criterion. Sainthood is not reserved for the spiritually elite. It belongs to every believer because every believer is "in Christ Jesus."

If you love Christ, you are a saint. That might come as a surprise to those who know you best, but it's true nonetheless!

The hallmark of sainthood is holiness. In fact, the Greek word translated "saints" in Philippians 1:1 (*hagios*) literally means "holy ones." It is used throughout the New Testament to speak of anyone or anything that represents God's holiness: Christ as the Holy One of God, the Holy Spirit, the Holy Father, holy Scriptures, holy angels, holy brethren, and so on.

To God, you are "holy and beloved" in Christ (Col. 3:12). You have received a saintly calling (1 Cor. 1:2) and a saintly inheritance (Col. 1:12). You have "redemption, the forgiveness of sins" (Col. 1:14) and every other spiritual blessing (Eph. 1:3).

With that privilege comes the responsibility of living a holy life. That's why Scripture admonishes you to present your body as a living and holy sacrifice (Rom. 12:1) and to live in a manner worthy of your saintly status (Eph. 5:3).

The power for godly living is the Holy Spirit, who indwells you. As you yield to Him through prayer and obedience to God's Word, the characteristics of a true saint become increasingly evident in your life. Make that your commitment today.

❖❖❖

Suggestions for Prayer: Thank God for choosing you as one of His holy ones. ❖ Pray that your life will be a consistent testimony to the reality of true sainthood.

For Further Study: What are the privileges and responsibilities of saints as outlined in Psalm 34?

". . . saints . . . who are in Philippi" (Phil. 1:1).

❖❖❖

As you give toward the needs of others, God will supply your needs.

Perhaps more than any other New Testament church, the Philippian church was characterized by generous, sacrificial giving. Their support for Paul extended throughout his missionary travels and was a source of great joy to him. In addition to money, they also sent Epaphroditus, a godly man who ministered to Paul during his imprisonment (Phil. 2:25-30; 4:18).

Paul was selective about accepting financial support from churches because he didn't want to be a burden or have his motives misunderstood. First Corinthians 9:6-14 tells us he had the right to receive support from those he ministered to, but he waived that right so the gospel would not be hindered in any way. In 2 Corinthians 11:9 he says, "When I was present with you and was in need, I was not a burden to anyone . . . in everything I kept myself from being a burden to you, and will continue to do so."

Similarly he wrote to the Thessalonians, "We did not act in an undisciplined manner among you, nor did we eat anyone's bread without paying for it, but with labor and hardship we kept working night and day so that we might not be a burden to any of you" (2 Thess. 3:7-9).

In contrast, Paul's willingness to accept support from the Philippian church speaks of the special trust and affection they shared.

Apparently the Philippians' generosity was so great, it left them with needs of their own. Paul assured them that their sacrifices were well-pleasing to God and that He would supply all their needs according to His riches in Christ Jesus (Phil. 4:18-19).

Like the Philippians, you should be characterized by generous, sacrificial support of those who minister God's Word to you. Faithful pastors and elders are worthy of such honor (1 Tim. 5:17-18), and generous giving brings joy to you and to others.

❖❖❖

Suggestions for Prayer: Thank God for those who faithfully minister to you.
❖ Ask for wisdom in how you might best support the financial needs of your church.

For Further Study: Read 1 Corinthians 9:1-14, 2 Corinthians 9:6-14, and 1 Timothy 6:6-9. ❖ What attitudes and principles are reflected in those passages? ❖ How might you incorporate them into your financial practices?

> "... to all the saints ... including the overseers and deacons"
> (Phil. 1:1).

❖❖❖

Faithful spiritual leaders are worthy of your appreciation and esteem.

Paul's salutation includes the "overseers and deacons" at Philippi. That probably is not a reference to elders and deacons as we know them, but is a general reference to all the Philippian saints, including spiritual leaders (overseers) and those who followed (servants).

That implies unity and submission within the church, which brings joy to leaders and followers alike. Hebrews 13:17 emphasizes that point: "Obey your leaders, and submit to them; for they keep watch over your souls, as those who will give an account. Let them do this with joy and not with grief, for this would be unprofitable for you."

Spiritual leadership is a sacred responsibility. Leaders are to lead, feed, and guard the flock of God, which Christ "purchased with His own blood" (Acts 20:28). They are accountable to God Himself for the faithful discharge of their duties.

You have a sacred responsibility as well: to obey and submit to your leaders. Hebrews 13:7 says, "Remember those who led you, who spoke the word of God to you; and considering the outcome of their way of life, imitate their faith." Paul adds in 1 Thessalonians 5:12-13, "Appreciate those who diligently labor among you, and have charge over you in the Lord and give you instruction, and ... esteem them very highly in love because of their work."

Sadly, our society encourages criticism and mistrust of anyone in authority. Verbal assaults and character assassinations are common. Many within the church have adopted that attitude toward their spiritual leaders, whom they view as functionaries or paid professionals. Consequently, many churches today are weak and ineffective from disunity and strife. Many pastors suffer untold grief from disobedient and ungrateful people.

You must never succumb to that mentality. Your leaders deserve your appreciation and esteem, not because they are exceptionally talented or have winsome personalities, but because of the sacred work God has called them to do.

Your godly attitude toward spiritual leaders will contribute immeasurably to unity and harmony within your church.

❖❖❖

Suggestions for Prayer: Thank God for your spiritual leaders. Pray for them and encourage them often.

For Further Study: Read 1 Corinthians 9:3-14. ❖ What right was Paul discussing? ❖ What illustrations did he use?

"Grace to you and peace from God our Father and the Lord Jesus Christ" (Phil. 1:2).

❖❖❖

Nothing you face today is beyond the purview of God's grace and peace.

Paul's wonderful benediction for grace and peace was ever on his heart. He offered it in each of his epistles and expounded on it throughout his writings.

Grace is the outpouring of God's goodness and mercy on undeserving mankind. Every benefit and provision you receive is by God's grace. That's why Peter called it "the manifold grace of God" (1 Peter 4:10). Just as your trials are manifold or multifaceted, so God's multifaceted and all-sufficient grace is correspondingly available to sustain you.

Peace, as used in Philippians 1:2, speaks of the calmness and absence of strife characteristic of one in whom God's grace is at work. The New Testament also links it to mercy, hope, joy, and love. To experience those graces is to experience true peace.

It is said that when Bible translators were seeking a word or phrase for "peace" in the language of the Chol Indians of South Mexico, they discovered that the words for "a quiet heart" gave just the meaning they were looking for. That's an appropriate parallel because peace guards the soul against anxiety and strife, granting solace and harmony.

Colossians 3:15 says, "Let the peace of Christ rule in your hearts, to which indeed you were called in one body." In Philippians 4:6-7 Paul says to "be anxious for nothing, but in everything by prayer and supplication with thanksgiving let your requests be made known to God. And the peace of God, which surpasses all comprehension, shall guard your hearts and your minds in Christ Jesus."

Although "grace to you and peace" was a common greeting in the early church, it was an uncommon experience in the unbelieving world. The same is true today, because only those who belong to God the Father and the Lord Jesus Christ receive grace and peace.

Are you experiencing God's peace? Remember, nothing you face today is beyond the purview of God's all-sufficient grace and surpassing peace.

❖❖❖

Suggestions for Prayer: Read Ephesians 2:14-18, and praise God for Christ, who is your peace, and for His gracious work on your behalf.

For Further Study: What is the first step to acquiring peace (John 16:33; 1 Peter 5:14)? ❖ What does the God of peace desire to accomplish within you (1 Thess. 5:23; Heb. 13:20-21)?

"I thank my God in all my remembrance of you" (Phil. 1:3).

✧✧✧

A key to Christian joy is to recall the goodness of others.

Though Paul was under house arrest in Rome when he wrote to the Philippians, his mind wasn't bound. Often he reflected on his experiences with the Philippian Christians. As he did so, his thoughts turned to prayers of praise and thanksgiving for all the Lord had done through them.

I'm sure Paul remembered when he preached in Philippi and God opened Lydia's heart to believe the gospel (Acts 16:13-14). Subsequently everyone in her household was saved (v. 15). Surely her kindness and hospitality were bright spots in an otherwise stormy stay at Philippi.

He must also have remembered the demon-possessed girl whom the Lord delivered from spiritual bondage (v. 18), and the Philippian jailer who threw Paul and Silas into prison after they had been beaten severely (vv. 23-24). Perhaps the girl became part of the Philippian church—the text doesn't say. We do know that the jailer and his whole household were saved, after which they showed kindness to Paul and Silas by tending to their wounds and feeding them (vv. 30-34).

The many financial gifts the Philippians sent to Paul were also fond memories for him because they were given out of love and concern. That was true of their present gift as well, which was delivered by Epaphroditus and went far beyond Paul's need (Phil. 4:18).

Paul's gratitude illustrates that Christian joy is enhanced in your life by your ability to recall the goodness of others. A corollary is your ability to forgive shortcomings and unkindnesses. That goes against the grain of our "don't get mad—get even" society, but is perfectly consistent with the compassion and forgiveness God has shown you. Therefore, be quick to forgive evil and slow to forget good.

✧✧✧

Suggestions for Prayer: Take time to reflect on some people who have shown kindness to you and encouraged you in your Christian walk. Thank God for them. If possible, call them or drop them a note of thanks. Assure them of your prayers, as Paul assured the Philippians. ✧ If you harbor ill will toward someone, resolve it quickly, and begin to uphold that person in prayer.

For Further Study: Read Matthew 5:23-26; 18:21-35. What were our Lord's instructions regarding forgiveness and reconciliation?

". . . always offering prayer with joy in my every prayer for you all" (Phil. 1:4).

❖❖❖

Intercessory prayer is a powerful tool in the hands of a righteous person.

A story is told of a special nurse who knew the importance of intercessory prayer. Because each day she used her hands as instruments of God's love and mercy toward those in her care, she found it natural to use her hand as a scheme of prayer. Each finger represented someone she wanted to pray for. Her thumb was nearest to her and reminded her to pray for those who were closest and dearest. The index finger was used for pointing, so it stood for her instructors. The third finger was the tallest and stood for those in leadership. The fourth finger was the weakest, representing those in distress and pain. The little finger, which was the smallest and least important, reminded the nurse to pray for her own needs.

Undoubtedly that nurse knew the joy of praying for others. Paul knew it too. Given the same circumstances, a lesser man would be consumed with his own well-being, but Paul modeled what he teaches in Philippians 2:4: "Do not merely look out for your own personal interests, but also for the interests of others." Such an attitude is the heart of effective intercessory prayer.

Those who lack the joy of the Holy Spirit often harbor negative thoughts toward others, which debilitates compassion and hinders prayer. That's tragic because intercessory prayer is a powerful tool in the hands of righteous people (James 5:16).

Analyze your own prayers. Are they generous with praise to God for His goodness to others? Do you pray for the needs of others? Practice doing so, and the joy of intercession will be yours.

❖❖❖

Suggestions for Prayer: Pray for specific people and specific needs. ❖ Thank God for what you see Him doing in the lives of others.

For Further Study: John 17 is Christ's intercessory prayer for His disciples, including us (v. 20). After reading that chapter, complete the following statements ❖ Eternal life is _____. ❖ Christ's mission on earth was to _____. ❖ The world's reaction to Christ and His followers is_____.
❖ The best way to convince the world that Christ was sent by the Father is to
_____.

" . . in view of your participation in the gospel from the first day
until now" (Phil. 1:5).

❖❖❖

**You share in a sacred partnership with Christ and your
fellow-Christians for the advancement of the gospel.**

In recent years the Greek word *koinōnia* has become familiar to many
Christians as the New Testament word for "fellowship." However, it is also
translated "partnership" and "participation." In Philippians 1:5, Paul uses it
to emphasize the participation of the Philippians in common ministry goals.

Romans 12:13 gives one aspect of that partnership and participation: monetary contributions. That's one aspect of fellowship that the Philippian church
eagerly shared with Paul. As he says in Philippians 4:15-16, "At the first
preaching of the gospel, after I departed from Macedonia, no church shared
with me in the matter of giving and receiving but you alone; for even in
Thessalonica you sent a gift more than once for my needs." They were part-
ners in his ministry because their financial support made it possible for him
to preach the gospel more effectively.

The Philippians knew that Paul carried a tremendous burden in his heart
for all the churches. In listing many of the trials he endured as an apostle, he
added, "Apart from such external things, there is the daily pressure upon me
of concern for all the churches" (2 Cor. 11:28). The Philippian church eased
that burden somewhat by being committed to Paul, to his teaching, and to
godly living. That brought great joy to him.

How about you? Do your leaders derive encouragement and joy from your
participation in the gospel? Remember, you share in a sacred partnership with
Christ and your fellow-Christians in the advancement of the gospel, just as
the Philippians shared a partnership with Paul. Rejoice in that privilege, and
make the most of it today.

❖❖❖

Suggestions for Prayer: Thank the Lord for the Christian fellowship you
enjoy. ❖ Ask for wisdom on how you might advance the gospel more effectively. ❖ Always seek to ease the burden of your spiritual leaders by faithfully
participating in the ministry of your church as God has gifted you.

For Further Study: Read Ephesians 4:11-16. ❖ What is the goal of Christian
ministry? ❖ What is the role of a pastor/teacher in achieving that goal? ❖ What
is your role (see also Rom. 12:6-8; 1 Cor. 12:4- 11; 1 Peter 4:10-11)?

"I am confident of this very thing, that He who began a good work in you will perfect it" (Phil. 1:6).

❖❖❖

God always finishes what He starts.

All who love Christ desire to be like Him in spiritual perfection and absolute holiness. We want to please Him in every respect. However, that noble pursuit is often met with frustration and discouragement as human frailties and sin block our pathway.

Paul's cry in Romans 7 is ours as well: "That which I am doing, I do not understand; for I am not practicing what I would like to do, but I am doing the very thing I hate. . . . I find then the principle that evil is present in me, the one who wishes to do good. . . . Wretched man that I am! Who will set me free from the body of this death?" (vv. 15, 21, 24). His answer resonates with confidence and relief: "Thanks be to God through Jesus Christ our Lord!" (v. 25).

Paul was convinced that God always completes the good work of salvation He begins in every new believer—a work that progressively conforms us to the image of His Son (2 Cor. 3:18). That might seem like a painfully slow process at times, but be assured He will complete it. All whom He justifies will be glorified (Rom. 8:29-30).

In the meantime, you have an active role to play in the process. Paul called it "work[ing] out your salvation with fear and trembling" (Phil. 2:12). You must discipline yourself for holiness through prayer, Bible study, obedience, and accountability to other believers. All the resources you need are at your disposal as God Himself works in you to produce "His good pleasure" (Phil. 2:13).

Rejoice in knowing that you belong to God and that He is conforming you to the image of His Son. See every event of this day as part of that process. Yield to the Spirit's prompting, and take heart that God will accomplish His will.

❖❖❖

Suggestions for Prayer: Give thanks to God, who is able "to make you stand in the presence of His glory blameless with great joy" (Jude 24). ❖ Express the desire to discipline yourself for godliness. Ask for wisdom in taking advantage of all the spiritual resources available to you as a believer.

For Further Study: Read Hebrews 10:19-25. ❖ What should be your attitude when approaching God? ❖ What is your responsibility in light of God's promises?

"I am confident of this very thing, that He who began a good work in you will perfect it until the day of Christ Jesus" (Phil. 1:6).

❖❖❖

Someday God will glorify and reward every believer.

For Christians there's an element of truth to the bumper sticker that reads, "Please be patient, God isn't finished with me yet." We aren't what we used to be, but there's much to be done to make us all He wants us to be. Yet, God's work within us is so sure and so powerful that Scripture guarantees its completion.

Pondering that guarantee led Bible expositor F. B. Meyer to write: "We go into the artist's studio and find there unfinished pictures covering large canvas, and suggesting great designs, but which have been left, either because the genius was not competent to complete the work, or because paralysis laid the hand low in death; but as we go into God's great workshop we find nothing that bears the mark of haste or insufficiency of power to finish, and we are sure that the work which His grace has begun, the arm of His strength will complete" (*The Epistle to the Philippians* [Grand Rapids, Mich.: Baker, 1952], p. 28).

The completion of God's work in you will come at a future point in time that Paul calls "the day of Christ Jesus" (Phil. 1:6). Scripture also speaks of "the day of the Lord," which is the time of God's judgment on unbelievers. But "the day of Christ Jesus" refers to the time when believers will be fully glorified and then rewarded for their faithful service (cf. 1 Cor. 3:10-15). All your earthly cares will be gone, and God's promise to keep you from stumbling and make you stand in His presence "blameless with great joy" (Jude 24) will be fully realized.

Concentrating on what is wrong in your life might depress you, but focusing on the glorious day of Christ should excite you. Don't be unduly concerned about what you are right now. Look ahead to what you will become by God's grace.

❖❖❖

Suggestions for Prayer: Reflect on the joy that is yours because you belong to an all-powerful God who is working mightily in you. Express your joy and praise to Him. ❖ Read 1 Chronicles 29:11-13 as a prayer of praise to God.

For Further Study: Read Revelation 7:9-17 and 22:1-5. What glimpses do those passages give you of the activities of glorified believers in Heaven?

"It is only right for me to feel this way about you all, because I have you in my heart, since both in my imprisonment and in the defense and confirmation of the gospel, you all are partakers of grace with me. For God is my witness, how I long for you all with the affection of Christ Jesus" (Phil. 1:7-8).

❖❖❖

Often the strongest and deepest relationships are forged in the crucible of Christian ministry.

Undoubtedly there are people who occupy a special place in your heart. Perhaps you seldom see them or talk to them, but they are on your mind and in your prayers often.

That's how Paul regarded the Philippian believers, and it was right for him to do so because they were such an integral part of his life and ministry. They stood by him in every situation—even during his judicial proceedings and imprisonment in Rome.

The gratitude and joy Paul felt was more than an emotion. It was a moral obligation to praise God for what He had accomplished through them. That's the meaning of the Greek word translated "right" in verse 7.

"Heart" refers to the center of one's thoughts and feelings (cf. Prov. 4:23). Paul thought of the Philippians often and eagerly yearned for them with the affection of Christ Himself. In Philippians 4:1 he calls them "my beloved brethren whom I long to see, my joy and crown."

The mutual affection between Paul and the Philippians illustrates that often the strongest and deepest relationships are developed within the context of Christian ministry. There's a special camaraderie among people who work toward life's most noble goals and see God achieve eternal results through their efforts. Guard those relationships carefully, and cultivate as many as possible.

❖❖❖

Suggestions for Prayer: Make a list of those who share in your ministry. Also list some ways God has worked through you in recent weeks. Spend time thanking Him for both.

For Further Study: Barnabas was a faithful friend and ministry companion to Paul. Read Acts 4:36-37, 9:22-28, 11:19-30, and 13:1-3 and answer these questions: ❖ What does "Barnabas" mean? Did he live up to his name? ❖ How did Barnabas pave the way for Paul's ministry among the disciples at Jerusalem? ❖ What adventure did Paul and Barnabas share that began at Antioch?

"The blameless in their walk are [God's] delight" (Prov. 11:20).

❖❖❖

Your love for God brings Him joy.

Our focus so far this month has been on the joy we experience in knowing and serving Christ. Before we turn our attention to the theme of godliness, I want you to consider two additional aspects of joy: the joy of pleasing God, and how to lose your joy. Pleasing God is our topic for today.

Perhaps you haven't given much thought to how you can bring joy to God, but Scripture mentions several ways. Luke 15:7, for example, says, "There will be more joy in heaven over one sinner who repents, than over ninety-nine righteous persons who need no repentance." Verse 10 adds, "There is joy in the presence of the angels of God over one sinner who repents." Repentance brings joy to God.

Faith is another source of joy for God. Hebrews 11:6 says, "Without faith it is impossible to please Him." That's the negative side of a positive principle: when you trust God, He is pleased.

In addition to repentance and faith, prayer also brings God joy. Proverbs 15:8 says, "The sacrifice of the wicked is an abomination to the Lord, but the prayer of the upright is His delight."

Righteous living is another source of joy to God, as David acknowledges in 1 Chronicles 29:17: "I know, O my God, that Thou triest the heart and delightest in uprightness." Solomon added that those who walk blamelessly are God's delight (Prov. 11:20).

Repentance, faith, prayer, and righteous living all please God because they are expressions of love. That's the overarching principle. Whenever you express your love to Him—whether by words of praise or by acts of obedience—you bring Him joy.

Doesn't it thrill you to know that the God of the universe delights in you? It should! Let that realization motivate you to find as many ways as possible to bring Him joy today.

❖❖❖

Suggestions for Prayer: Thank God for the privilege of bringing Him joy. ❖ Thank Him for His grace, which enables you to love Him and to express your love in repentance, faith, prayer, and righteous living (cf. 1 John 4:19).

For Further Study: Read 1 Kings 3:3-15. ❖ What did Solomon request of God? ❖ What was God's response?

*"I have learned to be content in whatever circumstances I am"
(Phil. 4:11).*

❖❖❖

Discontent and ingratitude will steal your joy.

True joy is God's gift to every believer, and yet many Christians seem to lack it. How can that be? Did God fail them? No. As with peace, assurance, and other benefits of salvation, joy can be forfeited for many reasons. Willful sin, prayerlessness, fear, self-centeredness, focusing on circumstances, and lack of forgiveness are the main culprits.

Two of the most common joy-thieves are dissatisfaction and ingratitude. Both are by-products of the health, wealth, and prosperity mentality of our day. That teaching has produced a generation of Christians who are more dissatisfied than ever because their demands and expectations are higher than ever. They've lost their perspective on God's sovereignty and have therefore lost the ability to give thanks in all things.

In marked contrast, when Jesus taught about contentment and anxiety (Matt. 6:25-34), He spoke of food and clothing—the basic necessities of life. But preferences, not necessities, are the issue with us. We're into style, personal appearance, job satisfaction, earning power, bigger homes, and newer cars. In the name of greater faith we even demand that God supply more miracles, more wealth, and more power.

Amid all that, Paul's words sound a refreshing note of assurance and rebuke: "I have learned to be content in whatever circumstances I am" (Phil. 4:11). He made no demands on God but simply trusted in His gracious provision. Whether he received little or much made no difference to him. In either case he was satisfied and thankful.

Don't be victimized by the spirit of our age. See God's blessings for what they are, and continually praise Him for His goodness. In doing so you will guard your heart from dissatisfaction and ingratitude. More important, you will bring joy to the One who is worthy of all praise.

❖❖❖

Suggestions for Prayer: Pray that the Holy Spirit will produce in you a joy and contentment that transcends your circumstances. ❖ Make it a daily practice to thank God for specific blessings and trials, knowing that He uses both to perfect His will in you.

For Further Study: Read 1 Kings 18:1–19:8. ❖ How did Elijah deal with the false prophets of Baal? ❖ How did he deal with Jezebel's threat? ❖ What caused Elijah's shift from a spiritual high to a spiritual low?

"This I pray . . ." (Phil. 1:9).

✧✧✧

Your prayers reveal the level of your spiritual maturity.

A s we come to our study of godliness in Philippians 1:9-11, we note that this passage is a prayer. Typically, Paul's prayers reflected his concern that his readers mature spiritually. That is impossible without prayer, because spiritual growth depends on the Holy Spirit's power, which is tapped through prayer.

Prayer is so vital that Jesus instructed His disciples to pray "at all times" (Luke 18:1). Paul commands us to "pray without ceasing" (1 Thess. 5:17). Peter said we should be "of sound judgment and sober spirit for the purpose of prayer" (1 Peter 4:7).

Scripture gives many other commands to pray, but the true test of your spirituality is your compulsion to pray, not simply your obedience to commands. As a Christian you exist in a spiritual realm in which prayer is as natural as breathing is in the natural realm. Just as atmospheric pressure exerts force on your lungs, compelling you to breathe, so your spiritual environment compels you to pray. Resisting either brings devastating results.

The more you see life through God's eyes, the more you are driven to pray. In that sense your prayers reveal the level of your spiritual maturity. Paul prayed with urgency day and night because he shared God's love for His people and His concern for their spiritual maturity.

Examine your own prayers. Do you pray from a sense of duty, or are you compelled to pray? Do you pray infrequently or briefly? Do your prayers center on your own needs or the needs of others? Do you pray for the spiritual maturity of others? Those important questions indicate the level of your spiritual maturity and give guidelines for making any needed changes in your pattern of prayer.

✧✧✧

Suggestions for Prayer: Thank God for the privilege and power of prayer. ✧ If you have neglected prayer, or if your prayers have been centered on yourself rather than others, confess your sin and ask God to give you a sense of holy urgency in praying as you should. ✧ Is there someone for whom you should be praying more consistently?

For Further Study: Read Daniel 6:1-28. ✧ What was Daniel's pattern of prayer? ✧ What accusation did the political leaders bring against Daniel? ✧ What was the king's attitude toward Daniel? ✧ How did God honor Daniel's faith?

> *"This I pray, that your love may abound still more and more in real knowledge and all discernment" (Phil. 1:9).*

❖❖❖

Christian love operates within the parameters of Biblical knowledge and spiritual discernment.

As a Christian, you are a repository of divine love. More than anything else, your love for God and for other believers marks you as a true disciple of Jesus Christ (John 13:35).

In addition to possessing God's love, you have the privilege and responsibility of expressing it to others on His behalf. That's a sacred trust. Paul qualifies it in Philippians 1:9, which tells us that love is to operate within the sphere of Biblical knowledge and spiritual discernment. Those are the parameters that govern God's love.

No matter how loving an act or word might seem, if it violates knowledge and discernment, it is not true Christian love. Second John 5-11 illustrates that principle. Apparently some believers who lacked discernment were hosting false teachers in the name of Christian love and hospitality. John sternly warned them, saying, "If anyone comes to you and does not bring [sound doctrine], do not receive him into your house, and do not give him a greeting; for the one who gives him a greeting participates in his evil deeds" (vv. 10-11). That might sound extreme or unloving, but the purity of God's people was at stake.

In 2 Thessalonians 3:5-6, after praying for the Thessalonians' love to increase, Paul commanded them to "keep aloof" from so-called Christians who were disregarding sound teaching. That's not contradictory, because Christian love guards sound doctrine and holy living.

Unfortunately, today it is common for Christians to compromise doctrinal purity in the name of love and unity, or to brand as unloving some practices Scripture clearly commands. Both are wrong and carry serious consequences.

Be thoughtful in how you express your love. Abundantly supply it in accord with Biblical knowledge and discernment. Excellence and righteousness will result (Phil. 1:10-11).

❖❖❖

Suggestions for Prayer: Thank God for the love He's given you through His Spirit (Rom. 5:5). ❖ Ask for opportunities to show Christ's love to others. ❖ Pray that your love will be governed by convictions grounded in God's truth.

For Further Study: What do the following passages teach about love? How can you apply them to your life? Romans 12:9-10; 5:5; 1 John 4:7-10; Galatians 5:22; 1 Peter 1:22; 4:8.

". . . so that you may approve the things that are excellent"
(Phil. 1:10).

❖❖❖

In a world of mediocrity and confusion,
God calls you to excellence and discernment.

There's the story of a pilot who came on the loudspeaker midflight and said, "I have some good news and some bad news. The bad news is, we've lost all our instrumentation and don't know where we are. The good news is, we have a strong tailwind and are making great time." That's an accurate picture of how many people live: they have no direction in life, but they're getting there fast!

We as Christians are to be different because we have divine guidance and eternal goals. Our lives are to be marked by a confident trust in God and a pursuit of spiritual excellence.

"Excellent" in Philippians 1:10 speaks of things that are worthwhile and vital. "Approv[ing]" what is "excellent" refers to testing things as one would test a precious metal to determine its purity and value. It goes beyond knowing good from evil. It distinguishes between better and best. It involves thinking Biblically and focusing your time and energy on what really counts. It involves cultivating spiritual discipline and not being controlled by your emotions, whims, moods, or circumstances.

Many organizations and businesses have rightly adopted the motto "Commitment to Excellence" to convey their desire to provide the finest product or service possible. If secular-minded people strive for that level of achievement, how much more should Christians pursue excellence for the glory of God!

Look at your life. Is it filled with godly love, discernment, and the pursuit of excellence—or has worldly trivia crowded out those virtues?

❖❖❖

Suggestions for Prayer: Read Isaiah 12:1-6 as a psalm of praise to the God of excellence. ❖ Ask God to give you a heart constantly set on pursuing excellence for His glory.

For Further Study: Daniel was a man who pursued excellence. Read Daniel 1:1–2:23. ❖ What was Daniel's decision regarding the king's food and wine, and how did he handle the situation? ❖ How did Daniel and his three friends compare in wisdom and understanding to the magicians and conjurers? ❖ What principles do you see in those two chapters that apply to your life?

"... in order to be sincere and blameless until the day of Christ"
(Phil. 1:10).

❖❖❖

Seek to have a life that bears scrutiny.

In our society, those whose lives are marked by moral soundness, upright-ness, honesty, and sincerity are usually thought of as people of integrity. However, society's standards often fall far short of God's. Spiritual integrity calls for the highest possible standard of behavior and requires supernatural resources available only to those who trust in Him.

Paul's prayer in Philippians 1:9-10 outlines the path to spiritual integrity. It begins with "love" that abounds with "knowledge and all discernment" (v. 9) and progresses to the pursuit of excellence (v. 10). The result is sincerity and blamelessness—two characteristics of godly integrity.

The Greek word translated "sincere" in verse 10 speaks of genuineness and authenticity. It literally means "without wax" and is an allusion to the prac-tice of inspecting pottery by holding it up to the sunlight. In ancient times pot-tery often cracked during the firing process. Rather than discarding cracked pieces, dishonest dealers often filled the cracks with wax and sold them to unsuspecting customers. Holding a pot up to the sunlight revealed any flaws and protected the customer from a bad purchase.

Following that analogy, Biblical integrity requires that you be without wax, having no hypocrisy or secret sins that show up when you're under pressure or facing temptation.

"Blameless" speaks of consistency in living a life that doesn't lead others into error or sin. Your standard is to be the same away from church as it is at church.

Being blameless isn't easy in a world that unashamedly flaunts its sinful prac-tices. You must guard against losing your sensitivity to the heinousness of sin and unwittingly beginning to tolerate or even accept the sin that once shocked you. That's when you lose integrity and begin to cause others to stumble.

Diligently pursue integrity with a view toward glorifying Christ in all things until He returns!

❖❖❖

Suggestions for Prayer: Thank God that He is "able to keep you from stum-bling and to make you stand in His presence . . . blameless with great joy" (Jude 24). ❖ Prayerfully guard your heart and mind from the subtle evil influ-ences that can erode your integrity and make you ineffective for the Lord.

For Further Study: Read Genesis 39. ❖ How was Joseph's integrity chal-lenged? ❖ How did God honor Joseph's commitment to godly integrity?

". . . having been filled with the fruit of righteousness which comes through Jesus Christ" (Phil. 1:11).

❖❖❖

Bearing spiritual fruit is the acid test of a true believer.

After facing life-threatening situations, people often say, "I saw my entire life flash before my eyes." That's the picture we get in Philippians 1:11.

"The fruit of righteousness" refers to what is produced in you as you operate in love, pursue excellence, and maintain your integrity. It includes every attitude and action consistent with God's standard of what is right.

"Having been filled" speaks of something that happened in the past with continuing results. At your salvation the seed of righteousness was planted within you. It bears righteous fruit throughout your lifetime. On the day of Christ that fruit will confirm your salvation.

Fruitfulness has always been the acid test of true salvation. Jesus said, "If you abide in My word, then you are truly disciples of Mine" (John 8:31). When John the Baptist admonished his followers to "bring forth fruits in keeping with your repentance" (Luke 3:8), he was speaking of good deeds (vv. 10-14). Paul said we are God's "workmanship, created in Christ Jesus for good works, which God prepared beforehand, that we should walk in them" (Eph. 2:10). John said that all who profess Christ should live as He lived (cf. 1 John 2:6).

Bearing spiritual fruit is not something you can achieve on your own. It "comes through Jesus Christ" (Phil. 1:11). Jesus Himself said, "Abide in Me, and I in you. As the branch cannot bear fruit of itself, unless it abides in the vine, so neither can you, unless you abide in Me. I am the vine, you are the branches; he who abides in Me, and I in him, he bears much fruit; for apart from Me you can do nothing" (John 15:4-5).

You were redeemed to glorify God through righteous deeds. Make that your priority today.

❖❖❖

Suggestions for Prayer: Psalm 71 is a psalm of praise to God for His righteousness and faithful provisions. Read it and meditate on its truths. Then praise God for His righteousness toward you. ❖ Ask for opportunities to demonstrate righteousness to others today.

For Further Study: Read Proverbs 11:1-9, 15:8-9, and 21:2-3, noting the characteristics and benefits of righteousness.

". . . to the glory and praise of God" (Phil. 1:11).

❖❖❖

To glorify God is to reflect His character in your words and deeds.

Paul's prayer in Philippians 1:9-11 closes with a reminder that love, excellence, integrity, and righteousness bring glory and praise to God.

God's glory is a recurring theme in Paul's writings, and rightly so, because that is the Christian's highest priority. But what is God's glory, and what does it mean to bring Him glory? After all, He is infinitely glorious in nature, so we can't add anything to Him. And His glory can never be diminished, so it doesn't have to be replenished or bolstered.

In Exodus 33:18-19 Moses says to God, "'I pray Thee, show me Thy glory!' And [God] said, 'I Myself will make all My goodness pass before you, and will proclaim the name of the Lord before you; and I will be gracious to whom I will be gracious, and will show compassion on whom I will show compassion.'" In effect God was telling Moses that His glory is the composite of His attributes.

That suggests you can glorify God by placing His attributes on display in your life. When others see godly characteristics such as love, mercy, patience, and kindness in you, they have a better picture of what God is like. That honors Him. That's why it's so important to guard your attitudes and actions. Paul admonished Timothy to be exemplary in his "speech, conduct, love, faith, and purity" (1 Tim. 4:12). That should be true of every believer!

Another way to glorify God is to praise Him. David said, "Ascribe to the Lord, O sons of the mighty, ascribe to the Lord glory and strength. Ascribe to the Lord the glory due to His name; worship the Lord in holy array. . . . In His temple everything says, 'Glory!'" (Ps. 29:1-2, 9).

You cannot add to God's glory, but you can proclaim it in your words and deeds. What picture of God do others see in you? Does your life bring glory to Him?

❖❖❖

Suggestions for Prayer: In 1 Chronicles 16:8-36 David instructs Asaph and Asaph's relatives on how to glorify God. Using that passage as a model, spend time in prayer glorifying God.

For Further Study: Reread 1 Chronicles 16:8-36, noting any specific instructions that apply to you.

"We have not ceased to pray for you and to ask that you may be filled with the knowledge of His will in all spiritual wisdom and understanding" (Col. 1:9).

❖❖❖

Godly living results from being controlled by the principles of God's Word.

Paul's prayer for the Philippians (Phil. 1:9-11) is closely paralleled by his prayer for the Colossians (Col. 1:9-12). Both epistles were written from the same Roman prison at about the same time in Paul's life. Both prayers focus on godly living, but they approach it from slightly different perspectives.

The Philippians were gracious people who needed to exercise greater knowledge and discernment in their love. The Colossians also were gracious, but their devotion to Christ was being challenged by heretics who taught that Christ is insufficient for salvation and godly living. True spirituality, the false teachers said, is found in Christ plus human philosophy, religious legalism, mysticism, and/or asceticism. Paul encouraged the Colossian believers and refuted the false teachers by showing the utter sufficiency of Christ.

At the outset of his prayer Paul stressed the importance of being controlled by the knowledge of God's will (which is revealed in His Word). That's the meaning of the Greek word translated "filled" in verse 9. "Knowledge" translates a word that speaks of a deep, penetrating knowledge that results in behavioral change. "Spiritual wisdom and understanding" refers to knowledge that cannot be known through human reasoning or philosophy. It is imparted by the Holy Spirit Himself.

In effect Paul was saying, "I pray that you will be continually controlled by the life-transforming knowledge of God's will, which the Holy Spirit imparts as you prayerfully study and meditate on God's Word."

Scripture supplies the principles you need to live a godly life. And the Spirit gives you the power to do so. Many false teachers will try to divert you from the simplicity of devotion to Christ by offering you philosophy, psychology, and a myriad of other hopeless alternatives. Don't be victimized. In Christ you have everything you need!

❖❖❖

Suggestions for Prayer: Thank God for His all-sufficient Son and for the resources that are yours in Him. ❖ Ask for wisdom to apply those resources to every situation you face today.

For Further Study: Read Colossians 1:15–2:23. ❖ What was Christ's role in creation? ❖ What was Paul's goal as a minister? ❖ What warnings and commands did Paul give?

". . . so that you may walk in a manner worthy of the Lord, to please Him in all respects" (Col. 1:10).

❖❖❖

Your manner of life should be consistent with Christ's.

In Colossians 1:9 Paul speaks of being controlled by the knowledge of God's will. In verse 10 he speaks of walking in a manner worthy of the Lord. There is a direct cause-and-effect relationship between those verses. When you are controlled by the knowledge of God's will, you will walk in a manner worthy of the Lord.

The Greek word translated "walk" means "to order one's behavior." It's a common New Testament metaphor for one's lifestyle. Paul made a similar plea to the Thessalonians: "so that you may walk in a manner worthy of the God who calls you into His own kingdom and glory" (1 Thess. 2:12).

The thought of being worthy of the Lord might raise some eyebrows, because we usually relate worthiness to merit or something deserved. But that isn't Paul's point at all. The Greek word translated "worthy" in Colossians 1:10 speaks of something that weighs as much or carries the same value as something else. He isn't saying we deserve Christ, but that our conduct should be consistent with His.

That is also Peter's point in 1 Peter 2:21: "You have been called for this purpose, since Christ also suffered for you, leaving you an example for you to follow in His steps." John said, "The one who says he abides in [Christ] ought himself to walk in the same manner as He walked" (1 John 2:6). He added in 2 John 6, "Walk according to His commandments." That's how you demonstrate your love for Christ (John 14:15) and please Him in every respect.

As a word of encouragement, a worthy walk is not a walk of sinless perfection. That won't happen until you are fully glorified. But each day you are growing in godliness as a result of the Spirit's transforming work in you (2 Cor. 3:18). Be faithful to that process. Set your affections on Christ, look to His Word, and rejoice in the privilege of becoming more like Him today.

❖❖❖

Suggestions for Prayer: Thank God for the power and guidance of His Spirit in your life. ❖ Be diligent to confess your sin when you stray from a worthy walk.

For Further Study: Read Ephesians 4:1-3 and Philippians 1:27-30. ❖ What specific attitudes are involved in a worthy walk? ❖ Does a worthy walk eliminate the possibility of suffering or persecution? Explain.

". . . bearing fruit in every good work and increasing in the knowledge of God" (Col. 1:10).

❖❖❖

Your fruitfulness is directly related to your knowledge of divine truth.

Every farmer who enjoys a plentiful harvest does so only after diligent effort on his part. He must cultivate the soil, plant the seed, and then nurture it to maturity. Each step is thoughtful, disciplined, and orderly.

Similarly, bearing spiritual fruit is not an unthinking or haphazard process. It requires us to be diligent in pursuing the knowledge of God's will, which is revealed in His Word. That is Paul's prayer in Colossians 1:9, which he reiterates in verse 10.

The phrase "increasing in the knowledge of God" (v. 10) can be translated "increasing *by* the knowledge of God." Both renderings are acceptable. The first emphasizes the need to grow; the second emphasizes the role that knowledge plays in your spiritual growth.

As your knowledge of God's Word increases, the Holy Spirit renews your mind and transforms your thinking. As you gaze into the glory of the Lord as revealed in Scripture, you "are being transformed into the same image from glory to glory" (2 Cor. 3:18). You "have put on the new self who is being renewed to a true knowledge according to the image of the One who created him" (Col. 3:10).

One of Satan's ploys to retard spiritual productivity is to get Christians preoccupied with humanistic philosophy and other bankrupt substitutes for God's truth. That's why he planted false teachers at Colosse to teach that knowing God's will is inadequate for true spirituality. Paul refuted that claim by affirming that Christ is the fullness of Deity in bodily form (Col. 2:9). In Him "are hidden all the treasures of wisdom and knowledge" (Col. 2:3). *He is all you need!*

Scripture commands you to grow in the grace and knowledge of Jesus Christ (2 Peter 3:18). Is that characteristic of your life? Are you looking forward to a bountiful spiritual harvest?

❖❖❖

Suggestions for Prayer: Thank God for the privilege of knowing His will and studying His Word. ❖ Prayerfully guard your mind from sinful influences. Saturate it with God's truth.

For Further Study: Read the following passages, noting the effects of God's Word: Psalms 119:9, 105; Acts 20:32; Romans 10:17; 1 Thessalonians 2:13; 2 Timothy 3:14-17; Hebrews 4:12-13; 1 John 2:14.

*". . . strengthened with all power, according to His glorious might,
for the attaining of all steadfastness and patience" (Col. 1:11).*

❖❖❖

God always empowers you to do what He commands you to do.

An alarming number of Christians seem to lack spiritual stability. Many are "carried about by every wind of doctrine, by the trickery of men, by craftiness in deceitful scheming" (Eph. 4:14). Others lack moral purity. Many are driven by their emotions rather than sound thinking. Increasingly, therapists and psychologists are replacing pastors and Biblical teachers as the heroes of the faith. While we still proclaim a sovereign, all-powerful God, our conduct often belies our creed.

Despite our inconsistencies, the power for spiritual stability is ours in Christ as we allow the knowledge of His will to control our lives. Paul describes the working of that power in Colossians 1:11. There the Greek words translated "strengthened" and "power" speak of inherent power that gives one the ability to do something.

The phrase "according to" indicates that the power for spiritual stability is proportional to God's abundant supply—and that supply is inexhaustible! The literal Greek says you are being "empowered with all power according to the might of His glory." That thought is akin to Philippians 2:12-13, where Paul says that the power for working out your salvation comes from God, "who is at work in you, both to will and to work for His good pleasure."

In Colossians 1:11 the result of God's enabling is "the attaining of all steadfastness and patience." "Steadfastness" speaks of endurance regarding people; "patience" speaks of endurance regarding things or circumstances. When you are steadfast and patient, you are spiritually stable. Your responses are Biblical, thoughtful, and calculated—not worldly, emotional, or uncontrolled. You bear up under trials because you understand God's purposes and trust His promises.

Paul said, "Be strong in the Lord, and in the strength of His might" (Eph. 6:10). That is possible when you trust God and rely on the infinite power that is yours in Christ.

❖❖❖

Suggestions for Prayer: Perhaps you know someone who is struggling with spiritual instability. Pray for him or her, and ask God to use you as a source of encouragement.

For Further Study: Psalm 18 is a psalm of victory that David wrote after God delivered him from Saul. Read it, then answer these questions: ❖ What characteristics of God did David mention? ❖ How might those characteristics apply to situations you are facing?

". . . joyously giving thanks to the Father" (Col. 1:11-12).

❖❖❖

Joyous thanksgiving acknowledges God as the giver of every good gift.

The inseparable link between joy and thanksgiving was a common theme for Paul. In Philippians 4:4-6 he says, "Rejoice in the Lord always; again I will say, rejoice!. . . . Be anxious for nothing, but in everything by prayer and supplication with thanksgiving let your requests be made known to God." He told the Thessalonians to "rejoice always; pray without ceasing; in everything give thanks; for this is God's will for you in Christ Jesus" (1 Thess. 5:16-18).

As often as Paul expressed thanks and encouraged others to express theirs, he was careful never to attribute to men the thanks due to God alone. For example, in Romans 1:8 he says, "I thank my God through Jesus Christ for you all, because your faith is being proclaimed throughout the whole world." He thanked God, not the Roman believers, because he knew that faith is a gift from God.

That doesn't mean you can't thank others for the kindnesses they show, but in doing so you must understand that they are instruments of God's grace.

Thanking Him shows humility and acknowledges His rightful place as the Sovereign Lord and the giver of every good and perfect gift (James 1:17). Those who reject His Lordship and refuse to give Him thanks incur His wrath (Rom. 1:21).

Only those who love Christ can truly give thanks because He is the channel through which thanks is expressed to the Father. As Paul says in Colossians 3:17, "And whatever you do in word or deed, do all in the name of the Lord Jesus, giving thanks through Him to God the Father." Hebrews 13:15 adds, "Through [Christ] then let us continually offer up a sacrifice of praise to God, that is, the fruit of lips that give thanks to His name."

As one who is privileged to know the God of all grace, be generous in your praise and thanksgiving today. See everything as a gift from His hand for your joy and edification.

❖❖❖

Suggestions for Prayer: Read aloud Psalm 136 as a prayer of praise to God.

For Further Study: From Psalm 136 list the things that prompted the psalmist's thanksgiving. How can that psalm serve as a model for your own praise?

"The Father . . . has qualified us to share in the inheritance of the saints in light" (Col. 1:12).

❖❖❖

You are the recipient of a very special inheritance.

Perhaps you've had the disappointing and annoying experience of receiving in the mail an envelope that identifies you as the winner of a large sum of money or some other fantastic prize, only to open it and discover you hadn't won anything at all. It was simply a ploy to get you to enter a contest or purchase a product.

In a world filled with deception and unfulfilled expectations, it's wonderful to know that God's truthfulness and integrity never waver. Not only has He promised you an eternal inheritance, but He also has qualified you to share in it.

The Greek word translated "qualified" in Colossians 1:12 means "to make sufficient" or "to authorize." "Share" speaks of receiving an allotted portion. The idea is that God has authorized you to receive a portion of the blessings that belong to all who love Him.

In Ephesians 1:3 Paul says that your inheritance consists of "every spiritual blessing" in Heaven. It is a glorious inheritance of which the Holy Spirit Himself is the pledge (vv. 14, 18). In Colossians 3:24 Paul calls it an inheritance "from the Lord."

In Colossians 1:12 he further describes it as an inheritance "in light," which refers to its overall character or quality. In the New Testament, "light" is often used metaphorically of truth and purity. First John 1:5 says, "God is light, and in Him there is no darkness at all." Believers are those who walk in the light (v. 7). So an inheritance in light is a godly, true, and pure inheritance—one that is reserved in Heaven, where He who is the Light dwells (1 Peter 1:4; Rev. 21:23).

Your eternal inheritance is no empty promise. God has secured it by delivering you from the domain of darkness and transferring you to the Kingdom of His beloved Son, in whom you have redemption, the forgiveness of sin (Col. 1:13-14). Rejoice in God's grace. Live today as a child of light!

❖❖❖

Suggestions for Prayer: Thank God for the grace of salvation and the glory of your inheritance. ❖ Ask Him to use you today as a light to those who walk in darkness.

For Further Study: Using Ephesians 5:6-16 as your guide, contrast the characteristics of darkness and light.

"Pray at all times in the Spirit" (Eph. 6:18).

❖❖❖

Spiritual victory is directly related to the quality of your prayer life.

Prayer is communication with God; and like all communication, it can be developed to maximum efficiency or allowed to languish. Which you choose will determine the quality of your spiritual life.

Ironically, the freedom of worship we enjoy in our society and our high standard of living make it easy to become complacent about prayer and to presume on God's grace. Consequently, many who say they trust in God actually live as if they don't need Him at all. Such neglect is sinful and leads to spiritual disaster.

Jesus taught that "men ought always to pray, and not to faint" (Luke 18:1, KJV). "Faint" speaks of giving in to evil or becoming weary or cowardly. Paul added that we should "pray at all times in the Spirit . . . with all prayer and petition" and "be on the alert with all perseverance and petition for all the saints" (Eph. 6:18).

First Thessalonians 5:17 says, "Pray without ceasing." That doesn't mean to do nothing but pray. It simply means to live in a constant state of God-consciousness. If you see a beautiful sunrise or a bouquet of flowers, your first response is to thank God for the beauty of His creation. If you see someone in distress, you intercede on his or her behalf. You see every experience of life in relation to God.

God wants you to be diligent and faithful in prayer. With that goal in mind, we will devote this month to a study of prayer from two texts: Daniel's prayer in Daniel 9:1-19, and the Disciples' Prayer in Matthew 6:9-13. Both are models of majestic, effective prayer.

As we study those passages together, be aware of your own pattern of prayer. Examine it carefully for strengths and weaknesses. Be prepared to make any necessary changes.

❖❖❖

Suggestions for Prayer: Thank God for the privilege of communing with Him in prayer. ❖ Ask Him to reveal any areas in your praying that need to be strengthened.

For Further Study: Read Daniel 9:1-19. ❖ What prompted Daniel's prayer? ❖ What was Daniel's attitude toward God? Toward himself and his people? ❖ What did Daniel request?

"Men ought always to pray" (Luke 18:1, KJV).

✧✧✧

Prayer should never be limited to certain times, places, or circumstances.

As a child I was taught to pray with my head bowed, eyes closed, and hands folded. Even as a young man I thought that was the only acceptable mode of prayer.

In my seminary days I sang in a quartet that traveled to various churches throughout the United States. The first time I traveled with them we had a prayer meeting in the car, and the driver prayed with his eyes open. All of us were glad he did, but I wondered if God really heard his prayer.

I have since learned that praying with my eyes closed is a helpful way to avoid distractions, but it isn't mandated in Scripture—nor are most of the other limitations people often place on prayer. For example, some people want to limit prayer to a certain posture, but Scripture tells of people praying while standing, sitting, kneeling, looking upward, bowing down, and lifting up their hands.

Some try to limit prayer to certain times of the day, such as morning or evening. But in the Bible people prayed at all times: morning, evening, three times a day, before meals, after meals, at bedtime, at midnight, day and night, in their youth, in their old age, when troubled, and when joyful.

Similarly, Scripture places no limits on the place or circumstances of prayer. It tells of people praying in a cave, in a closet, in a garden, on a mountainside, by a river, by the sea, in the street, in the Temple, in bed, at home, in the stomach of a fish, in battle, on a housetop, in a prison, in the wilderness, and on a cross.

The point is clear: there is no specific correct mode or kind of prayer, and prayer isn't limited by your location or circumstances. You are to pray always. That includes any kind of prayer, on any subject, at any time of the day or night.

✧✧✧

Suggestions for Prayer: Make a list of your current plans, thoughts, and concerns. Have you made each of them a matter of prayer? Commit yourself to sharing every aspect of your life with God.

For Further Study: Read Psalm 136. Note how the Lord is intimately involved in the lives of His people.

"In the first year of Darius the son of Ahasuerus . . . I gave my attention to the Lord God to seek Him by prayer" (Dan. 9:1-3).

✧✧✧

Uncompromising prayer brings glory to God.

Daniel's prayer in Daniel 9:1-19 illustrates the key elements of effective intercessory prayer. Those elements will serve as the focus of our studies for several days, but first some background to Daniel's prayer will be helpful.

Verse 1 says that Daniel prayed in the first year of the reign of King Darius, the first great king of the Medo-Persian Empire. About sixty-five years earlier, God had punished the sinful kingdom of Judah by allowing King Nebuchadnezzar of Babylon to conquer Jerusalem and take Israelite captives back to Babylon.

Subsequently the Babylonian Empire fell to the Medo-Persian Empire. Darius conquered Babylon on the night King Belshazzar threw a drunken festival at which God wrote the doom of his kingdom on the wall (Dan. 5:24-28).

Daniel was among the captives originally transported to Babylon by Nebuchadnezzar. Throughout the lengthy captivity period, he never forgot he was God's child and always represented God properly despite his difficult circumstances. He was a man of uncommon wisdom and courage. His trust in God was unwavering and his commitment to prayer uncompromising—even when his prayers could have cost him his life (Dan. 6:4-11).

As a result, God protected him, exalted him, and was glorified through him—as evidenced by King Darius' decree that everyone in the kingdom was to fear and tremble before Daniel's great God (Dan. 6:26).

Since Daniel understood the priority of prayer, he refused to be intimidated or distracted from it. His commitment is worthy of imitation. Can that be said of you? If everyone followed your pattern of prayer, would God's Kingdom be strengthened?

✧✧✧

Suggestions for Prayer: Consistency is important in prayer. You might try praying for different requests on specific days. For example, on Mondays you could pray for your governmental leaders, on Tuesdays for your pastor and the ministries of your church, etc.

For Further Study: Read Daniel 6. ✧ What rank did Daniel hold? ✧ Why did King Darius want to promote Daniel? ✧ What was the reaction of the commissioners and satraps to Daniel's popularity? ✧ How did they deceive the king? ✧ How did God protect Daniel?

"I, Daniel, observed in the books the number of the years which was revealed as the word of the Lord to Jeremiah the prophet for the completion of the desolations of Jerusalem, namely, seventy years. So I gave my attention to the Lord God to seek Him by prayer and supplications" (Dan. 9:2-3).

❖❖❖

God's sovereignty doesn't eliminate the need for prayer.

Have you ever wondered if it's Biblical to pray for things God has already promised in His Word to do? Is it proper to pray, say, for the salvation of sinners, knowing that God will redeem all the elect anyway, or for Christ's return, knowing it is a sure thing? Daniel gives us a clear answer.

God prophesied through Jeremiah that the Babylonian Captivity would last seventy years (Jer. 25:11-12). When Daniel read that prophecy, he realized that the time was near for his people to return to their homeland. That inspired him to pray fervently.

In Daniel 9:19 he cries out, "O Lord, hear! O Lord, forgive! O Lord, listen and take action! For Thine own sake, O my God, do not delay." He was in tune with God's Word and understood that somehow his prayers were part of God's plan.

The exact relationship between God's sovereignty and our prayers is a mystery, but it is clear that somehow God's Word and our prayers are co-laborers in achieving God's will.

Like Daniel, you and I live in a time when many of God's promises seem near fulfillment. Never before have world events pointed so dramatically to the nearness of the return of our Lord. Consequently, this is not the time for complacency or over-enthusiastic speculation. It is the time for careful Bible study and fervent prayer.

❖❖❖

Suggestions for Prayer: Thank God for His faithfulness and the sure promises of His Word. ❖ Ask Him for spiritual wisdom and insight to discern His will and then live accordingly.

For Further Study: Jeremiah 24:1–25:13 gives some background to Judah's captivity in Babylon. After reading those verses, answer these questions: ❖ To what kind of fruit did God liken Judah? ❖ What did God say would happen to King Zedekiah? ❖ What warning did the prophets give to Judah? ❖ What was Judah's response? ❖ How would God deal with Babylon?

"The word of the Lord [came] to Jeremiah the prophet for the completion of the desolations of Jerusalem" (Dan. 9:2).

❖❖❖

Effective prayer is always consistent with God's will.

It is characteristic of God's people to identify with God's purposes and to conform their will to His. Learning to pray according to His will is a major step in that process because it drives you to the Word and demonstrates a humble, submissive heart.

Jesus emphasized the priority of God's will when He said, "I have come down from heaven, not to do My own will, but the will of Him who sent Me" (John 6:38). He accomplished that goal, saying to the Father, "I glorified Thee on the earth, having accomplished the work which Thou hast given Me to do" (John 17:4). Even when facing the horror of the cross, Jesus didn't waver. Instead He prayed, "Father, if Thou art willing, remove this cup from Me; yet not My will, but Thine be done" (Luke 22:42).

Jesus taught His disciples the same priority, instructing them to pray, "Our Father who art in heaven, hallowed be Thy name. Thy kingdom come. Thy will be done, on earth as it is in heaven" (Matt. 6:9-10).

Daniel knew what it meant to pray according to God's will. After reading the prophecy of a seventy-year Babylonian Captivity, he immediately accepted it as God's will and began to pray for its fulfillment. His prayer wasn't passive resignation to some act of fate beyond his control. It was active participation in God's plan as revealed in Scripture. He wasn't trying to change God's will, but was doing everything he could to see it come to pass. That's the essence of praying according to God's will.

When you pray according to God's will, you can be confident that He hears you and will grant your requests (1 John 5:14-15). Live in that confidence today!

❖❖❖

Suggestions for Prayer: Be a diligent student of the Word so you will know God's will. ❖ Ask God to reveal areas in which your will is not conformed to His. As He does, take immediate steps to deal with the situation.

For Further Study: Read Revelation 22:6-21, noting God's will for Christ's return and how we're to respond to it.

"I gave my attention to the Lord God to seek Him by prayer and supplications, with fasting, sackcloth, and ashes" (Dan. 9:3).

❖❖❖

The more you understand God's holiness, the more you'll recognize your own sinfulness.

People view prayer differently. For some it is a last resort after all human options have been exhausted: "All I can do now is pray for you!" Others liken it to a spiritual spare tire—something used only in the event of an emergency. Many who should thrive on prayer have been lulled into complacency by an affluent and godless society.

Daniel, however, saw prayer as an opportunity to express the passion and fervency of his heart to the God he loved and served. In Daniel 9:3 he says, "I gave my attention to the Lord God to seek Him." That implies he set apart a specific time to devote to thoughtful, earnest, and fervent prayer. That is further supported by the way he prepared himself through fasting and donning sackcloth and ashes—symbols of humility and deep contrition over sin.

It might seem unusual for a man of Daniel's spiritual stature to be overwhelmed by his sense of sin, but the closer one draws to God, the more aware he is of his sinfulness. We see that in Paul, who called himself the "foremost" of all sinners (1 Tim. 1:15). That might seem like a ridiculous statement to us, but Paul saw sin for what it was. So did Daniel.

The title "Lord God" in verse 3 emphasizes God's sovereign rule over all things. Daniel knew that God had permitted the Babylonian Captivity and that He alone could deliver His people from it. Consequently, Daniel gave the Lord his undivided attention as he prayed and sought mercy for himself and his people.

Daniel's fervency is a rebuke to much of the flippancy we hear in prayer today. It was profound because it was generated by God's Word and grounded in His will.

James 5:16 says, "The effectual fervent prayer of a righteous man availeth much" (KJV). Be like Daniel—a righteous person who prays fervently with great effect.

❖❖❖

Suggestions for Prayer: Ask God to give you a greater sense of fervency in prayer. ❖ Be sensitive to any sin that might be hindering your prayers.

For Further Study: Read Luke 11:5-13. ❖ What parable did Jesus tell to illustrate the benefits of humble, persistent prayer? ❖ How did Jesus contrast earthly fathers with their Heavenly Father?

"I prayed to the Lord my God and confessed" (Dan. 9:4).

❖❖❖

God will not respond to self-righteous prayers.

In Luke 18 Jesus told a parable to people who were trusting in their own self-righteousness. He said, "Two men went up into the temple to pray, one a Pharisee, and the other a tax-gatherer. The Pharisee stood and was praying thus to himself, 'God, I thank Thee that I am not like other people, swindlers, unjust, adulterers, or even like this tax-gatherer. I fast twice a week; I pay tithes of all that I get.' But the tax-gatherer, standing some distance away, was even unwilling to lift up his eyes to heaven, but was beating his breast, saying, 'God, be merciful to me, the sinner!' I tell you, this man went down to his house justified rather than the other; for everyone who exalts himself shall be humbled, but he who humbles himself shall be exalted" (vv. 10-14).

Apart from God's mercy we cannot enter into God's presence. The tax-gatherer knew that and pled for forgiveness. The Pharisee missed the point and went away without forgiveness.

Like the tax-gatherer, Daniel approached God with an attitude of confession and self-denial. He could have reminded God of his years of faithful service while in Babylon, but that didn't enter his mind. He knew that in himself there was nothing to commend him to God. His only thought was for mercy for himself and his people, so God's purposes could be realized through them.

As a Christian, you have the wonderful privilege of boldly entering into God's presence "with a sincere heart in full assurance of faith" (Heb. 10:22). That privilege is rooted in God's grace through Christ's sacrifice and leaves no room for presumption or self-righteousness. Always guard your attitude in prayer so you don't unwittingly slip into a Pharisaic mentality.

❖❖❖

Suggestions for Prayer: Memorize Psalm 117:1–118:1, and recite it often as a hymn of praise to the Lord.

For Further Study: Jesus had much to say about the self-righteous scribes and Pharisees of His day. Read Matthew 23, noting His scathing denunciations of their hypocritical attitudes and practices.

"I prayed to the Lord my God and confessed" (Dan. 9:4).

❖❖❖

Confession brings forgiveness and guards God's character.

Confessing your sins means you agree with God that you have offended His holy character and are worthy of punishment and in need of forgiveness. That's exactly what we see Daniel doing in verses 5-16. Verse 20 summarizes his prayer: "I was speaking and praying, and confessing my sin and the sin of my people Israel, and presenting my supplication before the Lord my God."

Unlike some who suffer God's chastening, Daniel didn't shift the blame for Israel's calamity. Instead he admitted that his people had willfully disobeyed God's Word and ignored His prophets, thereby bringing judgment upon themselves. Once they were a nation blessed by God; now they were aliens and captives in a foreign land. God had kept His promise to curse them if they disobeyed Him (Deut. 28:15).

In verses 12-15 Daniel analyzes the consequences of Israel's sin, which included her captivity and the guilt she bore for her arrogance and her reluctance to repent.

Verse 14 reflects perhaps the most important aspect of confession—Daniel's affirmation that "the Lord our God is righteous with respect to all His deeds which He has done." The Gentile nations knew that the Israelites were God's chosen people. Surely the fall of Jerusalem raised questions about God's character: What kind of God would stand idly by while His people are ravaged and His Temple plundered? What is the benefit of having a God like that? This, in effect, is Daniel's response: "God is righteous in *everything* He does. We deserve this punishment, so don't accuse Him of acting unjustly."

Confession therefore serves a dual purpose: it brings forgiveness, and it frees God to chasten us without bringing accusations of inequity or injustice upon Himself.

Daniel's prayer came at a special time in Israel's history, but undoubtedly confession was a regular part of his life. That should be your pattern as well. Don't wait until disaster strikes before you confess your sin. Make it a daily practice.

❖❖❖

Suggestions for Prayer: ❖ If you have not developed a systematic approach to prayer, the ACTS format is a good way to start. ❖ *Adoration*—praising God. ❖ *Confession*—confessing sin. ❖ *Thanksgiving*—expressing gratitude to God. ❖ *Supplication*—praying for others.

For Further Study: Read about David's sin in 2 Samuel 11:1–12:25 and his confession in Psalm 51. What are the similarities and differences between David's confession and Daniel's?

"We have sinned, committed iniquity, acted wickedly, and rebelled, even turning aside from Thy commandments and ordinances. . . . We have not listened to Thy servants the prophets. . . . Open shame belongs to us, O Lord . . . because we have sinned against Thee. . . . Indeed all Israel has transgressed Thy law and turned aside, not obeying Thy voice. . . . Thy people have become a reproach to all those around us" (Dan. 9:5-16).

✧✧✧

Others should be the primary focus of your prayers.

In verses 5-16 Daniel identifies with his people and intercedes on their behalf. That's a common practice in Scripture. For example, Moses interceded for the Israelites after they sinned by worshiping the golden calf (Ex. 32:11-13).

All Paul's recorded prayers are intercessions. In Ephesians 6:18 he instructs us to "be on the alert with all perseverance and petition for all the saints." In 1 Timothy 2:1-4 he says, "I urge that entreaties and prayers, petitions and thanksgivings, be made on behalf of all men, for kings and all who are in authority, in order that we may lead a tranquil and quiet life in all godliness and dignity. This is good and acceptable in the sight of God our Savior, who desires all men to be saved and to come to the knowledge of the truth."

Similarly, the Lord's prayers are replete with intercessions. Even when hanging in agony on the cross, He prayed for His persecutors: "Father, forgive them; for they do not know what they are doing" (Luke 23:34).

When God placed us into the Body of Christ, He made us dependent on one another. When one member suffers, all suffer with it; when one is honored, all rejoice with it (1 Cor. 12:26). That's why Jesus instructed us to pray, "Give *us* this day *our* daily bread. And forgive *us our* debts. . . . And do not lead *us* into temptation, but deliver *us* from evil" (Matt. 6:11-13, emphasis added).

Let your prayers reflect a corporate and selfless mentality that embraces the needs of others.

✧✧✧

Suggestions for Prayer: Thank God for the people who have prayed for you over the years. Be aware of those for whom you should be praying. ✧ Sometimes the demands of prayer can seem overwhelming because there's so much to pray for, but be faithful, knowing that your prayers are a delight to the Lord (Prov. 15:8).

For Further Study: Read John 17, noting how Jesus interceded for His disciples.

"Alas, O Lord, the great and awesome God, who keeps His covenant and lovingkindness for those who love Him and keep His commandments. . . . Righteousness belongs to Thee, O Lord. . . . To the Lord our God belong compassion and forgiveness" (Dan. 9:4, 7, 9).

✧✧✧

God's attributes authenticate your prayers.

Prior to the Babylonian Captivity, God had warned His people not to adopt the idolatrous ways of their captors, whose gods were idols that could neither hear nor deliver from distress (Isa. 46:6-7).

In marked contrast, our God loves us and delivers us from evil. When we confess our sins and intercede for others, He hears and responds. In Isaiah 45:21-22 He says, "There is no other God besides Me, a righteous God and a Savior; there is none except Me. Turn to Me, and be saved, all the ends of the earth; for I am God, and there is no other."

In his prayer Daniel mentions several attributes of God that have a direct bearing on answered prayer. In verse 4 he calls Him "the great and awesome God." That speaks of His power and majesty. You can pray with confidence because God is powerful enough to change your circumstances when it serves His purposes.

God's faithfulness is reflected in the phrase "who keeps His covenant" (v. 4). He always keeps His promises. He made a covenant with Israel that if they repented He would forgive them (Deut. 30:1-3). He promised never to forsake them (Deut. 31:6; cf. Heb. 13:5).

God's love is seen in His acts of mercy toward those who love Him (v. 4). His justice and holiness are inherent in the phrase "righteousness belongs to Thee" (v. 7). God's actions are always loving and righteous. He never makes a mistake (Gen. 18:25).

Verse 9 mentions two final attributes: compassion and forgiveness. "Compassion" is a synonym for mercy. "Forgiveness" means He pardons your wrongdoings by canceling the penalty that sin has charged to your account. He reconciles you to Himself in sweet communion.

What a gracious God we serve! Rejoice in His love, and lean on His promises. He will never fail you.

✧✧✧

Suggestions for Prayer: Praise God for His attributes of power, majesty, faithfulness, love, holiness, compassion, and forgiveness.

For Further Study: Read Isaiah 44, which sternly warns Israel to avoid the idolatry of Babylon during the Babylonian Captivity. ✧ What promises did God make to Israel? ✧ How did God characterize idolaters?

"O Lord, in accordance with all Thy righteous acts, let now Thine anger and Thy wrath turn away from Thy city Jerusalem, Thy holy mountain; for because of our sins and the iniquities of our fathers, Jerusalem and Thy people have become a reproach to all those around us. So now, our God, listen to the prayer of Thy servant and to his supplications, and for Thy sake, O Lord, let Thy face shine on Thy desolate sanctuary.

"O my God, incline Thine ear and hear! Open Thine eyes and see our desolations and the city which is called by Thy name; for we are not presenting our supplications before Thee on account of any merits of our own but on account of Thy great compassion. O Lord, hear! O Lord, forgive! O Lord, listen and take action! For Thine own sake, O my God, do not delay, because Thy city and Thy people are called by Thy name" (Dan. 9:16-19).

✧✧✧

God's glory must be the ultimate goal of every prayer request we make.

Someone once said, "Show me your redeemed life and I might believe in your Redeemer." That's a fair request! As Christians, we are Christ's ambassadors to a dying world. With His Spirit in our hearts and His Word in our hands, we are to speak His truth in love and live a life that lends credibility to what we say.

When we fail to do that, we dishonor God and provide ammunition for those who seek to discredit His work. That was certainly true of Israel. They were God's chosen people, and yet His name was blasphemed among the Gentiles because of Israel's unbelief and disobedience (Rom. 2:24).

Daniel knew Israel didn't deserve mercy, but he asked God to forgive and restore them to their homeland for His own name's sake. Therein would He be glorified.

When you pray according to God's will, fervently confessing your sins and interceding for others, you're following in the godly tradition of Daniel and every other saint who sought God's glory above all else. May it be so today!

✧✧✧

Suggestions for Prayer: Pray for the nation of Israel, that God might redeem many Jewish people for His name's sake (cf. Rom. 10:1).

For Further Study: Read Ezekiel 36:16-38. ✧ Why did God scatter Israel? Why will He regather her? ✧ How will the Gentile nations react to her regathering?

Jesus told us to "Pray, then, in this way: 'Our Father who art in heaven, hallowed be Thy name. Thy kingdom come. Thy will be done, on earth as it is in heaven. Give us this day our daily bread. And forgive us our debts, as we also have forgiven our debtors. And do not lead us into temptation, but deliver us from evil. For Thine is the kingdom, and the power, and the glory, forever. Amen'" (Matt. 6:9-15).

❖❖❖

Jesus gave six elements that constitute true prayer.

Many people have memorized the Disciples' Prayer so they can recite it often, but as beautiful as it is, it wasn't given for that purpose. In fact, after Jesus gave it, no one in the New Testament recited it—not even Jesus Himself (cf. John 17)!

The disciples didn't ask Jesus to teach them a prayer, but to teach them how to pray (Luke 11:1). There is a significant difference. Jesus preceded His prayer by saying, "Pray, then, in this way" (Matt. 6:9), which literally means, "Pray along these lines." His prayer was a general pattern for all prayer, and although it wasn't recited, its principles are evident in all New Testament prayers.

Christ's model prayer teaches us to ask God for six things: 1. that His name be honored, 2. that He bring His Kingdom to earth, 3. that He do His will, 4. that He provide our daily needs, 5. that He pardon our sins, and 6. that He protect us from temptation. Each request contributes to the ultimate goal of all prayer, which is to bring glory to God. The last three are the means by which the first three are achieved. As God provides our daily bread, pardons our sins, and protects us when we are tempted, He is exalted in His name, Kingdom, and will.

If you understand and follow Christ's pattern for prayer, you can be assured that you are praying as He instructed and that whatever you ask in His name, He will do, so "that the Father may be glorified in the Son" (John 14:13).

❖❖❖

Suggestions for Prayer: Do your prayers reflect the six elements outlined in the Disciples' Prayer? If not, work on making them a regular part of your prayers.

For Further Study: Read Matthew 6:1-8, where Jesus discusses some of the practices of the Jewish religious leaders. ❖ What practices and motives did He mention? ❖ How did He feel about their spiritual leadership?

"Our Father who art in heaven" (Matt. 6:9).

✧✧✧

**Prayer begins with the recognition that God is your Father
and has the resources to meet your needs.**

The term *Father* is one of the most commonly used terms in our prayers, and rightly so, because that's how Jesus taught us to pray. But as common as that term is to us, it was very uncommon to the people of Christ's day.

At that time, most of the people who worshiped false gods thought of them as distant, capricious, and immoral beings who were to be feared. Even the Jewish people, who should have understood the Fatherhood of God, had removed themselves from His Fatherly care through their sin and apostasy. Consequently He seemed remote to them. Even some who did claim God as their Father were rebuked by Christ, who called them children of the Devil because they rejected the Son (John 8:44).

Against that backdrop, Christ's teaching was revolutionary. He proclaimed God as a caring and gracious Father who desires intimate fellowship with His children. That fellowship can come only through faith in the Son.

Beyond that, Jesus revealed the Father's character in everything He said and did. When Philip asked Jesus to show him the Father, Jesus replied, "Have I been so long with you, and yet you have not come to know Me, Philip? He who has seen Me has seen the Father" (John 14:9).

Jesus also proclaimed God as a Father who has all the treasures of Heaven at His disposal and who makes them available to His children so they might glorify Him: "Your Father knows what you need, before you ask Him. . . . Do not be anxious. . . . But seek first His kingdom, and His righteousness; and all [you need] shall be added to you" (Matt. 6:8, 31, 33).

Your faith in Christ is what makes God your Heavenly Father. He loves you, listens to your prayers, and supplies your needs according to His abundant resources. Look to Him today, and live as a thankful, obedient child.

✧✧✧

Suggestions for Prayer: Thank God that He is your gracious and loving Father. ✧ Praise Him for the abundant blessings He gives to you.

For Further Study: Read Proverbs 3:5-6 and Matthew 7:7-11. ✧ What are you exhorted to do? ✧ What specifically will God do for you? ✧ How should those passages affect your relationship with God?

"Our Father who art in heaven" (Matt. 6:9).

✧✧✧

With God as your Father, your life has eternal significance.

Author H. G. Wells wrote of a man who had been overcome by the pressure and stress of modern life. His doctor told him his only hope was to find fellowship with God. The man responded, "What? That—up there—having fellowship with me? I would as soon think of cooling my throat with the Milky Way or shaking hands with the stars." Poet Thomas Hardy said prayer is useless because there's no one to pray to except "that dreaming, dark, dumb thing that turns the handle of this idle show." Voltaire described life as a bad joke. He added, "Bring down the curtain; the farce is done." Such is the blasphemy and despair of all who insist that God is uninvolved in human affairs.

The Greek and Roman philosophers of Jesus' day rejected the Fatherhood of God because it contradicted their philosophical systems. The Stoic philosophers taught that all of the gods were apathetic and experienced no emotions at all. The Epicurean philosophers taught that the supreme quality of the gods was complete calm or perfect peace. To maintain their serenity, they needed to remain totally isolated from the human condition.

Scripture refutes all such heresies by declaring that God is an intimate, caring Father. The significance of that truth is staggering. He conquers your fears and comforts you in times of distress. He forgives your sins and gives you eternal hope. He showers you with limitless resources and makes you the recipient of an imperishable inheritance. He grants you wisdom and direction through His Spirit and His Word. He will never leave or forsake you.

When you humbly approach God as your Father, you assume the role of a child who is eager to obey his Father's will and receive all the benefits of His grace. Let that take you beyond your present circumstances and motivate you to dwell on what's eternal.

✧✧✧

Suggestions for Prayer: Thank God for the joy and purpose He gives you each day. ✧ Commit yourself to pursuing His will today.

For Further Study: Read Exodus 3:1-5 and Isaiah 6:1-5. What attitude should you have when you pray to God? ✧ What does Hebrews 4:16 say you can receive when you approach God in prayer?

"Hallowed be Thy name" (Matt. 6:9).

❖❖❖

Prayer should always exalt God.

The Disciples' Prayer illustrates the priority that God should hold in our prayers. Jesus began by exalting the Father—"Hallowed be Thy name" (v. 9), then requested that the Father's Kingdom come and His will be done (v. 10). He concluded with an anthem of praise: "For Thine is the kingdom, and the power, and the glory, forever. Amen" (v. 13). His prayer literally begins and ends with God.

"Hallowed be Thy name" exalts the name of the Lord and sets a tone of worship and submission that is sustained throughout the prayer. Where God's name is hallowed, He will be loved and revered, His Kingdom eagerly anticipated, and His will obeyed.

"Thy name" speaks of more than a title such as "God," "Lord," or "Jehovah." It speaks of God Himself and is the composite of all His attributes. The Hebrews considered God's name so sacred they wouldn't even speak it, but they missed the point. While meticulously guarding the letters of His name, they slandered His character and disobeyed His Word. Because of them the name of God was blasphemed among the Gentiles (Rom. 2:24).

Psalm 102:15 says, "So the nations will fear the name of the Lord, and all the kings of the earth Thy glory." It's not the letters of God's name that the nations fear; it's the embodiment of all He is. As Jesus prayed, "I manifested Thy name to the men whom Thou gavest Me" (John 17:6). He did that by revealing who God is. John 1:14 says, "The Word became flesh, and dwelt among us, and we beheld His glory, glory as of the only begotten from the Father, full of grace and truth." Jesus told Philip, "He who has seen Me has seen the Father" (John 14:9). Jesus is the manifestation of all that God is.

Manifesting the priority of God in your prayers involves acknowledging who He is and approaching Him with a reverent, humble spirit that is yielded to His will. As you do that, He will hallow His name through you.

❖❖❖

Suggestions for Prayer: Praise God for His holiness. ❖ Ask Him to use you today to demonstrate His holiness to others.

For Further Study: Read Numbers 20. How did Moses show irreverence for God's name?

"Hallowed be Thy name" (Matt. 6:9).

❖❖❖

God is holy and deserves your highest respect and your humble obedience.

To most people the word *hallowed* elicits thoughts of Halloween, ivy-covered walls, or starchy religious traditions. But those are all far from its Biblical meaning. "Hallowed" in Matthew 6:9 translates a Greek word that means "holy." When Christ said, "Hallowed be Thy name," He was saying in effect, "May Your name be regarded as holy." When you hallow God's name, you set it apart from everything common and give Him the place He deserves in your life.

Throughout Scripture, holiness is attributed to persons or things that are consecrated to God's service. The Sabbath day, for example, was to be kept "holy"—set apart from the other days (Ex. 20:8). The Israelite priests were to be considered "holy" because they rendered special service to the Lord (Lev. 21:8). As believers in Christ, we are to be "holy" because we belong to God (1 Peter 1:15).

Holiness also speaks of moral excellence and purity. God is called "the Holy One" (1 Peter 1:15) not only because He is set apart from His creation, but also because He is pure and sinless in His character. That's why Isaiah pronounced a curse on himself when he saw the Lord and heard the angels crying out, "Holy, Holy, Holy, is the Lord of hosts, the whole earth is full of His glory" (Isa. 6:3-5). He was overcome with a sense of his own human sinfulness in the presence of a holy God.

Such a God deserves your highest respect and reverence. He is your gracious and loving Father, but He is also the sovereign, majestic God of the universe. Consequently, you must guard against thinking of Him as a buddy or addressing Him flippantly.

Additionally, He deserves your humble obedience. You hallow His name only when your life is marked by righteousness and moral excellence.

May that be true of you today, and may you seek to honor Him in all that you do!

❖❖❖

Suggestions for Prayer: Always approach God with a sense of respect and reverence. ❖ Think of specific ways you can hallow His name today. Ask Him for the grace to do so.

For Further Study: Read each of these verses, noting the specific ways you can glorify God: Joshua 7:19; Psalm 50:23; John 15:8; Romans 15:5-6; 1 Corinthians 6:20; Philippians 2:9-11; and 2 Thessalonians 3:1.

"Hallowed be Thy name" (Matt. 6:9).

❖❖❖

Sound theology that results in holy living hallows God's name.

We have learned that hallowing God's name requires setting it apart from everything common and giving Him first place in our lives. That starts with believing He exists. Hebrews 11:6 says, "He who comes to God must believe that He is."

Beyond mere belief, you must also know the kind of God He is. Many people who claim to believe in God aren't hallowing His name because they have erroneous concepts of who He is. The Israelites thought they were worshiping the true God when they bowed down to the golden calf (Ex. 32:4). The Jewish leaders of Jesus' day thought they worshiped the true God, but Jesus called them children of the Devil because they rejected God's Word (John 8:44, 47). Sound Biblical doctrine about God is essential to revering God properly.

Hallowing God's name also involves constantly being aware of His presence. That helps you focus on His priorities and to see every aspect of your life from His perspective. That's what David meant when he said, "I have set the Lord continually before me" (Ps. 16:8).

Obedience is another way to hallow God's name. Your theology might be flawless, and you may be constantly aware of His presence, but if you disobey Him, you dishonor Him. Jesus said, "Let your light shine before men in such a way that they may see your good works, and glorify your Father who is in heaven" (Matt. 5:16).

You are an instrument through whom God displays His holiness in the world. If His name is to be hallowed on earth as it is in Heaven, it must first be hallowed in your life. That occurs when you believe in Him, understand who He really is, maintain an awareness of His presence, and obey His Word.

That high calling sets you apart from every unbeliever (1 Peter 2:9-10). Live today in light of that glorious calling!

❖❖❖

Suggestions for Prayer: Ask God to help you be aware of His presence in every circumstance you face today. ❖ Pray that your life will manifest His holiness.

For Further Study: Read Exodus 32. ❖ Why did the Israelites build the golden calf? ❖ What was Moses' response when God threatened to destroy His people?

"Thy kingdom come" (Matt. 6:10).

❖❖❖

When you pray, "Thy kingdom come," you are praying for Christ to reign on earth as He already does in Heaven.

When we hear the word *kingdom*, we tend to think of medieval castles, kings, knights, and the like. But "kingdom" in Matthew 6:10 translates a Greek word that means "rule" or "reign." We could translate the phrase, "Thy reign come." That gives a clearer sense of what Christ meant. He prayed that God's rule would be as apparent on earth as it is in Heaven.

God's Kingdom was the central issue in Christ's ministry. He proclaimed "the gospel of the kingdom" (Matt. 4:23) and instructed His followers to make the Kingdom a priority in their own lives (Matt. 6:33). He told parables about its character and value (Matt. 13) and indicted the scribes and Pharisees for hindering those who sought to enter it (Matt. 23:13). After His death and resurrection, He appeared for forty days and gave the disciples further instruction about the Kingdom (Acts 1:2-3).

When we pray, "Thy kingdom come," we are praying for Christ's sovereign rule to be as established on earth as it is in Heaven. In one sense the Kingdom is already here—in the hearts of believers. That Kingdom consists of "righteousness and peace and joy in the Holy Spirit" (Rom. 14:17). But in another sense the Kingdom is yet future. In Luke 17:21 Jesus says, "Behold, the kingdom of God is in your midst" (cf. John 18:36). Their King was present, but they rejected Him. Someday He will return again to establish His Kingdom on earth and personally reign over it. That's the aspect of the Kingdom we pray for in Matthew 6:10.

Sin and rebellion are now rampant, but when Christ's Kingdom comes, they will be done away with (Rev. 20:7-9). In the meantime, the work of the Kingdom continues, and you have the privilege of promoting it through your prayers and faithful ministry. Take every opportunity to do so today, and rejoice in the assurance that Christ will someday reign in victory and will be glorified for all eternity.

❖❖❖

Suggestions for Prayer: Praise God for the glorious future that awaits you and all believers. ❖ Pray with anticipation for the coming of Christ's eternal Kingdom.

For Further Study: Read Matthew 13:1-52. What parables did Jesus use to instruct His disciples about the Kingdom of Heaven?

"Thy kingdom come" (Matt. 6:10).

❖❖❖

Relinquish your will to Christ's sovereign rule.

A ttempting to explain all that is involved in the phrase "Thy kingdom come" is like a child standing on a beach attempting to scoop the entire ocean into a little pail. Only in eternity will we grasp all that it encompasses, but the poem "His Coming to Glory," written by the nineteenth-century hymn-writer Frances Havergal, captures its essence:

> *Oh the joy to see Thee reigning,*
> *Thee, my own beloved Lord!*
> *Every tongue Thy name confessing,*
> *Worship, honor, glory, blessing*
> *Brought to Thee with glad accord;*
> *Thee, my Master and my Friend,*
> *Vindicated and enthroned;*
> *Unto earth's remotest end*
> *Glorified, adored, and owned.*

Psalm 2:6-8 reflects the Father's joy on that great day: "'I have installed My King upon Zion, My holy mountain.' 'I will surely tell of the decree of the Lord; He said to Me, "Thou art My Son, today I have begotten Thee. Ask of Me, and I will surely give the nations as Thy inheritance, and the very ends of the earth as Thy possession."'" God will give the kingdoms of the world to His Son, who will reign as King of kings and Lord of lords (Rev. 19:16).

With that promise in mind, beware of seeing prayer primarily as an opportunity to inform God of your own plans and to seek His help in fulfilling them. Instead pray, "Thy kingdom come," which is a request for Christ to reign. In its fullest sense this is an affirmation that you are willing to relinquish the rule of your own life so the Holy Spirit can use you to promote the Kingdom in whatever way He chooses.

That kind of prayer can be difficult because we tend to be preoccupied with ourselves. But concentrate on conforming your prayers to God's purposes. Then you will be assured that you are praying according to His will.

❖❖❖

Suggestions for Prayer: Praise God for the hope of Christ's future reign on earth. ❖ Ask Him to use you today as a representative of His Kingdom.

For Further Study: According to Ephesians 4:17–5:5, how should citizens of Christ's Kingdom behave?

"Thy kingdom come" (Matt. 6:10).

❖❖❖

Conversion to Christ involves three elements: invitation, repentance, and commitment.

Someday Christ will return to earth to reign in His Kingdom. In the meantime He rules in the hearts of those who love Him.

Before He ascended into Heaven, Jesus gave us a mandate to evangelize the lost and to teach them His Word (Matt. 28:19-20). When we do this, sinners are converted and are transferred from the kingdom of darkness to the Kingdom of Christ (Col. 1:13). That's how His Kingdom grows.

Conversion is a work of the Spirit in the heart of unbelievers. He uses a myriad of people and circumstances to accomplish that work, but common to every true conversion are three key elements: invitation, repentance, and commitment.

In Matthew 22:1-14 Jesus, by way of a parable, invites people to come into His Kingdom. As an evangelist, you too should not only present the gospel but are to invite others to respond to what they've heard.

In Mark 1:14-15 we read, "Jesus came into Galilee, preaching the gospel of God, and saying, 'The time is fulfilled, and the kingdom of God is at hand; repent and believe in the gospel.'" Repentance means to feel sorrow over your sin and to turn from it (2 Cor. 7:9-11).

True repentance results in a commitment to respond to the righteous demands of the gospel. In Mark 12:34 Jesus says to a wise scribe, "You are not far from the kingdom of God." The scribe had all the information necessary for entering the Kingdom. What he lacked was a commitment to act on what he knew. Luke 9:62 says, "No one, after putting his hand to the plow and looking back, is fit for the kingdom of God." You might know everything about the Kingdom, but Christ's rule is not established in your heart until you've made a complete commitment to it.

When you pray for Christ's Kingdom to come, you are praying an evangelistic prayer that you take part in answering. Be faithful to proclaim the gospel, and make intercession for unbelievers a regular part of your prayers.

❖❖❖

Suggestions for Prayer: Pray for unbelieving family and friends. ❖ Ask the Lord for the opportunity to share Christ with an unbeliever today.

For Further Study: Read John 4. ❖ How did Jesus broach the subject of salvation with the Samaritan woman? ❖ Did He extend an invitation to her? Explain. ❖ How did the townspeople react to her report about Jesus?

"Thy kingdom come" (Matt. 6:10).

❖❖❖

***The only acceptable response to Christ's offer of the Kingdom
is to receive it, value it, and pursue it!***

Many people who think they're Kingdom citizens will someday be shocked to discover they aren't. In Matthew 7:21 Jesus says, "Not everyone who says to Me, 'Lord, Lord,' will enter the kingdom of heaven; but he who does the will of My Father who is in heaven." Some people think highly of the Kingdom but never receive the King. They call Jesus "Lord" but don't do His will. Lip service won't do. You must receive the King and His Kingdom (John 1:12).

You must also value the Kingdom. In Matthew 13:44 Jesus says, "The kingdom of heaven is like a treasure." In verses 45-46 He compares it to a pearl that was so valuable, a merchant sold all he had to purchase it. That's the value of the Kingdom. It's worth any sacrifice you have to make.

Finally, you must continually pursue the Kingdom. In Matthew 6:33 Jesus says, "Seek first His kingdom, and His righteousness; and all these things shall be added to you." In context He was discussing the basic necessities of life such as food and clothing, reminding His disciples that their Heavenly Father knew their needs and would supply them if they simply maintained the proper priorities. Unbelievers characteristically worry about meeting their own needs (v. 32), but believers are to be characterized by trusting in God and pursuing His Kingdom.

Christ offers His Kingdom to everyone (Matt. 28:19). The only acceptable response is to receive it, value it, and pursue it. Is that your response? Have you received the Kingdom? Is it precious to you? I trust it is. If so, rejoice and serve your King well today. Make His Kingdom your top priority. If not, turn from your sin and submit your life to Christ, who loves you and longs to receive you into His eternal Kingdom.

❖❖❖

Suggestions for Prayer: Thank God for the heavenly citizenship you hold (Phil. 3:20-21). ❖ Ask Him to help you keep His priorities uppermost in your life.

For Further Study: Read Revelation 21–22. As you do, think of what eternity with Christ will be like. What aspects of eternity do you especially look forward to?

"Thy will be done, on earth as it is in heaven" (Matt. 6:10).

✧✧✧

Your prayers make a difference!

M atthew 6:10 literally says, "Whatever You wish to have happen, let it happen immediately. As Your will is done in Heaven, so let it be done on earth." That's a prayer of active commitment to God's will.

Many people don't pray like that because they don't understand God's character. They think their prayers don't matter and that God will impose His will on them no matter what they do. They tend to pray with passive resignation, indifference, or resentment.

I remember praying such a prayer. After my freshman year in college, I was in a serious auto accident. The driver lost control of the car at about seventy-five miles per hour, and it rolled several times before coming to a stop. I was thrown clear of the vehicle and ended up sliding down the highway on my backside for about a hundred yards. I lost a lot of skin and had some third-degree burns and other injuries, but fortunately I didn't break any bones.

I was conscious during the entire ordeal and vividly remember thinking, *All right, God. If You're going to fight this way, I give up! I can't handle this!* You see, I knew God was calling me into the ministry, but I'd been focusing my life in another direction.

I think God used that experience to get my attention, and my prayer of passive resignation soon turned to active commitment as He refined my heart and drew me to Himself.

Perhaps God has dealt severely with you, too. If so, it's only because He loves you and wants to produce the fruit of righteousness in you (Heb. 12:11). Don't despise His chastening, and don't be fatalistic or resentful in your prayers. Godly prayers make a difference (James 5:16); so commit yourself to praying expectantly, knowing that God is gracious and wise and always responds for His glory and your highest good (Rom. 8:28).

✧✧✧

Suggestions for Prayer: If you tend to pray with indifference, passive resignation, or resentment, ask God's forgiveness. Study His character, and cultivate deep communion with Him through disciplined, trusting prayer.

For Further Study: Read Luke 18:1-8. ✧ Why did Jesus tell this parable? ✧ What principles do you see here that apply to your life?

"Thy will be done, on earth as it is in heaven" (Matt. 6:10).

❖❖❖

Praying for God's will to be done on earth is an aggressive prayer.

M any people assume that somehow everything that happens is God's will. But that's not true. Lives destroyed by murderous aggressors and families broken by adultery aren't God's will. Children and adults ravaged by abuse or crippled by disease aren't God's will. He uses sin and illness to accomplish His own purposes (Rom. 8:28), but they aren't His desire.

Eventually God will destroy all evil and will fulfill His purposes perfectly (Rev. 20:10-14), but that hasn't happened yet. That's why we must pray for His will to be done on earth. We can't afford to be passive or indifferent in prayer. We must pray aggressively and not lose heart (Luke 18:1).

That's how David prayed. His passion for God's will compelled him to pray, "Make me understand the way of Thy precepts, so I will meditate on Thy wonders. . . . I shall run the way of Thy commandments, for Thou wilt enlarge my heart. Teach me, O Lord, the way of Thy statutes, and I shall observe it to the end. Give me understanding, that I may observe Thy law, and keep it with all my heart. Make me walk in the path of Thy commandments, for I delight in it" (Ps. 119:27, 32-35).

But David also prayed, "Let God arise, let His enemies be scattered; and let those who hate Him flee before Him. As smoke is driven away, so drive them away; as wax melts before the fire, so let the wicked perish before God. But let the righteous be glad; let them exult before God; yes, let them rejoice with gladness" (Ps. 68:1-3). He loved God's will, but he also hated everything that opposed it.

When you truly pray for God's will to be done, you are aggressively pursuing His will for your own life and are also rebelling against Satan, his evil world system, and everything else that is at odds with God's will.

❖❖❖

Suggestions for Prayer: Thank God for David's example and for others who demonstrate a passion for God's will. ❖ Ask for wisdom to see beyond your circumstances to what God wants to accomplish through them.

For Further Study: Read Psalm 119. ❖ How can God's Word help you know and obey God's will? ❖ What was the psalmist's attitude toward the Word?

"Give us this day our daily bread" (Matt. 6:11).

❖❖❖

God is glorified when He meets your needs.

In America, praying for our daily bread hardly seems necessary. Most people need to pray for self-control to avoid overeating! But Matthew 6:11 isn't talking about food only. It is a statement of dependency on God and an acknowledgment that He alone provides all of life's basic necessities.

Sad to say, however, many people today have reduced prayer to a means of self-fulfillment. Recently a woman sent me a booklet and wrote, "I don't think you understand the true resource we have in prayer. You should read this booklet." The booklet repeatedly emphasized our right as Christians to demand things from God. But that misses the point of prayer altogether, which is to glorify God (John 14:13). We are to give God the privilege of revealing His glory by meeting our needs in whatever way He chooses. If we demand things of Him, we are likely to become frustrated or to question Him when we don't get what we want. That's a serious sin!

David G. Myers, in his book *The Human Puzzle* (New York: Harper and Row, 1978), said: "Some petitionary prayers seem not only to lack faith in the inherent goodness of God but also to elevate humankind to a position of control over God. God, the Scriptures remind us, is omniscient and omnipotent, the sovereign ruler of the universe. For Christians to pray as if God were a puppet whose strings they yank with their prayers seems not only potentially superstitious but blasphemous as well. When prayer is sold as a device for eliciting health, success, and other favors from a celestial vending machine, we may wonder what is really being merchandised. Is this faith or is it faith's counterfeit, a glib caricature of true Christianity?"

Guard your prayers! Always be aware of the enormous privilege you have to approach the infinite God and to receive His gracious provisions. Yet, always do so with His glory as your highest goal.

❖❖❖

Suggestions for Prayer: Read Proverbs 30:8-9. What attitude toward God do those verses convey? Is that your attitude in prayer?

For Further Study: Read Matthew 6:19-34 and James 4:3. How might you respond to someone who says Christians have the right to demand favors from God?

"Give us this day our daily bread" (Matt. 6:11).

❖❖❖

God is the source of every good gift.

God has given us everything good to enjoy, including rain to make things grow, minerals to make the soil fertile, animals for food and clothing, and energy for industry and transportation. Everything we have is from Him, and we are to be thankful for it all.

Jesus said, "If you then, being evil, know how to give good gifts to your children, how much more shall your Father who is in heaven give what is good to those who ask Him!" (Matt. 7:11). James 1:17 says, "Every good thing bestowed and every perfect gift is from above, coming down from the Father of lights, with whom there is no variation, or shifting shadow." Paul added, "Everything created by God is good, and nothing is to be rejected, if it is received with gratitude: for it is sanctified by means of the word of God and prayer" (1 Tim. 4:4-5).

Sadly, unbelievers don't acknowledge God's goodness, though they benefit from it every day. They attribute His providential care to luck or fate and His gracious provisions to nature or false gods. They do not honor Him as God or give Him thanks (Rom. 1:21).

The great Puritan writer Thomas Watson wrote: "If all be a gift, see the odious ingratitude of men who sin against their giver! God feeds them, and they fight against him; he gives them bread, and they give him affronts. How unworthy is this! Should we not cry shame of him who had a friend always feeding him with money, and yet he should betray and injure him? Thus ungratefully do sinners deal with God; they not only forget his mercies, but abuse them. 'When I had fed them to the full, they then committed adultery [Jer. 5:7].' Oh, how horrid is it to sin against a bountiful God!—to strike the hands that relieve us!" (*The Lord's Prayer* [London: The Banner of Truth Trust, 1972], p. 197).

How sad to see such ingratitude, and yet how thrilling to know that the infinite God cares for us and supplies our every need. Don't ever take His provisions for granted! Look to Him daily, and receive His gifts with a thankful heart.

❖❖❖

Suggestions for Prayer: Be generous with your praise for God's abundant blessings.

For Further Study: Read Genesis 1:29-31, noting the variety of foods God created for your enjoyment.

"And forgive us our debts" (Matt. 6:12).

❖❖❖

Believers confess their sins; unbelievers deny theirs.

Christians struggle with sin. That surely comes as no surprise to you. As you mature in Christ, the frequency of your sinning decreases, but your sensitivity to it increases. That doesn't mean you are more easily tempted, but that you are more aware of the subtleties of sin and how it dishonors God.

Some people think you should never confess your sins or seek forgiveness, but the Lord instructed us to do so when He told us to pray, "And forgive us our debts" (Matt. 6:12). That's the believer's prayer for the Father's forgiveness.

John said, "If we say that we have no sin, we are deceiving ourselves, and the truth is not in us. If we confess our sins, He is faithful and righteous to forgive us our sins and to cleanse us from all unrighteousness. If we say that we have not sinned, we make Him a liar, and His word is not in us" (1 John 1:8-10). That passage doesn't tell us how to get saved, as many have taught. It tells us how to distinguish believers from unbelievers: believers confess their sins; unbelievers don't.

The phrase "forgive us" in Matthew 6:12 implies the need for forgiveness. "Debts" translates a Greek word that was used to speak of a moral or monetary debt. Here it refers to sins. When you sin, you owe to God a consequence or a debt because you have violated His holiness.

When you sin as a believer, you don't lose your salvation, but you will face God's chastening if you don't repent. Hebrews 12 says, "Those whom the Lord loves He disciplines, and He scourges every son whom He receives . . . . He disciplines us for our good, that we may share His holiness" (vv. 6, 10).

If you are harboring sin, confess it now, and allow God to cleanse you and use you today for His glory.

❖❖❖

Suggestions for Prayer: Write down why God's forgiveness is important to you, then express those thoughts to Him in praise.

For Further Study: Read Psalm 38. ❖ What physical and emotional ailments did David experience as a result of his sin? ❖ What was his attitude toward God as he confessed his sin?

"And forgive us our debts" (Matt. 6:12).

❖❖❖

Forgiveness removes the guilt and penalty of sin and restores intimacy with God.

Man's greatest problem is sin. It renders him spiritually dead, alienates him from God and his fellowman, plagues him with guilt and fear, and can eventually damn him to eternal Hell. The only solution is forgiveness, and the only source of forgiveness is Jesus Christ.

All sin is punishable by death (Rom. 6:23), but Christ bore the sins of the world, thereby making it possible for us to be forgiven and to have eternal life through faith in Him (John 3:16). What a glorious reality!

Scripture speaks of two kinds of forgiveness: judicial and parental. Judicial forgiveness comes from God the righteous Judge, who wiped your sin off the record and set you free from its punishment and guilt. At the moment of your salvation He forgave all your sins—past, present, and future—and pronounced you righteous for all eternity. That's why nothing can ever separate you from Christ's love (Rom. 8:38-39).

Parental forgiveness is granted to believers by their loving Heavenly Father as they confess their sin and seek His cleansing. That's the kind of forgiveness Jesus speaks of in Matthew 6:12.

When a child disobeys his father, the father/child relationship isn't severed. The child is still a member of the family, and there's a sense in which he is already forgiven because he's under the umbrella of his father's parental love. But some of the intimacy of their relationship is lost until the child seeks forgiveness.

That's the idea in Matthew 6:12. The sins you commit as a believer don't rob you of your salvation, but they do affect your relationship with God. He still loves you and will always be your Father, but the intimacy and sweet communion you once knew is jeopardized until you seek reconciliation by confessing your sins.

As a Christian, you are judicially forgiven and will never come into condemnation. But never presume on that grace. Make confession part of your daily prayers so sin will never erode your relationship with your Heavenly Father.

❖❖❖

Suggestions for Prayer: Thank God for His judicial forgiveness of all your sins. ❖ Ask Him to help you maintain the joy of your relationship with Him by quickly dealing with any sin that comes up in your life.

For Further Study: Read Psalm 32:1-7. ❖ How did David feel about forgiveness? ❖ What happened to David before he confessed his sin?

"And forgive us our debts, as we also have forgiven our debtors. . . . For if you forgive men for their transgressions, your heavenly Father will also forgive you. But if you do not forgive men, then your Father will not forgive your transgressions" (Matt. 6:12, 14-15).

❖❖❖

An unforgiving Christian is a contradiction in terms.

It's possible to confess your sins and still not know the joy of forgiveness. How? Failure to forgive others! Christian educator J. Oswald Sanders observed that Jesus measures us by the yardstick we use on others. Jesus didn't say, "Forgive us *because* we have forgiven others," but "Forgive us *as* we have forgiven others."

An unforgiving Christian is a contradiction in terms because we are the forgiven ones! Ephesians 4:32 says, "Be kind to one another, tender-hearted, forgiving each other, just as God in Christ also has forgiven you." God forgave us an immeasurable debt, saving us from the horrors of eternal Hell. That should be motivation enough to forgive any offense against us, and yet some Christians still hold grudges.

Here are three practical steps by which to deal with the sin of unforgiveness. First, confess it to the Lord, and ask Him to help you mend the relationship in question. Second, go to the person, ask for forgiveness, and seek reconciliation. You might discover that he or she wasn't even aware of the offense. Third, give the person something you highly value. This is a very practical approach based on our Lord's teaching that where your treasure is, there your heart will be also (Matt. 6:21). Whenever I've given a book or other gift to someone who had wronged me, I've felt a great sense of liberty in my spirit. In addition, my joy is compounded because I feel the joy of giving as well as the joy of forgiving.

Don't ever let a grudge stand between you and another person. It will rob you of the full joy of God's forgiveness.

❖❖❖

Suggestions for Prayer: Before praying, examine your heart. If you harbor bitterness toward another person, follow the procedure given above. Then pray, thanking the Lord for the joy of reconciliation.

For Further Study: Read the Parable of the Servant in Matthew 18:21-35. ❖ What question prompted the parable? ❖ How did the king respond to his servant's pleading? ❖ What did the servant do later on? Why was that wrong?

"And do not lead us into temptation, but deliver us from evil"
(Matt. 6:13).

❖❖❖

Have a healthy sense of self-distrust.

A t the moment of your salvation, judicial forgiveness covered all of your sins—past, present, and future. Parental forgiveness restores the joy and sweet fellowship broken by any subsequent sins. But concurrent with the joy of being forgiven is the desire to be protected from any future sins. That's the desire expressed in Matthew 6:13: "And do not lead us into temptation, but deliver us from evil."

That petition seems simple enough at first glance, but it raises some important questions. According to James 1:13, God doesn't tempt anyone to commit sin; so why ask Him to protect us from something He apparently wouldn't lead us into in the first place?

Some say the word "temptation" in Matthew 6:13 means "trials." But trials strengthen us and prove the genuineness of our faith. We are to rejoice in them, not avoid them (James 1:2-4).

Though the Greek word here can refer either to a trial or an enticement, the solution to this paradox has to do with the nature of the petition. This is not so much a technical theological statement as it is an emotional plea from one who hates sin and wants to be protected from it. Chrysostom, the early church father, said this petition is a natural appeal of human weakness as it faces danger (*Homily* 19.10).

I don't know about you, but I have a healthy sense of self-distrust. That's why I carefully guard what I think, say, watch, read, and listen to. If I sense spiritual danger I run into the presence of God and say, "Lord, I will be overwhelmed by this situation unless You come to my aid." That's the spirit of Matthew 6:13.

We live in a fallen world that throws temptation after temptation our way. Therefore it's only natural and proper for us as Christians to continually confess our sins, receive the Father's forgiveness, and plead with Him to deliver us from the possibility of sinning against Him in the future.

❖❖❖

Suggestions for Prayer: Thank the Lord that He loves you and ministers through you despite your human weaknesses. ❖ Ask Him to protect you today from any situation that might cause you to sin.

For Further Study: Read 1 Corinthians 10:13 and James 1:13-16. ❖ To what degree will God allow you to be tempted? ❖ What is a common source of temptation?

*"And do not lead us into temptation, but deliver us from evil"
(Matt. 6:13).*

❖❖❖

Don't let your trials turn into temptations.

When we hear the English word *temptation*, we usually think of a solicitation to evil. But "temptation" in Matthew 6:13 translates a Greek word that can refer either to a trial that God permits in order to refine your spiritual character (James 1:2-4) or a temptation that Satan or your flesh brings to incite you to sin (Matt. 4:1; James 1:13-15). Both are valid translations.

I believe "temptation" in Matthew 6:13 refers in part to trials. Even though we know God uses trials for our good, it's still good to pray that He won't allow us to be caught in a trial that becomes an irresistible temptation. That can happen if we're spiritually weak or ill-prepared to deal with a situation.

God will never test you beyond what you're able to endure (1 Cor. 10:13), but resisting temptation requires spiritual discipline and divine resources. Praying for God to deliver you from trials that might overcome you is a safeguard against leaning on your own strength and neglecting His power.

God tested Joseph by allowing him to be sold into slavery by his brothers, falsely accused by an adulterous woman, and unjustly imprisoned by a jealous husband. But Joseph knew that God's hand was on his life. That's why he could later say to his brothers, "You meant evil against me, but God meant it for good in order to . . . preserve many people alive" (Gen. 50:20). Joseph was ready for the test and passed it beautifully!

Jesus Himself was led by the Spirit into the wilderness to be tempted by the Devil (Matt. 4:1). God wanted to test Him to prove His virtue, but Satan wanted to tempt Him to destroy His virtue. Jesus, too, was victorious.

When you experience trials, don't let them turn into temptations. Recognize God's purposes and seek His strength. Learn from the example of those who have successfully endured the same trials. Be assured that God is in control and is using each trial to mold your character and to teach you greater dependence on Him.

❖❖❖

Suggestions for Prayer: Thank God for the trials He brings your way. ❖ Ask Him to help you see your trials as means by which He strengthens you and glorifies Himself.

For Further Study: Read Psalm 119:11, Matthew 26:41, Ephesians 6:10-18, and James 4:7. What do those verses teach you about dealing with temptation?

"For Thine is the kingdom, and the power, and the glory, forever. Amen" (Matt. 6:13).

❖❖❖

The Disciples' Prayer is a pattern to follow for life.

The implications of the Disciples' Prayer are profound and far-reaching. An unknown author put it this way:

"I cannot say 'our' if I live only for myself in a spiritual, watertight compartment. I cannot say 'Father' if I do not endeavor each day to act like His child. I cannot say 'who art in heaven' if I am laying up no treasure there.

"I cannot say 'hallowed be Thy name' if I am not striving for holiness. I cannot say 'Thy kingdom come' if I am not doing all in my power to hasten that wonderful day. I cannot say 'Thy will be done' if I am disobedient to His Word. I cannot say 'in earth as it is in heaven' if I will not serve Him here and now.

"I cannot say 'give us . . . our daily bread' if I am dishonest or an 'under the counter' shopper. I cannot say 'forgive us our debts' if I harbor a grudge against anyone. I cannot say 'lead us not into temptation' if I deliberately place myself in its path. I cannot say 'deliver us from evil' if I do not put on the whole armor of God.

"I cannot say 'thine is the kingdom' if I do not give to the King the loyalty due Him as a faithful subject. I cannot attribute to Him 'the power' if I fear what men may do. I cannot ascribe to Him 'the glory' if I am seeking honor only for myself. I cannot say 'forever' if the horizon of my life is bounded completely by the things of time."

As you learn to apply to your own life the principles in this marvelous prayer, I pray that God's Kingdom will be your focus, His glory your goal, and His power your strength. Only then will our Lord's doxology be the continual song of your heart: "Thine is the kingdom, and the power, and the glory, forever. Amen" (v. 13).

❖❖❖

Suggestions for Prayer: Ask God to use what you've learned from the Disciples' Prayer to transform your prayers.

For Further Study: Read John 17, noting the priorities Jesus stressed in prayer.

"When [Jesus] saw the multitudes, He went up on the mountain; and after He sat down, His disciples came to Him. And opening His mouth He began to teach them" (Matt. 5:1-2).

❖❖❖

Only Christians know true happiness because they know Christ, who is its source.

J esus' earthly ministry included teaching, preaching, and healing. Wherever He went, He generated great excitement and controversy. Usually great multitudes of people followed Him as He moved throughout the regions of Judea and Galilee. Thousands came for healing, many came to mock and scorn, and some came in search of truth.

On one such occasion Jesus delivered His first recorded message—the Sermon on the Mount (Matt. 5–7). In it He proclaimed a standard of living diametrically opposed to the standards of His day—and ours. Boldly denouncing the ritualistic, hypocritical practices of the Jewish religious leaders, He taught that true religion is a matter of the heart or mind. People will behave as their hearts dictate (Luke 6:45); so the key to transformed behavior is transformed thinking.

At the beginning of His sermon Jesus presented the Beatitudes (Matt. 5:3-12), a list of the godly attitudes that mark a true believer and ensure true happiness. The Greek word translated "blessed" in those verses speaks of happiness and contentment. The rest of the sermon discusses the lifestyle that produces it.

Jesus taught that happiness is much more than favorable circumstances and pleasant emotions. In fact, it doesn't depend on circumstances at all. It is built on the indwelling character of God Himself. As your life manifests the virtues of humility, sorrow over sin, gentleness, righteousness, mercy, purity of heart, and peace, you will experience happiness that even severe persecution can't destroy.

As we study the Beatitudes, I pray you will be more and more conformed to the attitudes they portray and that you will experience true happiness in Christ.

❖❖❖

Suggestions for Prayer: Ask the Holy Spirit to minister to you through our daily studies. Be prepared to make any attitude changes that He might prompt.

For Further Study: Read the Sermon on the Mount (Matt. 5–7). ❖ What issues did Christ address? ❖ How did His hearers react to His teaching? How do you?

"Blessed are the poor in spirit . . . those who mourn . . . the gentle . . . those who hunger and thirst for righteousness . . . the merciful . . . the pure in heart . . . the peacemakers . . . [and] those who have been persecuted for the sake of righteousness" (Matt. 5:3-10).

❖❖❖

By the world's standards, Christ's definition of happiness is shocking and contradictory!

A quiz in a popular magazine characterized happy people as those who enjoy other people but aren't self-sacrificing, who refuse to participate in negative feelings or emotions, and who have a sense of accomplishment based on their own self-sufficiency.

But Jesus described happy people quite differently. In fact, He characterized them as spiritual beggars who realize they have no resources in themselves. He said they are meek rather than proud, mournful over their sin, self-sacrificing, and willing to endure persecution to reconcile men to God.

By the world's standards, that sounds more like misery than happiness! But the people of the world don't understand that what is often thought of as misery is actually the key to happiness.

Follow the Lord's progression of thought: true happiness begins with being "poor in spirit" (v. 3). That means you have a right attitude toward sin, which leads you to "mourn" over it (v. 4). Mourning over sin produces a meekness that leads to hungering and thirsting for righteousness (vv. 5-6), which results in mercy, purity of heart, and a peaceable spirit (vv. 7-9)—attitudes that bring true happiness.

When you display those attitudes, you can expect to be insulted, persecuted, and unjustly accused (vv. 10-11) because your life will be an irritating rebuke to worldly people. But despite the persecution, you can "rejoice, and be glad, for your reward in heaven is great" (v. 12).

You are one of God's lights in a sin-darkened world (v. 14), and while most people will reject Christ, others will be drawn to Him by the testimony of your life. Be faithful to Him today, so He can use you that way.

❖❖❖

Suggestions for Prayer: Thank God for the grace He gives you, enabling you to have Beatitude attitudes. ❖ Ask Him to make you a bright light in someone's life today.

For Further Study: Read 1 Peter 2:19-23. ❖ How did Jesus respond to persecution? ❖ How should you respond?

"Blessed are the poor in spirit, for theirs is the kingdom of heaven" (Matt. 5:3).

❖❖❖

Poverty of spirit is a prerequisite to salvation and to victorious Christian living.

In Luke 18:9-14 Jesus tells of two men who went to the Temple to pray. One was a Pharisee, the other a tax collector. The Pharisee boasted to God about his self-righteous efforts; the tax collector humbly acknowledged his sin. The Pharisee was proud and went away still in sin; the tax collector was poor in spirit and went away forgiven.

The Greek word translated "poor" in Matthew 5:3 was used in classical Greek to refer to those reduced to cowering in dark corners of the city streets begging for handouts. Because they had no personal resources, they were totally dependent on the gifts of others. That same word is used in Luke 16:20 to describe a "poor" man named Lazarus.

The spiritual parallel pictures those who know they are spiritually helpless and utterly destitute of any human resources that will commend them to God. They rely totally on God's grace for salvation, and they also rely on His grace for daily living. Jesus called them happy people because they are true believers and the Kingdom of Heaven belongs to them.

The word translated "theirs" in Matthew 5:3 is emphatic in the Greek text: the Kingdom of Heaven definitely belongs to those who are poor in spirit. They have its grace now and will fully enjoy its glory later (1 John 3:1-2). That's cause for great joy!

Isaiah 57:15 says, "Thus says the high and exalted One who lives forever, whose name is Holy, 'I dwell on a high and holy place, and also with the contrite and lowly of spirit in order to revive the spirit of the lowly and to revive the heart of the contrite.'" David added, "The sacrifices of God are a broken spirit; a broken and a contrite heart, O God, Thou wilt not despise" (Ps. 51:17).

Like the humble tax collector, recognize your weaknesses and rely totally on God's resources. Then He will hear your prayers and minister to your needs. That's where happiness begins!

❖❖❖

Suggestions for Prayer: Thank God that when you come to Him in humility and contrition, He hears you and responds. ❖ Prayerfully guard your heart from the subtle influences of pride.

For Further Study: Read the following verses, noting God's perspective on pride: Proverbs 6:16-17; 8:13; 11:2; 16:5, 18-19.

> *"Blessed are the poor in spirit, for theirs is the kingdom of heaven" (Matt. 5:3).*

✧✧✧

If you are poor in spirit, certain characteristics will mark your life.

The Puritan writer Thomas Watson listed seven ways to determine if you are poor in spirit (*The Beatitudes* [Edinburgh: The Banner of Truth Trust, 1971], pp. 45-48): ✧ *You will be weaned from self.* Psalm 131:2 says, "Like a weaned child rests against his mother, my soul is like a weaned child within me." When you are poor in spirit, you will focus not on yourself but on glorifying God and ministering to others. ✧ *You will focus on Christ.* Second Corinthians 3:18 says that believers are "beholding as in a mirror the glory of the Lord, [and] are being transformed into the same image from glory to glory, just as from the Lord, the Spirit." When you are poor in spirit, the wonder of Christ captivates you. To be like Him is your highest goal. ✧ *You will never complain.* If you are poor in spirit, you accept God's sovereign control over your circumstances, knowing you deserve nothing anyway. Yet the greater your needs, the more abundantly He provides. ✧ *You will see good in others.* A person who is poor in spirit recognizes his own weaknesses and appreciates the strengths of others. ✧ *You will spend time in prayer.* It is characteristic of beggars to beg. Therefore you will constantly be in God's presence seeking His strength and blessing. ✧ *You will take Christ on His terms.* Those who are poor in spirit will give up anything to please Christ, whereas the proud sinner wants simply to add Christ to his sinful lifestyle. ✧ *You will praise and thank God.* When you are poor in spirit, you will be filled with praise and thanks for the wonder of God's grace, which He lavishes on you through Christ (Eph. 1:6).

Do those principles characterize your life? If so, you are poor in spirit and the Kingdom of Heaven is yours (Matt. 5:3). If not, you must seek God's forgiveness and begin to live as His humble child.

✧✧✧

Suggestions for Prayer: Ask the Holy Spirit to search your heart, revealing any attitudes or motives that displease Him. Seek His grace in changing them.

For Further Study: Read 3 John. Would you characterize Gaius as poor in spirit? Diotrephes? Explain.

*"Blessed are those who mourn, for they shall be comforted"
(Matt. 5:4).*

❖❖❖

**Human sorrow is a natural and healthy emotion,
but beware of mourning over unfulfilled sinful desires.**

Most people in our society have an amusement-park mentality. They spend much of their time and money on entertainment, wanting to enjoy life and avoid problems whenever possible. To them, Matthew 5:4 is a paradox. How can someone who mourns be happy? The answer lies in the difference between godly sorrow and human sorrow. Godly sorrow is sorrow over sin; human sorrow is sorrow over some tragic or disappointing turn of events (2 Cor. 7:8-11).

In Matthew 5:4 Jesus is referring to godly sorrow, which is our topic for tomorrow. But we all face human sorrow as well, so I want to discuss it briefly today.

Human sorrow is a natural emotion. Our Lord Himself was "a man of sorrows, and acquainted with grief" (Isa. 53:3). Many things can cause this. We might mourn out of love, disappointment, loneliness, or physical illness. There is nothing wrong with that kind of mourning. It is a God-given relief valve for the pain and sorrow in this fallen world, and it promotes the healing process.

Scripture gives many examples of human sorrow. Abraham wept when his wife, Sarah, died (Gen. 23:2). Through tears Jeremiah preached God's message of judgment (Jer. 9:1). Paul expressed his concern for the church with his tears (Acts 20:31). Those are natural, healthy expressions of human sorrow.

However, sorrow can also be caused by evil desires or by a lack of trust in God. King Ahab mourned to the point of sulking and not eating when he couldn't have another man's property (1 Kings 21:4). Some Christians mourn excessively when they lose a loved one. Forsaking the comfort of the Spirit, they focus only on their own grief. Extreme or prolonged manifestations of great sorrow are sinful and must be confessed rather than comforted.

God is gracious to His children amid times of human sorrow. Ultimately He will do away with mourning and pain forever (Rev. 21:4). Rejoice in that promise, and be comforted by His wonderful grace!

❖❖❖

Suggestions for Prayer: Thank God for the ministry of the Spirit, who is the great Comforter or Helper (John 14:16-17). When sorrow occurs, lean on the Spirit, feed your soul on God's Word, and commune with Him in prayer.

For Further Study: Read Psalm 55. How did David express his desire to escape his difficult situation? What was his final resolve?

"Blessed are those who mourn, for they shall be comforted"
(Matt. 5:4).

✧✧✧

When your sins are forgiven, you are a happy person!

Human sorrow involves mourning over some tragic or disappointing turn of events. At such times believers are assured of God's sustaining and comforting grace (2 Cor. 1:3-4). But when Jesus said, "Blessed are those who mourn, for they shall be comforted" (Matt. 5:4), He was referring to godly sorrow, which involves mourning over your sin.

"Mourn" in Matthew 5:4 translates the strongest Greek word used in the New Testament to express grief. It is often used of the passionate lament expressed over the loss of a loved one (e.g., Mark 16:10). David was expressing that kind of sorrow over his sin when he wrote, "When I kept silent about my sin, my body wasted away through my groaning all day long. For day and night Thy hand was heavy upon me; my vitality was drained away as with the fever-heat of summer" (Ps. 32:3-4). His grief and despair made him physically ill.

At that point David wasn't a happy person, but the blessing godly sorrow brings isn't found in the sorrow itself, but in God's response to it. As Paul said to the Corinthians, "I now rejoice, not that you were made sorrowful, but that you were made sorrowful *to the point of repentance*; for you were made sorrowful according to the will of God. . . . For the sorrow that is according to the will of God produces a repentance without regret, leading to salvation; but the sorrow of the world produces death" (2 Cor. 7:9-10, emphasis added). Godly sorrow is the path to repentance and forgiveness.

After David confessed his sin, he proclaimed with great joy, "How blessed is he whose transgression is forgiven, whose sin is covered! How blessed is the man to whom the Lord does not impute iniquity, and in whose spirit there is no deceit!" (Psalm 32:1-2). When you understand that your sins are forgiven, you are a happy person!

How do you deal with *your* sins? Do you deny them and try to hide them, or do you mourn over them and confess them (cf. Prov. 28:13)?

✧✧✧

Suggestions for Prayer: If you have allowed some sin to rob you of your happiness, don't let it continue a moment longer. Like David, confess your sin and know the joy of forgiveness.

For Further Study: Read Luke 15:11-24. How did the prodigal son deal with his sin?

"Blessed are those who mourn, for they shall be comforted"
(Matt. 5:4).

❖❖❖

Sin is a serious issue with God. He never winks at it or takes it lightly.

Satan desires to desensitize Christians to the heinousness of sin. He wants you to stop mourning over sin and start enjoying it. Impossible? Many who once thought so have fallen prey to its power. It usually doesn't happen all at once. In fact, the process can be slow and subtle—almost imperceptible. But the results are always tragic.

How can you remain alert to the dangers of sin and protect yourself from compromise? First, be aware of your sin. David said, "My sin is ever before me" (Ps. 51:3). Isaiah cried out, "Woe is me, for I am ruined! Because I am a man of unclean lips, and I live among a people of unclean lips" (Isa. 6:5). Peter said to Jesus, "Depart from me, for I am a sinful man, O Lord!" (Luke 5:8). Paul called himself the chief of sinners (1 Tim. 1:15). Those men shared a common awareness of their own sinfulness, and it drove them to God for forgiveness and cleansing.

Second, remember the significance of the cross. If you allow a pattern of sin to develop in your life, you've forgotten the enormous price Christ paid to free you from its bondage.

Third, realize the effect sin has on others. The psalmist said, "My eyes shed streams of water, because they do not keep Thy law" (Ps. 119:136). Jesus mourned over Jerusalem, saying, "O Jerusalem, Jerusalem, who kills the prophets and stones those who are sent to her! How often I wanted to gather your children together, the way a hen gathers her chicks under her wings, and you were unwilling" (Matt. 23:37). Your heart should ache for those who are enslaved to sin.

Finally, eliminate anything that hinders your sensitivity to sin, such as deliberately sinning, rejecting God's forgiveness, being proud, presuming on God's grace, or taking sin lightly. Such things will quickly dull your spiritual senses and give Satan the opportunity to lead you into greater sin.

❖❖❖

Suggestions for Prayer: Thank God that He brings comfort and happiness to those who mourn over their sin. ❖ Ask Him to guard your heart from anything that will diminish your sensitivity to the awfulness of sin.

For Further Study: Read 1 Samuel 15. ❖ What was Saul's sin? ❖ Did he mourn over his sin? Explain.

"Blessed are the gentle, for they shall inherit the earth" (Matt. 5:5).

❖❖❖

Gentleness is power under control.

The Greek word translated "gentle" in Matthew 5:5 speaks of humility, meekness, and non-retaliation—traits that in our proud society are often equated with weakness or cowardice. But in reality they are virtues that identify Kingdom citizens.

The same word was used by the Greeks to describe a gentle breeze, a soothing medicine, or a domesticated colt. Those are examples of power under control. A gentle breeze brings pleasure, but a hurricane brings destruction; a soothing medicine brings healing, but an overdose can kill; a domesticated colt is useful, but a wild horse is dangerous.

Christ Himself is the epitome of gentleness. Even when officially announcing His messiahship to Jerusalem, He humbly entered the city astride a donkey (Matt. 21:5). His behavior amid persecution was exemplary: "Christ . . . suffered for you, leaving you an example for you to follow in His steps, who committed no sin, nor was any deceit found in His mouth; and while being reviled, He did not revile in return; while suffering, He uttered no threats" (1 Peter 2:21-23).

Despite His humility and restraint, Jesus wasn't weak or cowardly. He never defended Himself, but when His Father's house was being desecrated, He made a whip and beat those who were defiling it (John 2:13-16; Matt. 21:12-13). He never shirked from pronouncing judgment on unrepentant sinners and never compromised His integrity or disobeyed His Father's will.

The hypocritical Jewish religious leaders expected that when Israel's Messiah came, He would commend them for their wonderful spirituality. Instead, Jesus condemned them and called them children of the devil (John 8:44). In retaliation they had Him murdered. His power was always under control; theirs wasn't.

Our society has little use for gentleness. The macho, do-your-own-thing mentality characterizes most of our heroes. But you are called to a higher standard. When you pattern your life after Jesus, you will have a significant impact on society and will know true happiness.

❖❖❖

Suggestions for Prayer: Thank God for the virtue of gentleness, which He is producing in you by the power of His Spirit. Follow Christ's example today so that gentleness will mark your character.

For Further Study: Read the following passages, noting the responsibilities and blessings that accompany self-restraint: Proverbs 16:32; Ephesians 4:1-2; Colossians 3:12; and Titus 3:1-2.

"Blessed are the gentle, for they shall inherit the earth"
(Matt. 5:5).

❖❖❖

Someday God will reverse the curse and return the earth to His people.

God said to Adam and Eve, "Be fruitful and multiply, and fill the earth, and subdue it; and rule over the fish of the sea and over the birds of the sky, and over every living thing that moves on the earth" (Gen. 1:28). But their sin cost them their sovereignty and brought a curse upon the earth (Gen. 3:17-18).

The Apostle Paul said, "The anxious longing of the creation waits eagerly for the revealing of the sons of God . . . in hope that the creation itself also will be set free from its slavery to corruption" (Rom. 8:19-21). Someday that curse will be reversed, and God's people will once again inherit the earth.

The Greek word translated "inherit" (Matt. 5:5) means "to receive an allotted portion." The earth is the allotted portion of believers, who will reign with the Lord when He comes in His Kingdom (Rev. 20:6). That's an emphatic promise in Matthew 5:5, which literally reads, "Blessed are the gentle, for *only* they shall inherit the earth."

Many Jewish people of Christ's day thought the Kingdom belonged to the strong, proud, and defiant. But Jesus said the earth will belong to the gentle, meek, and humble. Proud, self-righteous people don't qualify (cf. Luke 1:46-55). Jesus said, "Truly I say to you, unless you are converted and become [humble and submissive] like children, you shall not enter the kingdom of heaven" (Matt. 18:3).

As a recipient of God's promises, you should be thrilled knowing that you will inherit the earth and reign with Christ in His earthly Kingdom. Be encouraged to know that even when evil people and godless nations seem to prosper, God is in complete control and will someday establish His righteous Kingdom on earth.

Rejoice in that assurance, and seek to be all He wants you to be until that great day.

❖❖❖

Suggestions for Prayer: Thank God that all of creation will someday be freed from sin's corrupting influences. ❖ Praise Him for His mighty power, which will bring it all to pass.

For Further Study: Read 1 Corinthians 6:1-8. ❖ What issue did Paul address? ❖ How does the future reign of Christians apply to that issue?

"Blessed are those who hunger and thirst for righteousness, for they shall be satisfied" (Matt. 5:6).

✧✧✧

Only Christ can satisfy your deepest needs.

Within every man and woman is a hunger and thirst only God can satisfy. That's why Jesus said, "I am the bread of life; he who comes to Me shall not hunger, and he who believes in Me shall never thirst" (John 6:35).

Sadly, most people search for happiness in the wrong places. The prodigal son in Luke 15 is one example. He turned from God to pursue sinful pleasures, but he soon discovered that sin cannot satisfy a hungering soul. That's when he returned to his father's house, where he was given a great feast—a picture of salvation.

The rich fool in Luke 12 thought that amassing possessions was the key to happiness, saying to himself, "'What shall I do, since I have no place to store my crops? . . . This is what I will do: I will tear down my barns and build larger ones, and there I will store all my grain and my goods. And I will say to my soul, "Soul, you have many goods laid up for many years to come; take your ease, eat, drink and be merry."' But God said to him, 'You fool! This very night your soul is required of you; and now who will own what you have prepared?' So is the man who lays up treasure for himself, and is not rich toward God" (vv. 17-21). Unlike the prodigal son, the rich fool never turned to God in repentance. Consequently he lost everything.

The rich fool is typical of many people today who ignore Christ and attempt to fill the void with worldly pleasures. Most are oblivious to the eternal peril that awaits them if they don't repent.

Those who love God shun worldliness, pursue righteousness, and know the satisfaction that comes from pleasing Him. That's the essence of the Sermon on the Mount: "Seek first His kingdom, and His righteousness; and all [you need] shall be added to you" (Matt. 6:33). Keep that goal uppermost in your mind as you face the challenge of each new day.

✧✧✧

Suggestions for Prayer: Thank God that He satisfies the deepest desires of your heart.

For Further Study: Read Daniel 4:28-37. ✧ What was Nebuchadnezzar's sin? ✧ How did God punish Him? ✧ How did Nebuchadnezzar respond after being punished?

"Blessed are those who hunger and thirst for righteousness, for they shall be satisfied" (Matt. 5:6).

❖❖❖

Your appetite for righteousness should equal your appetite for food and water.

David was a man after God's own heart. In Psalm 63:1 he writes, "O God, Thou art my God; I shall seek Thee earnestly; my soul thirsts for Thee, my flesh yearns for Thee, in a dry and weary land where there is no water." He communed with God and knew the blessings of His sufficiency: "The Lord is my shepherd, I shall not want. . . . He leads me beside quiet waters. He restores my soul; He guides me in the paths of righteousness. . . . Thy rod and Thy staff, they comfort me" (Ps. 23:1-4). He endured unjust persecution for the Lord's sake: "Zeal for Thy house has consumed me, and the reproaches of those who reproach Thee have fallen on me" (Ps. 69:9).

David's zeal for God illustrates what Jesus meant when He said, "Blessed are those who hunger and thirst for righteousness" (Matt. 5:6). The words translated "hunger" and "thirst" speak of intense desire. They are present participles, which imply continuous action. The idea is paradoxical: the believer's continuous and intense desire for righteousness is continually satisfied by Christ.

J. N. Darby, an early leader of the Plymouth Brethren movement, said, "To be hungry is not enough; I must be really starving to know what is in [God's] heart towards me. When the prodigal son was hungry he went to feed upon husks, but when he was starving, he turned to his father" (quoted in Martyn Lloyd-Jones's *Studies in the Sermon on the Mount*, Vol. 1, p. 81). When you have that kind of desperation, only God can satisfy it.

Does your desire for righteousness drive you to Christ for satisfaction? I pray that the words of the psalmist will be yours as well: "As for me, I will behold thy face in righteousness; I shall be satisfied, when I awake, with thy likeness" (Ps. 17:15, KJV).

❖❖❖

Suggestions for Prayer: Ask God to use today's events to increase your hunger and thirst for righteousness. Look to Him in all things, knowing that He alone can satisfy.

For Further Study: Read Philippians 3:1-14. ❖ What does it mean to place confidence in the flesh? ❖ How did Paul define true righteousness?

> *"Blessed are those who hunger and thirst for righteousness, for they shall be satisfied" (Matt. 5:6).*

❖❖❖

Your relationship with God is the measure of your righteousness.

Righteousness" means "to be right with God." When you hunger and thirst for righteousness, you passionately desire an ongoing and ever-maturing relationship with God Himself.

Righteousness begins with salvation and continues in sanctification. Only after you abandon all self-righteousness and hunger for salvation will you be cleansed from sin and made righteous in Christ. Then you embark on a life-long process of becoming as righteous as Christ—a process that will culminate when you are fully glorified in His presence (Rom. 8:29-30; 1 John 3:2). There's always need for improvement in this life (Phil. 3:12-14), but satisfaction comes in communing with Christ and growing in His grace.

You can know if you're hungering and thirsting for righteousness by asking yourself some simple questions. First, are you dissatisfied with your sin? Self-satisfaction is impossible if you are aware of your sin and if you grieve when you fall short of God's holy standard.

Second, do external things satisfy your longings? A hungry man isn't satisfied until he eats. A thirsty man isn't satisfied until he drinks. When you hunger and thirst after righteousness, only God's righteousness can satisfy you.

Third, do you have an appetite for God's Word? Hungry people don't need to be told to eat. It's instinctive! Spiritual hunger will drive you to feed on the Word in order to learn what God says about increasing in righteousness.

Fourth, are you content amid difficulties? A hungry soul is content despite the pain it goes through, because it sees every trial as a means by which God is teaching greater righteousness. If you react with anger or resentment when things go wrong, you're seeking superficial happiness.

Finally, are your hunger and thirst unconditional? The rich young ruler in Matthew 19 knew there was a void in his life but was unwilling to give up his possessions. His hunger was conditional.

Christ will fully satisfy every longing of your heart, and yet you will also constantly desire more of His righteousness. That's the blessed paradox of hungering and thirsting after righteousness.

❖❖❖

Suggestions for Prayer: Read Psalm 112 as a hymn of praise to God.

For Further Study: Read the following verses, noting how God satisfies those who trust in Him: Psalm 34:10; 107:9; Isaiah 55:1-3; John 4:14; 6:35.

"Blessed are the merciful, for they shall receive mercy" (Matt. 5:7).

❖❖❖

Mercy is a characteristic of true believers.

Like the other Beatitudes, Matthew 5:7 contains a twofold message: to enter the Kingdom, you must seek mercy; once there, you must show mercy to others.

The thought of showing mercy probably surprised Christ's audience because both the Jews and the Romans tended to be merciless. The Romans exalted justice, courage, discipline, and power. To them mercy was a sign of weakness. For example, if a Roman father wanted his newborn child to live, he simply held his thumb up; if he wanted it to die, he held his thumb down.

Jesus repeatedly rebuked the Jewish religious leaders for their egotistical, self-righteous, and condemning attitudes. They were intolerant of anyone who failed to live by their traditions. They even withheld financial support from their own needy parents (Matt. 15:3-9).

Like the people of Jesus' time, many people today also lack mercy. Some are outright cruel and unkind, but most are so consumed with their quest for self-gratification that they simply neglect others.

Christians, on the other hand, should be characterized by mercy. In fact, James used mercy to illustrate true faith: "What use is it, my brethren, if a man says he has faith, but he has no works? Can that faith save him? If a brother or sister is without clothing and in need of daily food, and one of you says to them, 'Go in peace, be warmed and be filled,' and yet you do not give them what is necessary for their body, what use is that? Even so faith, if it has no works, is dead, being by itself" (James 2:14-17). He also said mercy is characteristic of godly wisdom: "The wisdom from above is first pure, then peaceable, gentle, reasonable, full of mercy and good fruits, unwavering, without hypocrisy" (3:17).

As one who has received mercy from God, let mercy be the hallmark of your life.

❖❖❖

Suggestions for Prayer: Thank God for His great mercy. ❖ Ask Him to give you opportunities to show mercy to others today.

For Further Study: Read Luke 10:25-37. ❖ Who questioned Jesus, and what was his motive? ❖ What characteristics of mercy were demonstrated by the Samaritan traveler? ❖ What challenge did Jesus give His hearer? Are you willing to meet that challenge?

"Blessed are the merciful, for they shall receive mercy" (Matt. 5:7).

✧✧✧

Mercy is compassion in action.

M ercy is not a human attribute. It is God's gift to those who seek Him. Psalm 103:11 says, "As the heaven is high above the earth, so great is his mercy toward them that fear him" (KJV).

The verb form of "merciful" appears many times in Scripture and means "to have mercy on," "to aid the afflicted," "to give help to the wretched," or "to rescue the miserable." In general it refers to anything you do to benefit someone in need. The adjective form is used only twice—here in Matthew 5:7 and in Hebrews 2:17, which reads, "[Christ] had to be made like His brethren in all things, that He might become a merciful and faithful high priest." Christ Himself is both the source and illustration of mercy.

Christ modeled mercy throughout His earthly ministry. He healed the sick and enabled the crippled to walk. He gave sight to the blind, hearing to the deaf, and speech to the mute. His redeeming love embraced sinners of all kinds. He wept with those in sorrow and comforted the lonely. He embraced little children and the elderly alike. His mercy was compassion in action!

Despite His abundant mercy, Jesus received no mercy from His enemies. They hated Him without cause, accused Him falsely, beat Him, nailed Him to a cross, spat upon Him, and cursed Him. Even then He sought mercy for them, praying, "Father, forgive them; for they do not know what they are doing" (Luke 23:34).

Some have paraphrased Matthew 5:7 to say that if you show mercy to others, they will show mercy to you. Now, that might happen in some isolated incidences, but in this jaded world that's not often the case—as Jesus' life clearly demonstrates. Many Christians have incurred slander, rebuke, lawsuits, and even death for their noble efforts. Jesus didn't guarantee merciful treatment from others. His emphasis was that *God* shows mercy toward those who show mercy to others.

Don't ever be reluctant to show mercy to others—even when they misunderstand or mistreat you. God will use your kindness for His glory and will reward you accordingly.

✧✧✧

Suggestions for Prayer: Praise Jesus for being willing to suffer death that you might receive mercy. ✧ Is there someone you might show mercy to today in some tangible way?

For Further Study: Read John 5:1-18. ✧ How did Christ demonstrate mercy to the sick man? ✧ How did the Jewish religious leaders react?

*"Blessed are the merciful, for they shall receive mercy"
(Matt. 5:7).*

❖❖❖

There are many ways to show mercy.

G od delights in mercy, and as a believer you have the privilege of showing mercy in many ways. In the physical realm you can give money to
the poor, food to the hungry, or a bed to the homeless. God has always wanted
His people to be that way. Deuteronomy 15 says, "If there is a poor man with
you . . . you shall not harden your heart, nor close your hand from [him]; but
you shall freely open your hand to him, and shall generously lend him sufficient for his need in whatever he lacks" (vv. 7-8). Verses 12-14 instruct
Israelites who release a slave to provide for the slave's needs. That was the
merciful thing to do.

In the spiritual realm you can show mercy by pitying the lost. St. Augustine
said, "If I weep for that body from which the soul is departed, how should I
weep for that soul from which God is departed?" (cited by Thomas Watson
in *The Beatitudes*, p. 144). We mourn over the dead, but do we mourn as much
for lost souls? When Stephen was being stoned, he pitied his wretched murderers, asking God to forgive them (Acts 7:60). Jesus did the same (Luke
23:34). That should be our attitude as well.

Another way of showing mercy is to rebuke sin. Second Timothy 2:24-25
says, "The Lord's bond-servant must not be quarrelsome, but be kind to all
. . . with gentleness correcting those who are in opposition, if perhaps God
may grant them repentance leading to the knowledge of the truth." It is merciful and loving to rebuke sinners because it gives them a chance to repent
and be forgiven.

Prayer is also an act of mercy, as is preaching the gospel. In fact, sharing
Christ with someone is the most merciful thing you can do!

There are many more ways to be merciful, but I hope these will stimulate
your thinking and will encourage you to discover as many ways as possible to
pass on the abundant mercy God has shown to you.

❖❖❖

Suggestions for Prayer: Thank God for the mercies you have received from
others. ❖ Take advantage of every opportunity to minister to others.

For Further Study: Determine who receives mercy according to the following verses: Matthew 6:14; Titus 3:5-6; Hebrews 4:14-16; James 2:13; and 1
Peter 2:9-10.

"Blessed are the merciful, for they shall receive mercy"
(Matt. 5:7).

❖❖❖

God commends merciful people but condemns the merciless.

Scripture shows that those whom God blessed most abundantly were abundantly merciful to others. Abraham, for example, helped rescue his nephew Lot even after Lot had wronged him. Joseph was merciful to his brothers after they sold him into slavery. Twice David spared Saul's life after Saul tried to kill him.

But just as sure as God's commendation is upon those who show mercy, His condemnation is upon those who are merciless. Psalm 109:14-16 says, "Let the iniquity of [the merciless person's] fathers be remembered before the Lord, and do not let the sin of his mother be blotted out . . . because he did not remember to show lovingkindness."

When judgment comes, the Lord will tell such people, "Depart from Me, accursed ones, into the eternal fire which has been prepared for the devil and his angels; for I was hungry, and you gave Me nothing to eat; I was thirsty, and you gave Me nothing to drink; I was a stranger, and you did not invite Me in; naked, and you did not clothe Me; sick, and in prison, and you did not visit Me" (Matt. 25:41-43). They will respond, "Lord, when did we see You hungry, or thirsty, or a stranger, or naked, or sick, or in prison, and did not take care of You?" (v. 44). He will reply that when they withheld mercy from those who represented Him, they were withholding it from Him (v. 45).

Our society encourages us to grab everything we can for ourselves, but God wants us to reach out and give everything we can to others. If someone wrongs you, fails to repay a debt, or doesn't return something he has borrowed from you, be merciful to him. That doesn't mean you should excuse sin, but you are to respond to people with a heart of compassion. That's what Christ did for you. Can you do any less for others?

❖❖❖

Suggestions for Prayer: If there is someone who has wronged you, pray for that person, asking God to give you a heart of compassion for him or her. Make every effort to reconcile as soon as possible.

For Further Study: Read Romans 1:29-31. How did Paul characterize the ungodly?

"Blessed are the pure in heart, for they shall see God" (Matt. 5:8).

✧✧✧

Legalism can't produce a pure heart.

By the time Jesus arrived, Israel was in a desperate condition spiritually. The Jewish people were in bondage to the oppressive legalism of the Pharisees, who had developed a system of laws that was impossible to keep. Consequently, the people lacked security and were longing for a Savior to free them from guilt and frustration. They knew God had promised a Redeemer who would forgive their sins and cleanse their hearts (Ezek. 36:25-27), but they weren't sure when He was coming or how to identify Him when He arrived.

The enormous response to John the Baptist's ministry illustrates the level of expectancy among the people. Matthew 3:5-6 says, "Then Jerusalem was going out to him, and all Judea, and all the district around the Jordan; and they were being baptized by him in the Jordan River, as they confessed their sins." The uppermost question in everyone's mind seemed to be, "How can I enter the Kingdom of Heaven?"

Jesus Himself was asked that question by many people in different ways. In Luke 10:25 a lawyer asks, "Teacher, what shall I do to inherit eternal life?" In Luke 18:18 a rich young ruler asks exactly the same thing. In John 6:28 a multitude asks, "What shall we do, that we may work the works of God?" Nicodemus, a prominent Jewish religious leader, came to Jesus at night with the same question, but before he could ask it, Jesus read his thoughts and said, "Unless one is born again, he cannot see the kingdom of God" (John 3:3).

As devoutly religious as those people might have been, they would remain spiritually lost unless they placed their faith in Christ. That's the only way to enter the Kingdom.

Still today many people look for relief from sin and guilt. God can use you to share Christ with some of them. Ask Him for that privilege, and be prepared when it comes.

✧✧✧

Suggestions for Prayer: Pray for those enslaved to legalistic religious systems. ✧ Be sure there is no sin in your life to hinder God's work through you.

For Further Study: Read Galatians 3. ✧ Why did Paul rebuke the Galatians? ✧ What was the purpose of the Old Testament Law?

"Blessed are the pure in heart, for they shall see God" (Matt. 5:8).

✧✧✧

There are basically only two kinds of religion in the world: those based on human achievement and those based on divine accomplishment.

Religion comes in many forms. Almost every conceivable belief or behavior has been incorporated into some religious system at some point in time. But really there are only two kinds of religion. One says you can earn your way to Heaven; the other says you must trust in Jesus Christ alone. One is the religion of human achievement; the other is the religion of divine accomplishment.

Those who rely on their achievements tend to compare themselves to others. But that's a relative, self-justifying standard because you can always find someone worse than yourself on which to base the comparison.

Jesus eliminated all human standards when He said, "You are to be perfect, as your heavenly Father is perfect" (Matt. 5:48). Even the Jewish religious leaders, who were generally thought to be the epitome of righteousness, didn't qualify according to that standard. In fact, Jesus told the people that their righteousness had to exceed that of the scribes and Pharisees if they wanted to enter Heaven (Matt. 5:20). That must have shocked them, but Jesus wasn't speaking of conformity to external religious ceremonies. He was calling for pure hearts.

God doesn't compare you to liars, thieves, cheaters, child abusers, or murderers. He compares you to *Himself.* His absolute holy character is the standard by which He measures your suitability for Heaven. Apart from Christ, everyone fails that standard because "all have sinned and fall short of the glory of God" (Rom. 3:23). But the glorious truth of salvation is that Jesus Christ came to earth to purify our hearts. He took our sin upon Himself, paid its penalty, then bestowed His own righteousness upon us (Rom. 4:24). He keeps us pure by continually cleansing our sin and empowering us to do His will.

Your faith in Christ—not your personal achievements—is what makes you pure. Let that truth bring joy to your heart and praise to your lips!

✧✧✧

Suggestions for Prayer: Thank the Lord for accomplishing salvation on your behalf and for granting you saving faith. ✧ Pray that your thoughts and actions today will evidence a pure heart.

For Further Study: Read Psalm 24:1-5 and Ezekiel 36:25-29. ✧ Who is acceptable to God? ✧ How does God purify the hearts of His people?

"Blessed are the pure in heart, for they shall see God" (Matt. 5:8).

❖❖❖

The way you think determines the way you behave.

God is concerned about the way you think. That's why Paul said, "Do not be conformed to this world, but be transformed by the renewing of your mind, that you may prove what the will of God is, that which is good and acceptable and perfect" (Rom. 12:2). In Philippians 4:8 he instructs us to think about that which is true, honorable, right, pure, lovely, of good repute, excellent, and praiseworthy.

When Jesus spoke of a pure heart in Matthew 5:8, He was talking about sanctified thinking. The Greek word translated "heart" is *kardia*, from which we get the word *cardiac*. While we often relate *heart* to the emotions (e.g., "He has a broken heart"), the Bible relates it primarily to the intellect (e.g., "Out of the heart come evil thoughts, murders, adulteries, fornications, thefts, false witness, slanders," Matt. 15:19). That's why you must "watch over your heart with all diligence" (Prov. 4:23).

In a secondary way, however, *heart* relates to the will and emotions because they are influenced by the intellect. If you are committed to something, it will affect your will, which in turn will affect your emotions.

The Greek word translated "pure" in Matthew 5:8 means "to cleanse." In the moral sense it speaks of being free from the filth of sin. It also refers to something that is unmixed, unalloyed, or unadulterated. Spiritual integrity and sincere motives are appropriate applications of its meaning to the Christian life.

Jesus was saying the Kingdom citizen is blessed because he or she has pure thoughts and pure motives that together produce holy living. Someone might claim to be religious and have pure motives, but if his behavior isn't righteous, his heart isn't fixed on God. Similarly, you can go to church, carry a Bible, and recite verses, but if your heart isn't clean, you haven't met God's standard.

You must do the will of God from a pure heart (Eph. 6:6). Toward that end, make David's prayer yours as well: "Create in me a clean heart, O God, and renew a steadfast spirit within me" (Ps. 51:10).

❖❖❖

Suggestions for Prayer: Memorize Psalm 19:14 and make it a part of your daily prayers.

For Further Study: Read the following verses, noting the characteristics of a pure heart: Psalm 9:1; 26:2; 27:8; 28:7; 57:7.

"Blessed are the pure in heart, for they shall see God" (Matt. 5:8).

✧✧✧

You have a part to play in becoming pure in heart.

Purifying a heart is the gracious and miraculous work of the Holy Spirit, but there are some things we must do in response to His prompting. First, we must admit we can't purify our own hearts. Proverbs 20:9 says, "Who can say, 'I have cleansed my heart, I am pure from my sin'?" The implied answer is, no one!

Next, we must put our faith in Jesus Christ, whose sacrifice on the cross is the basis for our cleansing. Acts 15:9 says that God cleanses hearts on the basis of faith. Of course, our faith must be placed in the right object. First John 1:7 says, "If we walk in the light as He Himself is in the light, we have fellowship with one another, and the blood of Jesus His Son cleanses us from all sin."

Finally, we must study the Bible and pray. The psalmist said we keep our way pure by keeping it according to God's Word, which we must treasure in our hearts (Ps. 119:9, 11). As we pray and submit to the Word, the Spirit purifies our lives.

That's how you acquire and maintain a pure heart. As a result you "shall see God" (Matt. 5:8). That doesn't mean you'll see Him with physical eyes, but rather with spiritual ones. You'll begin to live in His presence and will become increasingly aware of His working in your life. You'll recognize His power and handiwork in the beauty and intricacy of creation (Ps. 19). You'll discern His grace and purposes amid trials and will learn to praise Him in all things. You'll sense His ministry through other Christians and will see His sovereignty in every event of your life. Life takes on a profound and eternal meaning as you share Christ with unbelievers and see Him transform lives.

There's no greater joy than knowing you are pure before God and that your life is honoring to Him. May that joy be yours today, and may God use you in a powerful way for His glory!

✧✧✧

Suggestions for Prayer: Ask the Lord for continued grace to live a pure life so others will see Christ in you.

For Further Study: Read Isaiah 6:1-8. ✧ Describe Isaiah's vision of God. ✧ How did Isaiah respond to God's presence?

"Blessed are the peacemakers, for they shall be called sons of God" (Matt. 5:9).

❖❖❖

God's peace cushions the soul during difficult times.

I remember reading about what is called "the cushion of the sea." The ocean surface is often greatly agitated, but as you descend, the water becomes increasingly calm. At its greatest depths, the ocean is virtually still. Oceanographers dredging ocean bottoms have found animal and plant remains that appear to have been undisturbed for hundreds of years.

Similarly, Christians can experience a cushion of peace in their souls regardless of their troubled surroundings. That's because they belong to God, who is the source of peace; they serve Christ, who is the Prince of Peace; and they are indwelt by the Holy Spirit, who is the agent of peace. Galatians 5:22 says, "The fruit of the Spirit is love, joy, peace." When you become a Christian, God grants you the gift of peace.

God is not only the source of perfect peace but also its purest example. Everything He does is marked by peace. First Corinthians 14:33 says He is not a God of confusion but of peace. In Judges 6:24 He is called Jehovah-shalom, which means, "the Lord is peace." The Trinity is characterized by a total absence of conflict—perfect oneness, perfect righteousness, and absolute harmony. It is impossible for God to be at odds with Himself!

God wants everyone to know that kind of peace. He created the world with peace and sent His Son to offer peace. Someday Christ will return to establish His Kingdom and reign in peace for eternity.

In the meantime, turmoil exists for all who don't know Christ. They have no cushion for their souls. You, however, have peace with God through the death of Christ Jesus, and as you obey Him, His peace will continually reign in your heart. Don't ever let sin rob you of that blessed cushion. Only as you experience peace within yourself can you share it with others.

❖❖❖

Suggestions for Prayer: Thank God for the cushion of peace He has provided amid difficult circumstances. ❖ Ask God to use you as an instrument of His peace today.

For Further Study: Read Isaiah 57:15-21, noting how God encourages the repentant and warns the wicked in relation to peace.

"Blessed are the peacemakers, for they shall be called sons of God" (Matt. 5:9).

❖❖❖

True peace exists only where truth reigns.

People often define *peace* as the absence of conflict, but God sees it differently. The absence of conflict is merely a truce, which might end overt hostilities but doesn't resolve the underlying issues. A truce simply introduces a cold war, which often drives the conflict underground, where it smolders until erupting in physical or emotional disaster.

James 3:17 says, "The wisdom from above is first pure, then peaceable." Godly wisdom, purity, and peace go hand in hand. Peace is wisdom in action and is never established at the expense of righteousness. Peace brings righteousness to bear on the situation, seeking to eliminate the source of conflict and to create right relationships. Feuding parties will know true peace only when they are willing to admit that their bitterness and hatred are wrong and humbly seek God's grace to make things right.

Some people equate peacemaking with evading issues, but true peace can be very confrontational. In Matthew 10:34 Jesus says, "Do not think that I came to bring peace on the earth; I did not come to bring peace, but a sword." That may seem to contradict Matthew 5:9, but it doesn't. Jesus knew that sinful people have to be confronted with the truth before they can experience peace. That can be a painful and difficult process because people usually have a hostile reaction to the gospel before they finally embrace it. Even believers will sometimes react negatively when confronted with God's truth.

Being a Biblical peacemaker has its price. You can expect to upset unbelievers who openly oppose God's Word, as well as believers who compromise its truth for the sake of maintaining "peace" among people of differing doctrinal persuasions. Some will call you narrow-minded and divisive for dealing with controversial issues. Some will misunderstand your motives or even attack you personally. But that's been the path of every true peacemaker— including our Lord Himself. Take heart, and be faithful. Your efforts to bring peace show that you are a child of God.

❖❖❖

Suggestions for Prayer: Ask God for the boldness never to compromise His truth. ❖ Pray for those you know who are suffering for the sake of the gospel.

For Further Study: Read Luke 12:51-53, noting how the gospel can bring division even among families.

"Blessed are the peacemakers, for they shall be called sons of God" (Matt. 5:9).

❖❖❖

Sin and falsehood hinder true peace.

Just as righteousness and truth are the noble companions of peace, so sin and falsehood are its great hindrances. The prophet Jeremiah said, "The heart is more deceitful than all else and is desperately [evil]; who can understand it?" (Jer. 17:9). Jesus said, "From within, out of the heart of men, proceed the evil thoughts and fornications, thefts, murders, adulteries, deeds of coveting and wickedness, as well as deceit, sensuality, envy, slander, pride and foolishness. All these evil things proceed from within and defile the man" (Mark 7:21-23).

People with sinful hearts create a sinful society that resists true peace. Ironically, many who talk of peace will also pay huge sums of money to watch two men beat the daylights out of each other in a boxing ring! Our society's heroes tend to be the macho, hard-nosed, tough guys. Our heroines tend to be free-spirited women who lead marches and stir up contention. Psychologists and psychiatrists tell us to stand up for our rights and get everything we can for ourselves. That breeds strife and conditions people to reject the peace of the gospel.

Furthermore, the unbelieving world has never tolerated God's peacemakers. Christ Himself often met with violent resistance. His accusers said, "He stirs up the people" (Luke 23:5). Paul's preaching frequently created conflict as well. He spent much time under house arrest and in filthy Roman prisons. On one occasion his enemies described him as "a real pest . . . who stirs up dissension among all the Jews throughout the world" (Acts 24:5).

All who proclaim the gospel will eventually meet with opposition because sin and falsehood have blinded people's hearts to true peace. That's why Paul warned us that all who desire to be godly will suffer persecution (2 Tim. 3:12). You can avoid strife by remaining silent about the Lord, but a faithful peacemaker is willing to speak the truth regardless of the consequences. Let that be true of you.

❖❖❖

Suggestions for Prayer: Thank God for Christ, who is the solution for the world's problem of sin and falsehood. ❖ Follow Paul's example by praying for boldness to proclaim God's truth at every opportunity (Eph. 6:19).

For Further Study: Read Matthew 10:16-25, noting the kind of reception the disciples were to expect from unbelievers.

"Blessed are the peacemakers, for they shall be called sons of God" (Matt. 5:9).

✧✧✧

Christ's atonement made it possible for man to be at peace with God.

After World War II the United Nations was created to promote world peace. But since its inception in 1945 there has not been a single day of global peace. That's a sad commentary on man's inability to make peace. In fact, someone once quipped that Washington D.C., has so many peace monuments because they build one after every war!

It hasn't always been that way. Prior to the fall of man, peace reigned on the earth because all creation was in perfect harmony with its Creator. But sin interrupted peace by alienating man from God and bringing a curse upon the earth. Man couldn't know true peace because he had no peace in his heart. That's why Jesus came to die.

I once read a story about a couple at a divorce hearing whose conflict couldn't be resolved. They had a four-year-old boy who became distressed and teary-eyed over what was happening. While the couple was arguing, the boy reached for his father's hand and his mother's hand and pulled until he joined them.

In a sense that's what Christ did. He provided the righteousness that allows man and God to join hands. Romans 5:1 says that those who are "justified by faith . . . have peace with God through the Lord Jesus Christ." Colossians 1:20 says that God reconciled all things to Himself through the blood of Christ's sacrifice on the cross.

Yet on the surface, the scene at the cross wasn't peaceful at all. Pain, sorrow, humiliation, hatred, mockery, darkness, and death were oppressively pervasive. But through it all Christ was doing what He alone could do: making peace between man and God. He paid the supreme price to give us that precious gift.

In the future Jesus will return as Prince of Peace to establish a Kingdom that will usher us into an eternal age of peace. In the meantime He reigns over the hearts of all who love Him. Let His peace reign in your heart today!

✧✧✧

Suggestions for Prayer: Thank God for the peace of heart that comes from knowing Christ.

For Further Study: Read Philippians 4:6-9. What must a person do to know God's peace?

> *"Blessed are the peacemakers, for they shall be called sons of God" (Matt. 5:9).*

✧✧✧

You are a messenger of peace!

When Jesus said, "Blessed are the peacemakers, for they shall be called sons of God," He was referring to a special group of people whom God called to restore the peace that was forfeited because of sin. They may not be politicians, statesmen, diplomats, kings, presidents, or Nobel prize winners, but they hold the key to true and lasting peace.

As a Christian, you are among that select group of peacemakers. As such you have two primary responsibilities. The first is to help others make peace with God. There is no greater privilege. The best way to do that is to preach the gospel of peace with clarity, so people understand their alienation from God and seek reconciliation. Romans 10:15 says, "How beautiful are the feet of those who bring glad tidings of good things!" The early church preached peace through Christ, and that is your privilege as well.

Your second responsibility is to help reconcile believers to one another. That's a very important issue to God. He won't accept worship from those who are at odds with each other. They must first deal with the conflict (Matt. 5:23-24). That is especially true within a family. Peter warned husbands to treat their wives properly so their prayers wouldn't be hindered (1 Peter 3:7).

Peacemakers don't avoid spiritual conflicts. Rather, they speak the truth in love and allow the Spirit to minister through them to bring reconciliation. If you see someone who is alienated from God, you are to present him or her with the gospel of peace. If you see two Christians fighting, you are to do everything you can to help them resolve their differences in a righteous manner.

Of course, to be an effective peacemaker you must maintain your own peace with God. Sin in your life will disrupt peace and will prevent you from dispensing God's peace to others. Therefore continually guard your heart and confess your sin so God can use you as His peacemaker.

✧✧✧

Suggestions for Prayer: Pray for those close to you who don't know Christ. Take every opportunity to tell them of God's peace.

For Further Study: Read 2 Corinthians 5:17-21. ✧ How did Paul describe the ministry of reconciliation? ✧ What was Christ's role in reconciling man to God?

"Blessed are those who have been persecuted for the sake of right-eousness" (Matt. 5:10).

❖❖❖

There is a price to pay for being a Kingdom citizen.

Unlike many today who try to make the gospel palatable for reluctant sinners, Jesus made it clear that following Him had its price. Rather than acceptance, fame, prestige, and prosperity, you can expect rejection and persecution. That's not a popular approach to evangelism, but it's honest. Also, it ensures that no one will try to enter the Kingdom on the wrong basis.

Jesus wanted His hearers to count the cost of discipleship. He knew that many of them would be disowned by their families and excommunicated from the Jewish synagogues. Many would suffer persecution or martyrdom at the hands of the Roman government. They needed to count the cost!

Persecution *did* come to those early Christians. The Emperor Nero smeared many of them with pitch, crucified them, and then burned them to light his garden parties. He condemned Christians for refusing to worship him as a god and blamed them for the burning of Rome in A.D. 64. Christians were also accused of cannibalism because Jesus said, "He who eats My flesh and drinks My blood abides in Me, and I in him" (John 6:56). They were also said to be revolutionaries because they believed that God would one day destroy the earth.

The world's animosity toward Christians hasn't changed. You might not face the severe persecutions the first-century believers faced, but you will be persecuted (Phil. 1:29). Even new Christians often face difficulties. If they refuse to join their former friends in sinful activities, they might be rejected. If they work for a dishonest boss who expects them to participate in or condone his evil practices, they might be fired or have to quit their jobs. That might bring extreme financial hardship to their families.

God won't always shield you from persecution, but He will honor your integrity and give you strength to endure any trial that comes your way. Praise Him for His all-sufficient grace!

❖❖❖

Suggestions for Prayer: Pray for those you know who are suffering hardship for Christ's sake. ❖ Ask God for the wisdom and strength to face persecution with integrity and unwavering faith.

For Further Study: Read James 1:2-4 and 1 Peter 5:10. ❖ What purpose does suffering serve? ❖ How should you respond to suffering?

"Blessed are those who have been persecuted for the sake of right-eousness" (Matt. 5:10).

❖❖❖

***If you don't experience persecution,
people probably don't know you're a Christian.***

I heard of a man who was fearful because he was starting a new job with a group of unbelievers whom he thought might give him a bad time if they found out he was a Christian. After his first day at work his wife asked him how he got along with them. "We got along just fine," he said. "They never found out I'm a Christian."

Silence is one way to avoid persecution. Some other ways are to approve of the world's standards, laugh at its jokes, enjoy its entertainment, and smile when it mocks God. If you never confront sin or tell people that Jesus is the only way to Heaven, or if your behavior is so worldly no one can distinguish you from unbelievers, you will probably be accepted and won't feel the heat of persecution.

But beware, for Jesus said, "Woe to you when all men speak well of you. . . . Whoever is ashamed of Me and My words, of him will the Son of Man be ashamed when He comes in His glory" (Luke 6:26; 9:26). The last thing any-one should want is for Christ to pronounce a curse on them or to be ashamed of them. That's an enormous price to pay for popularity!

If you take a stand for Christ and manifest Beatitude attitudes, you will be in direct opposition to Satan and the evil world system. And eventually you will experience some form of persecution. That has been true from the very beginning of human history, when Abel was murdered by his brother Cain because Cain couldn't tolerate his righteousness.

You should never fear persecution. God will grant you grace and will never test you beyond what He enables you to endure (1 Cor. 10:13). Nor should you ever compromise Biblical truth in order to avoid persecution. In Philippians 1:29 Paul says persecution is as much a gift of God as salvation itself. Both identify you as a true believer!

❖❖❖

Suggestions for Prayer: Memorize 1 Peter 2:20-21. Ask God to continually grant you the grace to follow Christ's example when difficulties come your way.

For Further Study: Read 2 Corinthians 11:23-33, noting the severe persecu-tion Paul endured for Christ's sake.

"Blessed are those who have been persecuted for the sake of righteousness, for theirs is the kingdom of heaven. Blessed are you when men revile you, and persecute you, and say all kinds of evil against you falsely, on account of Me" (Matt. 5:10-11).

✧✧✧

When you speak out for Christ, you can expect harassment, insults, and slander.

Jesus mentioned three broad categories of suffering that Christians will experience. The first is *persecution.* "Persecuted" (Matt. 5:10) and "persecute" (v. 11) both come from the same Greek root, meaning "to pursue" or "to chase away." Over time it came to mean "to harass" or "to treat in an evil manner." Verse 10 literally reads, "Blessed are those who have been allowing themselves to be persecuted." You are blessed when people harass you for your Christian stance and you willingly accept it for the sake of your Lord.

The second form of suffering is *"insults"* (v. 11), which translates a Greek word that means "to reproach," "to revile," or "to heap insults upon." It speaks of verbal abuse—attacking someone with vicious and mocking words. It is used in Matthew 27:44 of the mockery Christ endured at His crucifixion. It happened to Him, and it will happen to His followers as well.

The final category Jesus mentioned is *slander*—people telling lies about you. That's perhaps the hardest form of suffering to endure because our effectiveness for the Lord is directly related to our personal purity and integrity. When someone's trying to destroy the reputation you worked a lifetime to establish, that is a difficult trial indeed!

If you're going through a time of suffering for righteousness' sake, take heart—the Lord went through it too, and He understands how difficult it can be. He knows your heart and will minister His super-abounding grace to you. Rejoice that you are worthy of suffering for Him and that the Kingdom of Heaven is yours.

✧✧✧

Suggestions for Prayer: Pray for those who treat you unkindly, asking God to forgive them and to grant them His grace. ✧ Pray that you might always treat others with honesty and fairness.

For Further Study: Throughout history God Himself has endured much mocking and slander. Read 2 Peter 3:3-9, then answer these questions: ✧ What motivates mockers? ✧ What do they deny? ✧ Why doesn't God judge them on the spot?

"Blessed are those who have been persecuted for the sake of right-eousness, for theirs is the kingdom of heaven. Blessed are you when men revile you, and persecute you, and say all kinds of evil against you falsely, on account of Me" (Matt. 5:10-11).

✧✧✧

The persecution you receive for proclaiming Christ is really aimed at Christ Himself.

Savonarola has been called "the Burning Beacon of the Reformation." His sermons denouncing the sin and corruption of the Roman Catholic Church of his day helped pave the way for the Protestant Reformation. Many who heard his powerful sermons went away half-dazed, bewildered, and speechless. Often sobs of repentance resounded throughout the entire congregation as the Spirit of God moved in listeners' hearts. However, some who heard him couldn't tolerate the truth and eventually had him executed.

Jesus said, "'A slave is not greater than his master.' If they persecuted Me, they will also persecute you" (John 15:20). Sinful people will not tolerate a righteous standard. Prior to Christ's birth, the world had never seen a perfect man. The more people observed Christ, the more their own sinfulness stood out in stark contrast. That led some to persecute and finally kill Him, apparently thinking that by eliminating the standard they wouldn't have to keep it.

Psalm 35:19 prophesies that people would hate Christ without just cause. That is true of Christians as well. People don't necessarily hate us personally, but they resent the holy standard we represent. They hate Christ, but He isn't here to receive their hatred, so they lash out at His people. For Savonarola that meant death. For you it might mean social alienation or other forms of persecution.

Whatever comes your way, remember that your present sufferings "are not worthy to be compared with the glory" you will one day experience (Rom. 8:18). Therefore, "to the degree that you share the sufferings of Christ, keep on rejoicing" (1 Peter 4:13).

✧✧✧

Suggestions for Prayer: When you suffer for Christ's sake, thank Him for that privilege, recalling how much He suffered for you.

For Further Study: Before his conversion, the Apostle Paul (otherwise known as Saul) violently persecuted Christians, thinking he was doing God a favor. Read Acts 8:1-3, 9:1-31, and 1 Timothy 1:12-17, noting Paul's transformation from persecutor to preacher.

> *"Blessed are you when men revile you, and persecute you, and say all kinds of evil against you falsely, on account of Me. Rejoice, and be glad, for your reward in heaven is great, for so they persecuted the prophets who were before you" (Matt. 5:11-12).*

❖❖❖

The sacrifices you make for Christ's sake in this life will be abundantly compensated for in Heaven.

God's promise for those who are persecuted for His sake is that their reward in Heaven will be great (Matt. 5:12). Jesus said, "Everyone who has left houses or brothers or sisters or father or mother or children or farms for My name's sake, shall receive many times as much, and shall inherit eternal life" (Matt. 19:29).

Focusing on that promise instead of your present circumstances is how you can experience happiness amid suffering. That was Paul's great confidence even as he faced certain death. In 2 Timothy 4:8 he declares, "In the future there is laid up for me the crown of righteousness, which the Lord, the righteous Judge, will award to me on that day; and not only to me, but also to all who have loved His appearing."

Another source of joy in trials is knowing that you share the fate of the prophets themselves (Matt. 5:12). Those godly men suffered untold hardships for proclaiming God's message. That's a noble group to be identified with!

One final word of encouragement from Matthew 5:11—persecution will not be incessant! Jesus said, "Blessed are you when . . ." The Greek word translated "when" means "whenever." You won't always be persecuted, but whenever you are, you will be blessed. In addition, God will govern its intensity so you will be able to bear it (1 Cor. 10:13). He knows your human weaknesses and will supply the necessary grace and peace to get you through. That's why you can rejoice when otherwise you might be devastated and filled with grief.

If you are willing to make sacrifices now, you will receive incomparable rewards in the future. How shortsighted are those who protect themselves now by denying Christ or by compromising His truth rather than sacrificing the present for the sake of eternal blessing and glory!

❖❖❖

Suggestions for Prayer: Thank God for the example of the prophets and others who have suffered for Him.

For Further Study: Read Matthew 21:33-39 and Hebrews 11:32-38. ❖ How did Jesus illustrate the persecution of God's prophets? ❖ What is Scripture's commendation to those who suffered for righteousness' sake?

> *"The names of the twelve apostles are these: The first, Simon, who is called Peter, and Andrew his brother; and James the son of Zebedee, and John his brother; Philip and Bartholomew; Thomas and Matthew the tax-gatherer; James the son of Alphaeus, and Thaddaeus; Simon the Zealot, and Judas Iscariot, the one who betrayed Him" (Matt. 10:2-4).*

✧✧✧

God uses unqualified people to accomplish His purposes.

We live in a qualification-conscious society. Almost everything you do requires you to meet someone else's standards. You must qualify to purchase a home, buy a car, get a credit card, or attend college. In the job market, the most difficult jobs require people with the highest possible qualifications.

Ironically, God uses unqualified people to accomplish the world's most important task: advancing the Kingdom of God. It has always been that way. Adam and Eve plunged the human race into sin. Lot got drunk and committed incest with his own daughters. Abraham doubted God and committed adultery. Jacob deceived his father. Moses was a murderer. David was too, as well as an adulterer. Jonah got upset when God showed mercy to Nineveh. Elijah withstood 850 false priests and prophets, yet fled in terror from one woman—Jezebel. Paul (Saul) murdered Christians. And the list goes on and on.

The fact is, no one is fully qualified to do God's work. That's why He uses unqualified people. Perhaps that truth is most clearly illustrated in the twelve disciples, who had numerous human frailties, different temperaments, different skills, and diverse backgrounds, and yet Christ used them to change the world.

This month you will meet the disciples one by one. As you do, I want you to see that they were common men with a very uncommon calling. I also want you to observe the training process Jesus put them through, because it serves as a pattern for our discipleship as well.

I pray that you will be challenged by their strengths and encouraged by the way God used them despite their weaknesses and failures. He will use you too as you continue yielding your life to Him.

✧✧✧

Suggestions for Prayer: Memorize Luke 6:40. Ask God to make you more like Christ.

For Further Study: Read 2 Timothy 1:3-5, noting the weaknesses Timothy may have struggled with, and how Paul encouraged him. How might Paul's words apply to you?

"Having summoned His twelve disciples . . ." (Matt. 10:1).

❖❖❖

A good example is the best form of teaching.

Matthew 10:1 is Christ's official commissioning of the twelve men He handpicked to serve beside Him during His earthly ministry. Mark 3:13 says He "summoned those whom He Himself wanted, and they came to Him." In John 15:16 He tells them, "You did not choose Me, but I chose you, and appointed you, that you should go and bear fruit." This is not their call to salvation but to service. With the exception of Judas, they were already saved. Before the foundation of the world God chose them to be redeemed in Christ, and they had responded accordingly. Now Jesus was calling them to a specific ministry.

God always chooses those who will be saved and serve within His church. But between salvation and service there must be a time of training. For the disciples it was a period of three years in which Jesus Himself trained them as they experienced life together from day to day. That's the best form of discipleship. Classrooms and lectures are helpful, but there's no substitute for having a living pattern to follow—someone who models Christian virtue and shows you how to apply Biblical principles to your life.

Paul understood the importance of such an example. In Philippians 4:9 he says, "The things you have learned and received and heard and seen in me, practice these things." He said to Timothy, "Let no one look down on your youthfulness, but rather in speech, conduct, love, faith and purity, show yourself an example of those who believe" (1 Tim. 4:12). Peter followed suit, admonishing the church elders not to lord their authority over those in their charge but to be godly examples (1 Peter 5:3).

Whether you've been a Christian for many years or just a short time, you are an example to someone. People hear what you say and observe how you live. They look for a glimpse of Christ in your life. What do they see? How would they do spiritually if they followed your example perfectly?

❖❖❖

Suggestions for Prayer: Thank the Lord for those who are examples of godliness to you.

For Further Study: What do the following verses indicate about your salvation? John 15:16; Romans 8:28; Ephesians 1:4; and 2 Thessalonians 2:13. ❖ According to Ephesians 2:10, why were you saved?

"Having summoned His twelve disciples . . ." (Matt. 10:1).

❖❖❖

Jesus can overcome any inadequacy you might have.

Most people think of the disciples as stained-glass saints who didn't have to struggle with the faults and frailties of normal people. But they had inadequacies just like we all do. Seeing how Jesus dealt with them gives us hope that He can use us too.

One inadequacy common to all the disciples was their lack of understanding. For example, Luke 18 tells us that Jesus gave them details about His future suffering, death, and resurrection, but they didn't understand anything He said (vv. 31-34). Jesus overcame their lack of understanding by constantly teaching them until they got it right.

Another inadequacy was their lack of humility. More than once they argued among themselves about who would be the greatest in the Kingdom of Heaven (e.g., Mark 9:33-37). Jesus dealt with their lack of humility by His own example. He likened Himself to a servant, and even washed their dirty feet (John 13).

In addition to their lack of understanding and humility, they also lacked faith. Jesus often said to them, "O men of little faith." In Mark 16:14 He rebuked them for not even believing the reports of His resurrection.

They also lacked commitment. Just prior to Christ's death Judas betrayed Him, Peter denied Him, and the others deserted Him. Jesus dealt with their lack of commitment by praying for them (e.g., Luke 22:31-32; John 17:15).

Finally, they lacked spiritual power, which Christ overcame by giving them the Holy Spirit.

Those are significant inadequacies, but despite all that, the book of Acts tells us that the disciples turned the world upside-down with their powerful preaching and miraculous deeds. They were so much like Christ that people started calling them Christians, which means "little christs."

Jesus still transforms inadequacies into victories. He does it through the Spirit, the Word, and prayer. Don't be victimized by your inadequacies. Make those spiritual resources the continual focus of your life.

❖❖❖

Suggestions for Prayer: Thank the Lord for your inadequacies because they help you realize your dependence on Him. ❖ Ask for grace always to rely on your spiritual resources rather than your human abilities.

For Further Study: Read Matthew 20:20-28. ❖ Who spoke to Jesus on behalf of James and John? ❖ What was His response? ❖ How did the other disciples respond? ❖ What was Jesus' concluding principle?

"Having summoned His twelve disciples, He gave them authority over unclean spirits, to cast them out, and to heal every kind of disease and every kind of sickness. Now the names of the twelve apostles are these . . ." (Matt. 10:1-2).

✧✧✧

Every disciple must also be a discipler.

Have you ever met someone who constantly absorbs what the church has to offer, yet never seems to plug into a ministry where he can give to others? I've met many people like that. Some have attended church for many years, and have even taken evangelism and other special training classes. But they never quite feel qualified to minister to others or even to share their testimony. Eventually that has a crippling effect on their spiritual lives and on the life of the church in general.

When Jesus called the disciples to Himself, He did so in order to train them for ministry. We see this in Matthew 10:1-2. The Greek word translated "disciples" means "learners." "Apostles" translates a Greek word meaning "to dispatch away from" or "to send." In classical Greek it refers to a naval expedition dispatched to serve a foreign city or country. Disciples are learners; apostles are emissaries. Jesus called untrained disciples, but He dispatched trained apostles. That's the normal training process.

In Matthew 28:19-20 Jesus says, "Go . . . and make disciples of all the nations, baptizing them in the name of the Father and the Son and the Holy Spirit, teaching them to observe all that I commanded you." Paul said to Timothy, "The things which you have heard from me in the presence of many witnesses, these entrust to faithful men, who will be able to teach others also" (2 Tim. 2:2).

As wonderful and important as it is to learn of Christ, you must never be content to be a disciple only. You must also be a discipler!

✧✧✧

Suggestions for Prayer: Memorize Matthew 28:18-20. If you aren't currently discipling someone, ask the Lord for an opportunity to do so.

For Further Study: An important part of discipleship is spending time with Christ. One way to do that is to read through the Gospels on a regular basis. You might want to obtain a harmony of the Gospels to help in your study. Tell a friend of your plan so he or she can encourage you and hold you accountable.

> *"The names of the twelve apostles are these: The first, Simon, who is called Peter, and Andrew his brother; and James the son of Zebedee, and John his brother; Philip and Bartholomew; Thomas and Matthew the tax-gatherer; James the son of Alphaeus, and Thaddaeus; Simon the Zealot, and Judas Iscariot, the one who betrayed Him" (Matt. 10:2-4).*

❖❖❖

Unity in the Spirit is the key to a church's overall effectiveness.

Unity is a crucial element in the life of the church—especially among its leadership. A unified church can accomplish great things for Christ, but disunity can cripple or destroy it. Even the most orthodox churches aren't immune to disunity's subtle attack because it often arises from personality clashes or pride rather than doctrinal issues.

God often brings together in congregations and ministry teams people of vastly different backgrounds and temperaments. That mix produces a variety of skills and ministries, but it also produces the potential for disunity and strife. That was certainly true of the disciples, which included an impetuous fisherman (Peter), two passionate and ambitious "sons of thunder" (James and John), an analytical, pragmatic, and pessimistic man (Philip), a racially prejudiced man (Bartholomew), a despised tax collector (Matthew), a political Zealot (Simon), and a traitor (Judas, who was in it only for the money and eventually sold out for thirty pieces of silver).

Imagine the potential for disaster in a group like that! Yet their common purpose transcended their individual differences, and by His grace the Lord accomplished through them what they never could have accomplished on their own. That's the power of spiritual unity!

As a Christian, you're part of a select team that is accomplishing the world's greatest task: finishing the work Jesus began. That requires unity of purpose and effort. Satan will try to sow seeds of discord, but you must do everything possible to heed Paul's admonition to be "of the same mind, maintaining the same love, united in spirit, intent on one purpose" (Phil. 2:2).

❖❖❖

Suggestions for Prayer: Pray daily for unity among the leaders and congregation of your church.

For Further Study: Read 1 Corinthians 3:1-9, noting how Paul addressed the issue of disunity in the Corinthian church.

The twelve apostles included "Simon, who is called Peter"
(Matt. 10:2).

◇◇◇

Jesus can make an impulsive and vacillating Christian as stable as a rock.

The first disciple Matthew's Gospel names is "Simon, who is called Peter." He was a fisherman by trade, but Jesus called him to be a fisher of men. John 1:40-42 records their first encounter: "One of the two who heard John [the Baptist] speak, and followed Him, was Andrew, Simon Peter's brother. He found first his own brother Simon, and . . . brought him to Jesus. Jesus looked at him, and said, 'You are Simon the son of John; you shall be called Cephas' (which translated means Peter)."

"Peter" means "stone." "Cephas" is its Aramaic equivalent. By nature Simon tended to be impulsive and vacillating. Apparently Jesus named him Peter as a reminder of his future role in the church, which would require spiritual strength and stability. Whenever Peter acted like a man of strength, Jesus called him by his new name. When he sinned, Jesus called him by his old name (e.g., John 21:15-17). In the Gospel of John, Peter is called "Simon Peter" seventeen times. Perhaps John knew Peter so well, he realized he was always drifting somewhere between sinful Simon and spiritual Peter.

For the next few days we will see how Jesus worked with Peter to transform him into a true spiritual rock. It was an amazing transformation, but not unlike what He desires to do in every believer's life.

You might not have the same personality as Peter, but the Lord wants you to be a spiritual rock just the same. Peter himself wrote, "You also, as living stones, are being built up as a spiritual house for a holy priesthood, to offer up spiritual sacrifices acceptable to God through Jesus Christ" (1 Peter 2:5). That occurs as you "grow in the grace and knowledge of our Lord and Savior Jesus Christ" (2 Peter 3:18). Make that your continual aim.

◇◇◇

Suggestions for Prayer: List the areas of your Christian walk that are inconsistent or vacillating. Make them a matter of earnest prayer, asking God for wisdom and grace as you begin to strengthen them.

For Further Study: First Peter was written to Christians in danger of severe persecution. Read that epistle, noting the keys to spiritual stability that Peter gives.

*The twelve apostles included "Simon, who is called Peter"
(Matt. 10:2).*

❖❖❖

God can use your natural abilities as a basis for your spiritual service.

Peter is a good illustration of how God builds a spiritual leader. He begins with a person's natural traits and works from there. Natural traits alone don't make a spiritual leader; the person must also be gifted and called by the Holy Spirit to lead in the church and to be a model of spiritual virtue. But often God endows future leaders with natural abilities that constitute the raw materials from which He builds spiritual ministries. That was certainly the case with Peter, who demonstrated the leadership qualities of inquisitiveness, initiative, and involvement.

Peter was always asking questions. In fact, the Gospel records show that he asked more questions than all the other disciples combined! People who aren't inquisitive don't make good leaders because they're not concerned about problems and solutions.

Initiative was another indicator of Peter's leadership potential. He not only asked questions, but also he was often the first to respond when Jesus asked questions (e.g., Matt. 16:15-16; Luke 8:45).

Also, Peter loved to be in the middle of the action, even when it got him into trouble. For example, we might criticize his lack of faith when he sank after walking on water, but remember, the rest of the disciples never even got out of the boat.

Peter was inquisitive, showed initiative, and sought to be involved. How about you? Are you inquisitive about God's truth? Do you take the initiative to learn about Him? Do you want to be involved in what He is doing? If so, you have the raw material for spiritual leadership. Continue to cultivate those qualities, allowing the Spirit to use you for God's glory.

❖❖❖

Suggestions for Prayer: Pray for your spiritual leaders. ❖ Ask God for opportunities to lead others in the way of righteousness. Use every opportunity to its fullest.

For Further Study: Read the following verses, noting the kinds of questions Peter asked: Matthew 15:15; 18:21; 19:27; Mark 13:2-4; John 21:20-22.

The twelve apostles included "Simon, who is called Peter"
(Matt. 10:2).

❖❖❖

Your present experiences contribute to your future leadership ability.

Stan Carder is a dear brother in Christ and one of the pastors on our church staff. Before coming to Grace Church he pastored a church in Montana. While there, he was riding one night in a truck that was involved in a very serious accident. Stan suffered a broken neck and other major injuries. As a result he underwent months of arduous and painful therapy.

That was one of the most difficult periods in Stan's life, and yet God used it for a specific purpose. Today, as pastor of our special-ministries department, Stan ministers to more than five hundred physically and mentally handicapped people. God needed a man with unique qualifications to show love to a group of very special people. He chose Stan and allowed him the necessary experiences to fit him for the task.

God doesn't always permit such serious situations, but He does lead each of us into life-changing experiences that heighten our effectiveness in ministry.

Peter had many such experiences. In Matthew 16:15-16, for example, God gave him special revelation about the deity of Christ. In Acts 10 God sent him to preach the gospel to Gentiles—something unheard of at the time because Jewish people resisted any interaction with Gentiles. Perhaps the most tragic experience of Peter's life was his denial of Christ. But even that only increased his love for Christ and his appreciation of God's grace. After His resurrection, Christ forgave him and restored him to ministry (John 21:15-19).

Peter's many experiences helped prepare him for the key role he was to play in the early church. Similarly, your experiences help prepare you for future ministry. So seek to discern God's hand in your circumstances, and rejoice at the prospect of becoming a more effective Christian.

❖❖❖

Suggestions for Prayer: Thank God for both the good and bad experiences you have, knowing that each of them is important to your spiritual growth (cf. James 1:2-4).

For Further Study: Read Acts 10, noting what Peter learned from his experience. ❖ What vision did Peter have? ❖ What was the point of the vision?

The twelve apostles included "Simon, who is called Peter"
(Matt. 10:2).

❖❖❖

Peter learned five lessons that every believer must also learn.

We have seen that God uses our experiences to mold us into more effective Christians and leaders. Using Peter as our example, let's briefly look at five lessons we can learn from our experiences—submission, restraint, humility, sacrifice, and love.

Leaders tend to be confident and aggressive, so they must learn to submit to authority. Jesus illustrated that by telling Peter to go fishing and to look for a coin in the mouth of the first fish he caught (Matt. 17:24-27). He was to use that coin to pay their taxes. Peter was a citizen of God's Kingdom, but he needed an object lesson in submitting to governmental authorities.

When the soldiers came to arrest Jesus, Peter grabbed a sword and would have fought the entire group if Jesus hadn't restrained him. Peter needed to learn to entrust His life to the Father, just as Christ was doing.

Peter bragged that he would never leave or forsake Christ—but he did. Perhaps humility was the most painful lesson he had to learn.

Jesus told Peter that he would die as a martyr (John 21:18-19). From that day forward Peter knew his life was on the line, and yet he was willing to make the necessary sacrifice and minister anyway.

Leaders tend to be task-oriented and often are insensitive to people. Peter was that way, so Jesus demonstrated love by washing his feet and by instructing him to do loving deeds for others (John 13:6-9, 34).

Submission, restraint, humility, sacrifice, and love should be characteristic of every believer—no matter what role he or she has within the Body of Christ. I pray they are characteristic of your life, and that you will constantly seek to grow in those graces as God continues His work in you.

❖❖❖

Suggestions for Prayer: Spiritual lessons are sometimes painful to learn, but God is patient and gracious. Thank Him for His patience, and thank Him also for Christ, who is the perfect example of what we should be.

For Further Study: Peter learned his lessons well. Read 1 Peter 2:13-18, 21-23; 4:8, 16; and 5:5. What can you learn from Peter's instructions on submission, restraint, love, sacrifice, and humility?

The twelve apostles included "Simon, who is called Peter"
(Matt. 10:2).

✧✧✧

God knows how to get results.

God makes leaders by taking people with the right raw material, putting them through the right experiences, and teaching them the right lessons. That's how He trained Peter, and the results were astonishing. In the first twelve chapters of Acts we see Peter initiating the move to replace Judas with Matthias, preaching powerfully on the Day of Pentecost, healing a lame man, standing up to the Jewish authorities, confronting Ananias and Sapphira, dealing with Simon the magician, healing Aeneas, raising Dorcas from the dead, and taking the gospel to the Gentiles. In addition, he wrote two epistles that pass on to us all the lessons he learned from Jesus. What a leader!

Peter was as much a model of spiritual leadership in death as he was in life. Jesus told him he would be crucified for God's glory, and early church tradition tells us that Peter was in fact crucified. But before putting him to death, his executioners forced him to watch the crucifixion of his wife. As he stood at the foot of her cross, he encouraging her by saying over and over, "Remember the Lord, remember the Lord." When it was time for his own crucifixion, he requested that he be crucified upside-down because he felt unworthy to die as his Lord had died. His request was granted.

Just as God transformed Peter from a brash and impulsive fisherman into a powerful instrument for His glory, so He can transform everyone who is yielded to Him.

You will never be an apostle, but you can have the same depth of character and can know the same joy of serving Christ that Peter knew. There's no higher calling in the world than to be an instrument of God's grace. Peter was faithful to that calling. May you be faithful too!

✧✧✧

Suggestions for Prayer: Praise God for the assurance that He will perfect the work He has begun in you (Phil. 1:6). ✧ Ask Him to use the experiences you have today as instruments that shape you more into the image of Christ.

For Further Study: Read John 21:18-23. ✧ How did Jesus describe Peter's death? ✧ What was Peter's reaction to Christ's announcement? ✧ What misunderstanding was generated by their conversation?

The twelve apostles included "Andrew" (Matt. 10:2).

❖❖❖

Leading others to Christ should be a top priority in your life.

A ndrew was Peter's brother and a native of Bethsaida of Galilee. From the very start we see him leading people to Christ—beginning with his own brother.

The Gospel of John records his first encounter with Jesus: "John [the Baptist] was standing, and two of his disciples [Andrew and John], and he looked upon Jesus as He walked, and said, 'Behold, the Lamb of God!' And the two disciples heard him speak, and they followed Jesus. . . . One of the two who heard John speak, and followed Him, was Andrew, Simon Peter's brother. He found first his own brother Simon, and said to him, 'We have found the Messiah' (which translated means Christ). He brought him to Jesus" (John 1:35-37, 40-42). Later Jesus called both Andrew and Peter to become His disciples, and they immediately left their fishing nets to follow Him (Matt. 4:20).

Our next glimpse of Andrew is in John 6:8-9. It was late in the day, and thousands of people who were following Jesus were beginning to get hungry, but there wasn't enough food to feed them. Then Andrew brought to Jesus a young boy with five barley loaves and two fish. From that small lunch Jesus created enough food to feed the entire crowd!

Andrew also appears in John 12:20-22, which tells of some Greeks who were traveling to Jerusalem to celebrate the Passover feast. They came to Philip and requested to see Jesus. Philip took them to Andrew, who apparently took them to Jesus.

Andrew didn't always know how Jesus would deal with a particular person or situation, but he kept right on bringing them to Him anyway. That's a characteristic every believer should have. Your spiritual gifts might differ from others, but your common goal is to make disciples (Matt. 28:19-20), and that begins with leading sinners to Christ. Make that your priority today!

❖❖❖

Suggestions for Prayer: When was the last time you told an unbeliever about Jesus? Pray for an opportunity to do so soon.

For Further Study: Do you know how to present the gospel clearly and accurately? As a review read Romans 3:19-28, 1 Corinthians 15:1-8, Ephesians 2:8-10, and Titus 3:4-7.

The twelve apostles included "Andrew" (Matt. 10:2).

✧✧✧

Andrew is a picture of all believers who humbly minister behind the scenes.

It's been said that no one likes playing second fiddle, but that wasn't Andrew's perspective at all. Growing up in the shadow of an aggressive, outspoken brother like Peter would be a challenge for anyone. Even in the Biblical record Andrew is known as "Simon Peter's brother" (e.g., John 1:40). Yet when Andrew met Jesus, his first response was to tell Peter, knowing full well that once Peter became a disciple he probably would run the group. But Andrew was a truly humble man who was more concerned about bringing people to Christ than about who was in charge.

Andrew's faith and openness prompted him to take advantage of every opportunity to lead others to Christ. He knew that the Lord's primary mission was to "the lost sheep of the house of Israel" (Matt. 10:6), but he led Gentiles as well as Jewish people to Christ (John 12:20-22). He had seen Jesus change water into wine at the wedding in Cana (John 2:1-11), so he knew Jesus could do much with very little. That must have been on his mind when he brought the boy with five barley loaves and two fish to Jesus, knowing it would take a miracle to feed the huge crowd with such a small offering (John 6:8-9).

Tradition tells us that just prior to his death, Andrew preached in a province in which the governor's wife heard the gospel and was saved. The governor demanded that she reject Christ, but she refused. In anger he had Andrew crucified on an X-shaped cross, on which Andrew hung for two days before dying. Even then his courage didn't fail. He preached the gospel from that cross—still trying to bring others to Christ.

Andrew symbolizes all those humble, faithful, and courageous Christians who labor behind the scenes. They're the backbone of every ministry and the ones on whom every leader depends. You might never be a prominent leader like Peter, but you can be a faithful, courageous servant like Andrew.

✧✧✧

Suggestions for Prayer: Thank the Lord for all the humble, faithful servants in your church. ✧ Ask Him to teach you greater openness and courage so you can serve Him more effectively.

For Further Study: Read Philippians 2:25-30, noting how Epaphroditus ministered to Paul.

The twelve apostles included "James the son of Zebedee"
(Matt. 10:2).

❖❖❖

God can use overzealous and ambitious people for His glory.

L ike Peter and Andrew, James and John were fishermen. One day as Jesus
walked the shores of the Sea of Galilee, He saw them in a boat with their
father Zebedee and some hired servants. When Jesus called them to follow
Him, they immediately left the boat and went with Him (Mark 1:19-20).

James and John were zealous and ambitious men—so much so that Jesus
nicknamed them "Boanerges," which means, "Sons of thunder" (Mark 3:17).
At times their great zeal got the better of them. In Luke 9:54, for example,
after a Samaritan village had rejected some of the disciples, James and John
asked Jesus for permission to call down fire from Heaven to incinerate the
whole village! On another occasion they sent their mother to ask Jesus to give
them the most prominent places in His Kingdom (Matt. 20:20-28). They
wanted power, prestige, and honor, but Jesus promised them suffering and, in
James's case, a martyr's grave.

James was probably the eldest of the two brothers. His name is listed first
whenever their names appear together in Scripture. Perhaps he was also the
most zealous and passionate of the two, since he was the first apostle to be
martyred. When King Herod decided to persecute the early church, he had
James put to death with a sword (Acts 12:2). When he saw how much that
pleased the Jewish people, he had Peter arrested but didn't kill him.
Apparently James was a bigger threat than Peter. That tells us something about
the powerful ministry he must have had.

Like James and John, some Christians have a zeal that prompts them to run
ahead of the Holy Spirit. If that's true of you, be thankful for your zeal, but
also be careful to allow the Spirit to govern what you do and say. However, if
you've slipped into spiritual complacency and your life isn't much of a threat
to Satan's kingdom, you need to repent and become more zealous for the
Lord!

❖❖❖

Suggestions for Prayer: Ask God to give you a holy zeal that's motivated by
love and governed by His Spirit.

For Further Study: Read John 2:12-22. ❖ How did Jesus demonstrate His zeal
for God's house? ❖ Why were His actions necessary?

*The twelve apostles included "James the son of Zebedee"
(Matt. 10:2).*

❖❖❖

Zeal without sensitivity can destroy your life and ministry.

There's the story of a Norwegian pastor whose motto was "All or nothing!" His life and preaching were stern, strong, powerful, uncompromising, and utterly insensitive. Reportedly the people in his church didn't care much for him because he didn't care much for them. In his zeal and ambition to advance the Kingdom and uphold God's standard, he neglected everything else—including his own family.

One day his little daughter became so ill, the doctor warned him that if he didn't move her out of the cold Norwegian air to a warmer climate she would die. He refused, telling the doctor, "All or nothing!" Soon his little girl died. His wife was so grief-stricken she would sit for hours holding her daughter's garments close to her heart, trying somehow to ease her pain.

When the pastor saw what his wife was doing, he gave the clothes to a poor woman in the street. All that remained was a little bonnet, which his wife had hidden so she would have some reminder of her precious daughter. When the pastor found it, he gave that away too, lecturing his wife on giving "all or nothing." Within a few months she too died—of grief.

Now that's an extreme example of insensitive zeal, and yet there are many pastors, evangelists, and other Christian workers who are so zealous for the Lord and so task-oriented, they don't see the pain their own families and congregations are suffering.

James could have been like that if he hadn't yielded his life to Christ. He began as a zealous and insensitive disciple, but God refined his character and used him in a marvelous way.

Examine your own ministries and motives. Are you sensitive to your family and the people with whom you serve? Zeal can be a wonderful quality, but it must be tempered with love and sensitivity.

❖❖❖

Suggestions for Prayer: If you have been insensitive to those around you, confess that to them, and ask the Lord to give you a greater sensitivity from now on.

For Further Study: Eli the priest was negligent and insensitive to his family. Read 1 Samuel 3:1–4:18. ❖ What did the Lord tell Samuel concerning Eli? ❖ What was the outcome of Israel's battles with the Philistines? ❖ How did Eli and his sons die?

The twelve apostles included "John" (Matt. 10:2).

❖❖❖

Seek to maintain a proper balance between truth and love.

Some people picture John as overly sentimental and egotistical, lying with his head on Jesus' shoulder and constantly referring to himself as "the disciple whom Jesus loved." But that's not an accurate characterization of this "Son of thunder"! He loved Jesus deeply and was amazed that Jesus loved him—especially after he wanted to burn up the Samaritans and then secure a prominent place for himself in Christ's Kingdom. Calling himself "the disciple whom Jesus loved" (e.g., John 21:20) was simply his way of marveling over God's grace in his life.

As much as he loved Jesus, John never allowed his love to deteriorate into mere sentimentalism. In fact, the proper balance between truth and love is the hallmark of his ministry. In his writings we find the word *love* more than eighty times and *witness* nearly seventy times. His profound love for Christ compelled him to be a teacher of love and a witness to the truth. To him, obedience to the truth was the highest expression of love. As 1 John 2:5 says, "Whoever keeps [God's] word, in him the love of God has truly been perfected."

John's greatest joy was to know that his spiritual children were "walking in the truth" (3 John 4). He firmly denounced anyone who attempted to divert them from that goal by denying or distorting God's Word.

Today media talk shows and other influences have blurred the lines between opinion and truth. One man's opinion is purported to be as good as the next, and there's little talk about what's right or wrong.

Truth suffers even within the church, because many Christians are willing to compromise it to avoid upsetting people. They forget that true love flourishes only in the atmosphere of Biblical truth (Phil. 1:9).

Amid such confusion, God calls you to speak the truth in love (Eph. 4:15). The world doesn't need another opinion—it needs God's absolute and authoritative Word!

❖❖❖

Suggestions for Prayer: Thank God for the gift of His love and the power of His truth. Ask Him to make you a person of ever-increasing Biblical integrity.

For Further Study: Read Revelation 2:1-7. ❖ What strengths did the church at Ephesus have? ❖ What did it lack? ❖ What did Jesus require of it?

The twelve apostles included "Philip" (Matt. 10:3).

❖❖❖

Friendships can provide the most fertile soil for evangelism.

Philip was probably a fisherman who was acquainted with Peter, Andrew, James, John, Nathanael, and Thomas prior to their all becoming disciples. We first meet him in John 1:43-46, which says, "The next day [after Jesus encountered Peter and Andrew], He purposed to go forth into Galilee, and He found Philip, and Jesus said to him, 'Follow Me.' Now Philip was from Bethsaida, of the city of Andrew and Peter. Philip found Nathanael and said to him, 'We have found Him, of whom Moses in the Law and also the Prophets wrote, Jesus of Nazareth, the son of Joseph. . . . Come and see.'"

Those brief verses reveal two things about Philip. First, he had a seeking heart. Apparently he and Nathanael had studied the Scriptures in anticipation of the Messiah's coming. When Jesus said, "Follow Me," Philip was ready. Jeremiah 29:13 describes such a person: "You will seek Me and find Me, when you search for Me with all your heart."

Second, he had the heart of an evangelist. The first thing he did after his own conversion was to lead Nathanael to Christ. Imagine his joy as he told his friend about the One for whom they had searched so long!

I believe friendships usually provide the best context for evangelism because you're introducing Christ into an already established relationship of love, trust, and mutual respect. After all, it's only natural to share the joy of your salvation with someone you love.

I pray that your joy overflows to those around you and that they are drawn to Christ because of your testimony.

❖❖❖

Suggestions for Prayer: Do you have unsaved friends? If so, be faithful in praying for their salvation and asking the Lord to use you as an instrument of His grace. If not, ask the Lord to bring unsaved people into your life so you can tell them about Christ.

For Further Study: The Samaritan woman Jesus met at Jacob's well spoke of Him not only to her friends but also to the entire city. Read John 4:1-42. ❖ What analogy did Jesus use in presenting the gospel to her? ❖ How did Jesus describe true worshipers? ❖ What was the reaction of the city people to the woman's testimony?

The twelve apostles included "Philip" (Matt. 10:3).

❖❖❖

Pessimism will blind you to the sufficiency of God's resources.

It's been said that an optimist sees a glass half full, while a pessimist sees it half empty. An optimist sees opportunities; a pessimist sees obstacles. In one sense Philip was an optimist. He recognized Jesus as the Messiah and immediately saw an opportunity to share his discovery with Nathanael. In another sense, Philip was a pessimist because on occasions he failed to see what Christ could accomplish despite the apparent obstacles.

On one such occasion Jesus had just finished teaching and healing a crowd of thousands of people. Night was falling, and the people were beginning to get hungry. Apparently Philip was responsible for the food, so Jesus asked him, "Where are we to buy bread, that these may eat?" (John 6:5). Philip said, "Two hundred denarii worth of bread is not sufficient for them, for every one to receive a little" (v. 7). In other words, "We don't have enough resources in our whole savings account to buy enough food for a group this size!" Philip's calculating, pragmatic, pessimistic mind could reach only one conclusion: this is an utter impossibility.

Jesus knew all along how He was going to solve the problem, but He wanted to test Philip's faith (v. 6). Philip should have passed the test because he had already seen Jesus create wine from water at the wedding at Cana (John 2:1-11). Despite Philip's failure, Jesus didn't give up on him. Instead, from five barley loaves and two fish He created enough food to feed the entire crowd, thus replacing Philip's pessimism with a reaffirmation of divine sufficiency.

There's a little of Philip in each of us. We've experienced God's saving power and have seen Him answer prayer, and yet there are times when we let pessimism rob us of the joy of seeing Him work through obstacles in our lives. Don't let that happen to you. Keep your eyes on Christ, and trust in His sufficiency. He will never fail you!

❖❖❖

Suggestions for Prayer: Memorize Ephesians 3:20-21. Recite it often as a hymn of praise and an affirmation of your faith in God.

For Further Study: Read Numbers 13–14. ❖ What kind of report did the pessimistic spies bring back from the Promised Land? ❖ How did the people react to their report? ❖ How did God react to their report?

The twelve apostles included "Bartholomew [Nathanael]" (Matt. 10:3).

❖❖❖

Prejudice can destroy relationships and prevent people from coming to Christ.

Prejudice is an uncalled-for generalization based on feelings of superiority. It is an ugly sin that has fueled hatred and conflicts for centuries, dividing entire nations and bringing untold misery. But prejudice is most damning when it blinds people to God's Word. The prophet Jonah was so prejudiced against the Assyrians, he refused to go to Nineveh to preach to them. Even after God convinced him to obey, he wanted to die because the people of Nineveh had repented and God had spared them.

Prejudice also reared its ugly head in Nathanael, whose last name was Bartholomew (meaning "son of Tolmai"). John 1:45-46 says, "Philip found Nathanael, and said to him, 'We have found Him, of whom Moses in the Law and also the Prophets wrote, Jesus of Nazareth, the son of Joseph.' And Nathanael said to him, 'Can any good thing come out of Nazareth?'" Nathanael was a student of the Word and was looking for the Messiah, but he couldn't understand how the Messiah could come from Nazareth.

Nazareth lay on the fringes of the Jewish world—the last stop before Gentile territory. Perhaps the people of Cana, Nathanael's hometown, were more refined and educated than the people of Nazareth. Whatever the cause, Nathanael's perspective seemed to be that nothing but trouble could come out of Nazareth.

Prejudice has blinded many people to the gospel. The Jewish religious leaders rejected Jesus because He didn't fit their idea of a Messiah, wasn't from Jerusalem, and wasn't trained in their synagogues. Fortunately, Nathanael's desire for truth overpowered his prejudice, and he came to Jesus.

Perhaps you have family or friends who are resisting the gospel because of prejudice. If so, don't be discouraged, and don't give up! Jesus broke through Nathanael's prejudice and redeemed him, and He has done the same for millions of others.

❖❖❖

Suggestions for Prayer: Pray for those you know who are blinded by prejudice, asking God to open their spiritual eyes to His truth. ❖ Confess any prejudice you might have in your own heart.

For Further Study: Practicing unity and humility is the best way to overcome prejudice within the Body of Christ. Read Ephesians 4:1-6 and Philippians 2:1-8. ❖ What attitudes did Paul encourage? Discourage? ❖ Whose example of humble service on behalf of others are we to follow?

The twelve apostles included "Bartholomew [Nathanael]" (Matt. 10:3).

❖❖❖

God knows your heart and will honor your search for truth.

Despite Nathanael's prejudice, Jesus knew he was an honest, sincere Jewish believer in whom there was no religious hypocrisy or deceit (John 1:47). He truly sought after God and looked forward to the Messiah's coming.

Most of the Jewish people of Jesus' day believed that every circumcised descendant of Abraham was a true Jew and a beneficiary of the Abrahamic Covenant. But in Romans 2:28-29 Paul explains that salvation is an issue of the heart, not of national origin: "He is not a Jew who is one outwardly; neither is circumcision that which is outward in the flesh. But he is a Jew who is one inwardly; and circumcision is that which is of the heart." Nathanael was such a man.

He was shocked when Jesus described him as "an Israelite indeed, in whom is no guile" (John 1:47) because they had never met before. He was equally shocked when Jesus said He saw him under a fig tree because Jesus was nowhere near that tree. Nathanael immediately realized that Jesus was omniscient—He knew everything! That's why he exclaimed, "Rabbi, You are the Son of God; You are the King of Israel" (v. 49). He had found the Messiah for whom he had searched so long!

The Lord's mention of the fig tree is significant. In that region fig trees were commonly used as a source of shade and outdoor shelter. Many of the houses in Palestine had only one room, so fig trees became a place to be alone for prayer and meditation on the Scriptures. Quite possibly Nathanael was under the fig tree searching the Scriptures and communing with God when Jesus saw his open heart and his desire to find the Messiah. Jesus personally answered Nathanael's prayer.

When Jesus looks into your heart, does He see a true believer in whom there is no hypocrisy? Nathanael wasn't perfect, but he loved God and was a diligent student of the Word. And the Lord did great things through him. I pray that is true of you as well.

❖❖❖

Suggestions for Prayer: Ask the Spirit to reveal and deal with any hypocrisy you might be harboring. ❖ Ask God to increase your desire and capacity to know and love Him.

For Further Study: Memorize Romans 12:1-2 as a defense against hypocrisy.

The twelve apostles included "Thomas" (Matt. 10:3).

❖❖❖

**The follower of Christ will have an intense desire
to be in Christ's presence.**

When you think of Thomas, you probably think of a doubter. But if you look beyond his doubt, you'll see he was characterized by something that should mark every true believer—an intense desire to be with Christ.

John 10:39-40 tells us Jesus and His disciples left Jerusalem because of threats on Jesus' life. While they were staying near the Jordan River, Jesus received word that His dear friend Lazarus was sick. He delayed going to Lazarus because He didn't want merely to heal him, but to raise him from the dead.

Lazarus lived in Bethany—just two miles east of Jerusalem. So when Jesus decided to go there, His disciples were deeply concerned, thinking it would surely be a suicide mission (John 11:8). Despite the danger, Thomas said, "Let us also go, that we may die with Him" (v. 16). That's a pessimistic attitude, but it also shows his courage and his desire to be with Christ, whether in life or death. An optimist would expect the best, making it easier to go. Thomas expected the worst but was willing to go anyway.

I believe Thomas couldn't bear the thought of living without Christ. He would rather die with Him than live without Him. That's also evident in John 14, where Jesus told the disciples He was going away to prepare a place for them. Thomas responded by saying in effect, "Lord, we don't know where you're going or how to get there. Please don't go somewhere we can't go!" (v. 5). He didn't understand what Jesus was going to do. All he knew was that he didn't want to be separated from his Lord.

Can you identify with Thomas? Is Christ such an integral part of your daily decisions and activities that life without Him is unthinkable? Do you love Him so much you long to see Him? That was Thomas's passion. May it be yours as well.

❖❖❖

Suggestions for Prayer: Thank the Lord for His presence and power in your life. ❖ Demonstrate your love for Him by communing with Him often.

For Further Study: Read John 14:1-31. ❖ What did Jesus say about His return? ❖ Who would comfort and instruct the disciples in Christ's absence?

The twelve apostles included "Thomas" (Matt. 10:3).

✧✧✧

Jesus can replace your doubts with hope.

When Jesus was crucified, Thomas was shattered. He loved Jesus deeply and wanted always to be with Him. He'd even been willing to die with Him, but now his greatest fear had been realized: Jesus was gone.

Thomas was not with the other disciples when Jesus appeared to them after His resurrection. John 20:25 says, "The other disciples therefore were saying to [Thomas], 'We have seen the Lord!' But he said to them, 'Unless I shall see in His hands the imprint of the nails, and put my finger into the place of the nails, and put my hand into His side, I will not believe.'" Thomas was emotionally spent and was unwilling to subject himself to any further pain. So he retreated behind a wall of empiricism, saying in effect, "I'm not going to believe this on your word alone. I need proof! I must see Jesus myself."

Because of that, people have labeled him "Doubting Thomas," but remember, *none* of the disciples believed the resurrection until Jesus appeared to them. Thomas wasn't a compulsive doubter—he was a loving pessimist.

As it turned out, Thomas didn't need as much proof as he thought. When Jesus finally appeared to him and invited him to touch His hands and side, Thomas didn't do either. Instead he immediately cried out, "My Lord and my God!" (v. 28)—which is the greatest single confession of faith ever made.

Thomas struggled with doubt because he didn't understand what Jesus had said about His own death and resurrection, and he wasn't with the other disciples when Jesus first appeared to them. He failed to understand God's Word and forsook the company of believers—two common mistakes that can lead to doubt.

Jesus doesn't condemn you when you have doubts. Instead, He gives you His Spirit, His Word, and the fellowship of His people to encourage and strengthen you. So, commune with the Spirit in prayer, know the Word well, and never forsake the fellowship of believers. That's how to change your doubts into hope!

✧✧✧

Suggestions for Prayer: Thank God for the presence of His Spirit, the power of His Word, and the fellowship of His people.

For Further Study: Read Luke 24:13-35. ✧ Why didn't the two disciples recognize Jesus? ✧ How did Jesus change their doubts to hope?

The twelve apostles included "Matthew the tax-gatherer"
(Matt. 10:3).

❖❖❖

God can use you despite your sinful past.

I remember reading a notice in a local newspaper announcing the opening of a new evangelical church in our community. It gave the date and time of the first services, then added, "Our special guest star will be . . ." and named a popular Christian celebrity. In its attempt to appeal to unbelievers or simply draw a large crowd, the church today commonly uses that kind of approach.

Jesus, however, used a different approach. None of His disciples were famous at all. In fact, rather than drawing a favorable crowd, some of them might have repelled or even incited anger and hatred among His Jewish audience. Matthew was such a man because he was a despised tax-gatherer—one of many Jewish men employed by Rome to collect taxes from his own people. As such he was regarded as a traitor by his own countrymen.

The Roman tax system allowed tax collectors to keep anything they collected in excess of what was owed to Rome. That encouraged bribes, extortion, and other abuses.

To compound the issue, Matthew was among those who had the prerogative of taxing almost anything they wanted to tax—roads, bridges, harbors, axles, donkeys, packages, letters, imports, exports, merchandise, and so on. Such men could accumulate enormous wealth for themselves. You might remember another tax-gatherer named Zaccheus, who is described in Luke 19:2 as a wealthy man. His salvation was evidenced by his offer to repay those he had defrauded fourfold (v. 8).

Some people think God can't use them because they're not famous or because of their past sins. But God has used Matthew, Zaccheus, and millions of others like them. Concentrate on your present purity, and let God bless your ministry as He sees fit.

❖❖❖

Suggestions for Prayer: Thank God that he has made you a new person in Christ (2 Cor. 5:17). Minister in light of that reality!

For Further Study: Read Luke 19:1-10. ❖ Where was Zaccheus when Jesus first spoke to him? ❖ What was the reaction of the crowd when Jesus went to Zaccheus' house? ❖ What prompted Jesus to say that salvation had come to Zaccheus?

May 23 MARVELING AT GOD'S FORGIVENESS (MATTHEW)

The twelve apostles included "Matthew the tax-gatherer"
(Matt. 10:3).

❖❖❖

Never lose your sense of awe over Christ's forgiveness.

Matthew describes himself as "Matthew the tax-gatherer" (Matt. 10:3). He is the only apostle whose name is associated here with an occupation. Apparently Matthew never forgot what he had been saved from and never lost his sense of awe and unworthiness over Christ's forgiveness.

Matthew 9:1-8, where he sets the scene of his own conversion, tells us Jesus forgave the sins of a paralytic man and then healed him of his paralysis. When the Jewish scribes accused Him of blasphemy for claiming to have the authority to forgive sins, He said to them, "Why are you thinking evil in your hearts? For which is easier, to say, 'Your sins are forgiven,' or to say, 'Rise, and walk'?" He wanted them to know that His miracles testified to His deity. As God, He could as easily forgive sins as He could heal diseases.

Immediately after that account, Matthew gave the account of his own call. It's as if he wanted his own salvation to serve as an illustration of Christ's ability to forgive even the vilest of sinners. Matthew 9:9 says, "As Jesus passed on from there, He saw a man, called Matthew, sitting in the tax office; and He said to him, 'Follow Me!' And he rose, and followed Him."

When the Pharisees questioned Jesus' practice of associating with tax-gatherers, He said to them, "It is not those who are healthy who need a physician, but those who are ill. . . . I did not come to call the righteous, but sinners" (vv. 12-13). The Pharisees were sick with sin but thought they were healthy. Matthew and his associates knew they were sinners who needed a Savior.

Do you share Matthew's humility and sense of awe at receiving Christ's precious gift of forgiveness? I pray that you do and that you are continually praising Him for it.

❖❖❖

Suggestions for Prayer: Thank God for the wonder of forgiveness. ❖ If you have lost your sense of awe over God's forgiveness, perhaps you're taking His grace for granted. Confess your apathy, and ask Him to give you a deep appreciation for the enormous price He paid for your salvation.

For Further Study: As a reminder of what Christ endured for you, read Matthew 26:17–27:56, which chronicles the events of His betrayal and crucifixion.

> *The twelve apostles included "James the son of Alphaeus"*
> *(Matt. 10:3).*

✧✧✧

God often uses ordinary people to accomplish great things.

L ike most Christians, James the son of Alphaeus is an unknown and unsung soldier of the cross. His distinguishing characteristic is obscurity. Nothing he did or said is recorded in Scripture—only his name.

In Mark 15:40 he is called "James the Less," which literally means "Little James." That could refer to his stature (he might have been short), his age (he might have been younger than James the son of Zebedee), or his influence (he might have had relatively little influence among the disciples).

In Mark 2:14 Matthew (Levi) is called "the son of Alphaeus." Alphaeus was a common name, but it's possible that James and Matthew were brothers, since their fathers had the same first name. Also, James's mother is mentioned in Mark 15:40 as being present at Christ's crucifixion, along with other women. She is referred to as the wife of Clopas in John 19:25. Since Clopas was a form of Alphaeus, that further supports the possibility that James and Matthew were related.

From those references we might conclude that James was a small, young man whose personality was not particularly powerful. If he was Matthew's brother, perhaps he was as humble as Matthew, willing to serve the Lord without any applause or notice. Whichever the case, be encouraged that God uses obscure people like James and rewards them accordingly. Someday James will sit on a throne in Christ's millennial Kingdom, judging the twelve tribes of Israel—just like the other, more prominent disciples (Luke 22:30).

No matter how obscure or prominent you are from a human perspective, God can use you and will reward you with a glorious eternal inheritance.

✧✧✧

Suggestions for Prayer: Thank the Lord for all those people unknown to you whom He has used to shape your life for His glory. ✧ Seek to be more like James, serving Christ faithfully without applause or glory.

For Further Study: Read Luke 9:23-25. What did Jesus say is necessary to be His disciple? ✧ Read Luke 9:57-62. What were those men unwilling to give up to follow Christ?

The twelve apostles included "Thaddaeus" (Matt. 10:3).

❖❖❖

Victorious Christian living requires great courage.

Thaddaeus was a man of many identities. In the *King James* translation of Matthew 10:3 he is called "Lebbeus, whose surname was Thaddeus." He is also called "Judas the son of James" (Luke 6:16; Acts 1:13) and "Judas (not Iscariot)" (John 14:22).

Judas, which means "Jehovah leads," was probably the name given him at birth, with Thaddaeus and Lebbeus added later as nicknames to reflect his character. Apparently *Thaddaeus* was the nickname given to him by his family. It comes from a Hebrew root word that refers to the female breast. Basically it means a "breast-child." Perhaps Thaddaeus was the youngest child in the family or was especially dear to his mother. *Lebbeus* comes from a Hebrew root that means "heart." Literally it means a "heart-child" and speaks of someone who is courageous. That nickname was likely given him by his friends, who saw him as a man of boldness and courage.

Early church tradition tells us that Thaddaeus was tremendously gifted with the power of God to heal the sick. It is said that a certain Syrian king named Adgar was very ill and sent for Thaddaeus to come and heal him. On his way to the king, Thaddaeus reportedly healed hundreds of people throughout Syria. When he finally reached the king, he healed him and then preached Christ to him. As a result, the king became a Christian. The country, however, was thrown into chaos, and a vengeful nephew of the king had Thaddaeus imprisoned, then beaten to death with a club. If that tradition is true, it confirms that Thaddaeus was a man of great courage.

It takes courage to die for Christ, but it also takes courage to live for Him. That's why Paul said that God hasn't "given us a spirit of timidity, but of power and love and discipline" (2 Tim. 1:7). Each day trust in God's promises and rely on His Spirit. That's how you can face each new challenge with courage and confidence.

❖❖❖

Suggestions for Prayer: Thank God for the courage He has given you in the past, and ask Him to help you face future spiritual battles without retreat or compromise.

For Further Study: Read Daniel 3:1-30. ❖ Why were Shadrach, Meshach, and Abednego punished by King Nebuchadnezzar? ❖ How did God honor their courage?

The twelve apostles included "Thaddaeus" (Matt. 10:3).

❖❖❖

If you love Christ, you will receive His Word and obey it.

Radio signals are fascinating. At any given moment every room in your house is filled with voices, music, and numerous other sounds; yet you can't hear them unless your radio is tuned to their frequency. That's a modern parallel to a spiritual truth Jesus taught in John 14:21: "He who has My commandments, and keeps them, he it is who loves Me; and he who loves Me shall be loved by My Father, and I will love him, and will disclose Myself to him." In effect Jesus was saying, "I reveal Myself to those who love Me— those whose spiritual receivers are tuned to My frequency. They receive My Word and obey it."

In the Biblical record Thaddaeus is a man of few words. His question in John 14:22 is the only thing he ever said that is recorded in Scripture. It was prompted by his perplexity over Jesus' statement in verse 21 to disclose Himself only to those who love Him. Thaddaeus asked, "Lord, what then has happened that You are going to disclose Yourself to us, and not to the world?"

Thaddaeus didn't understand Christ's statement because it wasn't consistent with his concept of the Messiah. Like the other disciples, he expected Jesus imminently to vanquish Roman oppression, free God's people, and establish an earthly kingdom wherein He would sit on the throne of David, reigning as Lord and Savior. How could He do that without revealing who He was to everyone?

In verse 23 Jesus responds by reiterating that only those who love Him will be able to perceive Him, and they are the ones within whom He and the Father would dwell.

That brief conversation between the Lord and Thaddaeus addresses the very heart of Christianity. It isn't those who say they love God who are true believers, but those who receive Christ and obey His Word. As Jesus said, "If anyone loves Me, he will keep My word" (v. 23).

Does obedience to the Word characterize your life? I pray it does. Remember, your obedience to Christ is the measure of your love for Him.

❖❖❖

Suggestions for Prayer: Thank God for His Word, by which the Spirit instructs you and empowers you to live an obedient life.

For Further Study: Read John 8:31-47. ❖ To whom was Jesus speaking? ❖ Why were they seeking to kill Him? ❖ How did Jesus characterize the Devil?

The twelve apostles included "Simon the Zealot" (Matt. 10:4).

❖❖❖

**Even people of vastly different backgrounds
can minister together for Christ.**

During the time between the Old and New Testaments, a fiery revolutionary named Judas Maccabaeus led the Jewish people in a revolt against Greek influences on their nation and religion. The spirit of that movement was captured in this statement from the apocryphal book of 1 Maccabees: "Be ye zealous for the law and give your lives for the covenant" (1 Maccabees 2:50). That group of politically-oriented, self-appointed guardians of Judaism later became known as the Zealots.

During the New Testament period, Zealots conducted terrorist activities against Rome to free Israel from Roman oppression, prompting Rome to destroy Jerusalem in A.D. 70 and to slaughter people in 985 Galilean towns.

After the destruction of Jerusalem, the few remaining Zealots banded together under the leadership of a man named Eleazar. Their headquarters was at a retreat called Masada. When the Romans laid siege to Masada and the Zealots knew defeat was imminent, they chose to kill their own families and to commit suicide themselves rather than face death at the hands of the Romans. It was a tragedy of monumental proportions, but such was the depth of their fiery zeal for Judaism and their hatred for their political enemies.

Before coming to Christ, Simon was a Zealot. Even as a believer, he must have retained much of his zeal, redirecting it in a godly direction. We can only imagine the passion with which he approached the ministry, having finally found a leader and cause transcending Judaism and political activism.

It's amazing to realize that Simon the Zealot and Matthew the tax-gatherer ministered together. Under normal circumstances Simon would have killed a traitor like Matthew. But Christ broke through their differences, taught them to love each other, and used them for His glory.

Perhaps you know believers who come from totally different backgrounds than yours. Do you have trouble getting along with any of them? If so, why? How can you begin to mend your differences? Be encouraged by the transformation Christ worked in Simon and Matthew, and follow their example.

❖❖❖

Suggestions for Prayer: Pray for a spirit of unity in your church.

For Further Study: According to Romans 12:9-21, what attitudes should you have toward others?

The twelve apostles included "Judas Iscariot, the one who betrayed Him" (Matt. 10:4).

❖❖❖

God works all things together for His purposes.

At one time the little town of Kerioth was a relatively obscure Judean town, but all that changed when it produced the most hated man who ever lived—Judas Iscariot.

The first mention of Judas is here in Matthew's list of disciples. We have no record of his call, but we know Jesus did call him along with the others, and even gave him authority to minister in miraculous ways (Matt. 10:1). His first name, Judas, is despised today, but it was a common name in the days of Christ. It is the Greek form of Judah—the land of God's people. Iscariot literally means, "a man from the town of Kerioth."

People commonly ask why Jesus would select such a man to be His disciple. Didn't He know how things would turn out? Yes, He did, and that's precisely why He chose him. The Old Testament said the Messiah would be betrayed by a familiar friend for thirty pieces of silver, and Jesus knew Judas was that man (John 17:12).

Some people feel sorry for Judas, thinking he was simply misguided or used as some kind of pawn in a supernatural drama over which he had no control. But Judas did what he did by choice. Repeatedly Jesus gave him chances to repent, but he refused. Finally Satan used him in a diabolical attempt to destroy Jesus and to thwart God's plan of salvation. The Devil's attempt failed, however, because God can use even a Judas to accomplish His purposes.

Undoubtedly there are people in your life who wish you harm. Don't be discouraged. They are as much a part of God's plan for you as those who treat you kindly. You must reach out to them just as Jesus reached out to Judas. God knows what He's doing. Trust Him, and rejoice as you see His purposes accomplished even through your enemies.

❖❖❖

Suggestions for Prayer: Praise God for His sovereign control over every circumstance and for the promise that His purposes will never be thwarted.

For Further Study: Read Matthew 26:14-50 and 27:1-10. ❖ How did Jesus reveal that it was Judas who would betray Him? ❖ What reaction did Judas have when he heard that Jesus had been condemned?

The twelve apostles included "Judas Iscariot, the one who betrayed Him" (Matt. 10:4).

❖❖❖

***Hypocrisy is a spiritual cancer that
can devastate lives and destroy ministries.***

On a recent trip to New Zealand I learned that sheepherders there use specially trained, castrated male sheep to lead other sheep from holding areas into the slaughtering room. Those male sheep are appropriately called "Judas sheep." That illustrates the commonness with which we associate Judas with deception and death. Pretending to be a friend of Jesus, Judas betrayed him with a kiss and became for all time and eternity the epitome of hypocrisy.

Several characteristics of spiritual hypocrisy are clearly evident in Judas' life. First, hypocritical people often seem genuinely interested in a noble cause. Judas probably didn't want the Romans to rule over Israel, and he saw in Christ an opportunity to do something about it. He probably had the common misconception that Jesus was immediately going to establish His earthly Kingdom and put down Roman oppression.

Second, hypocritical people demonstrate an outward allegiance to Christ. Many of those who followed Jesus in the early stages of His ministry deserted Him along the way (John 6:66). Not Judas. He stayed to the end.

Third, hypocritical people can appear to be holy. When Jesus told the disciples that one of them would betray Him, none of them suspected Judas. Even after Jesus identified Judas as His betrayer, the other disciples still didn't understand (John 13:27-29). Judas must have put on a very convincing act!

Fourth, hypocritical people are self-centered. Judas didn't love Christ; he loved himself and joined the disciples to gain personal prosperity.

Finally, hypocritical people are deceivers. Judas was a pawn of Satan, whom Jesus described as "a liar, and the father of lies" (John 8:44). Is it any wonder that his whole life was one deception after another?

Judas was an unbeliever, but hypocrisy can also thrive in believers if its telltale signs are ignored. Guard your motives carefully, walk in the Spirit each day, and immediately confess even the slightest hint of hypocrisy.

❖❖❖

Suggestions for Prayer: Ask God to purify your love for Him and to protect you from the subtle inroads of hypocrisy.

For Further Study: Read John 12:1-8. ❖ How did Mary demonstrate her love for Christ? ❖ What objection did Judas raise? ❖ What was his motive?

The twelve apostles included "Judas Iscariot, the one who betrayed Him" (Matt. 10:4).

✧✧✧

**God can use even an apostate like Judas
to teach us some important lessons.**

Judas is history's greatest human tragedy. He had opportunities and privileges known only to the other disciples, but he turned from them to pursue a course of destruction. Yet even from his foolishness we can learn some important lessons.

Judas, for example, is the world's greatest example of lost opportunity. He ministered for three years with Jesus Himself but was content merely to associate with Him, never submitting to Him in saving faith. Millions of others have followed his example by hearing the gospel and associating with Christians, yet rejecting Christ. Tragically, like Judas, once death comes, they too are damned for all eternity.

Judas is also the world's greatest example of wasted privileges. He could have had the riches of an eternal inheritance but instead chose thirty pieces of silver. In that respect he is also the greatest illustration of the destructiveness and damnation greed can bring. He did an unthinkable thing, and yet he has many contemporary counterparts in those who place wealth and pleasure above godliness.

On the positive side, Judas is the world's greatest illustration of the forbearing, patient love of God. Knowing what Judas would do, Jesus tolerated him for three years. Beyond that, He constantly reached out to him and even called him "friend" after his kiss of betrayal (Matt. 26:50).

If you've ever been betrayed by a friend, you know the pain it can bring. But the Lord's pain was compounded many times over because He knew ahead of time that He would be betrayed and because the consequences were so serious. Yet He endured the pain, because He loved Judas and knew that His own betrayal was a necessary part of the redemptive plan.

The sins that destroyed Judas are common sins that you must avoid at all costs! Use every opportunity and privilege God gives you, and never take advantage of His patience.

✧✧✧

Suggestions for Prayer: Thank Jesus for the pain He endured at the hands of Judas. ✧ Pray that you will never cause Him such pain.

For Further Study: Read 1 Timothy 6:6-19. ✧ What perils await those who desire wealth? ✧ Rather than pursuing wealth, what should you pursue? ✧ What attitude should wealthy people have toward their money?

"The names of the twelve apostles are these: The first, Simon, who is called Peter, and Andrew his brother; and James the son of Zebedee, and John his brother; Philip and Bartholomew; Thomas and Matthew the tax-gatherer; James the son of Alphaeus, and Thaddaeus; Simon the Zealot, and Judas Iscariot, the one who betrayed Him" (Matt. 10:2-4).

❖❖❖

In God's hands you can be a precious and effective instrument.

The story is told of a great concert violinist who wanted to prove a point, so he rented a music hall and announced that he would play a concert on a $20,000 violin. On concert night the music hall was filled to capacity with music lovers anxious to hear such an expensive instrument played. The violinist stepped onto the stage, gave an exquisite performance, and received a thunderous standing ovation. When the applause subsided, he suddenly threw the violin to the ground, stomped it to pieces, and walked off the stage. The audience gasped, then sat in stunned silence.

Within seconds the stage manager approached the microphone and said, "Ladies and gentlemen, to put you at ease, the violin that was just destroyed was a $20 violin. The master will now return to play the remainder of his concert on the $20,000 instrument." At the conclusion of his concert he received another standing ovation. Few people could tell the difference between the two violins. His point was obvious: it isn't the violin that makes the music; it's the violinist.

The disciples were like $20 violins that Jesus transformed into priceless instruments for His glory. I trust that you have been encouraged to see how God used them despite their weakness, and I pray that you have been challenged by their strengths. You may not be dynamic like Peter or zealous like James and Simon, but you can be faithful like Andrew and courageous like Thaddaeus. Remember, God will take the raw material of your life and will expose you to the experiences and teachings that will shape you into the servant He wants you to be.

Trust Him to complete what He has begun in you, and commit each day to the goal of becoming a more qualified and effective disciple.

❖❖❖

Suggestions for Prayer: Make a list of the character traits you most admire in the disciples. Ask the Lord to increase those traits in your own life.

For Further Study: Read 1 Timothy 1:12-17, noting Paul's perspective on his own calling.

"Prove yourselves doers of the word, and not merely hearers who delude themselves" (James 1:22).

❖❖❖

God wants you to know whether your faith is genuine or not.

Our studies this month center on James 1:19–2:26, which deals with the issue of true faith—a most important consideration indeed. Knowing your faith is genuine is a wonderful assurance, but thinking you're saved when you're not is the most frightening deception imaginable. In Matthew 7:21-23 Jesus speaks of those who call Him Lord and even do miracles in His name but aren't redeemed. Second Timothy 3:5 speaks of those who have "a form of godliness" but deny its power. They're religious but lost. Sadly, many people today are victims of the same deception. They think they're Christians, but they're heading for eternal damnation unless they recognize their true condition and repent.

Deception of that magnitude is a tragedy beyond description. But you need never fall prey to it because James gives a series of tests for true faith. This month we'll be applying one of those tests: your attitude toward God's Word. That's an especially crucial test because the Word is the agency of both your salvation and sanctification. The Holy Spirit empowered it to save you, and He continually works through it to conform you to the image of Christ. That's why Peter said, "You have been born again not of seed which is perishable but imperishable, that is, through the living and abiding word of God. . . . [Therefore] like newborn babes, long for the pure milk of the word, that by it you may grow in respect to salvation" (1 Peter 1:23–2:2).

Jesus Himself characterized believers as those who abide in His Word and obey His commandments. They receive the Word with an attitude of submission and humility. However, unbelievers resist and disobey the Word (John 8:31, 43-45). Psalm 119:155 says, "Salvation is far from the wicked, for they do not seek Thy statutes."

As you study this test of true faith, ask yourself, *Do I pass the test?* I pray that your answer will echo the words of the psalmist: "I have inclined mine heart to perform thy statutes forever, even unto the end" (Ps. 119:112).

❖❖❖

Suggestions for Prayer: Ask God for clarity and confidence about your faith in Christ.

For Further Study: Read the book of James, noting the instructions he gives regarding Christian living.

"This you know, my beloved brethren. But let every one be quick to hear, slow to speak and slow to anger; for the anger of man does not achieve the righteousness of God. Therefore putting aside all filthiness and all that remains of wickedness, in humility receive the word implanted, which is able to save your souls" (James 1:19-21).

❖❖❖

True believers receive God's Word.

The key word in today's passage is "receive" (James 1:21). Believers are to receive God's Word. That's what distinguishes them from unbelievers. Jesus said to a group of religious unbelievers, "Why do you not understand what I am saying? It is because you cannot hear My word. . . . He who is of God hears the words of God; for this reason you do not hear them, because you are not of God" (John 8:43, 47).

"Hear" in those verses doesn't refer to hearing with the ear only. Jesus' audience heard in that sense—even to the point of wanting to kill Him for what He said (v. 59); but they didn't receive and obey His words. By rejecting the truth, they proved themselves to be children of the Devil, who is "the father of lies" (v. 44).

Peter called God's Word the "imperishable," "living," and "abiding" seed that brings salvation (1 Peter 1:23). But receiving God's Word isn't limited to salvation alone. As a Christian, you have the Word implanted within you. Now you must nurture it by removing any weeds of filthiness and wickedness so it can produce the fruit of righteousness. That isn't a one-time effort but a lifestyle of confession, looking into God's Word, desiring His message, and longing to obey it. That doesn't mean you'll be sinlessly perfect, but your life will be marked by ever-increasing spiritual maturity and obedience to the Word. When you are disobedient, you should feel an enormous tension in your spirit until you repent and make things right.

Are you hearing and receiving God's Word in that way? Do those who know you best see you as a person whose life is governed by Biblical principles? Jesus said, "If you abide in My word, then you are truly disciples of Mine" (John 8:31). Receive His truth, and abide in it continually!

❖❖❖

Suggestions for Prayer: Ask the Lord to keep you sensitive to His Word in every situation you face today.

For Further Study: Read 1 Thessalonians 2:13-14, noting the Thessalonians' response to God's Word.

"This you know, my beloved brethren. But let every one be quick to hear" (James 1:19).

❖❖❖

Being quick to hear involves a proper attitude toward God's Word.

I t has been well said that either God's Word will keep you from sin or sin will keep you from God's Word. Apparently some of James's readers were allowing sin to keep them from receiving the Word as they should. God was allowing them to experience various trials so their joy and spiritual endurance would increase, but they lacked wisdom and fell into temptation and sin. James called them back to the Word and to a godly perspective on their circumstances.

James 1:19 begins with the phrase "This you know," which refers back to verse 18. They had experienced the power of the Word in salvation, and now James wants them to allow that Word to sanctify them. For that to occur, they must be "quick to hear, slow to speak and slow to anger" (v. 19).

Being "quick to hear" means you don't disregard or fight against God's Word. Instead, when trials or difficult decisions come your way, you ask God for wisdom and receive the counsel of His Word with a willingness to obey it. You're not like the disciples on the road to Emmaus, whom Jesus described as "foolish men and slow of heart to believe in all that the prophets have spoken" (Luke 24:25).

You should be "quick to hear" the Word because it provides nourishment for your spiritual life and is your weapon against all spiritual adversaries. It is the means by which you are strengthened and equipped for every good work (2 Tim. 3:16-17). It delivers you from trials and temptations and engages you in communion with the living God. The Word should be your most welcome friend!

Be "quick to hear," pursuing every opportunity to learn God's truth. Let the testimony of the psalmist be yours: "O how I love Thy law! It is my meditation all the day . . . . I have restrained my feet from every evil way, that I may keep Thy word. . . . How sweet are Thy words to my taste! Yes, sweeter than honey to my mouth!" (Ps. 119:97, 101, 103).

❖❖❖

Suggestions for Prayer: Thank God for His precious Word and for the marvelous transforming work it accomplishes in you.

For Further Study: Read Psalm 19:1-14. ❖ What terms did the psalmist use to describe God's Word? ❖ What benefits does the Word bring?

"Let every one be . . . slow to speak" (James 1:19).

❖❖❖

Don't rush into the role of a Bible teacher.

It is reported that when the Scottish Reformer John Knox was called to preach, he shed many tears and withdrew to the privacy of his room. He was grieved and greatly troubled at the prospect of such an awesome responsibility. Only the compelling grace of the Holy Spirit Himself enabled Knox to fulfill his calling.

John Knox understood the importance of being "slow to speak." He knew that God holds teachers of the Word accountable for what they say and will dispense a stricter judgment to them if they violate their ministry (James 3:1-2).

In one sense, God holds everyone accountable for what they say. You are to "let no unwholesome word proceed from your mouth, but only such a word as is good for edification according to the need of the moment, that it may give grace to those who hear" (Eph. 4:29). But being "slow to speak" doesn't refer to vocabulary or opinions. It refers to teaching the Word. You are to pursue every opportunity to hear God's Word but must exercise reluctance in assuming the role of a teacher. Why? Because the tongue reveals the subtle sins of one's heart and easily offends others (James 3:2).

Does that mean you should never teach the Bible? No, because God commands every believer to "make disciples . . . *teaching them to observe all*" that Jesus taught (Matt. 28:19-20, emphasis added). And the Spirit gifts many believers to be preachers and teachers of the Word. Paul said, "I am under compulsion; for woe is me if I do not preach the gospel" (1 Cor. 9:16).

You must take every opportunity to share the gospel with others; and if God has called and gifted you to teach the Word, be faithful to do so. But remember, those are serious and sacred responsibilities. Be sure your motives are pure and your teaching accurate. If someone is offended, let it be by the convicting power of the Word, not by something you said at an unguarded moment.

❖❖❖

Suggestions for Prayer: Ask the Lord to teach you to guard your tongue and to speak only what is edifying to others.

For Further Study: Read Proverbs 10:19, 13:3, 17:28, and 29:20, noting what each verse teaches about wise speech.

"Let every one be . . . slow to anger; for the anger of man does not achieve the righteousness of God" (James 1:19-20).

✧✧✧

If you resent God's Word, you cannot grow in righteousness.

Have you ever started reading your Bible, thinking everything was fine between you and the Lord, only to have the Word suddenly cut deep into your soul to expose some sin you had neglected or tried to hide? That commonly happens because God seeks to purge sin in His children. The Holy Spirit uses the Word to penetrate the hidden recesses of the heart and to do His convicting and purifying work. How you respond to that process is an indicator of the genuineness of your faith.

"Anger" in James 1:19-20 refers to a negative response to that process. It is a deep internal resentment accompanied by an attitude of rejection. Sometimes that resentment can be subtle. Paul described those who "will not endure sound doctrine; but wanting to have their ears tickled, they will accumulate for themselves teachers in accordance to their own desires" (2 Tim. 4:3). These are the people who drift from church to church in search of someone who will tell them what they want to hear, or a congregation that wants a pastor who will make them feel good about themselves instead of preaching the Word and setting a high standard of holiness.

Sometimes resentment toward the Word ceases to be subtle and turns to open hostility. That happened when the crowd that Stephen confronted covered their ears, drove him out of the city, and stoned him to death (Acts 7:57-60). Countless others throughout history have felt the fatal blows of those whose resentment of God's truth turned to hatred for His people.

Receiving the Word includes being "quick to hear" what it says and "slow to anger" when it disagrees with your opinions or confronts your sin. Is that your attitude? Do you welcome its reproof and heed its warnings, or do you secretly resent it? When a Christian brother or sister confronts a sin in your life, do you accept or reject their counsel?

✧✧✧

Suggestions for Prayer: Thank God for the power of His Word to convict you and drive you to repentance. Welcome its correction with humility and thanksgiving.

For Further Study: Read 2 Timothy 4:1-5, noting the charge Paul gave to Timothy and his reason for giving it.

"Putting aside all filthiness and all that remains of wickedness . . . receive the word" (James 1:21).

❖❖❖

You cannot receive God's Word and harbor sin at the same time.

When the psalmist said, "I have restrained my feet from every evil way, that I may keep Thy word" (Ps. 119:101), he was acknowledging a key principle of spiritual growth: you must set aside sin if you expect to benefit from God's Word. Peter expressed the same thought when he said, "Putting aside all malice and all guile and hypocrisy and envy and all slander, like newborn babes, long for the pure milk of the word, that by it you may grow in respect to salvation" (1 Peter 2:1-2). Likewise, James admonished us to put off sin and receive the Word (1:21).

Neither James nor Peter were addressing unbelievers, because without Christ people have no capacity to set sin aside or receive God's Word. But we as Christians are characterized by our ability to do both, and we must continually purify our lives through confession of sin, repentance, and right choices. That's why Paul said, "Just as you presented your members as slaves to impurity and to lawlessness, resulting in further lawlessness, so now present your members as slaves to righteousness, resulting in sanctification" (Rom. 6:19).

The Greek word translated "putting aside" in James 1:21 originally meant taking off dirty, soiled clothes. "Filthiness" translates a Greek word that was used of moral vice as well as dirty clothes. Its root word was sometimes used of ear wax, which impedes a person's hearing. Similarly, sin impedes reception of the Word. "Wickedness" speaks of any evil intent or desire. Together these words stress the importance of setting aside all evil actions and intentions.

Simply stated, you should never presume on God's grace by approaching His Word with unconfessed sin. David prayed, "Keep back Thy servant from presumptuous [deliberate] sins; let them not rule over me; then I shall be blameless" (Ps. 19:13). He wanted to be pure before the Lord. I pray that you share his desire and will always receive the Word in purity.

❖❖❖

Suggestions for Prayer: Memorize Psalm 19:14. Make it your prayer as you study God's Word.

For Further Study: Read Colossians 3:5-17. ❖ What does Paul admonish you to put off? Put on? ❖ Why is it important to heed his admonitions?

"In humility receive the word implanted, which is able to save your souls" (James 1:21).

✧✧✧

A humble heart is a teachable heart.

Scripture speaks of a past, present, and future aspect of salvation. You have been saved from the penalty of sin (salvation), are being saved from the power of sin (sanctification), and will ultimately be saved from the presence of sin (glorification). At first glance James 1:21 may sound like it's written to unbelievers, urging them to receive the Word, which is able to redeem them. But the phrase "save your souls" carries the idea that the implanted Word has the ongoing power to continually save one's soul. It's a reference to the present and ongoing process of sanctification, which is nurtured by the Spirit-energized Word of God.

The Word was implanted within you by the Holy Spirit at the time of your salvation. It is the source of power and growth for your new life in Christ. Your responsibility is to receive it in purity and humility so it can do its sanctifying work.

"Humility" in James 1:21 could be translated "meekness," "gentleness," or "having a willing spirit", but I prefer "teachability." If your heart is pure and humble, you will be teachable and will set aside all resentment, anger, and pride so you can learn God's truth and apply it to your life.

When Jesus said, "If you love Me, you will keep My commandments" (John 14:15), He was addressing this very issue. If you love Him, you will desire to obey Him and will receive His Word so you can know His will for your life. As you receive the Word, the Holy Spirit empowers you to live according to its principles.

Paul said, "Let the word of Christ richly dwell within you, with all wisdom teaching and admonishing one another . . . and whatever you do in word or deed, do all in the name of the Lord Jesus" (Col. 3:16-17). That's the essence of a Biblical lifestyle and the fruit of receiving the Word in humility. May God bless you with a teachable spirit and an ever-increasing love for His truth.

✧✧✧

Suggestions for Prayer: Ask God to keep your heart tender towards Christ and His Word.

For Further Study: Read Nehemiah 8. ✧ Who read God's Word to the people? ✧ How did the people respond? ✧ Would you characterize them as receivers of the Word? Explain.

"Prove yourselves doers of the word, and not merely hearers who delude themselves" (James 1:22).

✧✧✧

A doer of the Word obeys what Scripture says.

Effective Bible study is built on three key questions: What does the Bible say? What does it mean? How does it apply to my life? Each of those questions is important, but applying the Word must always be the highest goal. Knowledge without application is useless.

Both the Old and New Testaments emphasize the importance of applying Scripture. For example, just prior to leading the Israelites into the Promised Land, Joshua received this message from God: "This book of the law shall not depart from your mouth, but you shall meditate on it day and night, so that you may be careful to do according to all that is written in it; for then you will make your way prosperous, and then you will have success" (Josh. 1:8). That's a command to be a doer of the Word—one who receives, studies, and understands Scripture and then applies it to every aspect of his or her life. That was the key to Joshua's amazing success.

James 1:22 is a New Testament counterpart to Joshua 1:8 and is directed to every believer: "Prove yourselves doers of the word, and not merely hearers who delude themselves." It's not enough to hear the Word—you must also do what it says.

The phrase "doer of the word" doesn't refer to the person who obeys periodically, but the one who habitually and characteristically obeys. It's one thing to run in a race; it's something else to be a runner. It's one thing to teach a class; it's something else to be a teacher. Runners are known for running; teachers are known for teaching—it's characteristic of their lives. Similarly, doers of the Word are known for their obedience to Biblical truth.

Never be content to be a hearer of the Word only, but prove yourself a doer in the Christian life. Your claim to love Christ will mean something only if you obey what He says.

✧✧✧

Suggestions for Prayer: Memorize Joshua 1:8, and pray regularly that God will make you a faithful doer of the Word.

For Further Study: Read Psalm 1. ✧ What are the benefits of delighting in God's law? ✧ How does the psalmist characterize those who reject righteousness?

"Prove yourselves doers of the word, and not merely hearers who delude themselves" (James 1:22).

❖❖❖

**It's a delusion to think you can hear God's Word,
then disobey it without cost.**

Matthew 7:21-23 records the tragic results of spiritual delusion. Jesus says, "Not every one who says to Me, 'Lord, Lord,' will enter the kingdom of heaven; but he who does the will of My Father, who is in heaven. Many will say to Me on that day, 'Lord, Lord, did we not prophesy in Your name, and in Your name cast out demons, and in Your name perform many miracles?' And then I will declare to them, 'I never knew you; depart from Me, you who practice lawlessness.'"

Jesus made a clear distinction between those who merely claim to be Christians and those who truly are. The difference is, true believers do the will of the Father. In the words of James, they are doers of the Word, not merely hearers who delude themselves.

"Hearers" in James 1:22 translates a Greek word that speaks of auditing a class. Auditing students attend class and listen to the instructor but don't do any work. Consequently, they don't receive credit for the course. The phrase "delude themselves" speaks of being victimized by one's own faulty reasoning.

People who listen to God's Word but never obey it are spiritual auditors who delude themselves by thinking that hearing the Word is all God requires of them. Unfortunately, many churches are full of such people. They attend services and hear the sermons, but their lives never seem to change. They're content to hear the Word but never apply it. Like those whom Jesus condemned in Matthew 7, they've chosen religious activities over true faith in Christ.

How tragic to think you're saved, only to hear, "I never knew you; depart from Me, you who practice lawlessness" (Matt. 7:23). That will never happen if you're a doer of the Word.

❖❖❖

Suggestions for Prayer: Take advantage of every opportunity to respond to the Word in specific ways. Ask God for His grace to keep you faithful to that goal.

For Further Study: Read Matthew 7:13-29. ❖ How did Jesus describe false prophets? ❖ How can you discern a false from a true prophet? ❖ To what did Jesus liken those who hear His words and act on them? Why?

"If any one is a hearer of the word and not a doer, he is like a man who looks at his natural face in a mirror; for once he has looked at himself and gone away, he has immediately forgotten what kind of person he was" (James 1:23-24).

❖❖❖

Always respond immediately to what you know to be God's will for you.

M en, have you ever been at work and touched your face, only to realize that you forgot to shave? Perhaps you were distracted by your wife's call to breakfast or by one of the kids. Ladies, have you ever been out in public and suddenly realized that you forgot to apply some of your makeup? Those are common occurrences that illustrate what it means to hear God's Word but fail to respond.

James 1:23 says, "If any one is a hearer of the word and not a doer, he is like a man who looks at his natural face in a mirror." "Looks" doesn't refer to a casual glance but to a careful, cautious, observant stare. This person is taking a good, long look at himself. Hearers of the Word are not necessarily superficial or casual in their approach to Scripture. They can be serious students of the Word. And yet, the fact is, some seminary professors or Sunday school teachers are not true believers. Some even write commentaries and other Bible reference works. Your response to the Word—not your depth of study alone—is the issue with God.

Despite the hearer's lingering look, he failed to respond, and the image reflected in the mirror soon faded. That's reminiscent of Jesus saying, "When any one hears the word of the kingdom, and does not understand it, the evil one comes and snatches away what has been sown in his heart" (Matt. 13:19). The Word was sown, but it bore no fruit. The man looked into the mirror, but he made no corrections.

Perhaps there's something God's Word is instructing you to do that you've been putting off. If so, delay no longer. Don't be a forgetful hearer!

❖❖❖

Suggestions for Prayer: Ask God to teach you to be more disciplined in responding to the dictates of His Word.

For Further Study: Read Matthew 13:1-23, noting the various soils and what they represent.

"One who looks intently at the perfect law, the law of liberty, and abides by it, not having become a forgetful hearer but an effectual doer, this man shall be blessed in what he does" (James 1:25).

✧✧✧

God blesses you when you obey His Word.

James 1:21-24 contrasts hearers of the Word and doers of the Word. Hearers don't respond to Scripture or benefit from its truths, though they may study it in depth. Doers receive it in humility and obey its commands. James 1:25 adds that they are "blessed" in what they do. That means there is blessing in the very act of obedience.

James here calls Scripture "the perfect law, the law of liberty." It is "law" because it's God's obligatory behavioral code. Grace doesn't eliminate God's moral law; but it gives us the spiritual resources to obey it, and forgiveness when we fail. That's how Jesus fulfills the law in us (cf. Matt. 5:17).

Scripture is "the perfect law" because it is complete, sufficient, comprehensive, and without error. Through it God meets every need and fulfills every desire of the human heart. In addition, it is "the law of liberty." That may sound paradoxical, because we tend to think of law and freedom as opposites. But as you look intently into the Word, the Holy Spirit enables you to apply its principles to your life, thereby freeing you from the guilt and bondage of sin and enabling you to live to God's glory. That's true freedom!

"Looks intently" translates a Greek word that pictures bending down to examine something with care and precision. This implies humility and a desire to see clearly what Scripture reveals about your own spiritual condition. It's an attitude as well as an action.

As you study Scripture, let this be your underlying attitude: "Lord, as I gaze intently into Your Word, reveal the things in my life that need to be changed. Then grant me the grace to make those changes, so I can live more fully to Your glory."

✧✧✧

Suggestions for Prayer: Memorize Psalm 139:23-24, and make it your sincere prayer.

For Further Study: Read Hebrews 4:12-13. ✧ To what is God's Word compared? ✧ What effect does the Word have on those who are exposed to it?

"One who looks intently at the perfect law, the law of liberty and abides by it, not having become a forgetful hearer but an effectual doer, this man shall be blessed in what he does" (James 1:25).

❖❖❖

Doers of the Word are persevering learners.

The phrase "and abides by it" in James 1:25 demands our close attention. "Abide" translates a Greek word that means "to stay beside," "to remain," or "to continue." The idea is that a doer of the Word continually and habitually gazes into God's perfect law. In other words, he is a persevering learner.

When you have that level of commitment to the Word, you will be an effectual doer—one who is in union with God's will and seeks to obey it above all else. As you do that, God will bless you. That doesn't necessarily mean you'll be successful in the eyes of the world, but your priorities and perspectives will be right, and the Lord will honor what you do.

This verse is a call to carefully examine yourself in light of God's standards. That's not a popular thing in our society because many people have an aversion to serious spiritual thought and self-examination. I believe that's why Christian television, music, and other forms of entertainment are so popular. Escaping reality through entertainment is far more appealing to most people than gazing into the mirror of God's Word and having their spiritual flaws and blemishes exposed. But if you desire to be like Christ, you must see yourself for what you are and make any needed corrections. To do that, you must continually examine your life in the light of Scripture.

Can you imagine what the church would be like if every Christian did that? Can you imagine the changes in your own life if you did it more consistently? Only the Holy Spirit can enable you to be a doer of the Word. So, yield to His leading through prayer and confession as you continue to study and apply God's Word.

❖❖❖

Suggestions for Prayer: Whenever you study Scripture, ask the Spirit to illuminate your mind and heart and to use the Word to transform you more and more into the image of Christ.

For Further Study: Read Colossians 3:16-17, noting what Paul says about responding to the Word.

"If anyone thinks himself to be religious, and yet does not bridle his tongue but deceives his own heart, this man's religion is worthless" (James 1:26).

✧✧✧

Your speech reveals the condition of your heart.

In verse 22 James talked about the delusion of hearing the Word without obeying it. Here he talks about the deception of external religious activity without internal purity of heart.

That's a common deception. Many people confuse a love for religious activity with love for God. They may go through the mechanics of reading the Bible, attending church, praying, giving money, or singing songs, but in reality their hearts are far from God. That kind of deception can be very subtle. That's why James disregards mere claims to Christianity and confronts our motives and obedience to the Word. Those are the acid tests!

James was selective in the word he used for "religious." Rather than using the common Greek word that spoke of internal godliness, he chose a word that referred to external religious trappings, ceremonies, and rituals—things that are useless for true spirituality.

He focused on the tongue as a test of true religion because the tongue is a window to the heart. As Jesus said, "The mouth speaks out of that which fills the heart" (Matt. 12:34). Corrupt speech betrays an unregenerate heart; righteous speech demonstrates a transformed heart. It doesn't matter how evangelical or Biblical your theology is, if you can't control your tongue, your religion is useless!

You can learn much about a person's character if you listen long enough to what he says. In the same way, others learn much about you as they listen to what you say. Do your words reveal a pure heart? Remember Paul's admonition to "let no unwholesome word proceed from your mouth, but only such a word as is good for edification according to the need of the moment, that it may give grace to those who hear" (Eph. 4:29). Make that your goal each day, so you can know the blessing and grace of disciplined speech!

✧✧✧

Suggestions for Prayer: Ask the Lord to guard your tongue from speaking anything that might dishonor Him. Be aware of everything you say.

For Further Study: Read James 3:1-12. ✧ What warning does James give? ✧ What analogies does he use for the tongue?

"This is pure and undefiled religion in the sight of our God and Father, to visit orphans and widows in their distress, and to keep oneself unstained by the world" (James 1:27).

❖❖❖

True religion produces holiness and sacrificial love.

I n this verse James continues his practical and penetrating assessment of true faith. So far he has said in effect, "Don't just study the Bible—obey it! Don't just dabble in external religion—have pure speech!" Now he adds, "Don't just say you're religious—demonstrate sacrificial love! Don't just claim to love God—live a pure life!" Shallow claims to Christianity meant nothing to him. He wanted to see godly attitudes and righteous deeds.

The Apostle John used the same approach when he wrote, "The one who says he abides in [Christ] ought himself to walk in the same manner as He walked. . . . The one who loves his brother abides in the light and there is no cause for stumbling in him. But the one who hates his brother is in the darkness and walks in the darkness, and does not know where he is going because the darkness has blinded his eyes" (1 John 2:6, 10-11). "Light" in that passage represents truth and righteousness; "darkness" speaks of error and sin. If you are truly saved, you are in the light and will show it by your love for others.

In our society, the definition of religion is very broad. Almost any belief system qualifies. But to God, any religion that doesn't produce holiness and sacrificial love is not true religion. That narrows the field considerably because anyone who isn't saved through faith in Jesus Christ remains in bondage to sin and has no capacity to live a holy and selfless life.

How about you? Do you flee from sin and reach out to those in need? If so, you have true religion. If not, receive Christ now. He alone is the source of holiness and love.

❖❖❖

Suggestions for Prayer: If you are a believer, God's love is already shed abroad in your heart through the indwelling Holy Spirit (Rom. 5:5). Ask God to increase your capacity to love others as Christ loves you.

For Further Study: Read 1 John 3:10-18, noting John's comparison of the children of God with the children of the Devil.

"This is pure and undefiled religion in the sight of our God and Father, to visit orphans and widows in their distress" (James 1:27).

✧✧✧

Sacrificial love is the hallmark of true Christianity.

Recently a local newspaper reported the story of a young woman who had been brutally beaten, sexually assaulted, repeatedly stabbed, then dumped down a hillside and left for dead. Miraculously she survived the attack and crawled up the hill to a spot along the road where several people were parked enjoying the panoramic view of the city.

Covered with blood from head to foot, she went from car to car pleading for help, only to have one person after another roll up their windows and drive away. No one wanted to get involved. Finally someone came to her rescue and took her to a hospital where she was treated for her wounds. The article went on to describe the anger of her rescuer toward those who turned their backs on the woman's cries for help.

That tragic story illustrates the lack of compassion so prevalent in our society. Many people won't become involved—even when the lives of others are at stake. They're unwilling to risk personal injury or inconvenience, or perhaps they're just complacent and insensitive.

That should never be true of Christians! Jesus showed great compassion to those with special needs, and He expects us to do the same.

Just as James used the tongue to represent a pure heart (v. 26), so he uses widows and orphans to represent pure love. "To visit" means to bring love, pity, and care to them. Widows and orphans are an especially needy segment within the church. As such, they represent all who are destitute and unable to repay your kindness.

Let your love be sacrificial. Give with no intention of receiving anything in return. Generously invest your time and resources in ministering to those who have no resources of their own. That's the essence of true religion!

✧✧✧

Suggestions for Prayer: Is there someone in your neighborhood or church whom you can help today? Ask God for wisdom and discernment on how you might best demonstrate His love to that person.

For Further Study: Read Exodus 22:22-24, Deuteronomy 14:28-29, Psalm 68:5, Acts 6:1-6, and 1 Timothy 5:3-16, noting God's provisions for widows and orphans.

"This is pure and undefiled religion in the sight of our God and Father . . . to keep oneself unstained by the world" (James 1:27).

❖❖❖

God doesn't tolerate compromise with the world.

Keeping yourself "unstained by the world" is an important test of your spiritual condition. The Apostle John said, "Do not love the world, nor the things in the world. If anyone loves the world, the love of the Father is not in him" (1 John 2:15). At first glance that might sound contradictory since God Himself so loved the world that He gave His Son to die for it (John 3:16). But John 3:16 refers to the inhabited earth—the people for whom Christ died. First John 2:15 refers to the evil world system in which we live, which includes the lifestyles, philosophies, morality, and ethics of our sinful culture. That world and everything it produces is passing away (1 John 2:16-17).

James 4:4 says, "You adulteresses, do you not know that friendship with the world is hostility toward God? Therefore whoever wishes to be a friend of the world makes himself an enemy of God." Those are strong words, but compromise is intolerable to God. You can't be His friend and a friend of the world at the same time!

Separation from the world is the final element of true religion mentioned in James 1. Before progressing to chapter 2, take a final spiritual inventory based on the checklist provided in verses 26-27: 1. *Do you control your tongue?* Review the quality of your conversation often. What does it reveal about the condition of your heart? Are there speech habits you need to change? 2. *Do you demonstrate love for others?* Do you have a sincere desire to help those in need? When you do help, are your motives pure, or are you simply trying to soothe your conscience or make others think more highly of you? 3. *Do you remain unstained by the world?* What is your attitude toward the world? Do you want to win it for Christ and remain unstained by its evil influences, or do you want to get as much out of it as you possibly can?

❖❖❖

Suggestions for Prayer: If your spiritual inventory reveals any sinful motives or practices, confess them, and begin to change today.

For Further Study: Reread James 1:19-27, reviewing the principles you've learned from those verses.

"My brethren, do not hold your faith in our glorious Lord Jesus Christ with an attitude of personal favoritism" (James 2:1).

❖❖❖

Because God is impartial, we as Christians must be impartial too.

People are prone to treat others differently based upon external criteria such as looks, possessions, or social status, but God is utterly impartial. He never shows favoritism and always judges righteously.

Favoritism can be defined as a preferential attitude and treatment of a person or group over another having equal claims and rights. It is unjustified partiality. James 2:1-13 confronts this as sin and admonishes us to avoid it at all costs.

God's impartiality is seen throughout Scripture. For example, Moses said to the people of Israel, "The Lord your God is the God of gods and the Lord of lords, the great, the mighty, and the awesome God who does not show partiality, nor take a bribe. He executes justice for the orphan and the widow, and shows His love for the alien by giving him food and clothing. So show your love for the alien, for you were aliens in the land of Egypt" (Deut. 10:17-19). Jehoshaphat, king of Judah, warned his judges to rule without partiality because God Himself has "no part in unrighteousness, or partiality" (2 Chron. 19:7).

God's impartiality is also seen in His gracious offer of salvation to people of every race. In Acts 10:34-35 Peter says, "I most certainly understand now that God is not one to show partiality, but in every nation the man who fears Him and does what is right, is welcome to Him."

God is also impartial in judgment. Romans 2:9-11 says that God will bring "tribulation and distress for every soul of man who does evil . . . but glory and honor and peace to every man who does good. . . . For there is no partiality with God."

Our text is a timely admonition because prejudice, discrimination, and bigotry are ever-present evils in our society—both inside and outside the church. I pray that God will use these studies to guard you from favoritism's subtle influences and to strengthen your commitment to godly living.

❖❖❖

Suggestions for Prayer: Ask God to reveal any partiality you might be harboring. As He does, confess it and turn from it.

For Further Study: Read Ephesians 6:5-9 and 1 Timothy 5:17-21. How does God's impartiality apply to how you should respond to your co-workers and your church leaders?

"My brethren, do not hold your faith in our glorious Lord Jesus Christ with an attitude of personal favoritism" (James 2:1).

❖❖❖

Your true worth is based on the value of your soul, not on external considerations.

Jesus is "our glorious Lord" (James 2:1)—the Sovereign One who rules over all His creation, the One in whom the fullness of God's glory is revealed. John said, "The Word [Jesus] became flesh, and dwelt among us, and we beheld His glory, glory as of the only begotten from the Father, full of grace and truth" (John 1:14). Paul said, "In Him all the fulness of Deity dwells in bodily form" (Col. 2:9).

As God, Jesus shares the impartiality of the Father. He knows that a person's worth is based on the value of his soul, not on external considerations. That's why He always looks on the heart and never judges on externals alone.

That was evident in the way Jesus dealt with sinners when He was still on earth. He never hesitated to confront them—whether they were influential Jewish religious leaders or common folks. Even His enemies acknowledged His impartiality when they said, "Teacher, we know that You are truthful and teach the way of God in truth, and defer to no one; for You are not partial to any" (Matt. 22:16).

Like the Father, Jesus also extended the offer of salvation to men and women of every race, social class, and moral standing. That's illustrated by the parable He told in Matthew 22:1-14 about the marriage of a king's son (an illustration of Himself). The invited guests (Israel) didn't show up, so the king commanded his servants to go out and gather everyone they could find to furnish the wedding with guests. As a result, people of every station in life attended the wedding, just as people of every station in life are called to salvation.

As you have opportunities to minister to others today, don't be influenced by externals such as looks, clothing, or economic level. Do as Jesus did: treat them with compassion, and speak the truth without compromise.

❖❖❖

Suggestions for Prayer: Praise the Lord for His impartiality, and ask Him for special grace as you reach out to others today.

For Further Study: Read Matthew 20:1-16. How does that parable illustrate the impartiality of God?

"If a man comes into your assembly with a gold ring and dressed in fine clothes, and there also comes in a poor man in dirty clothes, and you pay special attention to the one who is wearing the fine clothes, and say, 'You sit here in a good place,' and you say to the poor man, 'You stand over there, or sit down by my footstool,' have you not made distinctions among yourselves, and become judges with evil motives?" (James 2:2-4).

❖❖❖

You must show equal respect to poor and rich alike.

Partiality is an age-old problem that exists in almost every area of life. Perhaps its most common manifestations are racial, religious, and socioeconomic discrimination. By implication James denounced partiality in any form, but in James 2:2-4 he specifically mentions preferential treatment of the rich over the poor. He knew such favoritism was devastating not only because it is sinful, but also because the majority of believers in the early church were poor, common people. Discriminating against them would have struck a blow at the very heart of the church!

From its inception the church has upheld the priority of ministering to the poor. Acts 2:44-45 says, "All those who had believed were together, and had all things in common; and they began selling their property and possessions, and were sharing them with all, as anyone might have need." Paul organized a relief fund for the needy saints in Jerusalem (1 Cor. 16:1-4), and during one severe famine, "in the proportion that any of the disciples had means, each of them determined to send a contribution for the relief of the brethren living in Judea. And this they did, sending it in charge of Barnabas and Saul to the elders" (Acts 11:29-30).

God has chosen the poor of this world to be rich in faith and heirs of the Kingdom, but some of James's readers were dishonoring them (vv. 5-6). That had to stop! We too must honor the poor by treating them with dignity rather than prejudice and by meeting their needs whenever possible. Be alert to those around you whom you might help in some practical way.

❖❖❖

Suggestions for Prayer: Ask the Lord to keep you sensitive to those around you, and for wisdom to know how to respond to their needs.

For Further Study: Read 1 Corinthians 1:26-29, noting the kinds of people God uses to accomplish His purposes.

"If a man comes into your assembly with a gold ring and dressed in fine clothes, and there also comes in a poor man in dirty clothes, and you pay special attention to the one who is wearing the fine clothes, and say, 'You sit here in a good place,' and you say to the poor man, 'You stand over there, or sit down by my footstool', have you not made distinctions among yourselves, and become judges with evil motives?" (James 2:2-4).

❖❖❖

Favoritism is motivated by an evil desire to gain some advantage for yourself.

The story is told of a pastor who never ministered to an individual or family in his church without first checking a current record of their financial contributions. The more generous they were with their money, the more generous he was with his time. That's an appalling and flagrant display of favoritism, but in effect it's the same kind of situation James dealt with in our text for today.

Picture yourself in a worship service or Bible study when suddenly two visitors enter the room. The first visitor is a wealthy man, as evidenced by his expensive jewelry and designer clothes. The second visitor lives in abject poverty. The street is his home, as evidenced by his filthy, smelly, shabby clothing.

How would you respond to each visitor? Would you give the rich man the best seat in the house and see that he is as comfortable as possible? That's a gracious thing to do if your motives are pure. But if you're trying to win his favor or to profit from his wealth, a vicious sin has taken hold of you.

Your true motives will be revealed in the way you treat the poor man. Do you show him equal honor, or do you simply invite him to sit on the floor? Anything less than equal honor reveals an evil intent.

Favoritism can be subtle. That's why you must be in prayer and in the Word, constantly allowing the Spirit to penetrate and purify your deepest, most secret motives.

❖❖❖

Suggestions for Prayer: Praise God for His purity. ❖ Ask Him always to control your motives and actions.

For Further Study: Some Christians confuse honor with partiality. Giving honor to those in authority is Biblical; showing partiality is sinful. Read 1 Peter 2:17 and Romans 13:1, noting the exhortations to honor those in authority over you.

"Listen, my beloved brethren: did not God choose the poor of this world to be rich in faith and heirs of the kingdom which He promised to those who love Him? But you have dishonored the poor man" (James 2:5-6).

❖❖❖

Showing favoritism to the rich is inconsistent with God's choice of the poor.

Wealth and poverty are not necessarily spiritual issues. Many wealthy people are godly Christians, and many poor people are unbelievers. But generally speaking, God has chosen poor people to populate His Kingdom. Jesus said, "It is hard for a rich man to enter the kingdom of heaven. And again I say to you, it is easier for a camel to go through the eye of a needle, than for a rich man to enter the kingdom of God" (Matt. 19:23-24). That's because rich people tend to be bound to this world and have a false sense of security. Many of them not only reject Christ but also persecute believers (cf. James 2:6-7).

James said, "Let the brother of humble circumstances glory in his high position; and let the rich man glory in his humiliation, because like flowering grass he will pass away" (James 1:9-10). Most rich people pursue greater wealth while passing by the true riches of the Kingdom. But like a delicate flower in the scorching summer sun, they will soon fade away, and their futile pursuits will die with them.

Regardless of your financial status, if you love God, you are rich in faith and an heir of His Kingdom (James 2:5). That means you're saved and will inherit the fullness of your salvation and the richness of God's eternal blessing. That's a marvelous truth!

Don't let riches cloud your good judgment. God expects Christians to honor and care for their poorer brothers and sisters in Christ. You can't do that if you're showing partiality to the rich.

❖❖❖

Suggestions for Prayer: If God has blessed you with more resources than you need, be grateful and ready always to share with those in need (1 Tim. 6:18). If you struggle to get by, thank Him for what He does provide and for teaching you greater dependence on Him.

For Further Study: Read 1 Timothy 6:6-19. ❖ What is God's standard of contentment? ❖ What pitfalls await those who desire wealth? ❖ What constitutes true riches?

"Is it not the rich who oppress you and personally drag you into court? Do they not blaspheme the fair name by which you have been called?" (James 2:6-7).

✧✧✧

You can't accomplish God's purposes by siding with His enemies.

Favoritism has a way of blinding its victims to reality. James wrote about Christians who were trying to impress a rich man so they could benefit from his wealth and social status (vv. 2-3). The rich man represented the enemies of Christ, and yet they gave him preferential treatment anyway. The poor man represented those whom God chose to be rich in faith and heirs of His Kingdom, and yet they treated him badly and dishonored him (v. 6). That's not only inconsistent, it's foolish! You can't accomplish God's purposes by siding with His enemies.

Some ungodly rich people tyrannized Christians by withholding their wages and even putting some to death (James 5:4-6). They forcibly dragged Christians to court to exploit them by some injustice or inequity. They blasphemed the fair name of Christ. The phrase "by which you have been called" (v. 7) speaks of a personal relationship. Typically new converts made a public proclamation of their faith in Christ at their baptism. From then on they were called "Christians," meaning "Christ's own," "Christ's ones," or "belonging to Christ." So when people slandered Christians, they were slandering Christ Himself!

That anyone could overlook those evils and show favoritism to the enemies of Christ shows the subtle and devastating power of partiality. Today the circumstances may be different, but the principles are the same. So for the sake of Christ and His people, remember the three reasons James gives for not showing partiality: 1. You and your brothers and sisters in Christ are one with the Lord Jesus Christ, who is the glory of God revealed (v. 1); 2. God has chosen the poor to receive eternal riches (v. 5); and 3. God has called you by His name (v. 7). If you desire to be like Christ, you cannot be partial. Be fair and impartial in all your interactions with others.

✧✧✧

Suggestions for Prayer: Is there a personal or business relationship in which you are showing favoritism in order to gain some advantage for yourself? If so, confess it to the Lord and correct it right away.

For Further Study: Read Romans 15:5-7. ✧ How should Christians treat one another? ✧ What impact will we have if we obey Paul's admonition?

"If . . . you are fulfilling the royal law, according to the Scripture, 'You shall love your neighbor as yourself,' you are doing well" (James 2:8).

❖❖❖

Love is the only antidote for partiality.

In Matthew 22:36 a lawyer asked Jesus which commandment was the greatest. Jesus answered, "'You shall love the Lord your God with all your heart, and with all your soul, and with all your mind.' This is the greatest and foremost commandment. The second is like it, 'You shall love your neighbor as yourself.' On these two commandments depend the whole Law and the Prophets" (vv. 37-40). Love for God and one's fellowman summarizes the intent of God's law and is the measure of true faith.

Jesus wasn't calling for the shallow, emotional, self-oriented love that is so prevalent in our society, but for a sacrificial quality of love that places the needs of others on par with your own. That kind of love is utterly incompatible with partiality, which seeks only to further its own selfish goals.

Showing partiality breaks God's law because it violates God's attributes, misrepresents the Christian faith, ignores God's choice of the poor, and condones the blasphemous behavior of the rich (James 2:1-7). But when you treat others impartially, you fulfill the royal law. "Royal" in James 2:8 translates a Greek word that speaks of sovereignty. The law was given by God, who is the supreme authority in the universe; so it is authoritative and binding. Love fulfills God's law because if you love someone, you won't sin against him.

Apparently not all of James's readers were showing partiality, so he commended them, saying they were "doing well." The Greek word translated "well" speaks of that which is excellent. They were doing an excellent thing because they were acting in a manner consistent with God's impartial, loving nature. That's God's call to every believer, for "the one who says he abides in [Christ] ought himself to walk in the same manner as He walked" (1 John 2:6). As you do, you fulfill God's law and thereby prove that your faith and love are genuine.

❖❖❖

Suggestions for Prayer: God's love is the only antidote for partiality. So pray each day that He will teach you how better to express His love to those around you.

For Further Study: Read the following verses, noting the characteristics of godly love: John 3:16; Ephesians 5:25-29; Philippians 1:9-11; and 1 John 5:1-3.

"If you show partiality, you are committing sin and are convicted by the law as transgressors. For whoever keeps the whole law and yet stumbles in one point, he has become guilty of all. For He who said, 'Do not commit adultery,' also said, 'Do not commit murder.' Now if you do not commit adultery, but do commit murder, you have become a transgressor of the law" (James 2:9-11).

❖❖❖

***You sin when you fall short of God's holy standard
or go beyond the limits of His law.***

Many people attempt to justify their sinfulness by categorizing sins according to their apparent severity. For example, telling a "little white lie" isn't as serious to them as committing perjury; cheating on their income tax isn't as serious as robbing a bank. Others see God's law as a series of detached injunctions and assume they can gain credit with God by keeping one law even if they break the others. In the final analysis, if the laws they don't break outweigh the laws they do, they think everything will be OK.

Apparently some of those to whom James wrote had the same misconceptions, believing sins like prejudice, partiality, and indifference to the poor weren't as serious as sins like murder and adultery. Or perhaps they believed they could make up for their favoritism by keeping God's law in other areas.

Both of those views are erroneous and potentially damning because God's law isn't a series of detached injunctions or a way of gaining credit with God. It's a unified representation of His holy nature. Even though all sins aren't equally heinous or damaging, from God's perspective every sin violates His standard. When you break one law, you break them all and are characterized as a sinner and transgressor.

"Sin" in verse 9 speaks of missing the mark and falling short of God's holy standard. "Transgressors" refers to going beyond the accepted limits. One says you've fallen short; the other says you've gone too far. Both are equal violations of God's holiness. You must see all sin as an affront to Him and must never compound your sin by attempting to hide it, justify it, or counterbalance it with good works.

❖❖❖

Suggestions for Prayer: Memorize 1 John 1:9, and always confess your sin whenever you violate God's holy law. ❖ Praise God for pitying our plight as sinners and for providing a Savior.

For Further Study: Read Galatians 3:10-29, noting the purpose of God's law.

"So speak and so act, as those who are to be judged by the law of liberty. For judgment will be merciless to one who has shown no mercy; mercy triumphs over judgment" (James 2:12-13).

❖❖❖

Showing mercy is characteristic of a regenerate person.

Divine judgment has never been a popular topic of conversation. Godly people throughout history have been ridiculed, persecuted, and even killed for proclaiming it. In their efforts to win the approval of men, false teachers question or deny it. But James 2:12-13 reminds us that judgment will come, so we'd better live accordingly.

The basis for divine judgment is God's Word, which James called "the law of liberty" (v. 12). It is a liberating law because it frees you from sin's bondage and from the curse of death and Hell. It is the agency of the Spirit's transforming work, cutting deep into your soul to judge your thoughts and motives (Heb. 4:12). It gives you the wisdom that leads to salvation and equips you for godly living (2 Tim. 3:15-17). It imparts truth and discernment, freeing you from error and spiritual deception. It is in every sense a law of freedom and liberation for those who embrace it.

The law liberates believers but condemns unbelievers. The phrase "judgment will be merciless to one who has shown no mercy" (v. 13) speaks of unrelieved judgment in which every sin receives its fullest punishment. That can only mean eternal Hell! If the Word is at work in you, its effects will be evident in the way you speak and act. If you are impartial and merciful to people in need, that shows you are a true Christian and have received God's forgiveness and mercy yourself. If you show partiality and disregard for the needy, the law becomes your judge, exposing the fact that you aren't truly redeemed.

Are you a merciful person? Do you seek to provide for others without favoritism? When you fail to do so, do you confess your sin and seek forgiveness and restoration? Those are marks of true faith.

❖❖❖

Suggestions for Prayer: Praise the Lord for His great mercy toward you, and be sure to show mercy to those around you.

For Further Study: Read Luke 1:46-55, 68-79. Follow Mary's and Zacharias' example by rejoicing over God's mercy toward His people.

"What use is it, my brethren, if a man says he has faith, but he has no works? Can that faith save him? . . . You see that a man is justified by works, and not by faith alone" (James 2:14, 24).

❖❖❖

True faith produces good works.

M any false teachers claim that you can earn your own salvation by doing good works. Most Christians understand the heresy of that teaching, but some become confused when they read that "a man is justified by works, and not by faith alone" (James 2:24). That seems to conflict with Paul's teaching on salvation by grace through faith.

But when properly understood, James' teaching on salvation is perfectly consistent with Paul's. Paul clearly taught salvation by grace. In Ephesians 2:8-9 he says, "By grace you have been saved through faith; and that not of yourselves, it is the gift of God; not as a result of works, that no one should boast." But Paul also taught that true salvation results in good works, for in the next verse he says, "We are His workmanship, created in Christ Jesus for good works, which God prepared beforehand, that we should walk in them."

In Titus 3:5 he says that God "saved us, not on the basis of deeds which we have done in righteousness, but according to His mercy." But Titus 2:11-12 clarifies that God's grace leads us "to deny ungodliness and worldly desires and to live sensibly, righteously and godly in the present age." That's the proper balance between faith and works.

James also taught salvation by grace. He said that God redeems sinners by the Word of truth and implants His Word within them to enable them to progress in holiness (James 1:18, 21). That's a divine work, not a human effort. James 2:14-24 follows that up by telling us how we can know that work has taken place: there will be more than just a proclamation of faith; there will be a faith that does good works.

Don't be confused by how faith relates to good works. Put the two together by being a living testimony to God's saving grace.

❖❖❖

Suggestions for Prayer: Thank God for the righteousness He is producing in your life. Look for specific ways to demonstrate your faith to those around you today.

For Further Study: Read John 8:31-32. ❖ What is the mark of a true disciple? ❖ What effect does God's Word have on those who heed what it says?

"What use is it, my brethren, if a man says he has faith, but he has no works? Can that faith save him? If a brother or sister is without clothing and in need of daily food, and one of you says to them, 'Go in peace, be warmed and be filled'; and yet you do not give them what is necessary for their body; what use is that? Even so faith, if it has no works, is dead, being by itself" (James 2:14-17).

✧✧✧

Dead faith is hypocritical, shallow, and useless.

Jesus said, "Let your light shine before men in such a way that they may see your good works, and glorify your Father who is in heaven" (Matt. 5:16). Your righteous deeds illuminate the path to God by reflecting His power and grace to others. That brings Him glory and proves your faith is genuine.

Your deeds also serve as the basis of divine judgment. If you practice righteousness, you will receive eternal life; if you practice unrighteousness, you will receive "wrath and indignation" (Rom. 2:6-8). God will judge you on the basis of your deeds, because what you do reveals who you really are and what you really believe. That's why any so-called faith that doesn't produce good works is dead and utterly useless!

James illustrates that point in a practical way. If someone lacks the basic necessities of life and comes to you for help, what good does it do if you simply wish him well and send him away without meeting any of his needs? It does no good at all! Your pious words are hypocritical and without substance. If you really wished him well, you would do what you could to give him what he needs! Your unwillingness to do so betrays your true feelings. Similarly, dead faith is hypocritical, shallow, and useless because it doesn't put its claims into action; indeed, it has no divine capacity to do so.

I pray that your life will always manifest true faith and that others will glorify God because of your good works.

✧✧✧

Suggestions for Prayer: Perhaps you know someone whose claim to Christianity is doubtful because his or her life doesn't evidence the fruit of righteousness. If so, pray for that person regularly and set an example by your own good works.

For Further Study: Read John 15:1-8. ✧ What illustration did Jesus use for spiritual fruitfulness? ✧ What is the prerequisite for fruitfulness?

"Someone may well say, 'You have faith, and I have works; show me your faith without the works, and I will show you my faith by my works.' You believe that God is one. You do well; the demons also believe, and shudder. But are you willing to recognize, you foolish fellow, that faith without works is useless?" (James 2:18-20).

❖❖❖

Even demonic faith is better than dead faith!

In recent years there has been an alarming rise in the number of professing Christians who believe there's no necessary relationship between what they believe and what they do. They say you can't judge a person's spiritual condition by what he or she does because salvation is a matter of faith alone—as if requiring works violates the principle of faith.

It was that kind of reasoning that prompted James to issue this challenge: "You have faith, and I have works; show me your faith without the works, and I will show you my faith by my works" (2:18). The Greek word translated "show" means "to exhibit," "to demonstrate," or "to put on display." His point is simple: it's impossible to verify true faith apart from holy living, because doctrine and deed are inseparable.

Can you know if someone is a Christian by watching his behavior? According to James, that's the *only* way to know! In verse 19 he says, "You believe that God is one. You do well; the demons also believe, and shudder." In other words, affirming orthodox doctrine isn't necessarily proof of saving faith. Demons believe in the oneness of God, and its implications fill them with fear, but they aren't saved. The phrase "you do well" is intentionally sarcastic. The implication is that demonic faith is better than non-responsive faith because at least the demons shudder, which is better than no response at all.

You can't be a Christian in creed only—you must be one in conduct as well! James makes that very clear. Don't be confused or deceived by those who teach otherwise. Continually aim your life at bringing glory to God through the obedient application of Biblical truth.

❖❖❖

Suggestions for Prayer: Reaffirm to the Lord your commitment to abide by His Word.

For Further Study: Read John 8:12-47. Make a list of doctrines and deeds that characterize dead faith and a corresponding list of those that characterize true faith.

"Was not Abraham our father justified by works, when he offered up Isaac his son on the altar? You see that faith was working with his works, and as a result of the works, faith was perfected; and the Scripture was fulfilled which says, 'And Abraham believed God, and it was reckoned to him as righteousness,' and he was called the friend of God. You see that a man is justified by works, and not by faith alone" (James 2:21-24).

❖❖❖

You are a friend of God if you love Him and obey His Word.

Can you imagine life without friends—those precious people who love you despite your failings and who stand by you through joys and sorrows—those to whom you've committed yourself and whose companionship you treasure? They are without question one of God's greatest gifts, and yet there is an even greater gift—friendship with God Himself.

Jesus spoke of such a friendship in John 15:13-16, describing it as one of intimacy, mutual love, sacrifice, and commitment. In verse 14 He says, "You are My friends, if you do what I command you." That's the kind of friendship Abraham demonstrated when he obeyed God and prepared to offer Isaac as a sacrifice (Gen. 22:3-10). Isaac was the son through whom God's covenant to Abraham would be fulfilled. Killing him would violate that covenant and call into question the character of God, whose Word forbids human sacrifice (Deut. 18:10). It took unquestioning trust for Abraham to obey God's command. When he did, his faith was on display for all to see.

The Greek word translated "justified" in James 2:21 has two meanings: "to acquit" (treat as righteous) or "to vindicate" (demonstrate as righteous). James emphasized the second meaning. When Abraham believed God, he was justified by faith and acquitted of sin (Gen. 15:6). When he offered up Isaac, he was justified by works in that his faith was vindicated.

Faith is always the sole condition of salvation, but saving faith never stands alone—it is always accompanied by righteous works. That's the test of true salvation and of friendship with God.

As a friend of God, treasure that relationship, and be careful never to let sin rob you of its fullest joy.

❖❖❖

Suggestions for Prayer: Praise God for the privilege of being His friend.

For Further Study: Read Genesis 22:1-19, noting the faith and obedience of Abraham.

"In the same way was not Rahab the harlot also justified by works, when she received the messengers and sent them out by another way? Just as the body without the spirit is dead, so also faith without works is dead" (James 2:25-26).

❖❖❖

True faith willingly makes whatever sacrifices God requires.

It's understandable that James would use Abraham as an illustration of living faith—especially to his predominately Jewish readers. Rahab, however, is a different story. She was a Gentile, a prostitute, a liar, and lived in the pagan city of Jericho. How could such a person illustrate true faith?

Rahab knew very little about the true God, but what she knew, she believed, and what she believed, she acted on. She believed that God had led His people out of Egypt and defeated the Amorite kings (Josh. 2:9-10). She openly confessed that the Lord "is God in heaven above and on earth beneath" (v. 11). Her faith was vindicated when she aided the Hebrew spies who entered Jericho just prior to Joshua's invasion.

Both Abraham and Rahab valued their faith in God above all else. Both were willing to sacrifice what mattered most to them. For Abraham it was Isaac; for Rahab it was her own life. Their obedience in the face of such great sacrifice proved the genuineness of their faith.

James calls each of us to examine ourselves to be sure we have a living faith. The acid test is whether your faith produces obedience. No matter what you claim, if righteousness doesn't characterize your life, your faith is dead, not living. James likened that kind of faith to hypocrites who offer pious words to the needy but refuse to meet their needs, to demons who believe the truth about God but are eternally lost, and to a lifeless, useless corpse. Those are strong analogies, but God does not want you to be deceived about the quality of your own faith.

I pray that you are rejoicing in the confidence that your faith is genuine. God bless you as you live each day in His wonderful grace.

❖❖❖

Suggestions for Prayer: Ask God for the grace and courage to make any sacrifice necessary as you live out your faith.

For Further Study: Read Joshua 2:1-24, 6:1-27, and Matthew 1:1-5. ❖ How did Rahab protect the spies? ❖ How did God bless Rahab?

"Coming to Him as to a living stone . . . you also, as living stones, are being built up as a spiritual house for a holy priesthood. . . . You are a chosen race, a royal priesthood, a holy nation, a people for God's own possession . . . you are the people of God . . . you have received mercy" (1 Peter 2:4-10).

❖❖❖

You have enormous privileges in Christs.

A university student once confessed to a pastor, "I've come to the conclusion that I don't believe in God." "I see," the pastor replied. "Please tell me about the God you don't believe in." The student proceeded to describe a vengeful, unfair, arbitrary, cosmic ogre who delighted in watching earthlings stumble through life in search of meaning and direction. After listening to that portrayal of God, the pastor wisely replied, "I don't believe in that God either."

Like that student, most people have a warped view of God because they can't see beyond their circumstances and the conditions that plague our fallen world. Their distorted worldview keeps them from understanding God's goodness and mercy. But we as believers understand because we see beyond the physical realm and experience His grace and kindness in many ways.

Scripture speaks pointedly about the duties and responsibilities of Christians, but all of that is balanced by the rights and benefits we have in Christ. In writing to Christians who were experiencing severe persecution, the Apostle Peter reminded them of their privileges and called them to praise God for His abundant grace (1 Peter 2:9). That is your calling as well.

This month we will consider many of those privileges, including your union with Christ, access to God, the priestly role, spiritual security, election, dominion, and inheritance. The implications of them all are staggering and should be a source of great joy and thanksgiving as you study them from God's Word.

❖❖❖

Suggestions for Prayer: Thank God for the privilege of being His child. ❖ Pray that He will strengthen and encourage you with the truths you learn from these studies. ❖ Regardless of your circumstances, learn to focus on God's glory and grace, allowing them continually to fill your heart with praise and worship.

For Further Study: Read 1 Peter 1:3-9 and 2:4-10. Make a list of the spiritual privileges Peter mentions.

". . . coming to [Christ] as to a living stone" (1 Peter 2:4).

❖❖❖

Jesus Christ is the source of every spiritual privilege.

Often Christians speak of salvation as "coming to Christ." That's an accurate, Biblical description, for Jesus Himself said, "Come to Me, all who are weary and heavy laden, and I will give you rest" (Matt. 11:28); "I am the bread of life; he who comes to Me shall not hunger, and he who believes in Me shall never thirst" (John 6:35); "If any man is thirsty, let him come to Me and drink" (John 7:37). Those are metaphors for salvation.

Coming to Christ initiates all your spiritual privileges because in Him God "granted to us everything pertaining to life and godliness" (2 Peter 1:3). Paul said, "Blessed be the God and Father of our Lord Jesus Christ, who has blessed us with every spiritual blessing in the heavenly places in Christ" (Eph. 1:3).

The Greek word translated "coming" in 1 Peter 2:4 conveys more than initially turning to Christ for salvation. It implies remaining with Him. In the Greek translation of the Old Testament this word was used of those who drew near to God for ongoing worship. It was also used of Gentile proselytes— those who chose to identify themselves with God's people.

When you came to Christ, a permanent relationship of intimate, personal communion was established. Before that, you were rebellious toward God, without hope, and alienated from God's promises. Now you've been born again to a living hope, you abide in Him and in His Word, and you have wonderful spiritual privileges.

Indeed, you are a privileged person, and the greatest of those privileges is your personal relationship with Christ Himself. Continue to draw near to Him today through prayer and worship.

❖❖❖

Suggestions for Prayer: Tell Jesus how much you love Him and how you want your relationship with Him to be all it should be.

For Further Study: Read Ephesians 2:1-22. ❖ How did Paul describe our spiritual condition before salvation? ❖ How are sinners reconciled to God? ❖ What analogy did Paul use to describe our relationship as Christians to Jesus Christ?

"... coming to [Christ] as to a living stone" (1 Peter 2:4).

❖❖❖

Jesus is the only source of eternal life and the foundation upon which the church is built.

Peter's description of Christ as "a living stone" is paradoxical because stones aren't alive. In fact, we sometimes speak of something being "stone dead." Yet Peter's symbolism is profound because it beautifully incorporates three realities about Christ.

First, Jesus is the long-awaited Jewish Messiah. The Old Testament referred to the Messiah as a "stone," and Peter incorporated those texts into His description of Jesus in 1 Peter 2:6-8: "Behold I lay in Zion a choice stone, a precious corner stone, and he who believes in Him shall not be disappointed" (Isa. 28:16); "The stone which the builders rejected, this became the very corner stone" (Ps. 118:22); and "a stone of stumbling and a rock of offense" (Isa. 8:14). The parallel is obvious and would be especially meaningful to Peter's Jewish readers. The expectations of pious Jews throughout history were realized in Christ. God had kept His promise to send the Messiah!

Second, Jesus is a "stone" in that He is the focal point of His spiritual house, the church. The Greek word translated "stone" in verse 4 sometimes referred to the stones used in building projects. They were cut and chiseled to fit perfectly into a specific location and were practically immovable. Not only is Jesus a stone; He is the cornerstone, which is the most important stone in the entire building. From Him the church draws its spiritual symmetry.

Finally, Jesus is "living." That's an appropriate description because everything Peter said in this epistle is based on the fact that Jesus is alive. That's the believer's hope and the basis for every spiritual privilege you have. You "have been born again to a *living* hope through the resurrection of Jesus Christ from the dead" (1 Peter 1:3, emphasis added).

Interestingly, the literal rendering of 1 Peter 2:4 is, "Coming to Him as to living stone." Christ is a unique stone—the stone that possesses life. All who come to Him receive eternal life (cf. 1 John 5:11).

❖❖❖

Suggestions for Prayer: Praise the Lord for His unchangeable character and irrevocable promises.

For Further Study: Read Acts 2:22-47. ❖ What was the central point in Peter's sermon? ❖ How did the people respond to his preaching? ❖ How many people were baptized? ❖ What were some of the activities of the early church?

". . . coming to [Christ] as to a living stone, rejected by men, but choice and precious in the sight of God" (1 Peter 2:4).

❖❖❖

God's view of Christ is the only accurate standard by which to measure Christ's worth.

I once read about a conversation in the Louvre Museum in Paris. One of the curators of the museum, a man with great appreciation for art, overheard two men discussing a masterpiece. One man said to the other, "I don't think much of that painting." The curator, feeling obliged to reply to the man's statement, said to him, "Dear sir, if I may interrupt, that painting is not on trial; you are. The quality of that painting has already been established. Your disapproval simply demonstrates the frailty of your measuring capability."

Similarly, Jesus is not on trial before men; men are on trial before Him. He has already been approved by the Father. Those who arrogantly dismiss Him as unworthy of their devotion simply demonstrate their inability to recognize the most precious treasure of all.

Peter said, "This is contained in Scripture: 'Behold I lay in Zion a choice stone, a precious corner stone, and he who believes in Him shall not be disappointed.' This precious value, then, is for you who believe. But for those who disbelieve, 'The stone which the builders rejected, this became the very corner stone,' and, 'a stone of stumbling and a rock of offense'" (1 Peter 2:6-8). By God's standards, Jesus is the perfect cornerstone. But the leaders of Israel had faulty standards of measurement. They inspected Him closely but rejected Him because He didn't fit their concept of a Savior. Sadly, millions of men and women throughout history have followed their lead.

As you tell others about Christ, many will evaluate Him by a wrong standard and will reject Him. Others will evaluate Him according to God's standard and will find Him precious beyond measure. In either case, be a faithful witness, knowing that someday His full value will be proclaimed by all (Phil. 2:10-11).

❖❖❖

Suggestions for Prayer: Make a list of Christ's attributes that are especially meaningful to you. Use each attribute as a focal point of prayer and worship.

For Further Study: Read Acts 4:1-13, noting how Peter applied the principles found in 1 Peter 2:4-8 to the Jewish leaders.

"You also, as living stones, are being built up as a spiritual house" (1 Peter 2:5).

✧✧✧

Christ is your life, and you are an integral part of what He is accomplishing in the world.

The Jewish culture of Peter's time centered on the Temple in Jerusalem. Apparently drawing from that picture, Peter used vivid language to teach that God no longer dwells in an earthly, material, temporal house but in a spiritual house. Christ is the cornerstone, and the spiritual house He is building is comprised of individual believers.

That analogy introduces us to the first spiritual privilege Christians enjoy: union with Christ Himself. That makes Christianity utterly unique among religions. Buddhists are not said to be in Buddha; Muslims are not in Muhammad, or even in Allah; a Confucian is not in Confucius. Only Christians are united with and receive their spiritual life from the object of their worship.

When you came to Christ, the living stone, you became a living stone yourself. You possess His resurrection life and draw from His spiritual resources. That's what Peter meant when he said that God "has granted to us His precious and magnificent promises, in order that by them you might become partakers of the divine nature" (2 Peter 1:4).

Ephesians 2:19-22 adds, "You are no longer strangers and aliens, but you are fellow citizens with the saints, and are of God's household, having been built upon the foundation of the apostles and prophets, Christ Jesus Himself being the cornerstone, in whom the whole building, being fitted together is growing into a holy temple in the Lord; in whom you also are being built together into a dwelling of God in the Spirit." Christ is the cornerstone of the church, built on the foundation of Biblical truth, which is the divine revelation given through the apostles and prophets. Rejoice in the privilege of being united with Christ and learning from His Word!

✧✧✧

Suggestions for Prayer: Thank God for selecting you as one of His spiritual stones. Seek His wisdom and grace in living each day to His glory.

For Further Study: Read Acts 17:24, 1 Timothy 3:15, and Hebrews 3:6, noting what they teach about God's spiritual house.

"You . . . are being built up as a spiritual house for a holy priest-hood, to offer up spiritual sacrifices acceptable to God through Jesus Christ" (1 Peter 2:5).

❖❖❖

Christ's death provided access to the Father for all believers.

Throughout history, false gods have been portrayed as remote, indifferent, and apathetic to human needs and generally unapproachable by the common masses. Out of fear a man might attempt to appease his idols, but he has no desire or capacity to draw near to them.

Even those in Old Testament times who worshiped the true God had limited access to Him. The average Jewish person could commune with God through prayer but was forbidden to approach Him physically. Only the high priest was allowed to enter into God's presence in the Holy of Holies—but only once a year, on the Day of Atonement. Even then he had to go through a ceremonial washing and offer a sacrifice for his own sin. If he failed to prepare himself properly, he could forfeit his life.

Anyone daring to usurp the office of a priest was also in danger of severe punishment by God. King Azariah (also called Uzziah) was afflicted with leprosy, King Saul's lineage was cursed, and Korah and his rebellious followers were destroyed when the ground opened and swallowed them.

However, we as Christians enjoy unlimited access to the Father through Jesus Christ. Hebrews 10:19-22 says, "Since therefore, brethren, we have confidence to enter the holy place by the blood of Jesus, by a new and living way which He inaugurated for us through the veil, that is, His flesh, and since we have a great priest over the house of God, let us draw near with a sincere heart in full assurance of faith."

As a member of God's royal priesthood, you can approach Him with confidence, knowing He loves and welcomes you into His presence as much as He welcomes His own Son. Take full advantage of that access by communing with Him in prayer and offering each day as a spiritual sacrifice to Him.

❖❖❖

Suggestions for Prayer: Praise Jesus for shedding His precious blood so you can have access to the Father. ❖ Praise the Father for being a personal and approachable God.

For Further Study: Read Exodus 19. ❖ What did God tell Moses? ❖ For what were the people to prepare themselves? ❖ Was God approachable to the people?

"You . . . are being built up as a spiritual house for a holy priest-hood, to offer up spiritual sacrifices acceptable to God through Jesus Christ" (1 Peter 2:5).

❖❖❖

***Christians share common spiritual characteristics
with Old Testament priests.***

Peter identified believers as holy priests, but many Christians don't really know what that means because priests aren't part of our culture as a whole.

The primary purpose of an Old Testament priest was to offer acceptable sacrifices to God on behalf of the people. Priests were chosen by God Himself, specially cleansed through prescribed ceremonies, clothed in a pre-scribed manner, and anointed with oil as symbolic of God's Spirit upon them. They were expected to obey God, love His Word, and walk with Him.

Faithful priests had a positive impact on believers and unbelievers alike. Malachi 2:6 says they "turned many back from iniquity." Verse 7 adds that "the lips of a priest should preserve knowledge, and men should seek instruc-tion from his mouth; for he is the messenger of the Lord of hosts."

Those qualifications are paralleled in Christians, whom God regards as the only true priests. You were chosen by Him from before the foundation of the world and were cleansed by the washing of regeneration and renewing by the Holy Spirit. You are clothed with the righteousness of Christ and anointed by the Holy Spirit. Your purpose is "to offer up spiritual sacrifices acceptable to God through Jesus Christ" (1 Peter 2:5).

Scripture tells you therefore to present your body as "a living and holy sac-rifice, acceptable to God, which is your spiritual service of worship" (Rom. 12:1). Obedience, love for the Word, and communion with God should char-acterize your life; saints and sinners alike should see Christ in you and be affected by what they see.

The priesthood of believers is a high and holy calling to which no one is suited apart from God's grace and power. But be assured that He who called you will accomplish His good pleasure in you. Be committed to that goal each day as you lean on His resources and trust in His sufficiency.

❖❖❖

Suggestions for Prayer: Thank God for the priesthood He has entrusted to you. Ask Him to use you today to influence others in godly ways.

For Further Study: Read Leviticus 8 and 9, which tell of the consecration and inauguration of the Aaronic priesthood.

"You . . . are being built up as a spiritual house for a holy priest-hood, to offer up spiritual sacrifices acceptable to God through Jesus Christ" (1 Peter 2:5).

❖❖❖

Spiritual sacrifices are acts of praise and worship offered to God through Jesus Christ.

The primary mission of a Hebrew priest was to offer acceptable sacrifices to God. That's why God gave detailed instructions regarding the kinds of sacrifices He required. For example, if a lamb was offered, it had to be per-fect—without deformity or blemish. Then it had to be sacrificed in a pre-scribed manner. It was a serious offense to offer sacrifices in an unacceptable manner—a mistake that cost Aaron's sons their lives (Lev. 10:1-2).

The Old Testament sacrificial system pictured the supreme sacrifice of Christ on the cross. When He died, the veil that separated the Holy of Holies from the rest of the Temple split in two, signifying personal access to God through Christ. From that moment on, the Old Testament sacrifices ceased to have meaning. As the writer of Hebrews said, "We have been sanctified through the offering of the body of Jesus Christ once for all. And every priest stands daily ministering and offering time after time the same sacrifices, which can never take away sins; but He, having offered one sacrifice for sins for all time, sat down at the right hand of God. . . . For by one offering He has perfected for all time those who are sanctified" (Heb. 10:10-14).

Christ's sacrifice was complete. Nothing further is needed for salvation. The spiritual sacrifices that believers are to offer aren't sacrifices for sin, but are rather acts of praise and worship that flow from a redeemed life. They're the fruit of salvation and are acceptable to God because they're offered through His Son.

Since Jesus is the only mediator between God and man, your access to God is through Him alone. Anything that pleases Him is acceptable to the Father. Seeking His will, His plans, and His Kingdom all are aspects of offering up acceptable spiritual sacrifices. In effect, your entire life is to be one continu-ous sacrifice of love and praise to God. May it be so!

❖❖❖

Suggestions for Prayer: When you pray, be sure everything you say and every request you make is consistent with Christ's will.

For Further Study: Read Hebrews 10:1-18, noting how Christ's sacrifice dif-fered from Old Testament sacrifices.

". . . to offer up spiritual sacrifices acceptable to God through Jesus Christ" (1 Peter 2:5).

✧✧✧

Every faculty you have is to be used for God's glory.

I n Romans 12:1 Paul pleads with believers to present their bodies to God as "a living and holy sacrifice," which is an appropriate and acceptable act of worship. But as someone has rightly said, the problem with living sacrifices is that they tend to crawl off the altar. That's because sacrificial living demands spiritual discipline and constant dependence on the Holy Spirit. We as Christians aren't always willing to do that.

According to Paul, the motivation and ability for self-sacrifice are found in the mercies we've already experienced in Christ. In Romans 1–11 he mentions several of these, including love, grace, peace, faith, comfort, power, hope, patience, kindness, glory, honor, righteousness, forgiveness, reconciliation, justification, security, eternal life, freedom, resurrection, sonship, intercession, and the Holy Spirit. Because you've received all that, you should gladly surrender every faculty you have for holy purposes.

"Body" in Romans 12:1 also includes your mind, for verse 2 says, "Do not be conformed to this world, but be transformed by the renewing of your mind, that you may prove what the will of God is, that which is good and acceptable and perfect." A transformed mind is the key to transformed behavior.

Prior to your salvation, you had neither the desire nor the ability to make such a sacrifice. But because you are a new creation in Christ, you are not to "go on presenting the members of your body to sin as instruments of unrighteousness; but . . . as instruments of righteousness to God" (Rom. 6:13). One practical implication of this is to abstain from sexual immorality. "Know how to possess [your] own body in sanctification and honor" (1 Thess. 4:3-4).

You are a holy priest, and your priestly work begins with presenting yourself as a living and holy sacrifice. Is that your desire? Are you a faithful priest?

✧✧✧

Suggestions for Prayer: Thank God for His bountiful mercies toward you. ✧ Commit this day to Him, asking for the grace to live a holy life.

For Further Study: Read Romans 6. ✧ What choices do you have as a believer that you didn't have as an unbeliever? ✧ What is the benefit of being God's slave?

". . . to offer up spiritual sacrifices acceptable to God through Jesus Christ" (1 Peter 2:5).

❖❖❖

Praise consists of reciting God's attributes and mighty works.

"Praise the Lord" is a common expression today. Some see it as a catchy slogan, others commercialize it, still others see it as nothing more than the letters "PTL." But despite such attempts to trivialize it, praising the Lord remains the believer's expression of love and gratitude to a God who has been abundantly gracious to him. That was the cry of David's heart when he said, "I will bless the Lord at all times; His praise shall continually be in my mouth. My soul shall make its boast in the Lord; the humble shall hear it and rejoice. O magnify the Lord with me, and let us exalt His name together" (Ps. 34:1-3). That will be the song of believers for time and eternity!

God desires and deserves your praise. That's why Hebrews 13:15 says, "Through [Christ] . . . let us continually offer up a sacrifice of praise to God, that is, the fruit of lips that give thanks to His name." But what is praise? Is it merely saying "praise the Lord" over and over again, or is there more to it?

Two aspects of praise are obvious in Scripture. First is reciting God's attributes. That was the typical means of praise in the Old Testament. For example, Psalm 104 says, "Bless the Lord, O my soul! O Lord my God, Thou art very great; Thou art clothed with splendor and majesty, covering Thyself with light as with a cloak" (vv. 1-2).

The second aspect of praise is reciting God's works. Psalm 107:21-22 says, "Let them give thanks to the Lord for His lovingkindness, and for His wonders to the sons of men! Let them also offer sacrifices of thanksgiving, and tell of His works with joyful singing."

Praise involves reciting God's attributes from a heart of love, giving Him honor and reverence for who He is. It also involves reciting what He has done on behalf of His people. Your praise should follow the same pattern, so it will be an acceptable spiritual sacrifice to your loving God.

❖❖❖

Suggestions for Prayer: Read Psalm 103 as a prayer of praise to God.

For Further Study: Scripture mentions other spiritual sacrifices that believers should offer. Read Romans 15:16, Ephesians 5:2, Philippians 4:10-18, Hebrews 13:16, and Revelation 8:3, noting what those sacrifices are.

"This is contained in Scripture: 'Behold I lay in Zion a choice stone, a precious corner stone, and he who believes in Him shall not be disappointed'" (1 Peter 2:6).

❖❖❖

Christ is the fulfillment of all Messianic promises, and in Him you are eternally secure.

First Peter 2:6 is a paraphrase of Isaiah 28:16, which says, "Thus says the Lord God, 'Behold, I am laying in Zion a stone, a tested stone, a costly cornerstone for the foundation, firmly placed. He who believes in it will not be disturbed.'" Isaiah was speaking of the Messiah—the coming Christ of God. Peter, writing under the inspiration of the Holy Spirit, applied Isaiah's prophecy to Jesus.

In Isaiah's prophecy, "Zion" refers to Jerusalem, which stands atop Mount Zion. Mount Zion is sometimes used figuratively in Scripture to refer to the New Covenant of grace, whereas Mount Sinai represents the Old Covenant of law. Isaiah was saying that God would establish the Messiah as the cornerstone of His New Covenant Temple, the church.

The analogy of believers as stones and Christ as the cornerstone would have great meaning for the Jewish people. When the Temple in Jerusalem was built, the stones used in its construction were selected, cut, and shaped in the stone quarry according to precise plans (1 Kings 6:7). Only then were they taken to the building site and set into place. The most important stone was the cornerstone, to which the various angles of the building had to conform.

God used a similar process to build His New Covenant Temple. Its stones (individual believers) are elect and shaped by the Holy Spirit to fit into God's master plan for the church. Jesus Himself is the precious cornerstone, specially chosen and prepared by the Father to be the standard to which all others conform. He is the fulfillment of all Messianic promises and the One in whom you can trust without fear of disappointment. That means you are secure in Him!

Live today in the confidence that Christ cannot fail. He will always accomplish His purposes.

❖❖❖

Suggestions for Prayer: Praise God for keeping His promises and for giving you security in Christ.

For Further Study: Read Galatians 4:21-31. ❖ Who was the bondwoman, and what did she represent? ❖ To whom did Paul liken believers?

"This precious value, then, is for you who believe" (1 Peter 2:7).

❖❖❖

Love for Christ is the primary characteristic of a true believer.

First Peter 2:7 speaks of the believer's affection for Christ as contrasted to an unbeliever's rejection of Him. The first part of that verse could be translated, "To you who believe, He is precious." "Precious" means "valuable," "costly," "without equal," or "irreplaceable." Christ is all that, but only believers recognize His supreme value and regard Him with affection.

Affection for Christ is the bottom-line characteristic of true believers. Believing in Him and loving Him are inseparable. In John 16:27 Jesus says, "The Father Himself loves you, because you have loved Me, and have believed." In Matthew 10:37 He says, "He who loves father or mother more than Me is not worthy of Me; and he who loves son or daughter more than Me is not worthy of Me." Believers have a compelling and surpassing love for Christ.

To His antagonists Jesus declared, "If God were your Father, you would love Me" (John 8:42). Anyone who truly loves God will love Christ. Those antagonists claimed to be children of God, but their deception was revealed when they tried to kill Jesus for preaching God's truth. They were in fact children of the Devil (v. 44).

In John 14 Jesus adds, "If you love Me, you will keep My commandments. . . . He who has My commandments, and keeps them, he it is who loves Me; and he who loves Me shall be loved by My Father, and I will love him. . . . If anyone loves Me, he will keep My word; and My Father will love him, and We will come to him, and make Our abode with him. He who does not love Me does not keep My words" (vv. 15, 21, 23-24).

Many people are confused about what it means to be a Christian. But you have the privilege of clarifying the issue as you esteem Christ highly, love Him deeply, and demonstrate your love by obeying His Word. May God bless you richly as you pursue that goal today.

❖❖❖

Suggestions for Prayer: Ask God to give you opportunities to demonstrate Christ's love in specific ways to those around you.

For Further Study: Read 1 John 4:7–5:3. ❖ How did John characterize God? ❖ What effect should your love for God have on your relationships with others? ❖ How did John define love?

"For those who disbelieve, 'the stone which the builders rejected, this became the very corner stone,' and, 'a stone of stumbling and a rock of offense'; for they stumble because they are disobedient to the word, and to this doom they were also appointed" (1 Peter 2:7-8).

❖❖❖

Rejecting Christ leads to spiritual damnation.

Israel was a unique nation, chosen by God to be the guardian of His Word and the proclaimer of His Kingdom. The Old Testament records His miraculous and providential care for her throughout the centuries, and the prophets told of One who would come as her great Deliverer. Israel eagerly awaited the promised Messiah.

But the story has a surprise ending. In the person of Jesus Christ, the Messiah finally came and presented Himself to Israel. The religious leaders examined Him carefully, measuring Him in every way they could. But He didn't fit their blueprint. They expected a reigning, political Messiah who would instantly deliver them from Roman oppression. They felt no need for a spiritual deliverer, so they rejected Him and tossed Him aside like a worthless rock.

That rejected cornerstone is precious to believers but remains "a stone of stumbling and a rock of offense" to unbelievers. A "stone of stumbling" was a stone on which someone tripped while walking along the road. A "rock of offense" was a rock large enough to crush a person. The point is, rejecting Christ brings spiritual devastation of enormous proportions.

All who reject Christ do so because they are disobedient to the Word. Rebellion against the written Word inevitably leads to rejection of the living Word. Of such people Peter said, "To this doom they were also appointed" (v. 8). They weren't appointed to reject Christ but to receive the judgment that their rejection demands. That's a frightening reality that should motivate you to take every opportunity to evangelize the lost.

❖❖❖

Suggestions for Prayer: If you have family or friends who are rejecting Christ, pray for them often, asking God to grant them saving faith.

For Further Study: Read Romans 9:30–10:17, noting Israel's false standard of righteousness and Paul's prayer for her salvation.

"You are a chosen race" (1 Peter 2:9).

❖❖❖

Election is the spiritual privilege from which all others flow.

Unlike those who are destined to destruction because of their rejection of Christ (1 Peter 2:8), Christians are an elect race of people, bound together by God's redeeming grace. That's cause for great celebration!

First Peter 2:9 is an allusion to Deuteronomy 7:6-9, which says, "You are a holy people to the Lord your God; the Lord your God has chosen you to be a people for His own possession out of all the peoples who are on the face of the earth. The Lord did not set His love on you nor choose you because you were more in number than any of the peoples, for you were the fewest of all peoples, but because the Lord loved you and kept the oath which He swore to your forefathers, the Lord brought you out by a mighty hand, and redeemed you from the house of slavery, from the hand of Pharaoh king of Egypt. Know therefore that the Lord your God, He is God."

Like Israel, the church is the redeemed community of God, "chosen according to the foreknowledge of God the Father, by the sanctifying work of the Spirit" (1 Peter 1:1-2). Before the foundation of the world, God placed His love on you, then brought you into His Kingdom by granting you saving grace. That's the doctrine of election.

Many people misunderstand election, but it's a wonderful doctrine that brings marvelous benefits. It exalts God by demonstrating His love and grace toward miserable sinners. It eliminates pride by affirming that you are totally dependent on God's grace. It should promote such gratitude in your heart that you long to live in holiness and serve Him at any price. It should also give you joy and strength, knowing that God will never let you go and His purposes will be accomplished in you. You can face any challenge with utmost confidence in His provisions.

Rejoice in your election. Worship God, and yield to His Spirit's leading, so His choice of you will be evident to all who know you.

❖❖❖

Suggestions for Prayer: What has the spiritual privilege of being chosen by God meant in your life? Express your answer to God in prayer, thanking Him for His wondrous grace.

For Further Study: Read Romans 5. What benefits of election does Paul mention?

"You are . . . a royal priesthood" (1 Peter 2:9).

❖❖❖

Christians serve the King and will someday reign with Him in His Kingdom.

In Exodus 19:5-6 God says to Israel, "If you will indeed obey My voice and keep My covenant, then you shall be My own possession among all the peoples . . . and you shall be to Me a kingdom of priests and a holy nation." They were to be both priests and royalty, but they violated the covenant and forfeited those privileges. Now, according to Peter, Christians are the royal priesthood of God.

The Greek word translated "royal" in 1 Peter 2:9 was used of a royal palace, sovereignty, crown, or monarchy. In this context it refers to royalty in general. We speak of the royal house of England or France, meaning not a building but a sphere of dominion. So it is with God's "spiritual house" (v. 5). Believers serve the King and will also reign with Him in His sphere of dominion.

That is affirmed elsewhere in Scripture. In the book of Revelation we read, "Thou hast made them to be a kingdom and priests to our God; and they will reign upon the earth" (Rev. 5:10); and, "Blessed and holy is the one who has a part in the first resurrection; over these the second death has no power, but they will be priests of God and of Christ and will reign with Him" (Rev. 20:6).

Your royal position has some practical implications for the way you live each day. For example, when dealing with the problem of litigation among Christians, Paul said: "Does any one of you, when he has a case against his neighbor, dare to go to law before the unrighteous, and not before the saints? Or do you not know that the saints will judge the world? And if the world is judged by you, are you not competent to constitute the smallest law courts? Do you not know that we shall judge angels? How much more, matters of this life?" (1 Cor. 6:1-3).

Never forget who you are in Christ, and don't let sin or the world distract you from your priestly role.

❖❖❖

Suggestions for Prayer: Memorize 1 Timothy 4:12. Ask God to make you a better example of one who represents His royal priesthood.

For Further Study: Read Genesis 14:18-20 and Hebrews 7:1-17. Who was Melchizedek, and what was unique about his priesthood?

"You are . . . a holy nation" (1 Peter 2:9).

✧✧✧

Holiness involves the decreasing frequency of sin and
the increasing frequency of righteousness.

C hristians are a holy nation—a people set apart from sin and Hell to an intimate relationship with God. Originally Israel was God's holy nation, but by unbelief she forfeited that privilege. Now the church, which consists of both Jews and Gentiles, is His unique people and will remain so until the nation of Israel repents and receives her Messiah at His return (Zech. 12:10).

Biblical holiness (sanctification) is often misunderstood, but it needn't be. When the Holy Spirit delivered you from the domain of darkness and transferred you into the Kingdom of Christ, you became His special possession. That doesn't mean you're sinlessly perfect, but it does mean you're no longer a slave to sin, the Devil, and death. That's *positional* sanctification. *Practical* sanctification is the decreasing frequency of sin and the increasing frequency of righteousness as you progress in your Christian walk.

Sanctification should not be confused with false standards of holiness, adopted by those who, like the Pharisees, attempt to be holy through external means, or who, like the Stoics, have a passionless devotion to duty, or who, like monks, isolate themselves from the world, or who, like quasi-Christian psychologists, replace sanctification with introspection, self-analysis, and improvement of one's self-image.

True holiness begins with a love for Christ Himself. That's what compels you toward greater sanctification.

Peter said that you were "chosen according to the foreknowledge of God the Father, by the sanctifying work of the Spirit, that you may obey Jesus Christ" (1 Peter 1:1-2). Christ Himself became to you "wisdom from God, and righteousness and sanctification, and redemption" (1 Cor. 1:30). In Him you were saved, which is the beginning of sanctification, and in Him you have every resource necessary for progressing in holiness.

✧✧✧

Suggestions for Prayer: Thank God for your positional holiness in Christ, for by it you are perfect in His sight. ✧ Thank Him for the Spirit's power in your life, which enables you to live in a manner pleasing to Him.

For Further Study: What do the following passages say about sanctification? Acts 15:7-9; 1 Thessalonians 4:3; Hebrews 10:14; 1 Peter 1:15-16.

"You are . . . a people for God's own possession" (1 Peter 2:9).

✧✧✧

Since God paid the price to redeem you, you belong to Him.

When Jesus said, "I am the good shepherd; and I know My own, and My own know Me" (John 10:14), He stated a truth that has been especially dear to me since the early years of my theological education. One of the pleasant memories from my seminary days is sitting in chapel and singing the hymn by the nineteenth-century lyricist Wade Robinson—"I Am His and He Is Mine." I may never fully comprehend the depths of what it means to belong to Christ, but I will forever glory in it.

The Greek word translated "possession" in 1 Peter 2:9 means "to purchase" or "to acquire for a price." Paul used it in Ephesians 1:14 to speak of "the redemption of God's own possession." Everyone is His by creation, but we as Christians are uniquely His because He paid the price to redeem us from the bondage of sin and death.

God's ownership of believers is emphasized throughout Scripture. Paul admonished elders to "shepherd the church of God which He purchased with His own blood" (Acts 20:28). He said to the Corinthians, "Do you not know that your body is a temple of the Holy Spirit who is in you, whom you have from God, and that you are not your own? For you have been bought with a price: therefore glorify God in your body" (1 Cor. 6:19-20). Titus 2:14 says that Christ "gave Himself for us, that He might redeem [or purchase] us from every lawless deed and purify for Himself a people for His own possession."

Isaiah 43:21 says, "The people whom I formed for Myself, will declare My praise." That was to be Israel's purpose, and it is yours as well. God chose you as His own possession and gave His Son to purchase your salvation. You are His eternally; so live accordingly, and rejoice in such a glorious privilege!

✧✧✧

Suggestions for Prayer: Make it your practice to praise God abundantly for the privilege of belonging to Him.

For Further Study: Read John 10:1-33. ✧ What characterizes the Good Shepherd? ✧ What did Jesus claim about His relationship with God the Father? ✧ How did the Jewish leaders react to His teaching?

". . . that you may proclaim the excellencies of Him who has called you out of darkness into His marvelous light" (1 Peter 2:9).

❖❖❖

**God has granted you the ability to understand
the truth and live accordingly.**

In the natural realm, darkness can be a debilitating and frightening thing. The story is told of a missionary who was on board ship one dark night when suddenly he was awakened by the frantic cry of "Man overboard!" Immediately he arose from his bunk, grabbed the portable lamp from its bracket, and held it at the window of his cabin.

He couldn't see anything, but the next morning he was told that the flash of his lamp through the porthole emitted just enough light to enable those on deck to see the missing man clinging to a rope. They rescued him seconds before his strength would have given out. The light had shone just in time to save the man's life.

In the spiritual realm, darkness is even more devastating because it represents sin with all its disastrous consequences. First John 1:5-6 says, "God is light, and in Him there is no darkness at all. If we say that we have fellowship with Him and yet walk in the darkness, we lie and do not practice the truth."

Unbelievers are characterized as children of darkness. They are enslaved to Satan, the prince of darkness, who blinds their minds so they don't see the light of Christ's glorious gospel (2 Cor. 4:4). They love darkness and reject light because they don't want their evil deeds to be exposed (John 3:19-20).

Christians, however, have been called "out of darkness into [God's] marvelous light" (1 Peter 2:9). That refers to God's taking the initiative to save us. As an unredeemed sinner, you could never have turned from darkness on your own because you had neither the ability nor the desire to do so. God had to grant you saving grace and the illumination of His Spirit so you could recognize truth and respond accordingly.

That blessed privilege is known only to Christians. What a joy it is to not only recognize God's truth but also to walk in it daily!

❖❖❖

Suggestions for Prayer: Thank God for illuminating your mind and enabling you to see spiritual truth. Pray diligently for others to be so illuminated.

For Further Study: Read 1 John 1:5—2:11. Contrast the children of darkness with the children of light.

"You once were not a people, but now you are the people of God;
you had not received mercy, but now you have received mercy"
(1 Peter 2:10).

✧✧✧

Because of God's compassion, He withholds the
just punishment of your sin.

Hosea had a unique role among the prophets. God used him and his adulterous wife, Gomer, as living illustrations of His love for unfaithful Israel. When Gomer gave birth to a daughter, the Lord told Hosea to name her Lo-ruhamah, which means "No mercy," because His mercy for Israel would soon come to an end. When Gomer later gave birth to a son, the Lord said to call him Lo-ammi, which means "Not mine," for He no longer considered Israel His people. Yet He offered this hope, saying, "It will come about that, in the place where it is said to them, 'You are not My people,' it will be said to them, 'You are the sons of the living God'" (Hos. 1:10).

In our Scripture for today, Peter applied that Old Testament text to the New Testament church, just as Paul did in Romans 9:25-26: "'I will call those who were not My people, "My people," and her who was not beloved, "Beloved." And it shall be that in the place where it was said to them, "You are not My people," there they shall be called sons of the living God.'" God rejected unbelieving Israel but extended His compassion to anyone willing to trust in Christ. It is particularly true that Gentiles in the church were once not the people of God but now have received mercy and are God's beloved children.

God's mercy includes His general providential care for all mankind, but Hosea, Peter, and Paul were speaking of His special compassion—first in salvation, then in daily blessings—for those who belong to Him. By it He withholds the punishment we deserve for our sins and grants us His lovingkindness instead.

As you reflect on God's mercy in your own life, let Psalm 136:1 be the song of your heart: "O give thanks unto the Lord; for he is good: for his mercy endureth forever" (KJV).

✧✧✧

Suggestions for Prayer: Memorize Psalm 59:16-17. Recite it often in praise to the Lord.

For Further Study: What do the following verses teach about God's mercy? Psalm 103:11; 2 Corinthians 1:3; Titus 3:5.

"... that you may proclaim the excellencies of Him who has called you out of darkness into His marvelous light" (1 Peter 2:9).

✧✧✧

You are an ambassador of the living God.

The privilege of proclaiming the excellencies of God takes us back to 1 Peter 2:9, but we consider it here because it summarizes the purpose of all our Christian privileges.

The Greek word translated "proclaim" is an unusual word used only here in the New Testament. It means "to advertise" or "to publish" and refers to making something known that would otherwise be unknown. "Excellencies" speak of powerful and heroic deeds. You are an ambassador of Christ, having the great privilege of proclaiming what God has done for His people.

That was an intrinsic part of Hebrew worship. For example, Psalm 103 says, "Bless the Lord, O my soul, and forget none of His benefits; who pardons all your iniquities; who heals all your diseases; who redeems your life from the pit; who crowns you with lovingkindness and compassion; who satisfies your years with good things, so that your youth is renewed like the eagle. The Lord performs righteous deeds, and judgments for all who are oppressed. He made known His ways to Moses, His acts to the sons of Israel. The Lord is compassionate and gracious, slow to anger and abounding in lovingkindness" (vv. 2-8).

It would be an honor to be an ambassador of the United States, representing this country's power and capabilities to other countries. But you have an even greater honor—to represent the power and capabilities of the living God. When you have an opportunity to speak for Him, you can rightly say, "I have the privilege of announcing the mighty and heroic deeds of the living God, who has called me into His service."

Because you are in Christ, you have glorious privileges that include union with God, access to the Father, spiritual sacrifices, security, affection, dominion, possession, holiness, illumination, and compassion. What greater honor can there be than to proclaim the excellencies of the One who has granted you such marvelous privileges?

✧✧✧

Suggestions for Prayer: Thank God for calling you to be His ambassador. ✧ Ask Him for the courage and integrity to represent Him well always.

For Further Study: Read Psalm 147, noting all the mighty deeds of God proclaimed there.

"Blessed be the God and Father of our Lord Jesus Christ, who according to His great mercy has caused us to be born again to a living hope through the resurrection of Jesus Christ from the dead, to obtain an inheritance which is imperishable and undefiled and will not fade away, reserved in heaven for you" (1 Peter 1:3-4).

❖❖❖

Victory over present circumstances comes when you focus on your eternal inheritance and praise God for it.

One amazing privilege you have as a Christian is to be the beneficiary of a rich and exciting spiritual inheritance. Jesus gave us a glimpse of its magnitude when He said, "The King will say to those on His right, 'Come, you who are blessed of My Father, inherit the kingdom prepared for you from the foundation of the world'" (Matt. 25:34). The Kingdom itself is part of your inheritance!

This inheritance is shared by every child of God. Hebrews 9:15 says that Christ "is the mediator of a new covenant, in order that . . . those who have been called may receive the promise of the eternal inheritance." Jesus commissioned Paul to preach to the Gentiles "so that they may turn from darkness to light and from the dominion of Satan to God, in order that they may receive forgiveness of sins and an inheritance among those who have been sanctified by faith in [Him]" (Acts 26:18).

No one can fully understand "all that God has prepared for those who love Him" (1 Cor. 2:9). Consequently, at times you might forget you're a child of the King and begin to act like this world is all you have to live for. God may even have to discipline you from time to time to correct your behavior. But someday you will be all God created you to be and will know the full glory of your inheritance. In the meantime, be diligent to "set your mind on the things above, not on the things that are on earth" (Col. 3:2). Focus on your inheritance, and praise God for it. That will help you see beyond your present circumstances to the glory that awaits you when Jesus calls you home.

❖❖❖

Suggestions for Prayer: Thank God for the rich inheritance that is yours in Christ.

For Further Study: Read 1 Peter 1. ❖ What spiritual privileges did Peter mention? ❖ What commands did he give? ❖ Is there any connection between those privileges and commands? Explain.

July 22 PRAISING GOD FOR YOUR ETERNAL INHERITANCE

"Blessed be the God and Father of our Lord Jesus Christ" (1 Peter 1:3).

❖❖❖

God has blessed you richly and is worthy of your praise.

The source of your eternal inheritance is God, whom Peter described in several ways. First, He is our "blessed" God (1 Peter 1:3). The Greek word translated "blessed" in that verse speaks of that which is worthy of blessing, adoration, praise, or worship. Peter's praise for God is an example for us to follow. Our God is especially worthy of our praise in light of the glorious inheritance He has granted us in His Son (v. 4).

"Father" to the Jewish people of Peter's day was a new designation for God. The most common Jewish blessings emphasized God as Creator of all things and Redeemer or Deliverer of His people from Egypt, but not as Father (e.g., Gen. 14:20; 24:27; Ex. 18:10). Yet now through Christ we "have received a spirit of adoption as sons by which we cry out, 'Abba! [Daddy!] Father!'" (Rom. 8:15).

As wonderful a reality as the Fatherhood of God is, Peter's reference was not primarily to God as *our* Father but as Christ's Father. Their unique relationship affirms Christ's deity (cf. John 10:30-33). God is the Father of believers in a secondary sense because He has redeemed us through Christ and has adopted us into His family (Gal. 4:4-6).

In referring to Christ as "our Lord Jesus Christ" (1 Peter 1:3), Peter amplifies His redemptive work. "Lord" speaks of His sovereign rulership; "Jesus" is His name as God in human flesh; and "Christ" identifies Him as the Messiah, the anointed King.

Peter's final description of Christ is seen in the pronoun "our." He is *"our* Lord Jesus Christ," a personal Lord and Savior—not some distant, impersonal deity. He created and redeemed you because He loves you and wants to be intimately involved in every aspect of your life.

What a glorious God we serve! Worship Him today as He deserves to be worshiped.

❖❖❖

Suggestions for Prayer: Bless God, who is your Father, your Redeemer, your constant companion, and the source of your eternal inheritance.

For Further Study: Read John 4:1-26. What did Jesus say about the Fatherhood of God?

". . . according to His great mercy" (1 Peter 1:3).

❖❖❖

**Every dimension of life, whether physical or spiritual,
is a testimony to God's mercy.**

When God saved you and granted you an eternal inheritance, it wasn't because you were special or more deserving of His love and grace than others. It was because He sovereignly chose to love you and to extend His great mercy to you. That's why Paul said, "God, being rich in mercy, because of His great love with which He loved us, even when we were dead in our transgressions, made us alive together with Christ (by grace you have been saved)" (Eph. 2:4-5). He "saved us, not on the basis of deeds which we have done in righteousness, but according to His mercy" (Titus 3:5).

Because of His great mercy, God addresses the pitiful condition of mankind. Unregenerate people are totally depraved, dead in trespasses, enslaved to sin, cursed to eternal damnation, unable to help themselves, and in desperate need of someone to show them mercy and compassion. That's the good news of the gospel: God loves sinners and extends mercy to anyone willing to trust in Him.

Mercy tempers God's justice. The Puritan writer Thomas Watson said, "Mercy sweetens all God's other attributes. . . . When the water was bitter, and Israel could not drink, Moses cast a tree into the waters, and then they were made sweet. How bitter and dreadful were the other attributes of God, did not mercy sweeten them! Mercy sets God's power [at] work to help us; it makes his justice become our friend; it shall avenge our quarrels" (*A Body of Divinity* [Edinburgh: The Banner of Truth Trust, 1978], p. 94).

The very fact that God permits us to live at all speaks of His mercy. Lamentations 3:22-23 says, "It is [because] of the Lord's mercies that we are not consumed, because his compassions fail not. They are new every morning: great is thy faithfulness" (KJV).

No matter what your situation is, God's mercy is more than sufficient for you. It "is great above the heavens" (Ps. 108:4, KJV). So be encouraged, and look to Him always.

❖❖❖

Suggestions for Prayer: Praise God for His great mercy, for by it you have received eternal life and an eternal inheritance.

For Further Study: Read Mark 10:46-52. How did Jesus' healing ministry demonstrate God's mercy?

"[God] caused us to be born again to a living hope through the resurrection of Jesus Christ from the dead" (1 Peter 1:3).

❖❖❖

Everyone receives an eternal inheritance—either Heaven or Hell.

We have seen several aspects of the believer's inheritance, and we will see more in future days. But realize that unbelievers also will receive an inheritance, for Jesus will say to them, "Depart from Me, accursed ones, into the eternal fire which has been prepared for the devil and his angels. . . . And these will go away into eternal punishment, but the righteous into eternal life" (Matt. 25:41, 46).

Only Christians have eternal life and a royal inheritance. When you received Jesus Christ as your Lord and Savior, you became a new creation in Christ, and your life began to center on Him rather than yourself. The Holy Spirit indwelt you and began to transform your attitudes and actions. That's the new birth! It's like starting all over again, only this time you're pursuing God's glory rather than worldly pleasures or goals.

Also, when you were saved you became an heir of God and a fellow-heir with Christ (Rom. 8:17). So the new birth was the means of your salvation and your eternal inheritance.

Having said that, I must admonish you, just as Paul admonished the Corinthians, to "test yourselves to see if you are in the faith; examine yourselves! Or do you not recognize this about yourselves, that Jesus Christ is in you—unless indeed you fail the test?" (2 Cor. 13:5). You will want to avoid ever being deluded about your relationship with Christ. When you trust in the living Lord, you have a living hope and a glorious eternal inheritance. Anything less results in an inheritance of eternal damnation.

Jesus said, "I am the resurrection, and the life; he who believes in Me shall live even if he dies" (John 11:25). Be sure your faith is firmly fixed on Him.

❖❖❖

Suggestions for Prayer: Pray for family and friends who don't know Christ. Ask the Lord to redeem them, so He will be glorified and they will become joint-heirs with Christ.

For Further Study: What do the following verses teach about the new birth? John 1:12-13; 3:3; 1 Peter 1:23.

> *". . . to obtain an inheritance which is imperishable and undefiled and will not fade away" (1 Peter 1:4).*

✧✧✧

**Unlike earthly treasures, your eternal inheritance
can never be taken away from you.**

Despite the benefits of bank accounts, stocks, bonds, and a myriad of other investment opportunities, every earthly inheritance eventually is lost. If someone doesn't steal it, or if it doesn't lose its value in a stock market crash or recession, death will separate it from you. It's inevitable! That's why Jesus said, "Do not lay up for yourselves treasures upon earth, where moth and rust destroy, and where thieves break in and steal. But lay up for yourselves treasures in heaven, where neither moth nor rust destroys, and where thieves do not break in or steal" (Matt. 6:19-20).

The influence of sin and corruption doesn't apply only to finances—it affects everything. Paul said, "The creation was subjected to futility . . . in hope that the creation itself also will be set free from its slavery to corruption into the freedom of the glory of the children of God. For we know that the whole creation groans and suffers the pains of childbirth together until now" (Rom. 8:20-22). Nothing on earth escapes sin's corruption.

But your eternal inheritance is not like earthly treasures. It is imperishable, undefiled, and unfading (1 Peter 1:4). "Imperishable" means it is incorruptible and unable to decay. The Greek word used describes a land that had never been ravaged or plundered by an invading army. The idea is that your spiritual inheritance is secure and can never be violated by an intruder—not even Satan himself. "Undefiled" speaks of something unpolluted by sin. "Will not fade away" suggests a supernatural beauty that time cannot impair. Peter used the same word in 1 Peter 5:4 to speak of the unfading crown of glory faithful church leaders will receive when Christ returns.

Your inheritance is unique among treasures. No one can steal it, and nothing can corrupt or diminish it in any way. It's yours to enjoy to its fullest throughout all eternity. Don't let the pursuit of perishable things distract you from the joy of eternal riches.

✧✧✧

Suggestions for Prayer: Ask the Lord to help you keep a proper perspective on what is of greatest value in His eyes.

For Further Study: Read Matthew 6:19-34. ✧ Why shouldn't you worry about the necessities of life? ✧ What priorities should you have?

". . . to obtain an inheritance which is . . . reserved in heaven for you, who are protected by the power of God through faith for a salvation ready to be revealed in the last time" (1 Peter 1:4-5).

❖❖❖

Your eternal inheritance is doubly secure:
it is reserved for you, and you are reserved for it.

When Peter wrote his first epistle, attitudes toward Christians in the Roman Empire were not at all favorable. Because they would not worship the emperor as a god or enter into other sinful pagan practices, Christians were looked upon with suspicion and disdain. In addition, Nero had blamed them for burning Rome (an act he himself perpetrated); so anger and hatred toward them was at its peak.

Peter wrote to encourage them—and all believers—to live out their faith amid persecution, just as Jesus had done when He suffered unjustly (cf. 1 Peter 2:21-23). He reminded them that despite the sufferings they might endure in this life, God will reward them with an inheritance that is eternally secure because it is reserved in Heaven for them.

"Reserved" in 1 Peter 1:4 indicates an inheritance that already exists, is presently protected, and will continually be protected. The place of its protection is Heaven, where "neither moth nor rust destroys, and where thieves do not break in or steal" (Matt. 6:20), and where "nothing unclean and no one who practices abomination and lying, shall ever come into it, but only those whose names are written in the Lamb's book of life" (Rev. 21:27). There is no safer place!

Not only is your inheritance protected for you, but also you are protected for it! That's what Peter meant when he said that it is "reserved in heaven for you, who are protected by the power of God through faith for a salvation ready to be revealed in the last time" (1 Peter 1:4-5). The omnipotent, sovereign power of God will continually protect you until His work is fully accomplished in your life. Then He will grant you glorification—the fullness of the salvation for which He redeemed you.

You needn't fear the loss of your inheritance. Instead, rejoice in the protection of our gracious God.

❖❖❖

Suggestions for Prayer: Thank God for His protection and for the assurance of your inheritance.

For Further Study: What do the following verses teach about the security of your salvation? Romans 8:31-39; Philippians 1:6; and Jude 24.

"In this you greatly rejoice" (1 Peter 1:6).

❖❖❖

Contemplating your eternal inheritance should give you joy that transcends any temporal circumstance.

Joy is a major theme in Scripture. The psalmist said, "Sing for joy in the Lord, O you righteous ones; praise is becoming to the upright" (Ps. 33:1); "My lips will shout for joy when I sing praises to Thee; and my soul, which Thou hast redeemed" (Ps. 71:23).

Even creation itself is said to rejoice in the Lord: "Thou dost make the dawn and the sunset shout for joy. . . . Let the heavens be glad, and let the earth rejoice; let the sea roar, and all it contains; let the field exalt, and all that is in it. Then all the trees of the forest will sing for joy before the Lord. . . . Let the mountains sing together for joy before the Lord; for He is coming to judge the earth" (Ps. 65:8; 96:11-13; 98:8-9).

Joy is the special privilege of every believer, regardless of his or her circumstances. You might suffer untold heartache and persecution for your faith in Christ, but amid the severest trials, God wants you to know profound joy. That's why Peter said, "To the degree that you share the sufferings of Christ, keep on rejoicing; so that also at the revelation of His glory, you may rejoice with exultation" (1 Peter 4:13).

First Peter 1:6-9 identifies five elements of your Christian life that should bring you joy amid trials. The first is your protected inheritance. That's what Peter referred to when he said, "In *this* you greatly rejoice" (v. 6, emphasis added). Other elements include a proven faith, a promised honor, a personal fellowship, and a present deliverance (vv. 6-9), which we will explore in coming days.

The Greek word translated "greatly rejoice" in 1 Peter 1:6 is not the usual Greek word for "rejoice." Peter here used a more expressive and intense word that speaks of one who is happy in a profound spiritual sense rather than in a temporal or circumstantial sense. That's the quality of joy God grants to those who trust in Him and who look beyond their temporal trials to the glory of their eternal inheritance. Let that be your focus as well.

❖❖❖

Suggestions for Prayer: Thank God for the joy that transcends circumstances.

For Further Study: Read John 16:16-22. ❖ According to Jesus, why would the disciples lament? ❖ What would bring them joy? ❖ What does their experience teach you about the basis for your joy as a Christian?

"In this you greatly rejoice, even though now for a little while, if necessary, you have been distressed by various trials, that the proof of your faith, being more precious than gold which is perishable, even though tested by fire, may be found to result in praise and glory and honor at the revelation of Jesus Christ" (1 Peter 1:6-7).

❖❖❖

Proven faith brings joy and confidence.

Although some Christians fear that trials and persecutions can only rob them of their joy, Peter taught just the opposite. In fact, he said that joy comes not *in spite of* trouble but *because of* trouble. That's because it's easy to lose your joy if you doubt your salvation; but when your faith has been tested and proven to be genuine, doubts will disappear, and you'll have joy and assurance.

Every trial you face is designed to test and perfect your faith, and God carefully controls their parameters to accomplish that purpose. Verse 6 specifies that they are temporary, necessary, distressing, and multi-faceted, but they should never diminish your joy. He won't allow you to undergo more than you can bear (1 Cor. 10:13).

Peter used the analogy of an assayer or goldsmith to illustrate the purging process that produces proven faith (v. 7). The fire symbolizes trials, and the gold symbolizes your faith. Just as the refiner's fire burns away the dross and leaves only pure gold, so God purges you through trials in order to reveal the purity of your faith.

That's an appropriate analogy because gold was the most precious of metals and the standard for all monetary transactions. But as valuable as gold is, proven faith is infinitely more precious. Gold is temporal and perishable; proven faith is eternal.

So don't fear trials when they come your way. Welcome them as opportunities to prove that your faith is real. Be encouraged that "after you have suffered a little [while], the God of all grace, who called you to His eternal glory in Christ, will Himself perfect, confirm, strengthen and establish you" (1 Peter 5:10).

❖❖❖

Suggestions for Prayer: If you are currently going through a time of testing, ask God for the grace and wisdom to pass the test. Thank Him in advance for the joy and confidence you'll gain when the test is over.

For Further Study: Read 2 Corinthians 11:23-28, noting the trials Paul endured for His faith in Christ.

". . . that the proof of your faith . . . may be found to result in praise
and glory and honor at the revelation of Jesus Christ" (1 Peter 1:7).

❖❖❖

Your future reward is directly related to your present service.

The joy you experience after your faith has been tested and proven genuine is largely due to your present blessings and assurance of salvation. But there's a future aspect as well—the joy of anticipating the reward you'll receive from Jesus when you see Him face to face and hear, "Well done, good and faithful servant! . . . Come and share your master's happiness!" (Matt. 25:21, NIV). Peter described it as the "praise and glory and honor [you'll receive] at the revelation of Jesus Christ" (1 Peter 1:7).

"Praise" in that text speaks of verbal commendation. To receive "glory" is to be made like Christ. Jesus is the incarnation of God's glory (John 1:14), and we know that when He appears, "we shall be like Him, because we shall see Him just as He is" (1 John 3:2). Paul spoke of those who "by perseverance in doing good seek for glory and honor and immortality" (Rom. 2:7). As a result they will receive what they seek (v. 10).

Peter probably used "honor" as a synonym for rewards, which God will grant to all who faithfully serve Him. I believe those rewards are various capacities for heavenly service and are directly related to the believer's service in this life. Jesus said, "Behold, I am coming quickly, and My reward is with Me, to render to every man *according to what he has done*" (Rev. 22:12, emphasis added). Paul said, "He who plants and he who waters are one; but each will receive his own reward *according to his own labor*" (1 Cor. 3:8, emphasis added).

God alone is worthy of praise, glory, and honor, but He will give you all three because you'll be in the image of Jesus Christ—sinless and fully glorified (1 John 3:2). Until that time, "watch yourselves, that you might not lose what we have accomplished, but that you may receive a full reward" (2 John 8).

❖❖❖

Suggestions for Prayer: Praise the Lord for the joy of anticipating your future reward.

For Further Study: Peter spoke of a time when Jesus will reward believers. What do the following verses teach about that time? Romans 8:18; 1 Corinthians 1:7-8; 2 Thessalonians 1:5-10; 1 Peter 4:10-13.

"Though you have not seen Him, you love Him, and though you do not see Him now, but believe in Him, you greatly rejoice with joy inexpressible and full of glory" (1 Peter 1:8).

❖❖❖

Fellowship with Christ is built on love, trust, and obedience.

The recipients of 1 Peter, like us, had never seen Christ, but they enjoyed fellowship with Him just the same. And their fellowship was genuine because it was marked by love, trust, and obedience.

The love Peter speaks of in 1 Peter 1:8 isn't shallow emotionalism or sentimentality. It's the love of the will—the love of choice. His readers had chosen to love Christ despite never having seen Him physically. Such love is marked by obedience, as Jesus affirms in John 14: "If you love Me, you will keep My commandments. . . . He who does not love Me does not keep My words" (vv. 15, 24). To have fellowship with Christ is to love and obey Him.

Another element of fellowship is trust. After hearing reports about Christ's resurrection, the disciple Thomas declared that he would trust Jesus only after seeing and touching Him. Jesus honored his wishes, saying, "Reach here your finger, and see My hands; and reach here your hand, and put it into My side; and be not unbelieving, but believing" (John 20:27). But then Jesus said, "Because you have seen Me, have you believed? Blessed are they who did not see, and yet believed" (v. 29). We as Christians are among those who believe in Christ without having seen Him.

The result of loving and trusting Christ is "joy inexpressible and full of glory" (1 Peter 1:8). This joy is something beyond the ability of speech and thought to convey. That's obvious even on the human level—as evidenced by the thousands of songs that have attempted to communicate the joy of being in love. "Full of glory" refers to the divine element in Christian joy. It's a supernatural endowment bestowed and energized by the Holy Spirit (Gal. 5:22).

Enjoying fellowship with Christ is one of the supreme privileges of your Christian life. Strengthen and enrich that fellowship by learning the Word and relying on the Spirit. As you do, you will learn to love and trust Christ more deeply.

❖❖❖

Suggestions for Prayer: Ask God to teach you how to love and trust Him more faithfully. Thank Him for the joy that comes as you do.

For Further Study: Memorize Matthew 22:37.

"... obtaining as the outcome of your faith the salvation of your souls" (1 Peter 1:9).

✧✧✧

Your present deliverance sets you free from the penalty and power of sin.

In 1 Corinthians 1:18 Paul says that "the word of the cross is to those who are perishing foolishness, but to us *who are being saved* it is the power of God" (emphasis added). That emphasizes the marvelous reality of the believer's present deliverance from sin. Peter stressed the same truth in 1 Peter 1:9, where he says that believers obtain as the outcome of their faith the salvation of their souls.

The Greek word translated "obtaining" literally means "presently receiving for yourselves." It speaks of obtaining something that is due you as a result of your faith in Christ. "Outcome of your faith" refers to the logical result or end of faith. "Souls" speaks of the whole person. The entire verse could be translated, "You rejoice because you have and continue to hold on to the logical result of your proven faith—your ongoing deliverance from sin."

You need ongoing deliverance because sin is an ongoing problem. You have new life in Christ, you are a new creature in Him, and you are no longer a slave to the penalty and power of sin; but you're not yet fully glorified. Consequently you're still subject to sin's influence. Paul personalized that struggle in Romans 7, where he says, "The good that I wish, I do not do; but I practice the very evil that I do not wish. . . . I find then the principle that evil is present in me, the one who wishes to do good. . . . Wretched man that I am! Who will set me free from the body of this death?" (vv. 19, 21, 24). The victory comes in verse 25, which says, "Thanks be to God through Jesus Christ our Lord!"

Jesus is the Great Deliverer, through whom you have victory over sin, death, and Hell. That's the last spiritual privilege in Peter's brief list, but it's by no means the least. As you love and trust Him, you'll know the joy of present deliverance.

✧✧✧

Suggestions for Prayer: Praise the Lord for your deliverance from sin's bondage.

For Further Study: Review all the spiritual privileges and sources of Christian joy we've discussed this month. Keep them fresh in your mind as you face the challenges of each new day.

"Let all that you do be done in love" (1 Cor. 16:14).

✧✧✧

The more you love God, the less you will sin.

Scripture and personal experience teach us that sin always has its consequences. When you harbor unconfessed sin, you dishonor God and forfeit the blessings and joy He desires for you. Prolonged sin might even bring His chastening through pain or illness.

That's what happened to Corinthian believers who partook of the Lord's Table in a sinful manner (1 Cor. 11:27-30). Paul warned the rest of the congregation to take careful spiritual inventory of themselves to avoid incurring a similar punishment. In chapter 13 he reveals the root of their problem, saying in effect, "Some of you are physically ill because you're sinning. Start loving God and one another as you should and your ailments will disappear."

Love is the antidote for sin. When a Pharisee asked Jesus which of the commandments was greatest, Jesus replied, "'You shall love the Lord your God with all your heart, and with all your soul, and with all your mind.' This is the greatest and foremost commandment. The second is like it, 'You shall love your neighbor as yourself.' On these two commandments depend the whole Law and the Prophets" (Matt. 22:37-40). If you love the Lord and your fellow men, you won't sin against them. That's why Paul said, "He who loves his neighbor has fulfilled the law. For this, 'You shall not commit adultery, You shall not murder, You shall not steal, You shall not covet,' and if there is any other commandment, it is summed up in this saying, 'You shall love your neighbor as yourself.' Love does no wrong to a neighbor; love therefore is the fulfillment of the law" (Rom. 13:8-10).

Love is your highest calling and the greatest contribution you can make to others. But it's possible to neglect it or misunderstand its characteristics. That's why we're going to spend this month exploring true love and how it functions. As we do, pray that your love for God and others will increase each day.

✧✧✧

Suggestions for Prayer: Ask God for a greater capacity to love Him, then demonstrate your love by obeying His Word.

For Further Study: Read 1 Corinthians 13, noting the characteristics of love.

"I show you a still more excellent way" (1 Cor. 12:31).

❖❖❖

Without love, spiritual gifts are meaningless.

First Corinthians 13 has been called a hymn of love, or a lyrical interpretation of the Sermon on the Mount—the Beatitudes set to music. It's a beautiful portion of Scripture that comes as a breath of fresh air in a book dealing with one problem after another.

This chapter has often been isolated from its context, but its real power lies in the balance and correction it gives to the rest of the book. The Corinthians, like all Christians, had been gifted by God at the moment of salvation to benefit the church in a special way. But many were abusing their gifts, seeking prominence for themselves rather than ministering to one another. So in chapter 12 Paul discusses the concept of spiritual gifts, in chapter 14 their proper use, and in chapter 13 the need to use them in love.

Like many Christians today, the Corinthians forgot that spiritual gifts can operate effectively only in a person who is truly spiritual. They had the gifts of the Spirit, but they weren't displaying the fruit of the Spirit (Gal. 5:22), the first of which is love.

In 1 Corinthians 13 Paul begins, "If I speak with the tongues of men and of angels, but do not have love, I have become a noisy gong or a clanging cymbal. And if I have the gift of prophecy, and know all mysteries and all knowledge; and if I have all faith, so as to remove mountains, but do not have love, I am nothing. And if I give all my possessions to feed the poor, and if I deliver my body to be burned, but do not have love, it profits me nothing." Love must be the motive and driving force behind everything we do!

How has God gifted you for ministry? Are you using your gifts in love?

❖❖❖

Suggestions for Prayer: Ask God to purify your love and make you a more effective minister of the gifts He has given to you.

For Further Study: Read 1 Corinthians 12. ❖ Who distributes spiritual gifts? ❖ Which gifts did Paul mention? ❖ What is their purpose?

"I show you a still more excellent way" (1 Cor. 12:31).

❖❖❖

**Biblical love is characterized by humility,
obedience to God, and self-sacrifice.**

In our society, *love* is a common word but an uncommon experience. Often those who use the word most understand it least. Many who think they've found love have really settled for something far less than God intended for them.

For many, love means a romantic or sexual relationship. While Scripture has much to say about intimacy within marriage, the word *love* takes on a different meaning in the New Testament. Even Ephesians 5:25 ("Husbands, love your wives") doesn't refer to romantic love.

Other common errors include equating love with emotionalism or sentimentality, or confusing it with a friendly spirit of tolerance and brotherhood toward others—often apart from any consideration for doctrinal purity or Biblical convictions. But Biblical love is none of those.

The "more excellent way" Paul refers to in 1 Corinthians 12:31 is love that comes from God Himself and conforms to His holy attributes. We have no capacity to generate this on our own. The Greek word for that kind of love is *agapé*, and it is characterized by humility, obedience to God, and self-sacrifice. John 13:1 says of Christ's love for His disciples, "He loved them to the end." That literally means He loved them to perfection—to the limits of love. In verses 4-5 He demonstrates His love by washing their feet. Love is humble. It focuses on meeting needs.

In addition, love is obedient and willing to make sacrifices for others. Jesus said, "If you love Me, you will keep My commandments" (John 14:15). God made the supreme sacrifice for us in that He "so loved the world, that He gave His only begotten Son" (John 3:16).

First Corinthians 13 applies to Christians of every generation because we all face the danger of misusing our spiritual gifts. As we study this and other passages about love, ask yourself if your love is all that God wants it to be. If not, take note of what changes you need to make in light of what you're learning.

❖❖❖

Suggestions for Prayer: Thank God for loving you. ❖ Ask Him for wisdom and grace to understand and walk in love.

For Further Study: Read John 14:23-24, noting how Jesus described those who love Him.

Love is...
- humble
- Obedient to God
- Self Sacrificing
- Focuses on meeting needs.

"Beloved, let us love one another, for love is from God. . . . We love, because He first loved us" (1 John 4:7, 19).

❖❖❖

True love cannot be generated on the human level. It's a gift from God.

Scripture often makes seemingly impossible demands of us. For example, Jesus said, "Love your enemies, and pray for those who persecute you" (Matt. 5:44). That's easy to say, but how is it possible? Our natural tendency is to love our friends and hate our enemies. But Jesus said, "If you love those who love you, what reward have you? Do not even the tax-gatherers do the same? And if you greet your brothers only, what do you do more than others? Do not even the Gentiles do the same?" (vv. 46-47).

Israel viewed tax-gatherers as traitors and Gentiles as spiritual outcasts. Yet even traitors and outcasts show love and kindness to those who reciprocate. Jesus calls us to a much higher standard of love—one that is impartial, like God demonstrates when He "causes His sun to rise on the evil and the good, and sends rain on the righteous and the unrighteous" (v. 45). As we see from God Himself, it extends even to those who aren't worthy: "God demonstrates His own love toward us, in that while we were yet sinners, Christ died for us" (Rom. 5:8).

Despite generations of rebellion and slander against His holy will and name, God sacrificed His beloved Son, thereby providing the means by which sinners can be saved. Out of love, Jesus willingly endured the pain and shame of the cross and paid the price of our redemption. Now that's divine love in action!

God commands you to love as He loves—impartially and sacrificially. That may sound impossible on the human level, but remember that God never requires you to do anything He hasn't already enabled you to do. At the moment of your salvation, the Holy Spirit took up residence within you and began producing the fruit of love (Gal. 5:22). You don't have to muster it on your own. All you have to do is invite the Spirit to take control, allowing Him to govern your thoughts and actions. As you do, His precious fruit will be multiplied in your life.

❖❖❖

Suggestions for Prayer: Thank God for the love of the Spirit He has placed within you. ❖ Ask Him for opportunities today to learn how to love more perfectly.

For Further Study: Memorize Galatians 5:22-23.

"If I speak with the tongues of men and of angels, but do not have love, I have become a noisy gong or a clanging cymbal" (1 Cor. 13:1).

❖❖❖

Love distinguishes true communication from useless chatter and meaningless noises.

Paul begins his discourse on love by stating the futility of languages without love. The Corinthians were enamored with the showy spiritual gifts, apparently to the neglect of those they deemed less spectacular (see 1 Cor. 12:12-31). One of the gifts they prized most highly was tongues, which was the Spirit-given ability to declare God's truth in a language unknown to the speaker but known to others who heard.

Tongues were a sign to provoke unbelieving Jewish people to consider the gospel (1 Cor. 14:21-22). Its first occurrence was on the Day of Pentecost when the Spirit enabled those assembled in the upper room to proclaim the mighty deeds of God in the native languages of the Jews gathered in Jerusalem at the time (Acts 2:4-11).

The "tongues of angels" Paul mentions in 1 Corinthians 13:1 isn't the gift of tongues, as some suppose. He was simply using an exaggeration to emphasize his point, saying in effect, "If I had the ability to communicate with *angels*, it wouldn't do any good without love."

In Paul's day, the worship of Cybele and Dionysus, two pagan gods, included speaking in ecstatic languages accompanied by blaring trumpets, smashing gongs, and clanging cymbals. I believe Paul was drawing from that well-known practice to say that whenever Christians attempt to minister apart from the Spirit and His love, it's no different than a pagan rite. It may look and sound like the real thing, but it's meaningless and useless for any spiritual benefit.

You should take advantage of every opportunity to minister your spiritual gifts to others. But as you do, be sure it's with love, in the energy of the Spirit, and in accordance with God's Word. Then you'll have maximum impact as Christ uses your efforts for His glory.

❖❖❖

Suggestions for Prayer: Ask God to convict you whenever you attempt to exercise your spiritual gifts without love.

For Further Study: Read Romans 12:1-31. ❖ What does Paul say about spiritual gifts? ❖ How are Christians to express brotherly love to one another?

"If I have the gift of prophecy . . . but do not have love, I am nothing" (1 Cor. 13:2).

✧✧✧

Love motivated God to communicate with fallen humanity. That must be your motivation too.

The word *prophecy* as used in 1 Corinthians 13:2 is the ability to publicly proclaim God's truth accurately and authoritatively. It's a greater gift than tongues because tongues were given as a sign to unbelieving Israel in the first century (1 Cor. 14:21-22), whereas prophecy instructs and edifies believers throughout the centuries. Paul said, "One who prophesies speaks to men for edification and exhortation and consolation [and] edifies the church" (1 Cor. 14:3-4).

Prophecy has two aspects: revelation and reiteration. When an Old or New Testament prophet received new information directly from God, that was revelation. Whenever that information was repeated through preaching or teaching, it was reiteration. For example, the sermons of Peter and Paul combine new revelation with a reiteration of Old Testament truth. That's a common element in New Testament preaching.

With the close of the New Testament canon, direct revelation from God ceased. All preaching and teaching today is reiteration. New Testament prophets policed one another to ensure that every prophecy was truly from God (1 Cor. 14:32). Today Scripture itself is the standard by which we test someone's message. As the prophet Isaiah said, "To the law and to the testimony! If they do not speak according to this word, it is because they have no dawn" (8:20).

Paul is saying in 1 Corinthians 13:2, "If I have the ability to speak direct revelation from God, or to reiterate divine truth forcefully and dramatically, but lack love, my ministry is meaningless." In its broadest sense, that principle applies to every believer because we all are proclaimers of God's Word. You might not teach a class or preach a sermon, but whenever you tell someone about Christ or share a Biblical principle, you're reiterating divine truth. That's why you must always "speak the truth in love" (Eph. 4:15). Then the Holy Spirit can empower your words to minister to others.

✧✧✧

Suggestions for Prayer: Ask God to help you guard your words, so that everything you say will be clothed in His love.

For Further Study: Read Deuteronomy 13:1-5 and 18:20-22. ✧ What tests did Moses give for determining false prophets? ✧ What punishment did false prophets receive?

"If I have the gift of prophecy . . . but do not have love, I am nothing" (1 Cor. 13:2).

❖❖❖

Love is an indispensable ingredient in the learning process.

I have the privilege of spending time each week with hundreds of young people who attend The Master's College. As I observe their progress, I see the impact godly teachers have had on their lives, and I'm convinced that students learn best when they know that their teachers genuinely care about them.

Isn't that true in any relationship? Don't you respond more readily to those who love you and have your best interests at heart? That's certainly true in ministry. Think of the pastors and teachers who have meant the most to you over the years. They're probably the ones who have loved you and ministered to you in special ways.

Whether it's a pastor, teacher, family member, or friend, whoever speaks to people on behalf of God must do so with genuine love and concern. That's the positive side of Paul's negative statement in 1 Corinthians 13:2. Jeremiah was such a man. He loved the people of Israel deeply and was grieved at their apostasy and impending judgment. "O that my head were waters," he said, "and my eyes a fountain of tears, that I might weep day and night for the slain of the daughter of my people!" (Jer. 9:1). That's the spirit of a loving prophet, and this was typical of Jeremiah's lament over his people's sin.

Loveless preaching and teaching misrepresent God's character and hinder the gospel; loving proclamation is winsome and effective. That doesn't mean that all who hear you will respond positively; quite the contrary. The people of Judah didn't listen to Jeremiah, so they incurred severe judgment. Similarly, some to whom you speak will politely reject what you say; others will react with hostility. But those who respond in faith will appreciate your loving concern for their spiritual well-being.

❖❖❖

Suggestions for Prayer: Thank God for those who have ministered to you in love. Seek to follow their example as you reach out to others.

For Further Study: Read Acts 20:19, 31, Romans 9:2-3, and 2 Corinthians 2:4, noting the things that prompted Paul to weep for the people to whom he ministered.

"If I . . . know all mysteries and all knowledge . . . but do not have love, I am nothing" (1 Cor. 13:2).

✧✧✧

True knowledge is always governed by love.

Christians should never take knowledge for granted. The ability to learn about Christ and to grow in His truth is a blessing beyond measure. Paul prayed that we would be "filled with the knowledge of [God's] will in all spiritual wisdom and understanding" (Col. 1:9). That's what enables us to live in a way that pleases God (v. 10).

But knowledge must be governed by love, just as love must be governed by knowledge. In Philippians 1:9 Paul says, "This I pray, that your love may abound still more and more in real knowledge and all discernment." In 1 Corinthians 13:2 he says that knowledge without love is nothing. That's a God-ordained balance you must maintain if you want to be effective for the Lord.

In 1 Corinthians 13:2 Paul uses a hypothetical illustration to emphasize the importance of love: "If I . . . know all mysteries and all knowledge . . . but do not have love, I am nothing." The Greek word translated "mysteries" in that verse is used throughout the New Testament to speak of redemptive truth that once was hidden but is now revealed. For example, Scripture speaks of the mystery of God in human flesh (Col. 2:2-3), of Christ's indwelling us (Col. 1:26-27), and of the church as Christ's Body (Eph. 3:3-6, 9).

"Knowledge" in 1 Corinthians 13:2 refers to facts that can be ascertained by investigation. It's impossible to know every mystery and every fact in existence in the universe, but even if you did, without love your knowledge would be useless. Knowledge alone breeds arrogance, but love builds others up (1 Cor. 8:1).

Maintaining a balance of knowledge and love is a practical principle that influences the decisions you make every day. For example, if you have a choice between going to a Bible class or helping a neighbor with some immediate need, the better choice is to help your neighbor. You will have other opportunities to learn the Word, but it might be some time before you have a chance to show Christian love to your neighbor.

✧✧✧

Suggestions for Prayer: Ask God for the wisdom to keep knowledge and love in proper balance.

For Further Study: Read Luke 10:25-37. ✧ How did the lawyer try to justify himself to Jesus? ✧ How did Jesus illustrate love for one's neighbor?

"If I have all faith, so as to remove mountains, but do not have love, I am nothing" (1 Cor. 13:2).

❖❖❖

Loveless faith is useless faith.

In Matthew 17:19 the disciples came to Jesus wanting to know why they couldn't cast a demonic spirit from a child. Jesus responded, "Because of the littleness of your faith; for truly I say to you, if you have faith as a mustard seed, you shall say to this mountain, 'Move from here to there,' and it shall move; and nothing shall be impossible to you" (v. 20). He repeated the same principle in Matthew 21:21—"Truly I say to you, if you have faith, and do not doubt, you shall . . . say to this mountain [the Mount of Olives], 'Be taken up and cast into the sea,' [and] it shall happen."

Those passages have puzzled many people because they've never seen anyone move a mountain. But Jesus wasn't speaking literally. Moving mountains would cause all kinds of ecological problems and would be a pointless miracle. The expression "able to move mountains" was a common figure of speech in that day, meaning "to surmount great obstacles." Jesus was speaking of those who have the gift of faith—those who can move the hand of God through unwavering prayer.

The gift of faith is the ability to believe that God will act according to His will, no matter the circumstances. People with that gift are prayer warriors and tend to stand as rocks when others around them are falling apart. They see God's power and purposes at work, and they trust Him even when others doubt.

But, says Paul, even if you have such faith, if you don't have love, you are nothing. That's a harsh rebuke, but it places the emphasis where it belongs—on our motives. The Corinthians' motives were evident in their selfish pursuit of the showy gifts.

What motivates you? Remember, without love it doesn't matter what gifts you have, how eloquent your speech is, what you know, or what you believe. Only love can validate your service to Christ.

❖❖❖

Suggestions for Prayer: Ask God for a greater capacity to trust Him and for the motivation to pray more fervently.

For Further Study: Read Hebrews 11, drawing from the examples of the people of great faith mentioned there.

"If I give all my possessions to feed the poor . . . but do not have love, it profits me nothing" (1 Cor. 13:3).

✧✧✧

**Love is characterized by self-sacrifice,
but not all self-sacrifice is an act of love.**

If you've ever donated to your church or another charitable organization out of obligation, peer pressure, legalism, guilt, a desire for recognition, or simply to earn a tax deduction, you know what it means to give without love. In our society it's easy to fall prey to that kind of giving because the needs are so great and fund-raisers appeal to every conceivable motive. In addition, many cults and false religions encourage the giving up of possessions and other sacrificial gestures as a supposed means of earning God's favor. But God is more interested in *why* you give than *what* you give.

Paul's hypothetical illustration in 1 Corinthians 13:3 is that of someone who sacrificed everything he had to feed the poor. The Greek word translated "to feed" means "to dole out in small quantities." Apparently this guy didn't simply write out a check for a food distribution program; he was personally involved in a long-term, systematic program that would eventually consume every resource he had.

Paul doesn't mention motives—only that this person lacked love. Consequently, the benefits of his benevolence were limited to the physical realm. Any spiritual benefits were forfeited.

Jesus, making a similar point, said, "Beware of practicing your righteousness before men to be noticed by them; otherwise you have no reward with your Father who is in heaven" (Matt. 6:1). If your motive for giving is to gain the approval of men, their accolades will be your only reward. If you're motivated by love for God, He will reward you abundantly (vv. 2-4).

When you give to the Lord, what is your motive? Do you want others to think more highly of you? Do you feel obligated? Those are subtle influences, so be sure to guard your motives carefully. Remember, the only acceptable motive is love.

✧✧✧

Suggestions for Prayer: Ask the Holy Spirit to keep you sensitive to the needs of others, enabling you always to give out of genuine love.

For Further Study: Read Luke 18:9-14. ✧ How did the Pharisee's prayer differ from the tax-gatherer's? ✧ How did God respond to each prayer?

"If I deliver my body to be burned, but do not have love, it profits me nothing" (1 Cor. 13:3).

❖❖❖

Wrong motives rob even the greatest sacrifice of its spiritual benefit.

So far in his denunciation of loveless ministries, Paul has addressed what we say, what we know, what we believe, and how we give. Now he comes to the apex of his argument—how we die. Many Christians have made the ultimate sacrifice of martyrdom, but even that is useless without love.

In Paul's time, many slaves were branded with a hot iron to identify them as belonging to their master. For that reason, some interpreters believe Paul was referring to becoming a slave when he spoke of delivering his body to be burned (1 Cor. 13:3). Others think he was speaking of burning at the stake— a death that many Christians suffered at the hands of their persecutors.

Although death by burning wasn't a common form of persecution until after Paul wrote to the Corinthians, I believe that's what he had in mind in this passage. In verses 1-2 he used extremes to make his point: speaking with the tongues of angels, knowing *all* mysteries and having *all* knowledge, having *all* faith, and giving *all* one's possessions to feed the poor. The horrible, agonizing pain associated with death by fire is consistent with those extremes.

Jesus called martyrdom the highest expression of love (John 15:13). But it isn't always a godly or loving thing to do. Many people have died for lesser reasons. You may recall stories of the Japanese *kamikaze* pilots in World War II or, more recently, monks or students who burned themselves in protest of some political or social injustice.

Even Christians aren't exempt from wrong motives. It is reported that many Christians in the early church developed a martyr complex, wanting to die for the faith so they could become famous like the martyrs before them. Many deeds that look sacrificial on the surface are really the products of pride.

If the ultimate sacrifice is useless without love, so is every lesser sacrifice. But love sanctifies them all. So let God's love govern everything you do!

❖❖❖

Suggestions for Prayer: Memorize Romans 5:8 as a reminder to praise God for the sacrifice He has made for you.

For Further Study: Read Revelation 2:1-7. ❖ What strengths did the church in Ephesus have? ❖ What did the Lord say about its one glaring weakness?

*"Love is patient . . . kind . . . not jealous . . . does not brag . . . is
not arrogant, does not act unbecomingly . . . does not seek its own,
is not provoked, does not take into account a wrong suffered, does
not rejoice in unrighteousness, but rejoices with the truth; bears
all things, believes all things, hopes all things, endures all things"
(1 Cor. 13:4-7).*

❖❖❖

***Love is difficult to define, but it can be described
by the behavior it produces.***

Paul painted a portrait of the kind of love Jesus wants to produce in every
believer. It is, in fact, a portrait of Christ Himself, who is love's highest
expression. Unlike most English translations, which include several adjec-
tives, the Greek forms of all those properties are verbs. They do not focus on
what love is so much as on what love does and does not do.

Set against the backdrop of the Corinthians' self-promoting behavior,
Paul's words are a strong rebuke. He says in effect, "Love is patient, but you
are impatient. Love is kind, but you are unkind toward those who disagree
with you. Love is not jealous, but you envy those with certain spiritual gifts.
Love does not brag, but you are proud of your theology. Love is not arrogant
and does not act unbecomingly, but often you are rude and ill-mannered
toward one another.

"Love does not seek its own, but you are self-centered. Love is not provoked, but you quarrel among yourselves. Love does not take into account a
wrong suffered, but you hold grudges against each other. Love does not rejoice
in unrighteousness, but you delight in one another's failures. Love rejoices
with the truth, but you distort and disobey God's Word.

"Love bears all things, but you are defensive and resentful. Love is eager
to believe the best about someone, but you are quick to assume the worst.
Love never gives up and can tolerate incredible opposition, but you are weak
and intolerant."

Paul wanted the Corinthians to see the deficiencies in their love in light of
the truth and then make the needed corrections. You and I must do the same.
So as we explore each of love's characteristics, ask the Holy Spirit to purify
your heart so others will clearly see Paul's portrait of love on display in you.

❖❖❖

Suggestions for Prayer: Read 1 Corinthians 13:4-7, substituting "Jesus" for
"love." Then praise Him for all His excellencies.

For Further Study: What does 1 John 3:13-18 teach about love?

"Love is patient" (1 Cor. 13:4).

✧✧✧

Love does not retaliate.

W e usually think of patience as the ability to wait or endure without complaint—either regarding people or circumstances. But the Greek word translated "patience" in 1 Corinthians 13:4 refers specifically to patience with people. It literally means "to be long-tempered," and it speaks of one who could easily retaliate when wronged but chooses not to.

That kind of patience is a spiritual virtue reflective of God Himself (cf. Gal. 5:22). It can't be duplicated on a purely human level. But for Christians, it's to be a way of life. Paul said, "I . . . entreat you to walk in a manner worthy of the calling with which you have been called, with all humility and gentleness, with patience, showing forbearance to one another in love" (Eph. 4:1-2).

God Himself is the supreme example of patience. Peter said, "[He] is patient toward you, not wishing for any to perish but for all to come to repentance" (2 Peter 3:9). Those who reject His grace are despising "the riches of His kindness and forbearance and patience" (Rom. 2:4).

In the Greco-Roman world of Paul's day, retaliating for a personal insult or injury was considered a virtue. Non-retaliation was interpreted as a sign of weakness. Our society is much the same. Our heroes tend to be those who fight back with physical strength or litigation. But that isn't God's perspective, nor was it Christ's in praying for His killers: "Father, forgive them; for they do not know what they are doing" (Luke 23:34).

As you consider your own patience, remember that retaliation isn't always blatant and forceful. It's often subtle—like withholding affection from your spouse when he or she has wronged you, or withdrawing from a friend who has hurt you. But godly love never retaliates. It cares more for the feelings of others than for its own.

Remember the Lord's patience toward you, and allow His Spirit to produce similar patience in you.

✧✧✧

Suggestions for Prayer: If you are harboring resentment toward someone who has wronged you, confess it to the Lord, and do everything you can to reconcile with that person.

For Further Study: Read Genesis 50:15-21. ✧ What fear did Joseph's brothers have? ✧ How did Joseph react to their plea for forgiveness? ✧ How did God use Joseph's brothers' sin to accomplish His own purposes?

"Love is kind" (1 Cor. 13:4).

❖❖❖

Kindness repays evil with good.

Two men going opposite directions on a narrow mountain trail met each other head-on. With a steep cliff on one side and sheer rock on the other, they were unable to pass. The harder they tried to squeeze past one another, the more frustrated they became. The situation seemed hopeless until one of them, without saying a word, simply laid down on the trail, allowing the other man to walk over him. That illustrates kindness, which doesn't mind getting walked on if it benefits someone else.

The Greek word translated "kind" in 1 Corinthians 13:4 literally means "useful," "serving," or "gracious." It isn't simply the sweet attitude we usually associate with kindness; it's the idea of being useful to others. It's the flip side of patience. Patience endures abuses from others; kindness repays them with good deeds.

God committed the supreme act of kindness when He provided salvation for lost sinners. Titus 3:3-5 says, "We also once were foolish ourselves, disobedient, deceived, enslaved to various lusts and pleasures, spending our life in malice and envy, hateful, hating one another. But when the kindness of God our Savior and His love for mankind appeared, He saved us."

Jesus said, "Take My yoke upon you, and learn from Me, for I am gentle and humble in heart; and you shall find rest for your souls. For My yoke is easy, and My load is light" (Matt. 11:29-30). The Greek word translated "easy" is translated "kind" in 1 Corinthians 13:4. Jesus was saying, "Trust in Me, and I'll redeem you and show you My kindness."

Since "you have tasted the kindness of the Lord" (1 Peter 2:3), you should be anxious to show kindness to others. That's what Paul wanted the Corinthian believers to do. He knew they had the capacity, but they needed to repent of their selfish ways and allow love to dominate their lives.

❖❖❖

Suggestions for Prayer: The evil world in which we live gives abundant opportunity for you to express kindness to others. Ask the Lord to help you take full advantage of every opportunity to do so today.

For Further Study: Read Matthew 5:38-48, noting the practical expressions of kindness Jesus instructed His followers to pursue.

"Love . . . is not jealous" (1 Cor. 13:4).

❖❖❖

Jealousy thrives in a climate of selfish ambition.

Jealousy is an insidious sin that cries out, "I want what you have, and furthermore I don't want you to have it." It replaces contentment with resentment and spawns a myriad of other sins.

The Corinthians were jealous of one another's spiritual gifts. First Corinthians 12:31 literally says, "You are earnestly desiring the showy gifts, but I show you a more excellent way." The Greek word translated "earnestly desiring" is translated "jealous" in 1 Corinthians 13:4. It means "to boil" and speaks of the inner seething that comes from wanting something that someone else has. In 1 Corinthians 3:3 Paul rebukes them for the jealousy and strife that existed among them.

Paul knew what it meant to be victimized by jealous people. During one of his imprisonments he candidly wrote, "Some, to be sure, are preaching Christ even from envy and strife, but some also from good will; the latter do it out of love, knowing that I am appointed for the defense of the gospel; the former proclaim Christ out of selfish ambition, rather than from pure motives, thinking to cause me distress in my imprisonment" (Phil. 1:15-17).

Paul's attitude toward those who envied him was exemplary: "Whether in pretense or in truth, Christ is proclaimed; and in this I rejoice, yes, and I will rejoice" (v. 18). He wasn't motivated by personal comfort or selfish ambition. He loved Christ deeply and wanted as many people as possible to hear the gospel. As long as Christ was being proclaimed, Paul was happy—regardless of his own circumstances or the motives of others. That should be your perspective too.

Love is the antidote for jealousy. When godly love governs your heart, you can rejoice in the spiritual successes of others, even when you know their motives are wrong. But if you seek prominence and selfish gain, you become an easy target for jealousy and resentment.

❖❖❖

Suggestions for Prayer: Confess any jealousy you might be harboring toward others. ❖ Ask God to deepen your love for Christ so jealousy can't gain a foothold in your heart in the future.

For Further Study: Read 2 Corinthians 11:2. Is there such a thing as godly jealousy? Explain.

"Love does not brag" (1 Cor. 13:4).

✧✧✧

Love exalts others; pride exalts self.

Most of us shy away from people who have an inflated view of themselves or place themselves at the center of every conversation. Yet perhaps you too struggle with the temptation to spend most of your conversations talking about yourself. Even if you would never openly brag about yourself, might you at times secretly resent others for not acknowledging your accomplishments? That's the subtlety of pride.

Boasting always violates love because it seeks to exalt itself at the expense of others—to make itself look good while making others look inferior. It incites jealousy and other sins. Sadly, boasting exists even in the church. That's why Paul exhorted us not to think more highly of ourselves than we ought to think, "but to think so as to have sound judgment, as God has allotted to each a measure of faith" (Rom. 12:3). The context of that statement is spiritual gifts, which can lead to pride if not governed by humility and love.

The Corinthians were spiritual show-offs—each vying for attention and prominence. Consequently their worship services were chaotic. First Corinthians 14:26 says, "When you assemble, each one has a psalm, has a teaching, has a revelation, has a tongue, has an interpretation." Apparently they all were expressing their spiritual gifts at the same time with no regard for anyone else. That's why Paul concluded, "Let all things be done for edification."

Their lack of love was obvious because people who truly love others don't exalt themselves. They regard others as more important than themselves, just as Christ did when He humbled Himself and died for our sins (Phil. 2:3-8).

Boasting about our spiritual gifts is absurd because we did nothing to earn them. They don't reflect our capabilities; they reflect God's grace. That's why Paul asked the Corinthians, "What do you have that you did not receive? But if you did receive it, why do you boast as if you had not received it?" (1 Cor. 4:7). That applies to physical capabilities as well as spiritual enablements. Everything you have is a gift from God. Therefore, "Let him who boasts, boast in the Lord" (1 Cor. 1:31).

✧✧✧

Suggestions for Prayer: Each day acknowledge your total dependence on God's grace. ✧ Praise Him for the gifts He has entrusted to you.

For Further Study: Note what God has to say about haughtiness in Proverbs 6:16-17, 16:18, 18:12, 21:3-4, and 21:24.

"Love . . . is not arrogant" (1 Cor. 13:4).

❖❖❖

Love is the key to effective ministry.

In 1 Corinthians 13:4 Paul says, "Love does not brag and is not arrogant." We often equate bragging and arrogance, but in this passage there is a subtle difference. The Greek word translated "brag" emphasizes prideful speech or actions; "arrogant" emphasizes the attitude of pride motivating those actions.

The prideful attitudes of the Corinthians were evident in several areas. In 1 Corinthians 4:18-21 Paul says, "Some have become arrogant, as though I were not coming to you. But I will come to you soon, if the Lord wills, and I shall find out, not the words of those who are arrogant, but their power. . . . What do you desire? Shall I come to you with a rod or with love and a spirit of gentleness?" Apparently some thought they no longer needed his instruction. "After all," they reasoned, "we've had the best teachers—Apollos, Peter, and even Paul himself [1 Cor. 1:12]; so what need do we have for more instruction?" The fact was, they had just enough knowledge to inflate their egos, but they were woefully ignorant of love (1 Cor. 8:1).

It was arrogance that led the Corinthian church to condone gross immorality: "It is actually reported that there is immorality among you, and immorality of such a kind as does not exist even among the Gentiles, that someone has his father's wife [incest]. And you have become arrogant, and have not mourned instead, in order that the one who had done this deed might be removed from your midst" (1 Cor. 5:1-2). They were too prideful to confront and correct that situation, so they bragged about it instead. Even pagans wouldn't tolerate that kind of behavior!

That's a tragic picture of people so blinded by pride that they refused to discern between good and evil. Consequently, all their spiritual activities were counterproductive. They were gifted by the Spirit and even flaunted their gifts, but they lacked the love that transforms a gifted person into an effective minister.

Learn from the Corinthians' mistakes. Never settle for mere spiritual activities. Let love motivate everything you do. Then God can honor your ministries and make them truly effective for His purposes.

❖❖❖

Suggestions for Prayer: Ask God to make you a more effective minister and to protect you from the blindness of arrogance.

For Further Study: What do the following proverbs say about pride? Proverbs 8:13; 11:2; and 29:23.

"[Love] does not act unbecomingly" (1 Cor. 13:5).

✦✦✦

Considerate behavior demonstrates godly love and adds credibility to your witness.

When I was a young child, I loved to slurp my soup. I didn't see any harm in it, even though my parents constantly objected. Then one evening I ate with someone who slurped his soup. He was having a great time, but I didn't enjoy my meal very much. Then I realized that proper table manners are one way of showing consideration for others. It says, "I care about you and don't want to do anything that might disrupt your enjoyment of this meal."

On a more serious note, I know a couple who got an annulment on the grounds that the husband was rude to his wife. She claimed that his incessant burping proved he didn't really love her. The judge ruled in her favor, stating that if the husband truly loved her, he would have been more considerate. That's a strange story but a true one, and it illustrates the point that love is not rude.

"Unbecomingly" in 1 Corinthians 13:5 includes any behavior that violates acceptable Biblical or social standards. We could paraphrase it, "Love is considerate of others." That would have been in stark contrast to the inconsiderate behavior of the Corinthians—many of whom were overindulging at their love feasts and getting drunk on the Communion wine (1 Cor. 11:20-22). Some women were overstepping bounds by removing their veils and usurping the role of men in the church (1 Cor. 11:3-16; 14:34-35). Both men and women were corrupting the worship services by trying to outdo one another's spiritual gifts (1 Cor. 14:26).

Undoubtedly the Corinthians justified their rude behavior, just as we often justify ours. But rudeness betrays a lack of love and is always detrimental to effective ministry. For example, I've seen Christians behave so rudely toward non-Christians who smoke that they destroyed any opportunity to tell them about Christ.

Be aware of how you treat others—whether believers or unbelievers. Even the smallest of courtesies can make a profound impression.

✦✦✦

Suggestions for Prayer: Ask the Holy Spirit to monitor your behavior and to convict you of any loveless actions. As He does, be sure to confess and forsake them.

For Further Study: Read Luke 7:36-50. How did Jesus protect the repentant woman from the Pharisee's rudeness?

"[Love] does not seek its own" (1 Cor. 13:5).

❖❖❖

Love transforms selfish people into self-sacrificing people.

From the time of Adam and Eve, replacing God with self has been at the root of all sin. Our first parents had only one restriction: "From the tree of the knowledge of good and evil you shall not eat, for in the day that you eat from it you shall surely die" (Gen. 2:17). But Eve believed the serpent's lie that God was trying to keep her from realizing her full potential (Gen. 3:5). She ate the forbidden fruit and gave some to Adam, and together they plunged the human race into sin and death.

Christ changed all that when He came, not "to be served, but to serve, and to give His life a ransom for many" (Matt. 20:28). Unlike Adam and Eve, He didn't seek His own comfort or gain but made whatever sacrifices were necessary to redeem lost sinners.

It is reported that the inscription on a tombstone in a small English cemetery reads, "Here lies a miser who lived for himself, / And cared for nothing but gathering wealth. / Now where he is or how he fares, / Nobody knows and nobody cares."

How tragic to spend your entire life enslaved to your selfishness! In contrast, a tombstone in the courtyard of St. Paul's Cathedral in London reads, "Sacred to the memory of General Charles George Gordon, who at all times and everywhere gave his strength to the weak, his substance to the poor, his sympathy to the suffering, his heart to God." The first tombstone testifies to the futility of greed and selfishness, the second to the glory of generosity and self-sacrifice.

Christ is the perfect example of self-sacrifice. If you love Him, you should be characterized by the same quality. Then others will see your genuineness and commitment to them and will by God's grace be drawn to your Lord.

What epitaph might your family and friends write about you? I pray it is one that glorifies God for the selfless love He demonstrated through you.

❖❖❖

Suggestions for Prayer: Thank God for those who have made significant sacrifices toward your spiritual growth. Seek to imitate their love.

For Further Study: List the fifteen qualities of love from 1 Corinthians 13:4-7, then determine how self-sacrifice relates to each one.

"[Love] is not provoked" (1 Cor. 13:5).

❖❖❖

Self-centered anger cannot coexist with love.

The great eighteenth-century preacher and theologian Jonathan Edwards had a daughter with an uncontrollable temper. When a young man asked Dr. Edwards for his daughter's hand in marriage, he said no. The young man was crushed. "But I love her, and she loves me," he pleaded. "That makes no difference," Edwards replied; "she isn't worthy of you." "But she is a Christian, isn't she?" the young man argued. "Yes," said Edwards, "but the grace of God can live with some people with whom no one else could ever live."

That may seem harsh, but Jonathan Edwards knew what his would-be son-in-law hadn't yet learned: the presence of selfish anger indicates the absence of genuine love. "Love," said Paul, "is not provoked." It isn't given to sudden outbursts of emotion or action. It doesn't respond in anger to offenses committed against it.

Paul wasn't talking about anger over sin and its terrible consequences. That's righteous indignation, which Christians are expected to have. When Jesus drove the merchants and moneychangers out of the Temple (John 2:14-15), He was genuinely angry because His Father's house was being desecrated. But He never reacted that way when He was personally attacked or maligned. In the same way, it's right for you to be angry when others are mistreated, when God is offended, or when His Word is misrepresented. But love always bears up under personal attacks.

Such graciousness is foreign to our society, which teaches us to fight for our personal rights and to retaliate when we don't get what we think we deserve. That has produced greedy and loveless people who want little more than personal success and comfort. Anyone who dares to stand in their way is in danger of incurring their wrath.

As a Christian, you must resist such influences by focusing on your spiritual duty rather than on your rights. If you expect nothing from the world, you won't be angered or disappointed when nothing comes. Remember, God is the giver of every good and perfect gift (James 1:17). So humble yourself before Him, and He will exalt you at the proper time (James 4:10).

❖❖❖

Suggestions for Prayer: Ask God for the grace to forgive those who wrong you.

For Further Study: According to Ephesians 4:26-27, how should you deal with anger?

"[Love] does not take into account a wrong suffered" (1 Cor. 13:5).

❖❖❖

If you love someone, you won't keep a record of their offenses.

It is reported that when the Moravian missionaries first went to the Eskimos, they couldn't find a word in that language for forgiveness. They had to combine a series of shorter words into one compound word: *Issumagijoujungnainermik.* Although the word appears formidable, its meaning is beautiful: "Not being able to think about it anymore."

You've probably noticed that unforgiving people usually have good memories. Some can hold a grudge for a lifetime. But love never keeps a record of wrongs committed against it. It forgives and is unable to think about them anymore.

That's what Paul had in mind when he said that love "does not take into account a wrong suffered" (1 Cor. 13:5). The Greek word translated "take into account" was used for entries in a bookkeeper's ledger. Those entries helped the bookkeeper remember the nature of each financial transaction. In contrast, love never keeps a record or holds others accountable for the wrongs they've committed against it.

The greatest example of that kind of love is God Himself. Romans 4:8 says, "Blessed is the man whose sin the Lord will not take into account." Second Corinthians 5:19 adds, "God was in Christ reconciling the world to Himself, not counting their trespasses against them."

Every sin we commit as believers is an offense against God, but He never charges them to our account. We are in Christ, who bore our penalty on the cross. When we sin, we are immediately forgiven.

If you love others, you'll forgive them as God has forgiven you. Instead of holding them accountable for their offenses, you'll look beyond their sin to their potential in Christ. You'll heed Paul's admonition to "be kind to one another, tender-hearted, forgiving each other, just as God in Christ also has forgiven you" (Eph. 4:32). That's the character of true love.

❖❖❖

Suggestions for Prayer: Is there someone from whom you've been withholding forgiveness? If so, recognize it as sin and confess it to the Lord. Then be reconciled to that person right away. ❖ Thank God that He doesn't keep an account of your sins (cf. Ps. 130:3-4).

For Further Study: What does Matthew 18:21-35 say about forgiving others?

"[Love] does not rejoice in unrighteousness" (1 Cor. 13:6).

❖❖❖

Love never justifies sin.

To most Christians, the idea of rejoicing over unrighteousness is repulsive because it suggests enjoying deliberate, wanton sin. We've seen sin's tragic effects on mankind and know how it offends God, so how could we ever rejoice in such a thing? But rejoicing in unrighteousness includes any attempt to justify sin in your own life or in the lives of others, and this can be a very subtle thing.

There are many ways to rejoice in unrighteousness. One is to exchange right for wrong. That's what the prophet Isaiah condemned when saying, "Woe to those who call evil good, and good evil; who substitute darkness for light and light for darkness" (Isa. 5:20). In our society, for example, virtues such as virginity and fidelity in marriage are branded as old-fashioned and prudish, while promiscuity and adultery are heralded as contemporary and liberating. Social pressures can cause undiscerning or weak Christians to yield to confused and godless moral standards.

Another way to rejoice in unrighteousness is to be undiscerning about what you expose yourself to. The humanistic philosophies and blatant immorality of our society can quickly dull your moral and spiritual senses. Therefore you must carefully evaluate what you read, view, and listen to. Does it denigrate God and exalt violence, crime, immorality, slander, and the like? If so, and you find that book or article entertaining, you are rejoicing in sin.

Some believers actually rejoice over the sins of others. That's what Jonah did when he refused to preach at Nineveh for fear the people would repent and God would forgive them. He preferred to see them continue in sin rather than reconcile with God. That attitude is not so far removed from today as we'd like to think. I've known professing Christians who wanted out of their marriages so badly that they hoped their spouses would commit adultery so they would feel justified in getting a divorce. What a convoluted perspective!

True love cannot rejoice in sin but glories whenever righteousness prevails. If you love God, the things that please Him will please you, and the things that offend Him will offend you. Let that always be your standard.

❖❖❖

Suggestions for Prayer: Ask God for the grace to live a life that pleases Him.

For Further Study: Read Matthew 18:15-20, carefully noting the procedure for confronting a sinning Christian.

"[Love] rejoices with the truth" (1 Cor. 13:6).

❖❖❖

Love never compromises God's Word.

Paul has just given us a list of things that love does not do: become jealous, brag, act arrogantly or unbecomingly, seek its own, become provoked, keep track of wrongs suffered, or rejoice in unrighteousness. Now he comes to the first of five things love does: "[Love] rejoices with the truth" (v. 6).

The contrast here is between love's inability to rejoice in unrighteousness and its joy when truth prevails. "Truth" refers to God's Word, which is the standard of righteousness. Paul could have said, "Love doesn't rejoice in unrighteousness but rejoices with righteousness," but he went beyond the mere deeds of righteousness and addressed its standard and motive.

Love won't tolerate false doctrine or sinful behavior, but it rejoices when God's Word is taught and obeyed. The psalmist said, "O how I love Thy law! It is my meditation all the day. Thy commandments make me wiser than my enemies. . . . I have more insight than all my teachers . . . . I understand more than the aged. . . . I have restrained my feet from every evil way, that I may keep Thy word. I have not turned aside from Thine ordinances, for Thou Thyself hast taught me. How sweet are Thy words to my taste! Yes, sweeter than honey to my mouth! From Thy precepts I get understanding; therefore I hate every false way" (Ps. 119:97-104). That's the testimony of one who rejoices in the truth.

Often Christians are willing to compromise sound doctrine for the sake of loving others. They believe that doctrinal precision is somehow divisive and unloving. But Scripture says, "This is love, that we walk according to His commandments. . . . For many deceivers have gone out into the world, those who do not acknowledge Jesus Christ as coming in the flesh. This is the deceiver and the antichrist. Watch yourselves, that you might not lose what we have accomplished, but that you may receive a full reward" (2 John 6-8).

Biblical love always operates within the parameters of God's Word and spiritual discernment (Phil. 1:9-10). The most loving thing you can do is live according to Biblical truth. Doctrinal compromise simply diminishes the quality of love and plays into the hands of the evil one.

❖❖❖

Suggestions for Prayer: Ask God for the wisdom and discernment needed to keep your love within its proper Biblical bounds.

For Further Study: Memorize Philippians 1:9-11.

"[Love] bears all things" (1 Cor. 13:7).

❖❖❖

Love confronts sin but protects the sinner.

In 1 Corinthians 13:7 Paul mentions four qualities of love that are closely related: bearing all things, believing all things, hoping all things, and enduring all things. That might sound like love is indiscriminate and accepting of anything that comes along, but "all things" in that verse is qualified by the context. Love rejects jealousy, bragging, arrogance, and so on (vv. 4-6); but it bears, believes, hopes, and endures all things that are within the parameters of God's Word.

"[Love] bears all things" speaks of love's willingness to cover sins and protect sinners from further harm. That's opposite our tabloid-mentality society in which gossip is big business and people seemingly have an insatiable appetite for exposés and "true confessions."

Love seeks to protect, not expose. It confronts and disciplines sin but never broadcasts failures or wrongs. It feels the pain of those it loves and is willing to take that pain upon itself when necessary—as Christ did when He suffered for our sins.

In the Old Testament, the mercy seat was the place where the blood of atonement was sprinkled to cover the sins of the people (Lev. 16:14). That covering prefigured the perfect covering of sin that Christ brought through His death on the cross (Rom. 3:25-26). All who trust in Him are forever covered with the mantle of God's love.

You cannot cover sins in the redemptive sense, but you can help protect and restore its victims. Proverbs 10:12 says, "Hatred stirs up strife, but love covers all transgressions." First Peter 4:8 says, "Above all, keep fervent in your love for one another, because love covers a multitude of sins."

When you hear of someone's sin, what is your first reaction? Do you think the worst of him or even gloat over his failures? Or do you expect the best and want to protect him from further exposure, ridicule, or harm? Are you willing to confront sin when necessary and even help bear the burden that person might be carrying? How you react indicates the quality of your love.

❖❖❖

Suggestions for Prayer: Thank God for covering your sins with Christ's blood. ❖ Commit yourself to loving others in a way that truly bears all things.

For Further Study: Read Isaiah 53:3-12. ❖ How is Christ pictured? ❖ What did He endure on your behalf?

"[Love] believes all things" (1 Cor. 13:7).

❖❖❖

Love always expects the best of others.

In Luke 15 Jesus tells a parable about a father who had two sons. The younger son asked for his share of the family inheritance, then left home and squandered it on sinful pursuits. When he realized his folly, he decided to return home and ask his father's forgiveness. So "he got up and came to his father. But while he was still a long way off, his father saw him, and felt compassion for him, and ran and embraced him, and kissed him. And the son said to him, 'Father, I have sinned against heaven and in your sight; I am no longer worthy to be called your son.' But the father said to his slaves, 'Quickly bring out the best robe and put it on him, and put a ring on his hand and sandals on his feet; and bring the fattened calf, kill it, and let us eat and be merry'" (vv. 20-23).

That's a beautiful illustration of love's eagerness to forgive, but it also implies another characteristic of love. While the son was still far away, the father saw him coming. How could that be? Because he was watching for his son—anticipating and longing for his return. Love forgives when wrongs are committed against it, but it also expects the best of others. That's what it means to "believe all things" (1 Cor. 13:7). That son had hurt his father deeply, but his father never lost hope that his son would return.

I know a Christian woman who has been married to an unbelieving husband for thirty years. Yet she continues to say, "He will come to Christ someday." She isn't blind to the situation, but her love for her husband has transformed her earnest desire into an expectation. She believes he will turn to Christ because love always expects the best.

Perhaps you have a spouse or child who is an unbeliever or has drifted away from the Lord. Don't lose heart! Expect the best, and let that expectation motivate you to pray more fervently and to set a godly example for your loved ones to follow.

❖❖❖

Suggestions for Prayer: Ask God to guard your heart from cynical and suspicious attitudes toward others.

For Further Study: Read Matthew 9:1-13, noting the attitudes of the Jewish scribes and Pharisees toward Jesus.

"[Love] hopes all things" (1 Cor. 13:7).

✧✧✧

Love refuses to take human failure as final.

Even when faith falters, hope comes to the rescue. It is that long rope that keeps us linked to the sovereignty and power of God.

The Apostle Peter wrote to believers who were experiencing severe trials. To encourage them he began, "Blessed be the God and Father of our Lord Jesus Christ, who according to His great mercy has caused us to be born again to a living hope through the resurrection of Jesus Christ from the dead" (1 Peter 1:3).

Our hope is "a *living* hope" because our God is a living God. No matter how bleak your situation might seem, God is at work to accomplish His purposes. As Christ hung on the cross, it seemed as if sin had finally triumphed over righteousness. But sin's finest hour became its death knell when Christ arose from the grave as the Lord of life and the Redeemer of His people. Now "He who raised Christ Jesus from the dead will also give life to your mortal [body] through His Spirit who indwells you" (Rom. 8:11). Trials and death have no power over you. They simply bring you closer to Christ.

When ministering to others, hope gives you confidence that as long as there is life, human failure is never final. God refused to accept Israel's failures; Jesus refused to accept Peter's; and Paul refused to accept that of the Corinthians. When your attempts to cover the sins of others have failed or your righteous expectations have been shattered, hope says, "Don't give up. God can still work this out for good."

Hope is illustrated in the true story of a dog who was abandoned at the airport of a large city. He stayed there for over five years, waiting for his master to return. People at the airport fed and cared for him, but he refused to leave the spot where he last saw his master. If a dog's love for his master can produce that kind of hope, how much more should your love for God produce abiding hope?

✧✧✧

Suggestions for Prayer: Praise God for His sovereignty and power and for the hope that is yours in Christ.

For Further Study: Read Psalm 42, noting how the psalmist related the distressing circumstances of his life to his hope in God.

"[Love] endures all things" (1 Cor. 13:7).

❖❖❖

Love triumphs over opposition.

Endurance is the final characteristic of love that Paul mentions in this passage. The Greek word translated "endures" is a military term that speaks of being positioned in the middle of a violent battle. It refers not to withstanding minor annoyances but to incredible opposition—without ceasing to love.

Stephen is a good example of enduring love. He preached God's message without compromise, but his enemies stoned him to death. His last act was to fall on his knees, crying out with a loud voice, "Lord, do not hold this sin against them!" (Acts 7:60). A lesser man might have hated his tormentors, but not Stephen. He forgave them and beseeched God to do likewise, following the example of his Lord, who on the cross prayed, "Father, forgive them; for they do not know what they are doing" (Luke 23:34). That's the endurance of godly love.

Love bears all hurts, sins, and disappointments. It never broadcasts them but makes every attempt to reconcile and restore sinners. Love believes the best about others and is never cynical or suspicious. Even when it's under severe attack, it forgives and clings to the hope of God's power and promises. That kind of love should characterize every believer.

Your love may not be perfect, but it should be obvious. If you're struggling with implementing love in some area of your life, remember these five keys:

- Acknowledge that love is a command (Rom. 13:8-10).
- Agree that you have the spiritual resources to love others as God loves you (Rom. 5:5).
- Understand that loving others is normal Christian behavior (1 John 4:7-10).
- Realize that love is the Spirit's work (Gal. 5:22).
- Be fervent in your love for others (1 Peter 1:22; 4:8).

Godly love should be your highest purpose and greatest joy (Matt. 22:36-40). As you love others, you glorify Christ and make Him known to the world.

❖❖❖

Suggestions for Prayer: Review the fifteen characteristics of love from 1 Corinthians 13:4-7, asking God to increase each of them in your life.

For Further Study: Reread each reference in the five keys for implementing love in your life, and commit at least one to memory.

"Hate evil, you who love the Lord" (Ps. 97:10).

❖❖❖

God's hatred for evil is an extension of His love.

After spending this month exploring fifteen characteristics of godly love, it might seem odd to shift suddenly to the topic of hatred. Additionally, "holy hatred" will sound like a contradiction in terms to those who view all hatred as evil. But love and hate are inseparable. You can't truly love something and be complacent about the things that oppose or threaten it.

If you love your spouse, you hate anything that would defile or injure him or her. If you love your children, you hate anything that would harm them. If you love good, you hate evil. If you love unity, you hate discord. If you love God, you hate Satan. That's why Scripture says, "Hate evil, you who love the Lord" (Ps. 97:10) and, "The fear of the Lord is to hate evil; pride and arrogance and the evil way, and the perverted mouth, I [God personified] hate" (Prov. 8:13).

Unquestionably God is a God of love. First John 4 says, "Beloved, let us love one another, for love is from God; and every one who loves is born of God and knows God. The one who does not love does not know God, for God is love. . . . Beloved, if God so loved us, we also ought to love one another. . . . And we have come to know and have believed the love which God has for us. God is love, and the one who abides in love abides in God, and God abides in him" (vv. 7-8, 11, 16).

How are we to respond to that love? The psalmist wrote, "From Thy precepts I get understanding; therefore I hate every false way. . . . I hate those who are double-minded, but I love Thy law. . . . I esteem right all Thy precepts concerning everything, I hate every false way. . . . I hate and despise falsehood, but I love Thy law" (Ps. 119:104, 113, 128, 163).

Is that your prayer? Do you hate the things that oppose God? Are you offended by what offends Him? Remember, holy hatred is as much a part of godly love as any of its other characteristics. If you love God, you must necessarily hate evil.

❖❖❖

Suggestions for Prayer: Ask God to increase your love for Him and your hatred for evil.

For Further Study: Meditate on Psalm 119:101-104, and commit it to memory.

"There are six things which the Lord hates, yes, seven which are an abomination to Him: haughty eyes, a lying tongue, and hands that shed innocent blood, a heart that devises wicked plans, feet that run rapidly to evil, a false witness who utters lies, and one who spreads strife among brothers" (Prov. 6:16-19).

❖❖❖

God is clear about the things that displease Him.

God hates sin in any form, but Proverbs 6:17-19 lists seven that are especially loathsome to Him. First is "haughty eyes" (v. 17), which pictures a proud and arrogant person with his nose in the air and his eyes uplifted. The pride in his heart is reflected in his mannerisms.

Pride is perhaps listed first because it is at the heart of all rebellion against God—beginning with Lucifer himself, who cried out against God, "I will ascend to heaven; I will raise my throne above the stars of God, and I will sit on the mount of assembly in the recesses of the north. I will ascend above the heights of the clouds; I will make myself like the Most High" (Isa. 14:13-14).

God also hates "a lying tongue" (v. 17). Men often toy with truth, denying or distorting it to gain some supposed advantage. But God can't tolerate deception of any kind. He expects us to live according to His truth.

Third, He hates murderous hands (v. 17). That speaks of people whose hatred and greed are so strong that they will kill rather than be denied what they want. God created life and established its sanctity. That's why He ordained that murderers be put to death (Gen. 9:6).

God also hates a wicked heart and malevolent feet (v. 18). Sometimes people fall into sin inadvertently. But these people carefully plot their sinful activities and then hurry to execute their plans.

Finally, God hates "a false witness" and a divisive spirit (v. 19). Bearing "false witness" means telling lies about an innocent party. That can obstruct justice, destroy a reputation, and even destroy a life. A divisive spirit is one who creates divisions where there should be unity.

Those sins characterize unbelievers, but Christians aren't immune from them. So be on guard not to stray into attitudes and actions that God hates.

❖❖❖

Suggestions for Prayer: If you are practicing any of those things, confess them and repent.

For Further Study: According to Philippians 2:1-5, how should Christians treat one another?

"Do not love the world, nor the things in the world. If any one loves the world, the love of the Father is not in him. For all that is in the world, the lust of the flesh and the lust of the eyes and the boastful pride of life, is not from the Father, but is from the world. And the world is passing away, and also its lusts; but the one who does the will of God abides forever" (1 John 2:15-17).

❖❖❖

If you love the world, you're engaging in a love God hates.

Satan, from the very beginning of his rebellious activities, has been developing an invisible spiritual system of evil designed to oppose God and enslave people to sin. The Apostle John identified that system as "the world" and warned us not to love it.

Satan has had many centuries to develop his evil system; so it is very effective on those who reject Christ. First John 5:19 explains that while we as Christians belong to God, "the whole world lies in the power of the evil one," whom Jesus called "the ruler of this world" (John 12:31). In John 8:44 He identified certain unbelievers as children of their father, the Devil, who is a "murderer" and "the father of lies." That's how completely unbelievers are identified with Satan.

As a believer, you are identified with God. You have been delivered out of the domain of darkness and placed into the Kingdom of Christ (Col. 1:13). You are from God and have overcome the evil one because the Holy Spirit who indwells you is greater than he who controls the world (1 John 4:4).

Sadly, Christians sometimes flirt with the very things they've been saved from. Don't do that! Satan and his system have nothing to offer you. They are doomed. First John 2:17 says, "The world is passing away, and also its lusts; but the one who does the will of God abides forever."

❖❖❖

Suggestions for Prayer: If you've been flirting with the world, ask God's forgiveness. ❖ Praise God that someday Satan and his evil system will be vanquished.

For Further Study: Read the epistle of 1 John, noting the contrasts between the children of God and the children of Satan.

"Do not love the world, nor the things in the world. If any one loves the world, the love of the Father is not in him" (1 John 2:15).

❖❖❖

The world is opposed to everything God stands for.

Loving the world begins with thinking that God doesn't know what's best for you and is trying to cheat you out of something you deserve. That thought soon blossoms into a willingness to disregard God's warnings altogether and take whatever Satan has to offer.

Love of the world started in the Garden of Eden and continues to this day. Genesis 3:6 says, "When the woman saw that the tree was good for food, and that it was a delight to the eyes, and that the tree was desirable to make one wise, she took from its fruit and ate; and she gave also to her husband with her, and he ate." What made them think the fruit was good for food or able to make them wise? God didn't tell them that. In fact, He warned them that they would die if they ate the fruit (Gen. 2:17). But Eve believed the serpent's lie, and Adam followed suit.

Satan continues to propagate his lies, but you needn't fall prey to them if you love God and remember that the world is opposed to everything He stands for. It is spiritually dead, void of the Spirit (John 14:17), morally defiled, and dominated by pride, greed, and evil desires. It produces wrong opinions, selfish aims, sinful pleasures, demoralizing influences, corrupt politics, empty honors, and fickle love.

You can't love the world and God at the same time, because love knows no rivals. It gives its object first place. If you love God, He will have first place in your life. If you love the world, the love of the Father isn't in you (1 John 2:15).

Galatians 1:3-5 explains that Jesus "gave Himself for our sins, that He might deliver us out of this present evil age, according to the will of our God and Father, to whom be the glory forevermore." Christ died to deliver us from Satan's evil system. What greater motivation could there be to reject the world and live to God's glory?

❖❖❖

Suggestions for Prayer: Ask God for greater wisdom and for grace to resist the world's influences.

For Further Study: According to Ephesians 6:10-18, how can you as a believer protect yourself against Satan's evil system?

"Be strong in the Lord, and in the strength of His might. Put on the full armor of God, that you may be able to stand firm against the schemes of the devil. For our struggle is not against flesh and blood, but against the rulers, against the powers, against the world-forces of this darkness, against the spiritual forces of wickedness in the heavenly places" (Eph. 6:10-12).

❖❖❖

Victory in battle comes when you identify the enemy, resist his attacks, and then take the initiative against him.

Our nation has known many wars, but Vietnam was an especially frustrating campaign. Thick jungle terrain made the enemy hard to find, and guerrilla warfare made him hard to fight. Many Vietnamese who peacefully worked the rice paddies by day donned the black garb of the Viet Cong soldier by night and invaded unsuspecting U.S. forces camped nearby. American public opinion was strongly anti-war, and morale among our troops was often low.

Spiritual warfare has similar parallels. Subtly and deceitfully, Satan disguises himself as an "angel of light" (2 Cor. 11:14) and "prowls about like a roaring lion, seeking someone to devour" (1 Peter 5:8). His emissaries disguise themselves as "apostles of Christ" and "servants of righteousness" (2 Cor. 11:13-15). It takes wisdom and discernment to identify them and to defend yourself against their attacks.

Most people are defenseless, however, because they scoff at the supernatural and deny the reality of spiritual warfare. They think Satan may be fine for movie plots and book sales but assume that only the superstitious and credulous take him seriously. Unfortunately, many Christians have succumbed to such persons' ridicule and have forsaken the battle.

Ephesians 6:10-24 reminds us that spiritual warfare is real and that God has given us all the resources we need—not only to defend ourselves, but also to take the initiative and win the victory over the forces of darkness.

I pray that our studies this month will encourage you in the battle and will challenge you to always have on "the full armor of God, that you may be able to stand firm against the schemes of the devil" (Eph. 6:11).

❖❖❖

Suggestions for Prayer: Seek discernment and grace to identify the enemy and to stand against him courageously.

For Further Study: Read Ephesians 6:10-24. What armor has God supplied to protect you in spiritual warfare?

"Be strong in the Lord, and in the strength of His might. Put on the full armor of God, that you may be able to stand firm against the schemes of the devil" (Eph. 6:10-11).

✧✧✧

Adequate preparation is the key to spiritual victory.

The Gulf War introduced some highly sophisticated weapons that had never been proven under live battle conditions. Most of the troops hadn't experienced war either. Yet, troops and machinery combined in a display of military conquest unparalleled in history.

Thorough preparation proved to be an indispensable element in that overwhelming victory. That included developing and testing high-tech weaponry, recruiting and training troops, and engaging in mock battles. Generals know that if they dare enter a battlefield ill-prepared, they're destined for defeat. Consequently, they do everything possible to prepare their troops for victory.

Similarly, your success in spiritual warfare is directly proportional to your preparedness. You must "be strong in the Lord, and in the strength of His might" (Eph. 6:10) and must also put on your armor (v. 11). God is your strength and source of victory, but you must trust Him and must appropriate your spiritual resources. As Oliver Cromwell said, "Trust in God and keep your powder dry."

If you delay preparation until the battle is upon you, it's too late. If your armor isn't in place, you're vulnerable to the arrows of the enemy. If you neglect prayer, worship, Bible study, accountability, and the other disciplines of faith, you can't expect to prevail when spiritual skirmishes arise.

No soldier who values his own life would step onto a battlefield unprepared. How much more should soldiers of Christ prepare themselves to fight against Satan's forces! Be diligent. Christ guarantees ultimate victory, but you can lose individual battles if you're unprepared. It's even possible to lapse into periods of spiritual lethargy, indifference, impotency, and ineffectiveness, but that's utterly inconsistent with your mandate to "fight the good fight" (1 Tim. 1:18).

Don't be caught off-guard! Keep your armor on, and remain alert to the advances of the enemy.

✧✧✧

Suggestions for Prayer: Ask God to keep you alert to the reality of spiritual warfare and to the need to be prepared at all times for battle. ✧ Thank Him for the times He protected you when your armor wasn't as secure as it needed to be.

For Further Study: Memorize 2 Timothy 2:4 as a reminder to be spiritually prepared at all times.

"Be strong in the Lord, and in the strength of His might. Put on the full armor of God, that you may be able to stand firm against the schemes of the devil" (Eph. 6:10-11).

❖❖❖

In Christ you have every resource necessary for spiritual victory.

Satan opposes God and wants to prevent believers from glorifying Him. One way he does that is by convincing them that he is either so formidable they could never defeat him, or so weak they can fight him in their own strength.

Second Corinthians 10:4 says, "The weapons of our warfare are not of the flesh, but divinely powerful for the destruction of fortresses." Human resources alone can never defeat a spiritual enemy, but divine resources can. That's why it's crucial to understand the resources you have in Christ that ensure spiritual victory.

In Ephesians 1:3 Paul says you have received all the blessings of Heaven through Christ. That includes being forgiven and redeemed (vv. 6-7) and receiving knowledge, understanding, and wisdom (vv. 17-18). Within you resides the Holy Spirit (v. 13), who strengthens you and accomplishes more than you can ask or think (3:16, 20).

Believers represent the awesome power of God in this world—the same power that raised Christ from the dead, seated Him at the right hand of the Father, and subjected all things under His feet (Eph. 1:19-22). He is the Sovereign Lord against whom no one can successfully stand. That's why Paul exhorted us to "be strong in *the Lord*, and in the strength of *His* might" (Eph. 6:10, emphasis added). We find this strength by putting on the armor He has supplied: truth, righteousness, peace, faith, salvation, and the Word, and using it all with prayer. Then, no matter what direction the enemy approaches from or how subtle his attacks may be, we'll be able to stand firm.

Satan's attacks are complex and subtle. His ways of working in this world are cunning and deceitful. Since it's impossible to analyze and anticipate his every offense, focus on strengthening your defenses by understanding your spiritual resources and using them each day.

❖❖❖

Suggestions for Prayer: Ask God to increase your understanding of spiritual warfare. ❖ Seek wisdom in applying your resources in the most effective ways. ❖ When you face spiritual battles, confide in a Christian friend who will pray with you and encourage you.

For Further Study: According to Matthew 4:1-11, how did Jesus deal with Satan's attacks?

"Be strong in the Lord, and in the strength of His might. Put on the full armor of God" (Eph. 6:10-11).

❖❖❖

Spiritual victory is not passive; it involves the discipline of daily obedience to Christ and His Word.

When I was a child, my father and I watched a boxing match on television. After going through the ritual of punching the air, kicking his feet, and putting rosin on his shoes, one of the fighters knelt in the corner and crossed himself. I asked my dad if that helped. He said, "It does if he can punch. If he can't punch, it doesn't help at all."

That illustrates a point we touched on yesterday and will explore further today: God's part and our part in spiritual warfare. Many Christians believe spiritual victory comes simply by surrendering more completely to God. They quote verses like 2 Chronicles 20:15 to support their view: "The battle is not yours but God's." "Stop struggling and striving," they say. "Instead, yield and completely surrender yourself to God. He alone does the fighting and gives the victory."

Such people are often called "Quietists" because they view the Christian's role in spiritual warfare as passive or quiet. Their anthem is, "Let go and let God."

But Scripture gives a very different view of the believer's role. It pictures the Christian life as a war, a race, and a fight. We depend on God's energy, power, and strength, but we are by no means passive. We're commanded to apply ourselves to good deeds, resist the Devil, bring our bodies under subjection, walk in wisdom, press toward the prize, cleanse ourselves from all filthiness of flesh and spirit, work out our salvation with fear and trembling, and perfect holiness in the fear of God. Those are calls to fervent action.

In Ephesians 6:10-11 Paul says, "Be strong in the . . . strength of His might. Put on the full armor of God." That's the balance. God supplies the resources; we supply the effort.

❖❖❖

Suggestions for Prayer: Thank God for the strength He gives for spiritual victory. ❖ Ask for His wisdom in living a balanced Christian life.

For Further Study: Read 2 Peter 1:3-7. ❖ What does God supply for Christian living? ❖ What must you as a believer supply?

"Be strong in the Lord, and in the strength of His might . . . . For our struggle is not against flesh and blood, but against the rulers, against the powers, against the world forces of this darkness, against the spiritual forces of wickedness in the heavenly places" (Eph. 6:10, 12).

❖❖❖

Spiritual warfare can be intense, but God's grace enables you to prevail against Satan's attacks.

Through the ages Satan has accused, besieged, and battered believers in an effort to prevent them from living to the glory of God. He attempts to snatch the gospel message from a person's heart even before salvation occurs (Matt. 13:19). He bombards believers with false doctrine, trying to confuse and distract them from Biblical truth (Eph. 4:14).

Martin Luther reported that his conflict with Satan became so intense that at one point it was as if he could see him. In anger over Satan's incessant attacks, Luther picked up his inkwell and threw it at him. It hit the wall with a resounding crash, splattering ink throughout the room. The stains remained for many years, reminding all who saw them of how vivid spiritual conflict can be.

You may not have experienced anything like the intensity of Martin Luther's conflict, but spiritual warfare is just as real for you as it was for him. You are in mortal combat with Satan and his evil forces. That's why Paul said, "Our struggle is not against flesh and blood, but against . . . spiritual forces of wickedness in the heavenly places" (Eph. 6:12).

"Struggle" in that verse speaks of life-and-death, hand-to-hand combat—the kind Jesus Himself experienced while on earth. He met opposition and persecution at every turn. The same was true of Paul and the other apostles as they dealt with Jewish religionists, heathens, sorcerers, and demon-possessed people who tried in vain to thwart the apostles' missionary efforts.

Satan's onslaughts may seem overwhelming at times, but don't be discouraged. See them for what they are—a defeated foe's last-ditch efforts to inflict damage on the conquering army. The Lord will strengthen and protect you, just as He has protected all believers before you.

❖❖❖

Suggestions for Prayer: Praise God for being your protector and the source of spiritual victory.

For Further Study: Read Acts 4:1-22. ❖ What kind of opposition did Peter and John face? ❖ How did they respond to the Jewish Council's order not to preach the gospel?

"Stand firm against the schemes of the devil" (Eph. 6:11).

❖❖❖

Keep your spiritual armor on at all times.

Every battle has an offensive and defensive strategy. Paul outlines the Christian's offensive strategy in 2 Corinthians 10:3-5: "Though we walk in the flesh, we do not war according to the flesh, for the weapons of our warfare are not of the flesh, but divinely powerful for the destruction of fortresses. We are destroying speculations and every lofty thing raised up against the knowledge of God, and we are taking every thought captive to the obedience of Christ."

Our defensive strategy is to rely on Christ's strength and put on our spiritual armor (Eph. 6:10-11). Paul was probably chained to a Roman soldier when he wrote to the Ephesians; so he had a ready illustration of spiritual armament at hand. But unlike Roman soldiers, who removed their armor when off-duty, Christians must remain fully protected at all times. That thought is captured in the Greek word translated "put on" in Ephesians 6:11, which carries the idea of permanence—putting it on once and for all.

"Stand firm" in verse 11 translates a military term that speaks of holding your ground while under attack. When properly employed, your spiritual armor serves as a lifelong companion that enables you to fight against the forces of evil and to do so without retreat. Just as Jesus personally instructed the churches in Thyatira and Philadelphia to hold fast until He returns (Rev. 2:25; 3:11), so He also instructs us to stand our ground without wavering.

Similar New Testament exhortations call us to hold fast to Biblical truth (1 Cor. 15:2), to that which is good (1 Thess. 5:21), to our confidence in Christ (Heb. 3:6), and to our confession of faith (Heb. 4:14). Those are marks of a strong and stable believer against whom the schemes of Satan have little effect.

❖❖❖

Suggestions for Prayer: Is there an area of your Christian life in which you're not standing as firm as you should—perhaps prayer, Bible study, or personal ministry? If so, confess it to the Lord, and begin to strengthen that area today. Don't give Satan a weakness to attack.

For Further Study: Memorize 1 John 4:4 as a reminder of God's power in your life.

"Stand firm against the schemes of the devil" (Eph. 6:11).

✧✧✧

Satan opposes everything God does.

The believer's conflict with the forces of darkness is rightly called spiritual warfare since Satan and his evil world system are hostile toward everything God does. By nature they are anti-God and anti-Christ.

Satan is the antithesis of every godly attribute. God is holy; Satan is evil. God is love; Satan is the embodiment of hatred. God redeems His children; Satan damns his. Jesus reveals grace and truth (John 1:17), but Satan "does not stand in the truth, because there is no truth in him. Whenever he speaks a lie, he speaks from his own nature; for he is a liar, and the father of lies" (John 8:44).

God gives life, whereas Satan breeds death (Heb. 2:14). God produces "love, joy, peace, patience, kindness, goodness, faithfulness, gentleness, self-control" (Gal. 5:22-23). Satan produces "immorality, impurity, sensuality, idolatry, sorcery, enmities, strife, jealousy, outbursts of anger, disputes, dissensions, factions, envyings, drunkenness, carousings, and things like these" (vv. 19-21).

God uses trials to prove the genuineness of your faith and to increase your joy and spiritual endurance (James 1:3). Satan uses temptation in an attempt to destroy your faith and silence your testimony. God grants freedom from the bondage of sin, while Satan wants to enslave you to sin for all eternity (2 Tim. 2:26).

Jesus is your "Advocate," pleading your cause before the Father (1 John 2:1). Satan is an "accuser," blaming you incessantly for things God has already forgiven (Rev. 12:10).

Because Satan opposes everything God does, he'll also oppose God's children. When he does, don't be overly concerned or think of it as odd or unfair. Expect trials, be prepared, and rejoice, because they show you're a threat to Satan's system and an asset to Christ's Kingdom.

✧✧✧

Suggestions for Prayer: Thank God for the joy of knowing Christ and being free from sin's bondage. ✧ Ask Him to use you today in a powerful way for His glory.

For Further Study: Read Romans 14:17 and 1 John 2:16-17. What characterizes the Kingdom of God? The evil world system of Satan?

"Stand firm against the schemes of the devil" (Eph. 6:11).

✧✧✧

One of Satan's most effective tactics is to challenge God's credibility.

Paul's exhortation to "stand firm against the schemes of the devil" (Eph. 6:11) refers to the various tactics Satan employs in spiritual warfare. One of his tactics is to call God's character and motives into question by raising doubts about His Word.

He used that approach in the Garden of Eden when he said to Eve, "Indeed, has God said, 'You shall not eat from any tree of the garden'?" (Gen. 3:1). In one brief statement Satan disputed and distorted God's Word. God didn't forbid them to eat from *any* tree. They could eat freely from every tree except one—the tree of the knowledge of good and evil (2:16-17).

Satan followed his distortion with an outright denial of God's Word: "You surely shall not die!" (3:4). He implied that God lied when He said sin would result in death. Satan then went on to tell Eve that if she ate the fruit, she would in fact become like God Himself (v. 5). The implication is that God was withholding something good from Eve, and to keep her from seeking it, He had intimidated her with empty threats of death and judgment.

Do you see the insidious nature of Satan's approach? Tragically, Eve didn't. Rather than trusting and obeying God, she believed Satan's lies and concluded that the tree was "good for food," "a delight to the eyes," and "desirable to make one wise." Then "she took from its fruit and ate" (v. 6).

Satan deceives and spreads his lies from generation to generation (2 Cor. 11:14). Although he is subtle, his attempts to discredit God by disputing, distorting, and denying His Word should be obvious to discerning Christians.

Don't be victimized by Satan's attacks. Become strong in the Word through systematic Bible study. Yield to the Spirit's control through prayer and obedience to Biblical principles.

✧✧✧

Suggestions for Prayer: Ask God for the discernment to recognize Satanic deceptions, and for the wisdom to pursue truth. ✧ Pray for God's enabling as you discipline yourself for diligent Bible study.

For Further Study: Read 1 John 2:12-14. How did John describe those who are strong in the Word?

"Stand firm against the schemes of the devil" (Eph. 6:11).

❖❖❖

Satan wants to catch you off-guard.

Yesterday we saw how Satan attacks God's Word. Today we will see how he attacks God's people. Persecution, peer pressure, and preoccupation are three weapons he employs with great effectiveness.

Persecution should never take Christians by surprise, because Scripture repeatedly warns us that it will come. For example, 2 Timothy 3:12 says, "Indeed, all who desire to live godly in Christ Jesus will be persecuted." Yet, such warnings are often overlooked in the health, wealth, and prosperity climate of contemporary Christianity.

As the greed perpetuated by such a movement continues its assault on Christian virtue, many professing believers have come to expect a pain-free, trouble-free life. When trials come, they're caught off-guard and are often disillusioned with the church or with God Himself. Some prove to be phony believers, whom Jesus described in His parable of the four soils—people who initially respond to the gospel with joy, yet fall away when affliction or persecution arises because of the Word (Matt. 13:21).

Satan also uses peer pressure as an effective weapon. Many people never come to Christ for fear of losing their friends or being thought of as different. Even Christians sometimes struggle with peer pressure, compromising God's standards to avoid offending others.

Another weapon is preoccupation with the world. Often the hardest place to live the Christian life is in the easiest place. For example, becoming a Christian in America isn't the life-threatening choice it is in some parts of the world. Some who stand boldly against persecution or peer pressure might falter in a climate of acceptance. Often that's when the danger of spiritual complacency and preoccupation with the world is greatest.

To guard against those attacks, remember that God uses persecution to mature you and bring glory to Himself. Also, make a conscious choice each day to please God rather than people. Finally, evaluate your priorities and activities carefully. Fight the tendency to become preoccupied with things unrelated to God's Kingdom.

❖❖❖

Suggestions for Prayer: Ask God to keep you spiritually alert throughout this day, so the enemy doesn't catch you off-guard.

For Further Study: Read Matthew 26:31-56. What might the disciples have done to avoid being caught off-guard?

September 10 MAINTAINING SPIRITUAL EFFECTIVENESS

"Stand firm against the schemes of the devil" (Eph. 6:11).

❖❖❖

Satan wants to render you ineffective for Christ.

In 1 Corinthians 16:9 Paul says, "A wide door for effective service has opened to me, and there are many adversaries." That's typical of spiritual warfare. The more opportunities you have to serve Christ, the more adversaries you'll face. That's because Satan seeks to hinder your spiritual service.

Often seminary students ask me if ministry becomes easier over the years. In one sense it does because you learn better study skills, time management, and the like. But in a greater sense it becomes more difficult because as you labor in the Word, contend for souls, and struggle against your own weaknesses, Satan opposes you at every turn.

You can sense something of the difficulty of ministry in Paul's words to the Thessalonians: "Having thus a fond affection for you, we were well-pleased to impart to you not only the gospel but also our own lives, because you had become very dear to us. For you recall, brethren, our labor and hardship, how working night and day so as not to be a burden to any of you, we proclaimed to you the gospel of God" (1 Thess. 2:8-9). To the Ephesian elders he said, "Be on the alert, remembering that night and day for a period of three years I did not cease to admonish each one with tears" (Acts 20:31).

Every sphere of ministry is important—whether you're a pastor, homemaker, factory worker, or student. Consequently, every ministry encounters opposition as Satan attempts to cause friction and discouragement within families, churches, and workplaces. Thus, believers must be humble and gentle toward one another, "being diligent to preserve the unity of the Spirit in the bond of peace" (Eph. 4:3). When we do that, the Body of Christ is strengthened, and Satan can't gain a foothold.

Ministry is hard work, and the obstacles are great, but the victories are even greater. So be faithful, knowing that God will reward you richly.

❖❖❖

Suggestions for Prayer: Thank God for the privilege of serving Him, even during the hard times. ❖ Thank Him for the encouragement you receive from His Spirit, His Word, and your fellow-believers.

For Further Study: According to Romans 8:18, what was Paul's perspective on difficulties?

> *"Our struggle is not against flesh and blood, but against the rulers, against the powers, against the world-forces of this darkness, against the spiritual forces of wickedness in the heavenly places" (Eph. 6:12).*

❖❖❖

Don't confuse prisoners of war with the enemy.

Sometimes in the heat of battle we might lose perspective on who the real enemy is. Ephesians 6:12 reminds us that our struggle isn't against sinful people, but against the evil system and the supernatural forces that influence their attitudes and actions.

In his assault on the Kingdom of God, Satan has assembled a highly organized army of fallen angels. Paul categorized them as "rulers . . . powers . . . world-forces of this darkness . . . spiritual forces of wickedness in the heavenly places" (Eph. 6:12).

That isn't a detailed description of Satan's hierarchy but simply a general indication of its power and sophistication. Apparently "rulers" and "powers" are high-ranking demons. "World forces of this darkness" are possibly demons who infiltrate various political systems of the world, attempting to direct human leaders to oppose God's plans. An example is a demon called "the prince of the kingdom of Persia" in Daniel 10:13 who withstood God's angelic messenger to Daniel until Michael the archangel came to the rescue. "Spiritual forces of wickedness in the heavenly places" perhaps refers to demons involved in the most vile and perverted kinds of sins—gross immorality, occultic practices, Satan worship, and the like.

Those who reject Christ and God are unwitting prisoners of war—captured and mobilized by the enemy to accomplish his purposes. Tragically, when he's finished with them he'll abandon them, and they will go to an eternal Hell.

You probably know unbelievers who enjoy ridiculing your faith and making life difficult for you. Although that is hard to take, be patient, and don't become embittered toward them. Ask God to make you an instrument of His love as you reach out to them. Also pray that God will remove their spiritual blindness, so they can see beyond Satan's lies and recognize their need for a Savior.

❖❖❖

Suggestions for Prayer: Praise God for delivering you from "the domain of darkness" and transferring you into "the kingdom of His beloved Son" (Col. 1:13). ❖ Ask Him to use you today to break through Satan's deception in someone's life.

For Further Study: Read 2 Corinthians 4:3-7, noting why people reject the gospel.

"Take up the full armor of God, that you may be able to resist in the evil day, and having done everything, to stand firm" (Eph. 6:13).

✧✧✧

Spiritual warfare isn't as much a frontal attack on Satan's domain as it is the ability to resist his advances.

Spiritual warfare has become a popular topic in recent years. Books, tapes, and seminars on the subject abound, but there is still much confusion. Some say we must rebuke and bind Satan in order to thwart his power and influence. Others say we must expel demonic spirits through "deliverance ministries." Still others encourage us to band together to aggressively assault the strongholds of supposed territorial demons.

But spiritual warfare isn't an outright frontal attack on the forces of darkness. Scripture says, "Submit . . . to God. Resist the devil and he will flee from you" (James 4:7); "Be on the alert. Your adversary, the devil, prowls about like a roaring lion, seeking someone to devour. But resist him, firm in your faith" (1 Peter 5:8-9). The idea that Christians have the authority to rebuke or bind Satan is foreign to Scripture. Even Michael the archangel treated him with more respect than that (Jude 9).

Spiritual victory involves submitting to God, pursuing His will, keeping your spiritual armor on, being on the alert for Satan's attacks, and then standing firm and resisting him "in the evil day" (Eph. 6:13).

"Evil day" is a general reference to the sin that exists in this world. As "the god of this world" (2 Cor. 4:4), Satan will continue to produce evil until he and his forces are cast into the lake of fire (Rev. 20:10-15). Then "the evil day" will give way to an eternal age of righteousness.

Countless people have pastored churches, taught Sunday school classes, led Bible studies, sung in choirs, and been involved in every conceivable area of ministry only to one day abandon their ministries and embrace the world. Somehow they stopped resisting the Devil and lost the courage to stand firm.

How about you? Is your commitment strong? Are you willing to stand firm for the Lord today?

✧✧✧

Suggestions for Prayer: Ask God for the grace to boldly resist whatever might challenge your faith today.

For Further Study: Read 1 Corinthians 9:23-27. ✧ What was Paul's great fear? ✧ What measures did he take to ensure spiritual victory? ✧ Are you taking the same measures?

"Stand firm therefore, having girded your loins with truth"
(Eph. 6:14).

◇◇◇

Truthfulness is the best defense against Satan's lies.

The first piece of armor Paul mentions in Ephesians 6:14 is the belt of truth. Roman soldiers of his day wore a tunic, which was a large square piece of material with holes for the head and arms. A belt kept the tunic from flying loosely and getting in the way in the midst of battle.

The phrase "having girded your loins" was commonly used for gathering up the loose material of one's tunic or robe when preparing for battle or travel. It speaks of preparedness, as in Exodus 12:11, where God tells the children of Israel to gird their loins for their exodus from Egypt. Jesus used it in a figurative sense in Luke 12:35, where He warns us to gird our loins or "be dressed in readiness" for His second coming. Peter said we're to gird our minds for action (1 Peter 1:13).

The Greek word translated "truth" in Ephesians 6:14 can refer either to the content of that which is true or to an attitude of truthfulness. Both are implied in the verse. In Ephesians 4 Paul combines both aspects in warning us not to be "tossed here and there by waves, and carried about by every wind of doctrine, by the trickery of men, by craftiness in deceitful scheming" (vv. 14-15). Instead, we are to embrace sound doctrine and always speak the truth in love.

The way to defend yourself against the cunning deceptions of Satan is to gird yourself with a thorough knowledge of God's Word and a firm commitment to obedience. Yet many Christians remain vulnerable because they're unwilling to do that.

Paul exhorted the Philippians to excel in "knowledge" and "discernment" and to remain "sincere and blameless" until in Christ's presence (Phil. 1:9-10), and you must do the same. Never be content with your present level of spirituality. Keep learning and growing. Demonstrate an attitude of truthfulness that reveals your commitment to God's Word and your readiness for battle.

◇◇◇

Suggestions for Prayer: Is your life characterized by truthfulness? If not, you're a ready target for Satan's schemes. Confess this to the Lord, and ask Him to cleanse your heart and to give you a love for His truth. Begin today to apply His Word to your life.

For Further Study: Read verses 1-4 and 13-15 of 2 Corinthians 11, noting the tactics of Satan and his servants.

"Stand firm therefore . . . having put on the breastplate of right-eousness" (Eph. 6:14).

❖❖❖

True righteousness begins with a right relationship with God.

A Roman soldier would often engage his enemy in hand-to-hand combat. At such times, the weapon of choice was the short sword, with which he sought to penetrate his opponent's vital organs. For his own protection he wore a molded metal breastplate that extended from the base of his neck to the top of his thighs. It helped deflect any attacks aimed at his heart and abdomen.

The Roman breastplate has great symbolism in Paul's analogy because to the Jewish people the heart represented man's mind and thinking processes; the intestinal area or bowels represented the seat of feelings and emotions. Proverbs 23:7 says, "As [a man] thinketh in his heart, so is he" (KJV). Jeremiah 17:9 says, "The heart is more deceitful than all else and is desperately sick; who can understand it?" Jesus added, "From within, out of the heart of men, proceed the evil thoughts" (Mark 7:21).

During spiritual warfare, Satan's primary attacks target your thinking and emotions. If he can condition you to think and feel contrary to God's Word, he has won a significant victory. That's why he attempts to fill your mind with lies, immorality, false doctrine, and half-truths. He tries to blur the line between righteousness and sin by surrounding you with evil influences that increase your tolerance for sin. He clothes offensive sin in the blinding garment of entertainment. He puts it to music and masks it in humor to confuse you and deaden your spiritual senses. Satan wants to corrupt your emotions and draw you into sinful desires.

Putting on the breastplate of righteousness begins with a right relationship with God, who is the source of true righteousness. From that relationship flows the commitment to cultivate righteousness in your own life by learning and applying His Word. Therein lies the protection you need to safeguard your mind and emotions from Satanic deceptions.

❖❖❖

Suggestions for Prayer: Focus on strengthening your relationship with God today. Commune with Him in prayer. Meditate on His Word. Seek His grace in responding thoughtfully and righteously to the temptations you face.

For Further Study: Read Proverbs 10, noting Solomon's description of right-eous people.

*"Stand firm therefore . . . having put on the breastplate of right-
eousness" (Eph. 6:14).*

❖❖❖

Practical righteousness is moment-by-moment obedience to God.

We've seen the importance of putting on the breastplate of righteousness as protection against Satan's attempts to pervert your thinking
and emotions. But Scripture speaks of three kinds of righteousness: self-righteousness, imputed righteousness, and practical righteousness. Which did
Paul have in mind in Ephesians 6:14?

Paul wasn't speaking of self-righteousness because that is what the breastplate of righteousness is designed to protect you from. Self-righteousness
deceives a person into thinking, "I can please God and reach Heaven on my
own merit." But Isaiah said, "All our righteous deeds are like a filthy garment"
(Isa. 64:6). Far from getting you to Heaven, self-righteousness will condemn
you to eternal Hell because it rejects the merits of Christ's atonement.

Similarly, Paul wasn't speaking of imputed righteousness—the righteousness of Christ granted to every believer at the moment of salvation. This is
also called "positional righteousness" because it results from your position or
standing in Christ. Second Corinthians 5:21 says that God made Christ, "who
knew no sin to be sin on our behalf, that we might become the righteousness
of God in Him." Every believer is clothed in the garment of Christ's righteousness. You don't put that on. It's already yours in Christ.

Only practical righteousness remains—that which flows from obedience to
God's Word. Although in God's eyes you are righteous in Christ, you must also
pursue righteous behavior. In other words, your practice should match your position. That's what Paul meant when he said, "Work out your salvation with fear
and trembling" (Phil. 2:12). John added that "the one who says he abides in
[Christ] ought himself to walk in the same manner as He walked" (1 John 2:6).

As you learn to live in obedience to God's Word, you'll be protected by the
breastplate of righteousness.

❖❖❖

Suggestions for Prayer: Ask the Spirit to help you search your heart and to
reveal any self-righteous attitudes that might be making you vulnerable to
Satan's attacks. Confess them, and then praise Christ for the true righteousness that is yours in Him.

For Further Study: Read Romans 3:10-23. What kind of righteousness did
Paul describe here?

September 16 A RIGHTEOUSNESS THAT GLORIFIES GOD

"Stand firm therefore . . . having put on the breastplate of right-eousness" (Eph. 6:14).

✧✧✧

A righteous life testifies to God's transforming power and brings Him glory.

We've seen the importance of donning the breastplate of righteousness, but Scripture also discusses the consequences of failing to do so. These consequences serve as warnings to anyone who is prone to neglect righteousness.

If you're not committed to righteousness, you not only make yourself spiritually vulnerable, but you also forfeit some of God's wonderful blessings. David prayed, "Restore to me the joy of Thy salvation" (Ps. 51:12). His sin had robbed him of his joy and assurance. That's true of us as well, because joy is directly proportional to obedience. If you're pursuing greater righteousness, you'll know greater joy.

You might also forfeit some of your heavenly reward. John said, "Watch yourselves, that you might not lose what we have accomplished, but that you may receive a full reward" (2 John 8). I believe that New Testament rewards are various capacities for service in Heaven. The greater your reward, the greater your capacity to serve God. Somehow your current righteousness and faithfulness to God affect what you will do for all eternity. Don't allow sin and negligence to diminish your reward!

Without righteousness you will also suffer loss of opportunity to glorify God. When thinking or behaving unrighteously, you violate your reason for existence, which is to glorify God in everything (1 Cor. 10:31). Instead of exalting Him, you bring reproach on His name. Instead of causing others to see your good works and glorify your Father in Heaven (Matt. 5:16), you breed confusion and mockery.

Peter says to us, "Beloved, I urge you as aliens and strangers to abstain from fleshly lusts, which wage war against the soul. Keep your behavior excellent among the Gentiles, so that . . . they may on account of your good deeds, as they observe them, glorify God in the day of visitation" (1 Peter 2:11). When unbelievers scrutinize your life, what do you see? Does your righteousness testify to God's saving and sanctifying grace?

✧✧✧

Suggestions for Prayer: Ask God to give you an increased hunger and thirst for righteousness as you seek to live to His glory today.

For Further Study: Memorize 2 Corinthians 5:21 as a reminder of God's marvelous grace to you.

"Stand firm . . . having shod your feet with the preparation of the gospel of peace" (Eph. 6:14-15).

❖❖❖

Standing firm while in the conflict requires the right kind of spiritual footwear.

I'll never forget a game that took place at the Rose Bowl during my college football days. Being wintertime and late in the football season, the field was in bad shape from several days of rain and an entire season of wear and tear. However, the grounds crew painted the field green; so it looked much better than it actually was. I had two pairs of football shoes—one with long spikes for bad turf and one with short spikes for good turf. Thinking the field looked pretty good, I opted to wear the short spikes.

On the opening kickoff I caught the ball on the 4 yard line, took two steps, and immediately landed on my backside. That's not unusual after a tackle, but in this case there wasn't an opponent in sight! I had slipped in the mud; my shoes had betrayed me.

Proper shoes are important in athletics and are even more important when you're fighting for your life. Roman soldiers took great care in selecting just the right shoe. Typically they wore a thick-soled semi-boot with straps securing it to the leg. On the bottom of the soles were hobnails that protruded like the cleats of a track or baseball shoe. The thick soles protected the feet from injury; the hobnails provided traction when maneuvering on the soil.

The Christian's spiritual footwear is the "gospel of peace" (Eph. 6:15). Romans 5:1 says, "Having been justified by faith, we have peace with God through our Lord Jesus Christ." God has reconciled you to Himself through the death of His Son (v. 10). Once you were His enemy; now you are His child. Once He opposed you; now He is on your side.

No matter how difficult your circumstances may be or how many opponents come against you, realize that the invincible God of the universe is on your side. He makes war against His enemies (Rev. 2:16), and against Him no one can stand. So stand firm in that confidence. Focus on your Great Ally rather than on your feeble enemies.

❖❖❖

Suggestions for Prayer: Thank God for His peace, presence, and protection in your life.

For Further Study: Read Judges 7. How did Gideon demonstrate his confidence that God was on his side?

"In addition to all, taking up the shield of faith with which you will be able to extinguish all the flaming missiles of the evil one" (Eph. 6:16).

◇◇◇

Intense spiritual warfare calls for intense trust in God.

A n on-duty Roman soldier was always dressed for battle, but he didn't employ his shield, helmet, and sword until the fighting started. But we as Christians must be ready for battle at all times because our enemy is relentless. We can't afford to overlook a single piece of armor or to slip into complacency or neglect.

In that regard, Ephesians 6:16 says in effect, "Now that you've prepared for battle by girding your loins with truth, protecting your vital organs with the breastplate of righteousness, and securing your feet with the gospel of peace, don't forget to take up your shield."

Two types of shields were commonly used by Roman soldiers. One was a small, lightweight, round shield that was strapped to the soldier's left forearm and was used to parry blows during hand-to-hand combat. The other, which Paul refers to here, was a large shield measuring about four and a half feet high and two and a half feet wide. It was made of sturdy wood covered with metal and a thick layer of oil-treated leather. The metal deflected arrows, while the oily leather extinguished the fiery pitch with which arrows were commonly swabbed. That type of shield was ideal for full-body protection.

In the initial stages of a battle, the front-line soldiers knelt behind their large shields to protect themselves and to provide a defense barrier for the troops behind them who were firing offensive weapons. The goal was to inch their way forward as a human wall until they could engage the enemy in hand-to-hand combat.

As a believer, the shield that protects you is your faith in God. If you never question His character, power, or Word, you'll never fall victim to Satan's attacks. That doesn't mean he won't besiege you; but when he does, his assaults will be ineffective.

◇◇◇

Suggestions for Prayer: Faith is a precious gift from God (Phil. 1:29). Thank Him for it, and ask for wisdom to apply it properly when spiritual struggles come (James 1:5).

For Further Study: Read Romans 8:31-39. ◇ Meditate on the victory you have in Christ. ◇ What effect should that have on your daily living?

"In addition to all, taking up the shield of faith with which you will be able to extinguish all the flaming missiles of the evil one" (Eph. 6:16).

❖❖❖

Don't elevate Satan's will above God's will in your life.

In Ephesians 6:16 Paul characterizes Satan as "the evil one" who attacks believers with flaming missiles. The Greek word translated "evil one" literally means "bad," "vile," or "wretched." All are apt descriptions of the archenemy of our souls, who seeks to maim and destroy us spiritually.

The term "flaming missiles" pictures one of the Roman weapons of Paul's day—arrows that had pitch-soaked cotton material affixed to their tips. In battle they were set on fire and shot at the enemy. As the arrow hit its target, flaming pitch spread onto clothing and other flammable surfaces. Under such attacks a Roman soldier without a shield was in a perilous situation indeed.

Satan's flaming arrows come in many forms: solicitations to impurity, selfishness, doubt, fear, disappointment, greed, vanity, covetousness, and the like. But whatever the specific form, all are seducing temptations aimed at eliciting ungodly responses.

Your faith protects you from such attacks when you elevate God's will above Satan's in your life. When tempted by Satan, Jesus responded by saying in effect, "I will not violate my Father's will by yielding to your devious schemes. In His own time He will feed Me, anoint Me as Messiah, and give Me the kingdoms of the world. I will not elevate your will and timing above His" (Matt. 4:1-11).

When the enemy suggested that Jesus make bread out of stones, Jesus could have created food. He is the Messiah and the sovereign Lord over the kingdoms of the world. But He trusted the Father and yielded to His will, even though it meant personal discomfort and, eventually, the cross. When Satan saw that Jesus' trust in the Father was unshakable, he left Him (v. 11). That's the power of faith.

I pray that you will show similar strength in times of testing. Satan will flee from you if you "resist him, firm in your faith" (1 Peter 5:9).

❖❖❖ .

Suggestions for Prayer: Praise Jesus for His sinless character and His example of how to triumph over temptation.

For Further Study: Memorize James 4:7 as a reminder of the importance of resisting Satan.

"Take the helmet of salvation" (Eph. 6:17).

❖❖❖

***Discouragement and doubt are deflected
when you know you're secure in Christ.***

The Roman soldier's helmet was a crucial piece of armor designed to deflect blows to the head—especially the potentially lethal blow of a broadsword. Soldiers of that day carried a swift and precise dagger designed for close-quarter, hand-to-hand combat. But they also carried a giant broadsword, which was a two-edged, three- to four-foot-long sword. It had a massive handle that, similar to a baseball bat, was held with both hands. With it they could take broad swipes from side to side or deliver a crushing blow to an opponent's skull.

To protect us from Satan's crushing blows, Paul tells us to "take the helmet of salvation." Considering all he's been telling us so far, he was not saying, "Oh, by the way, go get saved." Paul was addressing believers. Unbelievers don't have to put on spiritual armor. They aren't even in the battle. Satan doesn't attack his own forces.

In 1 Thessalonians 5:8 Paul describes the helmet of salvation as "the hope of salvation." That implies that Satan's most fierce and powerful blows are directed at the believer's assurance and security. Therefore Paul was encouraging believers to have confidence in the salvation they already possess. He knew that doubting their security in Christ would render them ineffective in spiritual warfare, just as a blow to the head renders one's physical body incapable of defending itself.

As a believer, you should have the assurance that you are secure in Christ. If you don't, you haven't put your helmet on, and that makes you vulnerable to discouragement and doubt. Romans 8:29-30 assures us that *all* whom God justifies, He sanctifies and glorifies. No one is lost in the process.

Jesus said, "My sheep hear My voice, and I know them, and they follow Me; and I give eternal life to them; and they shall never perish, and no one shall snatch them out of My hand" (John 10:27-28). That's a wonderful promise. So don't let your enemy rob you of the joy and assurance of knowing you belong to Christ, for the Lord will never let you go (Heb. 13:5).

❖❖❖

Suggestions for Prayer: Praise God for your eternal security in Christ!

For Further Study: Read John 6:37-40. ❖ Who receives eternal life? ❖ How does Christ respond to those who come to Him?

"Take the helmet of salvation" (Eph. 6:17).

❖❖❖

The key to conquering doubt is to focus on the preserving power of God.

Doubt comes to Christians in many ways. After you've sinned, your conscience might hiss at you, saying, "Surely you're not a Christian. Why would God save you anyway? You don't deserve His mercy. You're not good enough. How presumptuous to think God could ever use you!" Such doubts are common among Christians who focus on their performance rather than on God's power.

All too often we're quick to acknowledge God's power to save us but slow to understand His power to keep us. To complicate matters, many Christians believe they can lose their salvation; so they live in constant fear of falling away from the faith. Still others have never learned what Scripture teaches about their security in Christ. They're so intent on pleasing God through their own efforts that they lose sight of grace and drift into a subtle works-righteousness mentality.

Your performance doesn't determine your standing in Christ; your standing in Christ determines your performance. Good works are the necessary result of salvation (Eph. 2:10), but they don't save you or keep you saved. That's God's work.

Jude said, "Now to Him who is able to keep you from stumbling, and to make you stand in the presence of His glory blameless with great joy . . ." (v. 24). "Able" in that verse translates a Greek word that speaks of power. "Keep" literally means "to secure in the midst of an attack." "Stumbling" refers to falling into sin. Together they say that God is powerful enough to prevent you from stumbling into sin and falling away from Him, no matter how intense Satan's attacks might be. He will continue to protect and cleanse you until the day you enter His glorious Heaven perfected.

Sin is a serious issue, and you should never take it lightly. But when you do sin, remember that as a believer you're immediately cleansed by the blood of Jesus Christ (1 John 1:7). Always confess your sins and turn from them, but never doubt God's power or willingness to keep you saved. Trust in His grace, not in your ability to perform.

❖❖❖

Suggestions for Prayer: Praise the Lord for continually cleansing your sin.

For Further Study: Memorize Jude 24-25, and recite those verses often as a reminder of God's power and majesty.

"Take the helmet of salvation" (Eph. 6:17).

❖❖❖

Your helmet of salvation protects you from discouragement and despair.

We've seen how Satan attacks believers with his two-edged sword of doubt and discouragement. But he doesn't stop there. He tries to take you beyond discouragement and on to despair by robbing you of hope. Unless you're careful, his attacks will be successful when you're battle-weary.

The prophet Elijah is an illustration of that truth. The highlight of his ministry came atop Mount Carmel, where he slew 450 prophets of Baal (1 Kings 18:40). And yet immediately after that great victory, he fled for his life because Queen Jezebel threatened to kill him (1 Kings 19:1-3).

He ran from Mount Carmel into the wilderness of Beersheba, where he "sat down under a juniper tree; and he requested for himself that he might die, and said, 'It is enough; now, O Lord, take my life, for I am not better than my fathers'" (v. 4). He went on to moan, "I have been very zealous for the Lord, the God of hosts; for the sons of Israel have forsaken Thy covenant, torn down Thine altars and killed Thy prophets with the sword. And I alone am left; and they seek my life, to take it away" (v. 10).

Elijah lost hope because he failed to see his circumstances through the eyes of faith; he was attempting to fight the battle on his own. He allowed himself to become emotionally, physically, and spiritually spent, and he became overwhelmed with self-pity. He felt utterly alone.

But God hadn't abandoned Elijah. He was still in control, and His people were numerous (v. 18). Elijah had, in effect, removed his helmet of salvation and received a near-fatal blow to his confidence in God's blessing on his life.

There may be times when, like Elijah, you lose your confidence and doubt God's faithfulness. At such times, putting on the helmet of salvation means taking your eyes off your circumstances and trusting in God's promises. You may not always sense His presence or understand what He's doing, but be assured that He will never leave you or forsake you (Heb. 13:5); His purposes will always be accomplished (Rom. 8:28).

❖❖❖

Suggestions for Prayer: Praise God for His unchanging character and irrevocable promises.

For Further Study: Read Isaiah 40:29-31 and Galatians 6:9. ❖ What promises are given in those passages? ❖ In what specific ways do they apply to your life?

*"Take . . . the sword of the Spirit, which is the word of God"
(Eph. 6:17).*

❖❖❖

God's Word is your primary offensive spiritual weapon.

All the armor Paul lists in Ephesians 6 is defensive, with one exception: the sword of the Spirit. That's your offensive weapon for defeating Satan.

We've seen that Roman soldiers carried two swords—the large broadsword and the small dagger. The Greek word translated "sword" in verse 17 refers to the dagger, which was anywhere from six to eighteen inches in length and was carried in a sheath or scabbard at the soldier's side.

The dagger was a common weapon. The Roman soldiers who arrested Jesus in the Garden of Gethsemane were each armed with one (Matt. 26:47). Peter used one to cut off the ear of the high priest's servant (Matt. 26:51). A dagger was used to kill James, the brother of John (Acts. 12:2). Hebrews 11:37 tells us that such a weapon was used against various heroes of the faith.

"The sword of the Spirit" isn't a direct reference to the Holy Spirit as such. The implication is that since our enemy is spiritual, our weapons also must be spiritual (2 Cor. 10:4). Our sword is spiritual because it is the Word given by the Holy Spirit. He inspired its writing, and through it He convicts and redeems sinners (John 16:8; Heb. 4:12-13). The Word abides in you and transforms you. It supplies everything you need for a godly, victorious life. It builds you up and produces holiness (Acts 20:32). And it equips you for good works by teaching, reproving, correcting, and training you in righteousness (2 Tim. 3:16-17).

The Bible is a powerful and effective weapon. The question is, Do you know how to use it? Do you diligently study it and apply its principles to your life? Do you have a storehouse of Biblical truth to draw from in the heat of battle?

The Roman dagger was a precision weapon aimed at a specific spot to produce a specific result. Similarly, the sword of the Spirit is most effective when you apply specific Biblical principles to specific situations in your life. Do you do that?

❖❖❖

Suggestions for Prayer: Ask God to increase your desire to know His Word. ❖ Ask for wisdom in applying what you already know to the decisions and situations you'll face today.

For Further Study: Read 1 Peter 1:22–2:3. How are believers to approach the Word?

"Take . . . the sword of the Spirit, which is the word of God"
(Eph. 6:17).

❖❖❖

To wield the sword of the Spirit is to apply specific Biblical principles to
specific situations.

J esus gave us the perfect example of skillful and precise use of the sword
of the Spirit. Following His baptism, "Jesus was led up by the Spirit into
the wilderness to be tempted by the devil. And after He had fasted forty days
and forty nights, He then became hungry. And the tempter came and said to
Him, 'If You are the Son of God, command that these stones become bread'"
(Matt. 4:1-3).

Satan was challenging Christ's trust in His Heavenly Father's power and
provisions. God had just announced that Jesus was His Son (Matt. 3:17).
Would He now abandon Jesus and let Him starve in the wilderness? Satan
urged Jesus to take matters into His own hands and supply His own needs.
After all, Satan implied, doesn't the Son of God deserve better than this?

Jesus didn't act on His own authority or demand that God give Him what
He deserved. Instead, He demonstrated His trust in God and rebuked Satan
for his evil intents: "It is written, 'Man shall not live on bread alone, but on
every word that proceeds out of the mouth of God'" (v. 4). That's a specific
verse applied to a specific situation. Jesus responded the same way to Satan's
other temptations (vv. 7, 10).

Scripture gives many general principles for Christian living, but the sword
of the Spirit is a precise weapon. We must learn to apply the appropriate
Biblical principles to any given situation. That's what the psalmist meant
when he wrote, "How can a young man keep his way pure? By keeping it
according to Thy word. . . . Thy word I have treasured in my heart, that I may
not sin against Thee" (Ps. 119:9, 11).

Do you know where to go in the Bible to defend yourself against sorrow,
discouragement, apathy, lust, or pride? If not, you're attempting to do spiritual battle unarmed.

❖❖❖

Suggestions for Prayer: Thank God for His precious Word and the study
resources that are available to Bible students today. ❖ Renew your commitment
to daily systematic Bible study.

For Further Study: Read Psalm 119:97-105. Is that your attitude toward
Scripture?

"Take . . . the sword of the Spirit, which is the word of God"
(Eph. 6:17).

❖❖❖

**Your attitude toward Scripture will determine
your effectiveness in spiritual battle.**

I remember enjoying the observations of a perceptive man who was gazing at a beautiful garden. First he saw a butterfly flitting from flower to flower. It spent a few seconds on the edge of each but derived no particular benefit from any of them.

Next he saw a botanist with large notebook and microscope in hand. As the botanist carefully observed each flower and plant, he made copious entries in his book. But after hours of meticulous study, most of what he learned was shut up in his book. Very little remained in his mind.

Then came a little bee. When it entered a flower, it emerged laden with pollen. It had left the hive that morning empty but would return full.

When it comes to Bible study, some people are like butterflies, going from one favorite verse to another, one seminar to another, or one book to another. They're very busy and expend much energy but have little to show for their efforts. They remain unchanged in any significant way because they never really delve into the Word wholeheartedly. They're content to simply flutter around the edges.

Others, like the botanist, may study in great depth but never apply it to their lives. I know of entire commentaries written by unbelievers. In some cases their grasp of Scripture is exceptional, but they know nothing of true love for God and obedience to Biblical truth. What a tragedy! But you don't have to be a Biblical scholar to make that mistake. You need only to fail to apply what you learn to your life.

Rather, strive to be like the bee, spending time in the Word—reading, studying, taking notes—then emerging fuller than when you began. Your mind will be filled with wisdom and Biblical insights. Your life will be sweeter and purer because the Word has done its work (1 Cor. 2:13).

Are you a butterfly, a botanist, or a bee?

❖❖❖

Suggestions for Prayer: Thank God for the opportunities He gives you to study His Word. Take full advantage of them.

For Further Study: According to James 1:22-25, what's the difference between someone who merely hears the Word and someone who obeys it?

"Take . . . the sword of the Spirit, which is the word of God"
(Eph. 6:17).

✧✧✧

Despite Satanic opposition, God's Word will
accomplish its work in His people.

In Matthew 13 Jesus tells the Parable of the Sower and the Seed: "Behold, the sower went out to sow; and as he sowed, some seeds fell beside the road, and the birds came and devoured them. And others fell upon the rocky places, where they did not have much soil; and immediately they sprang up. . . . But when the sun had risen, they were scorched; and because they had no root, they withered away. And others fell among the thorns, and the thorns came up and choked them out. And others fell on the good soil, and yielded a crop" (vv. 3-8).

Jesus went on to explain that the seed is the truth of God's Word. Satan and his demonic forces can snatch it away from those who hear it but don't understand what it means. They can bring affliction and persecution against those who have an emotional commitment only, thereby causing them to lose heart and fall away. In some cases they choke out the Word with worry and "the deceitfulness of riches" (vv. 19-22).

But truly repentant sinners receive and nurture gospel truth, just as prepared soil receives and nurtures seed. They hear it, understand it, receive it, and produce spiritual fruit (v. 23).

Proclaiming the gospel is an important aspect of taking up the sword of the Spirit (Eph. 6:17). As you do, others will be saved and will join God's army. But be warned: Satan never gives up territory without a fight. Some of the people you witness to will forget what you tell them. Others will refuse to turn from worldly influences. Still others may respond emotionally but without a genuine commitment to serving Christ and forsaking sin.

Those spiritual battles should compel you to bathe your evangelism in prayer and to undergird it with a clear gospel presentation. If people understand precisely what it means to receive Christ, and if their hearts are prepared by the Holy Spirit, they'll not be so easily victimized by Satanic opposition.

✧✧✧

Suggestions for Prayer: Ask the Lord to give you an opportunity to share Christ with someone today or to encourage a struggling believer.

For Further Study: Read 1 Thessalonians 3:1-8. ✧ What was Paul's concern for the Thessalonian believers? ✧ What did he do to eliminate his concern?

"With all prayer and petition pray at all times" (Eph. 6:18).

❖❖❖

Make prayer an ongoing part of your day.

As important as prayer is to your Christian life, you might expect Paul to list it as another piece of spiritual armor, but he doesn't. Instead, he makes it all-pervasive by instructing us to "pray at all times." That's our spiritual lifeline—the air our spirits breathe. The effectiveness of each piece of armor is directly related to the quality of our prayers.

We see the importance of prayer throughout the New Testament. Jesus instructed His disciples to be on the alert at all times, praying so they would have strength to face the trials and temptations that lay ahead (Luke 21:36). The apostles devoted themselves to prayer (Acts 6:4), as did godly people like Cornelius (Acts 10:2). Every Christian is to be continually devoted to prayer (Rom. 12:12).

In Philippians 4:6 Paul says, "Be anxious for nothing, but in everything by prayer and supplication with thanksgiving let your requests be made known to God." He told the Thessalonians to "pray without ceasing" (1 Thess. 5:17) and instructed men everywhere to "pray, lifting up holy hands" (1 Tim. 2:8).

Jesus and Paul not only exhorted believers to pray but also modeled diligent prayer in their own lives. Jesus often went for extended periods of time alone to pray. Paul wrote often of his own fervent prayers on behalf of others (cf. Col. 1:9; Philem. 4).

As a child, you may have been taught that prayer is reserved for mealtimes, bedtimes, or church services. That's a common misconception many children carry into their adult years. But believers are to be in constant communication with God, which is simply the overflow of seeing all of life from His perspective. Just as you would discuss your everyday experiences and feelings with a close friend, so you're to discuss them with God.

God loves you and wants to share your every joy, sorrow, victory, and defeat. Be conscious of His presence today, and take advantage of the sweet communion He offers.

❖❖❖

Suggestions for Prayer: Thank God He's always available to hear your prayers. ❖ Ask Him to give you a desire to commune with Him more faithfully.

For Further Study: What do the following verses say about the most appropriate times for prayer? Psalm 55:16-17; Daniel 6:10; Luke 6:12; 1 Timothy 5:5.

"With all prayer and petition pray at all times in the Spirit, and with this in view, be on the alert with all perseverance and petition for all the saints" (Eph. 6:18).

❖❖❖

Your desire to know God should motivate you toward fervent prayer.

Man's highest purpose is to know God. Jesus prayed to the Father, saying, "This is eternal life, that they may know Thee, the only true God, and Jesus Christ whom Thou hast sent" (John 17:3). Of us He said, "I am the good shepherd; and I know My own, and My own know Me" (John 10:14). John added that "we know that the Son of God has come, and has given us understanding, in order that we might know Him who is true, and we are in Him who is true, in His Son Jesus Christ" (1 John 5:20).

Every Christian knows God through salvation, but beyond that lies an intimate knowledge of God. That should be the quest of every believer. Moses prayed, "Let me know Thy ways, that I may know Thee, so that I may find favor in Thy sight" (Ex. 33:13). David entreated his son Solomon to "know the God of your father, and serve Him with a whole heart and a willing mind" (1 Chron. 28:9). Even the Apostle Paul, who perhaps knew Christ more intimately than any human being thus far, never lost his passion for an even deeper knowledge (Phil. 3:10).

Such passion is the driving force behind powerful prayer. Those who know God best pray most often and most fervently. Their love for Him compels them to know and serve Him better.

How about you? Is your knowledge of God intimate? Does the character of your prayers reveal that you're in the process of knowing God?

Paul's admonitions to "pray at all times in the Spirit" and to "be on the alert with all perseverance and petition for all the saints" (Eph. 6:18) presuppose that you know God and desire to see His will fulfilled in His people. If not, you'll never appreciate the importance of interceding on behalf of others.

❖❖❖

Suggestions for Prayer: The martyred missionary Jim Elliot once prayed, "Lord, make my life a testimony to the value of knowing You." Let that be your prayer each day.

For Further Study: Read 1 Chronicles 28. ❖ What did God forbid David to do? ❖ What would happen to Solomon if he failed to know and serve God?

"With all prayer and petition pray at all times in the Spirit, and with this in view, be on the alert with all perseverance and petition for all the saints" (Eph. 6:18).

❖❖❖

**God wants you to look beyond your own problems
and pray for the needs of others.**

The great preacher D. Martyn Lloyd-Jones wrote, "Before the outbreak of the Spanish Civil War, in Barcelona, Madrid and other places, there were psychological clinics with large numbers of neurotics undergoing drug treatments and others attending regularly for psychoanalysis and such like. They had their personal problems, their worries, their anxieties, their temptations, having to go back week after week, month after month, to the clinics in order to be kept going.

"Then came the Civil War; and one of the first and most striking effects of that War was that it virtually emptied the psychological and psychiatric clinics. These neurotic people were suddenly cured by a greater anxiety, the anxiety about their whole position, whether their homes would still be there, whether their husbands would still be alive, whether their children would be killed.

"Their greater anxieties got rid of the lesser ones. In having to give attention to the bigger problem they forgot their own personal and somewhat petty problems" (*The Christian Soldier: An Exposition of Ephesians 6:10 to 20* [Grand Rapids: Baker, 1978], p. 357).

That's a negative illustration of a positive principle: your own problems pale as you pray in the Spirit on behalf of others. Praying "in the Spirit" (Eph. 6:18) is praying in concert with the Holy Spirit—in harmony with His Person and will. It's synonymous with praying according to God's will (1 John 5:14).

The Holy Spirit intercedes for you (Rom. 8:26-27), and you are to intercede for others. That's not always easy in our contemporary religious environment where self-centeredness is praised rather than shunned and more and more professing Christians are embracing the health, wealth, and prosperity heresy. But God's mandate is for us to love one another, pray for one another, and look out for one another's interests (Phil. 2:3-4). Let that mandate govern all your relationships.

❖❖❖

Suggestions for Prayer: Make a list of people for whom you want to intercede. ❖ Spend time praying for each person, asking God to show you specific ways to minister to his or her needs.

For Further Study: Read Philippians 2:1-11. ❖ What should be your attitude toward other believers? ❖ How did Christ set an example of proper attitudes?

*"Finally, be strong in the Lord, and in the strength of His might"
(Eph. 6:10).*

❖❖❖

You can be victorious!

This month we've learned many things about spiritual warfare that I pray will better equip you for victory in your Christian life. In concluding our brief study of Ephesians 6:10-18, here are some key principles I want you to remember: ❖ Remember that Satan is a defeated foe. Jesus came to destroy the Devil's works (1 John 3:8) and will someday cast him into eternal Hell (Rev. 20:10). ❖ Remember the power of Christ in your life. John said, "Greater is He who is in you than he who is in the world" (1 John 4:4). The same power that defeated Satan indwells you. Consequently, you are never alone or without divine resources. ❖ Remember to resist Satan. You have the power to resist him; so don't acquiesce to him by being ignorant of his schemes or by deliberately exposing yourself to temptation. ❖ Keep your spiritual armor on at all times. It's foolish to enter combat without proper protection. ❖ Let Christ control your attitudes and actions. The spiritual battle we're in calls for spiritual weapons (2 Cor. 10:3-4); so take "every thought captive to the obedience of Christ" (v. 5). Feed on the Word, and obey its principles. ❖ Pray, pray, pray! Prayer unleashes the Spirit's power. Be a person of fervent and faithful prayer (cf. James 5:16).

God never intended for you to live in spiritual defeat. I pray you'll take advantage of the resources He has supplied, so your life will honor Him. Enjoy sweet victory every day!

❖❖❖

Suggestions for Prayer: Thank God for His promise of ultimate victory in Christ.

For Further Study: Read Ephesians 6:10-18. ❖ Review each piece of armor. ❖ Is any piece missing from your personal defense system? If so, determine what you will do to correct the deficiency.

"[The Bereans] were more noble-minded than those in Thessalonica, for they received the word with great eagerness, examining the Scriptures daily, to see whether these things were so" (Acts 17:11).

❖❖❖

God honors spiritual discernment.

On his second missionary journey Paul, accompanied by Silas, preached the gospel of Jesus Christ in the city of Thessalonica. They weren't there long before the gospel took root and many turned from their idolatry "to serve a true and living God" (1 Thess. 1:9). In 1 Thessalonians 2:13 Paul says, "We also constantly thank God that when you received from us the word of God's message, you accepted it not as the word of men, but for what it really is, the word of God." Their open response to God's Word made them an example to all the believers in that area (1 Thess. 1:7).

But as exemplary as the Thessalonians were, their fellow-believers in Berea were even more so. God called them "noble-minded" (Acts 17:11). They were eager to hear what Paul and Silas had to say but tested it against God's prior revelation in the Old Testament before receiving it as a message from God. They had learned to examine everything carefully and to "hold fast" to the truth (1 Thess. 5:21).

The church today, however, has an appalling lack of that kind of discernment. Many believers are duped by novel teachings and outright heresies. They're "tossed here and there by waves, and carried about by every wind of doctrine" (Eph. 4:14). We desperately need a new breed of Bereans who will raise high the banner of sound doctrine and never compromise it.

With that goal in mind, our studies this month will focus on the character and benefits of God's Word. You'll learn that it's the source of spiritual growth, spiritual service, blessing, victory, truth, and knowledge. You'll see its infallibility, inerrancy, authority, inspiration, and sufficiency.

I pray that by this month's end, your commitment to learning and applying Biblical truth will be stronger than ever and that you will indeed be a modern-day, noble-minded Berean.

❖❖❖

Suggestions for Prayer: Ask God to give you a greater love for His wonderful Word.

For Further Study: Read Acts 17:1-15. ❖ Why did Paul and his companions leave Thessalonica and Berea? ❖ What do Paul's experiences tell you about what you might expect as you share Christ with others?

October 2 PROGRAMMING YOUR SPIRITUAL COMPUTER

"Be filled with the knowledge of [God's] will in all spiritual wisdom and understanding, so that you may walk in a manner worthy of the Lord" (Col. 1:9-10).

✧✧✧

Godly behavior is the result of godly thinking.

Perhaps you've heard computer buffs use the term G.I.G.O.: "garbage in, garbage out." Input determines output. What you feed into a computer is what you'll get out.

Similarly, what you program into your mind will eventually influence your behavior. That's why you must expose your mind to things that are "true," "honorable," "right," "pure," "lovely," "of good repute," "excellent," and "worthy of praise" (Phil. 4:8). As one preacher put it, "You should be so saturated with God's Word that your blood is 'bibline.' If you cut yourself, you should bleed Bible verses!" His exaggeration reveals his passion for God's truth—a passion every believer should share.

Paul prayed that we would "walk in a manner worthy of the Lord, to please Him in all respects, bearing fruit in every good work and increasing in the knowledge of God; [and be] strengthened with all power . . . for the attaining of all steadfastness and patience, joyously giving thanks to the Father" (Col. 1:10-12).

Those are marvelous Christian characteristics, but how are they achieved? Verse 9 gives us the answer: "Be filled with the knowledge of [God's] will in all spiritual wisdom and understanding." The Greek word translated "filled" speaks of influence or control. It's the same word Paul uses in Ephesians 5:18: "Be filled with [controlled by] the Spirit." When you're filled with the Spirit, He governs your choices. Similarly, when you're filled with the knowledge of God's will, your choices reflect godly wisdom and understanding.

The phrase "spiritual wisdom and understanding" indicates more than merely knowing God's Word. It speaks of applying it to your life under the Spirit's power and direction.

As you prayerfully saturate your mind with God's Word, it begins more and more to control your thinking and behavior. And the Spirit uses the Word to renew your mind and to protect you from conformity to worldly attitudes and actions (Rom. 12:2).

✧✧✧

Suggestions for Prayer: Ask the Holy Spirit to control every aspect of your life today. ✧ Be diligent to apply the appropriate Biblical principles to every circumstance you face.

For Further Study: Memorize Philippians 4:8 as a reminder to feed your mind with the things that produce godliness.

"My Word . . . shall not return to Me . . . without accomplishing what I desire" (Isa. 55:11).

"Man does not live by bread alone, but . . . by everything that proceeds out of the mouth of the Lord" (Deut. 8:3).

❖❖❖

God's Word is both productive and nourishing.

The Bible contains many precious promises, two of which relate specifically to itself. First, the prophet Isaiah said that the Word is productive: "As the rain and the snow come down from heaven, and do not return there without watering the earth, and making it bear and sprout, and furnishing seed to the sower and bread to the eater; so shall My word be which goes forth from My mouth; it shall not return to Me empty, without accomplishing what I desire, and without succeeding in the matter for which I sent it" (Isa. 55:10-11).

As you administer the Word, it may encourage a fellow-Christian, bring a sinner to repentance, or even confirm an unbeliever in his sin. Whatever the response, be assured that the Word always accomplishes its intended purpose.

The Word is like a messenger that runs to do God's work: "He sends forth His command to the earth; His word runs very swiftly. He gives snow like wool; He scatters the hoarfrost like ashes. He casts forth His ice as fragments; who can stand before His cold? He sends forth His word and melts them; He causes His wind to blow and the waters to flow. He declares His words to Jacob, His statutes and His ordinances to Israel" (Ps. 147:15-19). Just as God sends the natural elements to accomplish His purposes, He also sends His Word.

The Word is also nourishing. Moses wrote, "Man does not live by bread alone, but man lives by everything that proceeds out of the mouth of the Lord" (Deut. 8:3). God's Word feeds believers, causing spiritual growth.

How should you respond to such a powerful and productive Word? Trust it, so you can live each day in confidence. Proclaim it, so others will come to know its Author. Obey it, so it can continue its transforming work in you, making you more like Christ each day.

❖❖❖

Suggestions for Prayer: God's promises are intended to bring you great joy and encouragement. List seven promises that are especially meaningful to you. Use one each day for one week as a focal point for prayer and praise.

For Further Study: What promises does Jesus make in John 14:1-14?

"Be diligent to present yourself approved to God as a workman who does not need to be ashamed, handling accurately the word of truth" (2 Tim. 2:15).

✧✧✧

The Holy Spirit protects you from false doctrine, but that doesn't eliminate the need for diligent Bible study.

For the next few days we'll consider several benefits of Bible study. Today we'll address the broader question of why Bible study is necessary at all.

Perhaps you know believers who think Bible study is unnecessary. Bible reading, they say, is sufficient because we have the Holy Spirit, who teaches us all things. Often they cite 1 John 2:27 in support of their view: "As for you, the anointing [the Holy Spirit] which you received from [God] abides in you, and you have no need for anyone to teach you; but as His anointing teaches you about all things, and is true and is not a lie, and just as it has taught you, you abide in Him."

That passage, however, isn't implying that Bible study or Bible teachers aren't necessary. On the contrary, John was exhorting his readers to abide in what they'd already learned (v. 24) and to shun only those teachers who deny Christ and try to deceive believers.

The Holy Spirit is the believer's resident lie detector, granting discernment to shield him or her from false doctrine. Although a Christian may be temporarily confused by false teachers, ultimately he can never drift into apostasy or deny Christ. If anyone does depart from the faith, his departure is proof that he was never a true believer in the first place (v. 19).

The Spirit protects you from error, but you must fulfill your responsibility as a student of the Word. Even a man of Timothy's spiritual stature needed to study the Word diligently and to handle it accurately (2 Tim. 2:15).

I pray that the psalmist's attitude toward Scripture will be yours as well: "O how I love Thy law! It is my meditation all the day" (Ps. 119:97).

✧✧✧

Suggestions for Prayer: Thank God for His precious Word. ✧ Ask Him to give you a deeper love for its truths.

For Further Study: Read Titus 1:7-16 and 2 Timothy 2:2. ✧ What skills must an overseer have regarding God's Word? ✧ Why are those skills necessary? ✧ Do those skills apply to church leaders only? Explain. ✧ Are you skilled in handling God's Word?

October 5

"Like newborn babes, long for the pure milk of the word, that by it you may grow in respect to salvation" (1 Peter 2:2).

❖❖❖

Scripture is our source of spiritual growth.

A newborn baby was abandoned in a pile of trash in a city alley. The mother had obviously left it there to die. The infant was near death when someone heard its faint cry and summoned medical help. The child survived, but only because it received the attention and nourishment it needed.

That situation has a spiritual parallel, which Peter used to illustrate the believer's dependence on God's Word. If a baby is deprived of nourishment, it will soon die. Similarly, if a Christian doesn't feed on the Word, he or she will languish spiritually and will become ineffective for the Lord. On the positive side, a believer should long for God's Word as intently as a newborn baby longs for its mother's milk.

Scripture draws on the parent/child metaphor in other ways as well, referring to Christians as being born again (John 3:7; 1 Peter 1:3), children of God (Rom. 8:16; 1 John 3:1), and adopted sons (Rom. 8:15; Eph. 1:5). Just as it is natural for biological children to grow and mature, Christians also have the capacity for spiritual growth. In fact, we're commanded to "grow in the grace and knowledge of our Lord and Savior Jesus Christ" (2 Peter 3:18).

The Word of God is the mainstay of your spiritual diet. It's your primary source of nourishment. Paul said, "As you . . . have received Christ Jesus the Lord, so walk in Him, having been firmly rooted and now being built up in Him and established in your faith, just as you were instructed" (Col. 2:6-7). "Your faith" in that context refers to the content of Christianity—the doctrines of Scripture. As your knowledge and application of Biblical principles increase, you will become more and more grounded in truth and steadfast in Christ.

❖❖❖

Suggestions for Prayer: If you've lost your appetite for God's Word, it may be because of sin (1 Peter 2:1). If so, ask God to cleanse your heart and to give you a renewed longing for His truth. Then commit yourself to daily time in the Word.

For Further Study: Read Acts 20:32 and 1 Thessalonians 2:13, noting the effect Scripture has on believers.

"All Scripture is inspired by God and profitable . . . that the man of God may be adequate, equipped for every good work" (2 Tim. 3:16-17).

❖❖❖

Scripture equips you for spiritual service.

Each week I have the privilege of interacting with more than one hundred students at The Master's Seminary. One of my greatest joys is seeing their determination to do God's work in God's way.

That attitude is the key to success in ministry, as Joshua learned when he assumed leadership over the Israelites after Moses' death. At that point God said to him, "This book of the law shall not depart from your mouth, but you shall meditate on it day and night, so that you may be careful to do according to all that is written in it; for then you will make your way prosperous, and then you will have success" (Josh. 1:8).

This is how Paul described spiritual success to Timothy: "In pointing out [the things I have said] to the brethren, you will be a good servant of Christ Jesus, constantly nourished on the words of the faith and of the sound doctrine which you have been following" (1 Tim. 4:6).

"Servant" speaks of one who oversees and dispenses the goods and property of another. A good spiritual servant is one who knows and dispenses God's Word. Whatever level of ministry you pursue, you must conform to Biblical teaching. To do that, you must know what God says about ministering to His people.

I've met many people who love the Lord and want desperately to serve Him effectively, but they haven't taken time to learn the principles that govern spiritual ministry. Consequently they're ill-prepared and in some cases unwittingly participating in activities that actually violate God's Word.

Don't let that happen to you. God's Word supplies all the strength, instruction, and comfort you need to serve Christ properly. Study it thoroughly, and follow it closely.

❖❖❖

Suggestions for Prayer: Thank God for every ministry opportunity He gives you. ❖ Ask Him to help you see any areas of your service that might need to be corrected, and then respond accordingly.

For Further Study: According to Philippians 1:12-18, is it possible to minister with impure motives? Explain.

"Blessed are those who hear the word of God, and observe it"
(Luke 11:28).

❖❖❖

Obeying Scripture brings spiritual blessing.

When Scripture speaks of a person's being "blessed," it usually refers to the reception of some temporal or spiritual benefit. It also includes the joy and sense of well-being that comes with knowing that God is at work on your behalf.

The psalmist wrote, "How blessed is the man who does not walk in the counsel of the wicked, nor stand in the path of sinners, nor sit in the seat of scoffers! But his delight is in the law of the Lord, and in His law he meditates day and night. And he will be like a tree firmly planted by streams of water, which yields its fruit in its season, and its leaf does not wither; and in whatever he does, he prospers" (Ps. 1:1-2). Those who know and obey God's Word will be blessed. The psalmist likened them to a strong, productive, prosperous tree.

James added, "One who looks intently at the perfect law, the law of liberty [God's Word], and abides by it, not having become a forgetful hearer but an effectual doer, this man shall be blessed in what he does" (James 1:25). Again, the very act of obedience brings blessing.

John opens the book of Revelation with this promise: "Blessed is he who reads and those who hear the words of the prophecy, and heed the things which are written in it" (Rev. 1:3). Jesus closed Revelation with the same promise: "Blessed is he who heeds the words of the prophecy of this book" (Rev. 22:7). Obedience and blessing always go hand in hand.

As a Christian, you've been blessed "with every spiritual blessing in the heavenly places in Christ" (Eph. 1:3). Every spiritual resource is yours. Even in times of sorrow and persecution, God's blessing rests on you (1 Peter 4:14). But you can forfeit His blessings by neglecting His Word or by committing other sinful acts. So guard your heart carefully, and continue in the Word. As you do, your joy will be boundless!

❖❖❖

Suggestions for Prayer: Make a list of specific ways in which the Lord has blessed you in recent days. Praise Him for each one.

For Further Study: Read James 1:12, 1 Peter 3:14, and 1 Peter 4:14. How does God's blessing apply when you're suffering unjustly?

*"How can a young man keep his way pure? By keeping it accord-
ing to Thy word. . . . Thy word I have treasured in my heart, that
I may not sin against Thee" (Ps. 119:9, 11).*

❖❖❖

Scripture is the source of spiritual victory.

Many Christians struggle with spiritual defeat or recurring sins because they haven't learned to apply Biblical principles to specific situations. Perhaps they don't know God's will because they haven't matured in the Word. Or maybe they know what He expects of them, but they disregard His counsel. In either case, the result is the same.

Jesus Himself repelled Satan's attacks by quoting specific portions of Scripture that applied to specific temptations (Matt. 4:1-11). He knew the Word, believed it, and refused to compromise its principles. In so doing, He set a pattern for us to follow.

Using metaphorical language, the Apostle John emphasized the priority of the Word when he described three levels of spiritual maturity: children, young men, and fathers. In 1 John 2:13 he says, "I have written to you, children, because you know the Father." Spiritual children aren't yet mature in their faith, but they know who their Heavenly Father is. They know they belong to God.

John continues: "I have written to you, young men, because you are strong, and the word of God abides in you, and you have overcome the evil one" (v. 14). Spiritual young men are healthy, vibrant, and aggressive because the Word abides in them—it has found a home in their hearts. They're victorious over the evil one because their doctrine is sound and they've cultivated spiritual wisdom and discernment (Phil. 1:9). They recognize Satan's lies and reject them.

First John 2:14 also says, "I have written to you, fathers, because you know Him who has been from the beginning." Spiritual fathers have a deep, mature relationship with God that comes from prolonged time in prayer and the Word.

Which of those terms best describes you—spiritual child, young man, or father? What specific things can you do today to move toward a more mature and victorious Christian life?

❖❖❖

Suggestions for Prayer: Ask God to help you love Him more deeply and to know His Word more completely. Therein is the key to spiritual victory.

For Further Study: Memorize Psalm 119:11. Recite it often as a reminder of the priority of hiding God's Word in your heart.

"Concerning you, my brethren, I myself also am convinced that you yourselves are full of goodness, filled with all knowledge, and able also to admonish one another" (Rom. 15:14).

❖❖❖

Scripture is the source of godly counsel.

In recent years the question of who is competent to counsel has become an important issue in the church. Many pastors and other church leaders have curtailed their counseling ministries or stopped them altogether. They've been made to feel inadequate for not having formal training in psychological counseling techniques.

Behind this movement away from pastoral counseling is the subtle implication that the Holy Spirit and Scripture are incapable of addressing the deepest needs of the human heart. It is claimed that only secular psychology dispensed by trained analysts can do that.

But the truth is, the heart of man is "more deceitful than all else and is desperately sick; who can understand it?" (Jer. 17:9). No one. That includes humanistic counselors. Verse 10 says, "I the Lord search the heart, I test the mind." Only God can understand the human heart.

David prayed, "O Lord, Thou hast searched me and known me. Thou dost know when I sit down and when I rise up; Thou dost understand my thought from afar. Thou dost scrutinize my path and my lying down, and art intimately acquainted with all my ways. . . . Where can I go from Thy Spirit? Or where can I flee from Thy presence?" (Ps. 139:1-3, 7).

Only God knows what's in a person's heart. Only His Spirit working through His Word can penetrate one's deepest thoughts and motives to transform the heart and renew the mind (Heb. 4:12; Rom. 12:2).

Professional psychologists are no substitute for spiritually gifted people who know the Word, possess godly wisdom, are full of goodness, and are available to help others apply divine truth to their lives (Rom. 15:14).

When people come to you for counsel, the best thing you can do is show them what God's Word says about their problem and how it applies to their situation. But you can't do that unless you know the Word and are allowing it to do its work in you first. Then you'll be in a position to counsel others more effectively.

❖❖❖

Suggestions for Prayer: Thank God for the wise and all-sufficient counsel of His Word. ❖ Reaffirm your commitment to share it at every opportunity.

For Further Study: According to Psalm 119:24, on what did the psalmist rely for his counsel?

*"Thy law is truth. . . . And all Thy commandments are truth. . . .
The sum of Thy word is truth" (Ps. 119:142, 151, 160).*

❖❖❖

Scripture is the source of divine truth.

It amazes me how people can spend so much time searching for truth but ignore the Bible. In his poem *Miriam,* John Greenleaf Whittier reflected on the same conundrum:

*We search the world for truth. We cull
The good, the pure, the beautiful,
From graven stone and written scroll,
From all old flower-fields of the soul;
And, weary seekers of the best,
We come back laden from the quest,
To find that all the sages said
Is in the Book our mothers read.*

God never intended for truth to be mysterious or unattainable. His Word is a repository of truth, containing every principle we need for life and thought.

But knowing truth begins with knowing God, who is its Author. First John 5:20 says, "We know that the Son of God has come, and has given us understanding, in order that we might know Him who is true, and we are in Him who is true, in His Son Jesus Christ. This is the true God and eternal life."

The psalmist proclaimed, "The works of His hands are truth and justice; all His precepts are sure. They are upheld forever and ever; they are performed in truth and uprightness" (Ps. 111:7-8).

As Christians, we are those who walk in truth. That's how Jesus described us when He prayed to the Father: "Sanctify them in the truth; Thy word is truth" (John 17:17). Similarly John said, "I have no greater joy than this, to hear of my children walking in the truth" (3 John 4). In contrast, unbelievers "suppress the truth in unrighteousness," thus making themselves targets for the wrath of God (Rom. 1:18).

To love God is to love truth; to love truth is to love the Word. May you walk in the truth of God's Word today and every day.

❖❖❖

Suggestions for Prayer: Thank God for the privilege of knowing Him and being able to walk in His truth.

For Further Study: How does Jesus describe the Holy Spirit in John 14:17, 15:26, and 16:13?

"God, after He spoke long ago to the fathers in the prophets in many portions and in many ways, in these last days has spoken to us in His Son" (Heb. 1:1-2).

❖❖❖

Scripture is the storehouse of divine revelation.

For decades liberal theologians have misrepresented the Bible as merely a collection of man's religious thoughts and aspirations. But Scripture is much more than that. It is in fact divine revelation—God's self-disclosure through His Spirit to the human authors. Man could never know God's identity, attributes, perspectives, or commands if God hadn't revealed them to him. Nor could man know his own origin, purpose, or destiny.

Paul said, "'Things which eye has not seen and ear has not heard, and which have not entered the heart of man, all that God has prepared for those who love Him.' For to us God revealed them through the Spirit" (1 Cor. 2:9-10). In 2 Timothy 3:16 he adds, "All Scripture is inspired by God and profitable for teaching, for reproof, for correction, for training in righteousness." God inspired every word of Scripture and speaks on every page.

Hebrews 1 speaks of two general means by which God revealed Himself: Old Testament revelation ("long ago," v. 1) and New Testament revelation ("in His Son," v. 2). First He spoke to the Jewish fathers through the Old Testament prophets "in many portions." That refers to all the books of the Old Testament. "In many ways" speaks of the specific means by which He communicated: visions, prophecies, parables, types, symbols, ceremonies, theophanies, and audible voice.

From the close of the Old Testament to the arrival of John the Baptist, there were approximately four hundred years during which God was silent. But that silence was shattered when John announced the coming of Christ. From that time on, God spoke through His Son. The Gospels record His life and teachings, the book of Acts shows the propagation of His teachings through the apostles and early church, the epistles apply His teachings to everyday life, and Revelation tells of His triumphant return and the consummation of divine revelation.

Isn't it wonderful to know God's perspective on life and history?

❖❖❖

Suggestions for Prayer: Thank God that His Word is a lamp to your feet and a light to your path (Ps. 119:105).

For Further Study: According to Deuteronomy 29:29, what is the purpose of divine revelation?

"Contend earnestly for the faith which was once for all *delivered to the saints" (Jude 3, emphasis added).*

❖❖❖

Scripture contains everything you need to know for godly living.

For many years I've watched with deep concern as a significant number of Christians have drifted from a thoughtful, Biblical, God-centered theology to one that is increasingly mystical, non-Biblical, and man-centered. One of the most disturbing indicators of this trend is the proliferation of extra-Biblical revelations that certain people are claiming to receive directly from God.

Such claims are alarming because they dilute the uniqueness and centrality of the Bible and cause people to lean on man's word rather than God's. They imply that Scripture is insufficient for Christian living and that we need additional revelation to fill the gap.

But God's Word contains everything you need to know for spiritual life and godly living. It is "inspired by God and profitable for teaching, for reproof, for correction, for training in righteousness," so that you may be fully "equipped for every good work" (2 Tim. 3:16-17). What more is necessary?

When the Apostle John died, apostolic revelation came to an end. But that written legacy remains as the standard by which we are to test every teacher and teaching that claims to be from God (1 Thess. 5:21; 1 John 4:1). If a teaching doesn't conform to Scripture, it must be rejected. If it does conform, it isn't a new revelation. In either case, additional revelation is unnecessary.

God went to great lengths to record and preserve His revelation, and He jealously guards it from corruption of any kind. From Moses, the first known recipient of divine revelation, to the Apostle John, the final recipient, His charge remained the same: "You shall not add to the word which I am commanding you, nor take away from it, that you may keep the commandments of the Lord your God which I command you" (Deut. 4:2; cf. Rev. 22:18-19).

Don't be swayed by supposed new revelations. Devote yourself to what has already been revealed.

❖❖❖

Suggestions for Prayer: Ask God to guard your heart from confusion and to help you keep your attention firmly fixed on His Word.

For Further Study: According to 2 Timothy 4:1-4, why must we preach and uphold God's Word?

"All Scripture is inspired by God and profitable for teaching, for reproof, for correction, for training in righteousness; that the man of God may be adequate, equipped for every good work" (2 Tim. 3:16-17).

✧✧✧

God's Word is inspired.

Second Timothy 3:16 speaks of the inspiration of Scripture. "Inspired" is the translation of a Greek word that literally means "God-breathed." Every word of Scripture is from the mouth of God!

Theologians speak of inspiration as the mysterious process by which God worked through the authors of Scripture to produce inerrant and divinely authoritative writings. Inspiration is a mystery because Scripture doesn't explain specifically how it occurred. The only glimpse we have is from 2 Peter: "Know this first of all, that no prophecy of Scripture is a matter of one's own interpretation, for no prophecy was ever made by an act of human will, but men moved by the Holy Spirit spoke from God" (1:20-21).

"Interpretation" speaks of origin. Scripture didn't originate on the human level but with the Holy Spirit, who "moved" upon the authors to write it (v. 21). "Moved" is the translation of a nautical term that describes the effects of wind upon a ship as it blows against its sails and moves it through the water. Similarly, the Spirit moved on the Biblical writers to produce the Word of God in the language of men.

The human authors of Scripture knew they were writing God's Word, and they did so with confidence and authority. Often they cited or alluded to one another as authoritative agents of divine revelation (e.g., 2 Peter 3:15-16).

On a personal level, inspiration guarantees that what Scripture says, God says. It's His counsel to you; so you can study and obey it with full assurance that it is true and will never lead you astray.

✧✧✧

Suggestions for Prayer: Praise the Lord for His inspired Word. ✧ Reaffirm your commitment to live according to its principles today.

For Further Study: Often the New Testament affirms the inspiration of the Old Testament by attributing Old Testament quotations to God Himself. For example, compare these Old Testament passages with their New Testament counterparts: Genesis 2:24 with Matthew 19:4-5; Psalm 2:1-2 with Acts 4:25-26; Isaiah 55:3 with Acts 13:34; Psalm 16:10 with Acts 13:35; Psalm 95:7-11 with Hebrews 3:7-11. ✧ How might you respond to someone who says that the Bible is merely the words of devout religious men?

October 14 RALLYING AROUND THE WORD

"Every word of God is tested [pure, flawless]" (Prov. 30:5).

❖❖❖

God's Word is without error.

The term *inerrancy* conveys the belief that the original writings of Scripture are wholly true in everything they teach—whether doctrine, history, science, geography, geology, or any other discipline or knowledge. It also applies to accurate copies of those original writings.

Inerrancy is an unpopular concept with some people because they believe it isn't really important. But consider the implications. No Christian would deny that our relationship to Jesus Christ is of utmost importance. But how can we know Him except as He is presented in the Bible? He is our Lord, and we must obey His commandments (Heb. 5:9). How can we know what He commands if we doubt His Word?

Others reject inerrancy because they think it's divisive. But inerrancy should be a rallying point for evangelicals, not a dividing point. What unifying factor do we have if we can't agree on the truth of divine revelation?

Still others withhold judgment on the issue, thinking it's a technical matter that is best decided by Biblical scholars. On the contrary, it is the most basic of all matters. It's nothing less than asking, "Is there a sure word from God?"

Inerrancy isn't simply a matter of theological debate. It's a matter of God's character. God cannot lie (Titus 1:2; Heb. 6:18); therefore His Word is true. Jeremiah 10:10 says that the Lord is "the true God" or the God of truth. The Apostle John said, "God is true" (John 3:33). And Jesus defined eternal life as knowing "the only true God" (John 17:3). Christ came so we might "know Him who is true . . . the true God and eternal life" (1 John 5:20).

Don't be shaken by those who attack the integrity of Scripture. As you have opportunity, study any problem passages so you'll know firsthand what the issues and proposed solutions are. And remember, Scripture was given by inspiration of the Holy Spirit, who is "the Spirit of truth" (John 16:13). He cannot err.

❖❖❖

Suggestions for Prayer: If Psalm 119:12-16 reflects the intent of your heart, read it to the Lord as a prayer of praise and commitment.

For Further Study: According to Matthew 22:29 and John 17:17, what was Jesus' view of Scripture?

The law of the Lord is perfect. . . . The commandment of the Lord is pure. . . . The judgments of the Lord are true; they are righteous altogether" (Ps. 19:7-9).

✧✧✧

God's Word is infallible.

Infallibility refers to the truth of Scripture as a whole, whereas inerrancy focuses on the accuracy of every single word. Like inerrancy, infallibility is grounded in the character of God. God cannot lie and does not change (1 Sam. 15:29). He is thoroughly consistent in everything He does, and His Word reflects those characteristics. The psalmist wrote, "The sum of Thy word is truth, and every one of Thy righteous ordinances is everlasting" (Ps. 119:160). Paul said, "The Law is holy, and the commandment is holy and righteous and good" (Rom. 7:12).

Jesus said He didn't come to abolish the law or the prophets (sections of the Old Testament) but to fulfill them. He promised that everything in Scripture will be fulfilled (Matt. 5:17-18). John 10:35 declares that the authority of Scripture "cannot be broken." It is binding and cannot be destroyed, abolished, or done away with. God's Word is indestructible, authoritative, and infallible.

On a practical level, *infallibility* means that you can trust the Bible. It will never deceive you or give you counsel that will later prove to be erroneous. That was the confidence of the psalmist when he wrote, "Establish Thy word to Thy servant, as that which produces reverence for Thee. Turn away my reproach which I dread, for Thine ordinances are good. Behold, I long for Thy precepts; revive me through Thy righteousness. May Thy lovingkindnesses also come to me, O Lord, Thy salvation according to Thy word; so I shall have an answer for him who reproaches me, for I trust in Thy word. And do not take the word of truth utterly out of my mouth, for I wait for Thine ordinances. So I will keep Thy law continually, forever and ever. And I will walk at liberty, for I seek Thy precepts. I will also speak of Thy testimonies before kings, and shall not be ashamed. And I shall delight in Thy commandments, which I love" (Ps. 119:38-47).

✧✧✧

Suggestions for Prayer: Praise God that His Word is utterly trustworthy.

For Further Study: Memorize Psalm 119:165 as a reminder of the infallibility of God's Word.

"Listen, O heavens, and hear, O earth; for the Lord speaks" (Isa. 1:2).

✧✧✧

God's Word is the only source of divine authority.

We might assume that those who affirm the inspiration, inerrancy, and infallibility of God's Word would automatically submit to its authority. But that isn't always the case. Even those who hold to a high view of Scripture sometimes fail to obey it. We need to be reminded that the authority of God's Word isn't simply a doctrine to be affirmed but a priority to be pursued.

Israel fell into the trap of holding to a high view of Scripture while failing to abide by its statutes. To them Paul said, "If you bear the name 'Jew,' and rely upon the Law, and boast in God, and know His will, and approve the things that are essential, being instructed out of the Law, and are confident that you yourself are a guide to the blind, a light to those who are in darkness, a corrector of the foolish, a teacher of the immature, having in the Law the embodiment of knowledge and of the truth, you therefore, who teach another, do you not teach yourself? . . . You who boast in the Law, through your breaking the Law, do you dishonor God? For 'the name of God is blasphemed among the Gentiles because of you'" (Rom. 2:17-21, 23-24).

Israel's sin led unbelievers to blaspheme God. That's analogous to our society in which the Lord is constantly ridiculed because of the sins of His people.

You are the only Bible some unbelievers will ever read, and your life is under scrutiny every day. What do others learn from you? Do they see an accurate picture of your God?

Christians will always be maligned, but let it be for righteousness' sake, not because of sin. As Peter said, "Keep your behavior excellent among [unbelievers], so that in the thing in which they slander you as evildoers, they may on account of your good deeds, as they observe them, glorify God" (1 Peter 2:12).

✧✧✧

Suggestions for Prayer: Confess any areas of your life where you are being disobedient to God's Word. ✧ Seek His grace and power to live each day as one who truly respects the authority of God's Word.

For Further Study: Read 1 Corinthians 10:1-13. What purpose does the Old Testament record of Israel's punishments serve for us?

"The law of the Lord is perfect, restoring the soul; the testimony of the Lord is sure, making wise the simple. The precepts of the Lord are right, rejoicing the heart; the commandment of the Lord is pure, enlightening the eyes. The fear of the Lord is clean, enduring forever; the judgments of the Lord are true; they are righteous altogether.

"They are more desirable than gold, yes, than much fine gold; sweeter also than honey and the drippings of the honeycomb. Moreover, by them Thy servant is warned; in keeping them there is great reward.

"Who can discern his errors? Acquit me of hidden faults. Also keep back Thy servant from presumptuous sins; let them not rule over me; then I shall be blameless, and I shall be acquitted of great transgression.

"Let the words of my mouth and the meditation of my heart be acceptable in Thy sight, O Lord, my rock and my redeemer" (Ps. 19:7-14).

❖❖❖

God's Word addresses the soul's every need.

King David was a man of stark contrasts. He knew the humility of shepherding a flock and the prestige of reigning over a nation. He experienced glorious triumphs and bitter defeats. He sought after God, yet also suffered immense guilt and pain from immorality and murder. That led to even his own son's seeking to take his life. Some of his psalms reflect great hope and others despair. But through it all he continued to look to God, being assured of God's sovereignty and the sufficiency of His divine resources.

In Psalm 19 David penned the most monumental statement ever made on the sufficiency of Scripture. As we study it in the days ahead, keep in mind that every need of your soul or inmost being is ultimately spiritual, and God has supplied sufficient resources to meet those needs completely. That was David's confidence. May it be yours as well.

❖❖❖

Suggestions for Prayer: Throughout our study of Psalm 19, ask God to give you fresh insights that will enable you to appreciate and rest more fully in His gracious provisions.

For Further Study: Reread Psalm 19:1-14. ❖ What terms did David use for God's Word? ❖ What benefits does the Word bring to believers? ❖ Are you enjoying those benefits?

"The law of the Lord is perfect, restoring the soul" (Ps. 19:7).

❖❖❖

**God can transform you through His Word into
the person He wants you to be.**

Many today doubt the power of Scripture in dealing with the deeper aspects of the human heart and mind. The Bible may be helpful for certain superficial or "spiritual" problems, they say, but it's too simplistic and inadequate for the more complex psychological issues of modern man. The truth is, however, the best psychology can do is to modify external behavior. It cannot redeem and transform the soul. Only God can do that through the power of His Word.

That's the truth behind Psalm 19:7, which calls Scripture "the law of the Lord," thus emphasizing its didactic nature. It is the sum of God's instruction to man, whether for creed (what we believe), character (what we are), or conduct (what we do).

The law of the Lord is "perfect." That represents a common Hebrew word that speaks of wholeness, completeness, or sufficiency. Commentator Albert Barnes wrote that Scripture "lacks nothing [for] its completeness; nothing in order that it might be what it should be. It is complete as a revelation of Divine truth; it is complete as a rule of conduct. . . . It is absolutely true; it is adapted with consummate wisdom to the [needs] of man; it is an unerring guide of conduct. There is nothing there which would lead men into error or sin; there is nothing essential for man to know which may not be found there" (*Notes on the Old Testament: Psalms*, Vol. 1 [Grand Rapids, Mich.: Baker, 1974], p. 171).

Man's reasoning is imperfect, but God's Word is perfect, containing everything necessary for your spiritual life. It is so comprehensive that it can restore your soul. That is, it will convert, revive, refresh, and transform every aspect of your being to make you precisely the person God wants you to be.

Don't look to impotent human alternatives when God's Word stands ready to minister to your every need. Spiritual warfare is fought with spiritual weapons, not fleshly techniques, theories, or therapies (2 Cor. 10:4).

❖❖❖

Suggestions for Prayer: Ask God to keep you focused on His counsel regarding every situation you face today.

For Further Study: Memorize 2 Corinthians 9:8 as a reminder of God's super-abounding grace to you.

"The testimony of the Lord is sure, making wise the simple"
(Ps. 19:7).

❖❖❖

God's Word imparts wisdom and knowledge beyond
the realm of mere human understanding.

David's characterization of God's Word as "the testimony of the Lord" (Ps. 19:7) speaks of its role as God's witness to who He is and what He requires of us. In addition, it's a "sure" witness. That means it's unwavering, immovable, unmistakable, reliable, and trustworthy.

Peter made the same point when, after recounting his incredible experience with Christ on the Mount of Transfiguration (2 Peter 1:16-18), he said, "but we have a testimony more sure than that—the prophetic word" (v. 19, literal translation). The testimony of God's written Word is a surer and more convincing confirmation of God's truth than even apostolic experiences with Christ Himself!

Perhaps that's why our Lord prevented the two disciples on the Emmaus Road from recognizing Him as He gave them a Biblical basis for the things they had seen and heard (Luke 24:27). Their faith and preaching were to be based on Scripture, not merely on their own personal experiences—no matter how profound or moving those experiences may have been.

The benefit of God's sure Word is that it makes the simple wise (Ps. 19:7). It takes undiscerning, ignorant, and gullible people and teaches them profound truth from God that they can apply to their lives. As they do this, they become skilled in the art of godly living.

That was the psalmist's joy when he wrote, "Thy commandments make me wiser than my enemies, for they are ever mine. I have more insight than all my teachers, for Thy testimonies are my meditation. I understand more than the aged, because I have observed Thy precepts" (Ps. 119:98-100).

Applying that principle to New Testament believers, Paul prayed that we would be "filled with the knowledge of [God's] will in all spiritual wisdom and understanding" (Col. 1:9). As that occurs, we're enabled to "walk in a manner worthy of the Lord [and] to please Him in all respects" (v. 10). That's the outworking of godly wisdom and the key to holy living.

❖❖❖

Suggestions for Prayer: Pray that God's wisdom will increase and abound in your life today and every day.

For Further Study: Read Luke 24:13-35, noting how Jesus ministered the Word to the disciples on the Emmaus Road.

"The precepts of the Lord are right, rejoicing the heart"
(Ps. 19:8).

❖❖❖

Knowing your life is on the right track is a source of great joy.

What brings you joy? Your answer will reveal much about your priorities and about the direction your life is heading spiritually.

The psalmist wrote, "How blessed [happy] is the man who does not walk in the counsel of the wicked, nor stand in the path of sinners, nor sit in the seat of scoffers! But his delight is in the law of the Lord, and in His law he meditates day and night. And he will be like a tree firmly planted by streams of water, which yields its fruit in its season, and its leaf does not wither; and in whatever he does, he prospers" (Ps. 1:1-3).

That psalmist knew that true joy and happiness come from knowing God and abiding in His Word. That was David's confidence when he wrote, "The precepts of the Lord are right, rejoicing the heart" (Ps. 19:8).

"Precepts" in that verse speaks of divine principles and guidelines for character and conduct. God created you and knows how you must live to give glory to Him. And He revealed in His Word every precept you must know to do so.

Every divine precept is "right." It shows you the path that is right and true. What a wonderful confidence that is! While many around you may be discouraged or despondent because of their lack of direction and purpose, God's Word is a lamp to your feet and a light to your path (Ps. 119:105). It guides you through the difficult mazes of life and gives your life eternal significance. Don't live simply for your own pleasures. Your life has a high and holy purpose, and each day can be filled with joy as you see that purpose unfold.

❖❖❖

Suggestions for Prayer: Ask God to help you be mindful of your eternal purpose today and every day. ❖ Ask Him to direct you to someone who needs Christ and is sensing a lack of purpose in his or her life.

For Further Study: Read Colossians 3:1-4. ❖ How did Paul describe Christ? ❖ What should be the focus of your thinking? ❖ Are you heeding Paul's exhortation?

October 21

*"The commandment of the Lord is pure, enlightening the eyes"
(Ps. 19:8).*

❖❖❖

Obedience to the Word is the hallmark of a true believer.

It isn't popular these days to speak of God's Word as a book of command-ments. Commands imply law, and we're accustomed to grace. But the fact is, both the Old and New Testaments contain many commandments that all God's people are to obey.

The Apostle John said, "By this we know that we have come to know Him, if we keep His commandments. The one who says, 'I have come to know Him,' and does not keep His commandments, is a liar, and the truth is not in him; but whoever keeps His word, in him the love of God has truly been per-fected" (1 John 2:3-5). John equated the commandments of God with the Word of God.

Jesus Himself said, "If you love Me, you will keep My commandments" (John 14:15), and "He who has My commandments and keeps them, he it is who loves Me; and he who loves Me shall be loved by My Father" (v. 21). If you truly love Christ, your life will be characterized by a pattern of obedience to His Word.

Every commandment of God is "pure," the psalmist said (Ps. 19:8). Its effect is "enlightening the eyes." God's Word brings spiritual truth into clear focus. Not every passage of Scripture is easy to understand, but taken as a whole, the message of the Bible is clear to the regenerate mind.

But as clear as the Bible is to believers, unredeemed people can't under-stand it. To them it's foolishness because their minds are unenlightened (1 Cor. 2:14). In their spiritual blindness they choose humanistic philosophical speculations over God's Word. But as a believer, you are continually being enlightened by the truths of God's Word as the Holy Spirit enables you to understand them and apply them to your life.

Your ability to understand the Word is a priceless gift. Take advantage of it daily by expanding your Bible knowledge and increasing your obedience.

❖❖❖

Suggestions for Prayer: Thank the Lord for opening your mind to the truths of His Word. ❖ Commit yourself to discovering at least one additional truth from Scripture each day.

For Further Study: Read 1 Corinthians 2:14-16. What comparison did Paul make between the natural (unregenerate) man and the spiritual (regenerate) man?

"The fear of the Lord is clean, enduring forever" (Ps. 19:9).

❖❖❖

Fearing God leads to reverential attitudes and actions.

In the Old Testament, to fear God was to view Him with reverential awe and to bow to His sovereign authority. In Psalm 34 David wrote, "Come, you children, listen to me; I will teach you the fear of the Lord. Who is the man who desires life, and loves length of days that he may see good? Keep your tongue from evil, and your lips from speaking deceit. Depart from evil, and do good; seek peace, and pursue it" (vv. 11-14). His son Solomon added, "The fear of the Lord is the beginning of knowledge. . . . Fear the Lord and turn away from evil" (Prov. 1:7; 3:7).

The concept of fearing God isn't limited to the Old Testament. Paul said, "Work out your salvation with fear and trembling" (Phil. 2:12), "Let us cleanse ourselves from all defilement of flesh and spirit, perfecting holiness in the fear of God" (2 Cor. 7:1), and "Be subject to one another in the fear of Christ" (Eph. 5:21).

Our fear of God compels us to worship Him and to conform our lives to His will. If you fear Him, pleasing Him will be your greatest delight, and displeasing Him your greatest disappointment.

In Psalm 19:9 David uses "fear" as a synonym for God's Word, implying that Scripture is God's manual on how to worship Him. "Clean" is a comprehensive term that speaks of the absence of sin, corruption, filthiness, defilement, imperfection, and error. The message Scripture conveys is always "flawless, like silver refined in a furnace of clay, purified seven times" (Ps. 12:6, NIV).

Because it is so perfect, Scripture endures forever (Ps. 19:9). That's why Jesus said, "Heaven and earth will pass away, but my words will not pass away" (Mark 13:31). It never needs to be updated to accommodate contemporary thinking. It stands forever, authoritative and unyielding. Those who judge it, slander it, or ignore it are in grave peril. It is far better to fear God and to bow to His revealed will.

❖❖❖

Suggestions for Prayer: Read Psalm 33 as a prayer of praise to the Lord.

For Further Study: Memorize Proverbs 3:5-7 as a reminder always to seek God's will and approval.

"The judgments of the Lord are true; they are righteous altogether" (Ps. 19:9).

❖❖❖

God's Word is true and produces righteousness in the believer's life.

The inability of human wisdom to produce right living was reaffirmed in my thinking as I read a contemporary psychiatrist's book on how to overcome depression. The doctor's first suggestion was to shout "Cancel!" every time you have a negative thought. She also recommended playing a tape recording of positive messages while you sleep at night and listening to positive music during the day.

Cultivating a meaningful spiritual philosophy was another of her suggestions. She said any will do—as long as it works for you—but cautioned against those that speak of sin and guilt. Her final point was to find the spiritual light within yourself.

That kind of advice is foolish because it has no basis in truth. The best it can do is mask a few symptoms. It cannot cure the illness.

Jesus illustrated the hopelessness of searching for truth through such means when He said to a group of unbelievers, "Why do you not understand what I am saying? It is because you cannot hear My word. You are of your father the devil . . . [who] does not stand in the truth, because there is no truth in him. Whenever he speaks a lie, he speaks from his own nature; for he is a liar, and the father of lies. But because I speak the truth, you do not believe Me. . . . He who is of God hears the words of God; for this reason you do not hear them, because you are not of God" (John 8:43-47).

Unbelievers don't see the truth of God's Word for what it is. But believers hear the truth and receive it. Like David, they acknowledge that "the judgments of the Lord are true; they are righteous altogether" (Ps. 19:9).

"Judgments" in that context speaks of ordinances or divine verdicts from the Supreme Judge. "Righteous altogether" implies that Scripture produces comprehensive righteousness in all who receive it. Together these words emphasize that true righteousness originates from God's Word and flows through His people.

❖❖❖

Suggestions for Prayer: Praise God for giving you the truth that produces righteousness.

For Further Study: What do the following verses say about God's righteous Word? Psalm 119:89, 128, 137-138, 142, and 160.

"[The judgments of the Lord] are more desirable than gold, yes, than much fine gold; sweeter also than honey and the drippings of the honeycomb" (Ps. 19:10).

❖❖❖

You should value Scripture more than all earthly treasures.

I have a friend who has a beautiful collection of rare Bibles. My favorite is one of the earliest printed copies, dating back to sixteenth-century England. The first time I held it in my hands I noticed that the top third of every page was covered with a dark stain. Tears filled my eyes when I realized it was from the blood of its original owner.

My friend explained that when Bloody Mary ruled England, she delighted in terrorizing Protestants and murdering as many as she could. Her soldiers would execute their victims through some bloody means, then take his or her Bible and dip it into the blood. Some of those Bibles have been preserved and are known as Martyrs' Bibles. Scientists have confirmed that the dark stains on every page of my friend's Bible are, indeed, human blood.

That same Bible is well-worn from being studied. And many of its pages have water stains on them—perhaps from tears. Obviously it was someone's most precious possession, and his or her blood is there to prove it.

Psalm 19:10 captures the heart of such people, extolling the preciousness of God's Word. To David, Scripture was more valuable than the best gold and the purest honey. Meditating on it meant more to him than the richest and sweetest things in life. He knew its ability to satisfy every spiritual appetite.

As precious as God's Word is, many Christians take it for granted and become complacent in their studies. Some go for long periods without gaining fresh insights from its pages.

Perhaps you know someone who is in that situation. If so, ask the Lord for wisdom as you gently encourage him or her toward greater faithfulness in the Word. At the same time be careful not to become negligent yourself.

❖❖❖

Suggestions for Prayer: Thank God for the example of those who have loved His Word to the cost of their lives. ❖ Ask Him to give you the desire to feed on His truth daily and the drive to satisfy that desire.

For Further Study: Read 1 Peter 2:1-2 as a reminder to keep your heart sensitive to the precious gift of God's Word.

"By [Thy judgments] Thy servant is warned; in keeping them there is great reward" (Ps. 19:11).

✧✧✧

Heeding God's warnings brings spiritual protection and great joy.

Psalm 19:11 concludes David's hymn on the sufficiency of Scripture. How appropriate that it ends noting the value of God's warning, because guarding His people against temptation, sin, error, foolishness, false teachers, and every other threat to their spiritual well-being is a major concern to God.

For example, God said to the prophet Ezekiel, "Now as for you, son of man, I have appointed you a watchman for the house of Israel; so you will hear a message from My mouth, and give them warning from Me" (33:7). The great tragedy of the Old Testament is that Israel rejected God's "statutes and His covenant which He made with their fathers, and His warnings with which He warned them" (2 Kings 17:15).

The Apostle Paul defined his ministry as that of proclaiming Christ and warning "every man and teaching every man with all wisdom" (Col. 1:28). After exhorting the Thessalonian church to maintain sexual purity, Paul added, "The Lord is the avenger in all these things, just as we also told you before and solemnly warned you" (1 Thess. 4:6).

He also warned the Ephesian church, saying, "I know that after my departure savage wolves will come in among you, not sparing the flock; and from among your own selves men will arise, speaking perverse things, to draw away the disciples after them. Therefore be on the alert, remembering that night and day for a period of three years I did not cease to admonish [warn] each one with tears" (Acts 20:29-32). He did that by declaring to them the whole counsel of God (v. 27).

The warnings of Scripture aren't intended to frustrate or stifle you. On the contrary, when you heed them, they shelter you from spiritual harm and bring the joy of knowing you're in God's will. That's the "great reward" David speaks of in Psalm 19:11. May you earn it, as he eventually did, through heeding God's Word in every aspect of life.

✧✧✧

Suggestions for Prayer: Overwhelmed with the sufficiency of God's Word, David prayed, "Let the words of my mouth and the meditation of my heart be acceptable in Thy sight, O Lord, my rock and my redeemer" (Ps. 19:14). Make that your prayer as well.

For Further Study: Re-read Psalm 19:7-11, reviewing each characteristic and benefit of Scripture. Think carefully about how they apply to your life.

"From childhood you have known the sacred writings which are able to give you the wisdom that leads to salvation through faith which is in Christ Jesus" (2 Tim. 3:15).

✧✧✧

Planting and nurturing the seed of God's Word in a child's mind can produce an abundant spiritual harvest.

Not long ago I met with a group of Christian leaders to consider several candidates for a significant ministry position. During our meeting it dawned on me that each candidate's father was a prominent pastor. Each candidate had grown up in a family that daily taught and exemplified Biblical truth.

That illustrates the enormous impact a Christian heritage can have on a person—whether he pursues the pastorate or not. And by no means is it fathers only who influence their children toward righteousness. Quite the contrary; a godly mother usually has far more opportunity to do so.

Dr. G. Campbell Morgan had four sons—all of whom followed his example by becoming ministers. It's reported that at a family reunion a friend asked one of the sons, "Which Morgan is the greatest preacher?" "That's easy," the son replied. "Mother!"

Timothy knew the benefits of a spiritual heritage like that. His mother, Eunice, and his grandmother, Lois (2 Tim. 1:5) taught him the sacred writings, which give the wisdom that leads to salvation (2 Tim. 3:15). Even as a child, Timothy was being equipped for the ministry to which God would later call him. The spiritual training he received as a child—and the reservoir of Biblical knowledge he accumulated in those early years—were crucial elements in his adult ministry.

If you are a parent, the most precious gift you can give your child is a godly upbringing that will serve as the foundation for his or her future ministries.

✧✧✧

Suggestions for Prayer: Praise God for those who have instructed you in the Word and encouraged you in righteousness. ✧ If you are a parent, pray that your children will exceed you in the faith. ✧ Be faithful to pray for the young people around you and to set a godly example for them to follow.

For Further Study: Read 1 Samuel 1:1–2:10. What characteristics of a godly mother did Hannah display?

"All Scripture is inspired by God and profitable for teaching, for reproof, for correction, for training in righteousness" (2 Tim. 3:16).

✧✧✧

Scripture is a manual of divine truth.

This month we've considered many benefits of Scripture. Second Timothy 3:16 lists four more that will be the focus of our studies as we draw this month to a close: teaching truth, reproving sin and error, correcting behavior, and training in righteousness. We've touched on each of those to some extent in our past studies, but they warrant additional discussion from this verse, which is Scripture's most concise statement on its own power and purpose.

First, the Bible is profitable for teaching. The Greek word translated "teaching" refers more to content than to the process of teaching. Scripture is God's manual of divine truth for patterning your thoughts and actions.

As a believer, you have the capacity to understand and respond to Scripture. That's because the Holy Spirit indwells you and imparts spiritual discernment, wisdom, and understanding (1 John 2:27). You have "the mind of Christ" (1 Cor. 2:16).

But having the ability to understand spiritual truth doesn't guarantee you'll exercise that ability. God said to the Israelites through the prophet Hosea, "My people are destroyed for lack of knowledge" (4:6). His truth was available to them, but they ignored it and lived in disobedience.

I've heard many people lament that they could have avoided much grief if only they had known the Bible more thoroughly—if only they had taken the time to learn what God expected of them in a particular situation. Perhaps you've felt that way. The best way to avoid making that mistake in the future is to faithfully, prayerfully, patiently, and thoroughly saturate your mind with Biblical truth now, and then discipline yourself to live according to its principles. Now that's the challenge of a lifetime, but it's the only way to profit from Biblical teaching and to avoid unnecessary heartaches.

I pray that you will be encouraged today as you study God's Word and diligently apply it to your life.

✧✧✧

Suggestions for Prayer: Ask God to use the circumstances you face today to draw you closer to Him and to motivate you to dig deeper into His Word.

For Further Study: Read Exodus 24:1-8. What was the Israelites' response to God's Word? What is yours?

"All Scripture is . . . profitable for . . . reproof" (2 Tim. 3:16).

❖❖❖

Scripture is the standard by which you must measure all teaching.

In November of 1978, United States Representative Leo Ryan of California visited the People's Temple (a California-based cult) in Guyana. He went to investigate reports that some of the people were being held there against their will. The world was soon shocked to learn that the congressman and his party had been ambushed and killed.

Even more shocking was the grim discovery that followed a few days later. Authorities who entered the compound at Jonestown, Guyana, were horrified to find the bodies of 780 cult members who had been shot or had committed suicide by drinking cyanide-laced punch. Their leader, the Reverend Jim Jones, was found lying near the altar—dead from a single bullet wound to the head.

For many, it was the first time they had witnessed the deadly effect of Satanic teaching. Editorials and articles for months attempted to explain how such appalling deception and genocide could occur in this day and age. But as tragic as the Jonestown deaths were, most observers missed the greatest tragedy of all—the spiritual damnation into which Jim Jones, David Koresh, and all other false teachers lead their followers.

Spiritual deception is a very serious issue to God. That's why in Scripture He lays down the truth and reproves anything contrary to it. The Greek word translated "reproof" in 2 Timothy 3:16 means "to rebuke or confront someone regarding misconduct or false teaching."

If you have a thorough grasp of Scripture, you have a standard by which to measure all teaching. Then you can easily recognize false doctrine and can avoid spiritual deception. That's what John had in mind when he said, "I have written to you, [spiritual] young men, because you are strong, and the word of God abides in you, and you have overcome the evil one" (1 John 2:14).

False religions will always attempt to distort Scripture because they must eliminate God's truth before they can justify their own lies. Beware of their subtleties, and be strong in God's Word.

❖❖❖

Suggestions for Prayer: Thank the Lord for protecting you from spiritual deception. ❖ Pray for anyone you may know who has fallen victim to false teaching. Take every opportunity to impart God's truth to them.

For Further Study: Read 2 Corinthians 11:1-4, 13-15. How did Paul describe false teachers?

"All Scripture is . . . profitable for . . . reproof" (2 Tim. 3:16).

❖❖❖

**People who aren't interested in holy living
will avoid being exposed to sound doctrine.**

Paul instructed Timothy to "preach the word; be ready in season and out of season; reprove, rebuke, exhort, with great patience and instruction" (2 Tim. 4:2). He knew a time was coming when many people would reject sound doctrine and, "wanting to have their ears tickled, [would] accumulate for themselves teachers in accordance to their own desires; and . . . turn away their ears from the truth, and will turn aside to myths" (vv. 3-4).

That's certainly true of our day. Many who profess to love Christ seem intolerant of His Word. Often they fall into spiritual complacency and surround themselves with teachers who tell them exactly what they want to hear. If they can't find a comfortable message, they drift from church to church or simply abandon it altogether.

Such people have exchanged conviction for comfort and need to examine themselves to see if they are genuine believers (2 Cor. 13:5). Their attitude toward the Word is in stark contrast to those who truly love Christ and come to the Word with an earnest desire to learn its truths and live accordingly.

But even true believers can fall into the trap of negligence and compromise. Perhaps you've noticed how sinning Christians often try to avoid exposure to God's Word. Sometimes they'll temporarily stop attending church or Bible studies. They also try to avoid other believers—especially those who will hold them accountable to what they know to be true.

But like any loving parent, God won't allow His children to remain in sin for long without disciplining them (Heb. 12:5-11). Sooner or later they must repent and be reconciled to Him.

An important element in reconciling sinning Christians to God is the faithful prayers of other believers. God may choose to use you in that way; so always be ready to pray and be eager to restore others in a spirit of gentleness (Gal. 6:1).

❖❖❖

Suggestions for Prayer: Do you know a Christian who is being disobedient to God's Word? If so, ask God to bring him or her to repentance. Assure the person of your prayers and concern, and be available to be further used in the restoration process if the Lord wills.

For Further Study: What does Matthew 18:15-20 say about how to confront a sinning Christian?

"All Scripture is . . . profitable for . . . correction" (2 Tim. 3:16).

❖❖❖

God's Word strengthens the repentant sinner.

If you're a gardening buff, you know that skillful pruning promotes the overall growth and productivity of a plant. Jesus assumed His audience knew as much when He said, "I am the true vine, and My Father is the vinedresser. Every branch in Me that does not bear fruit, He takes away; and every branch that bears fruit, He prunes it, that it may bear more fruit. You are already clean because of the word which I have spoken to you" (John 15:1-3).

Jesus was comparing believers to branches, which the Father prunes for maximum productivity. The Word is His pruning shear, which He applies with skill and precision to remove our imperfections and to promote godliness. He wants to eliminate anything from our lives that may restrict our spiritual growth.

The word translated "correction" in 2 Timothy 3:16 speaks of the strengthening work of God's Word. Scripture not only exposes your sin, but it also strengthens you and restores you to a proper spiritual posture. It convicts you and then gives you instruction to build you up again.

Job 17:9 says, "The righteous shall hold to his way, and he who has clean hands shall grow stronger and stronger." Paul added, "I commend you to God and to the word of His grace, which is able to build you up and to give you the inheritance among all those who are sanctified" (Acts 20:32).

As the Spirit uses Scripture to expose sin in your life, forsake that sin, and follow what Scripture says to do instead. You will be strengthened in your spiritual walk as a result. To aid in that process, be "constantly nourished on the words of the faith and . . . sound doctrine" (1 Tim. 4:6).

I firmly believe that any weaknesses you have can become areas of great strength as you allow God's Word to do its sanctifying work within you.

❖❖❖

Suggestions for Prayer: Thank God for the strengthening and restoring power of His Word. ❖ If there's an area of your life that is weak and vulnerable to temptation, confess it to the Lord, and begin today to strengthen it according to the Word.

For Further Study: Read Ephesians 1:18-23 and 3:14-21. ❖ What did Paul pray for? ❖ How did God demonstrate His power toward believers? ❖ Is God's power sufficient for all your spiritual needs? Explain.

"All Scripture is . . . profitable for . . . training in righteousness"
(2 Tim. 3:16).

❖❖❖

God's Word nourishes your spiritual life.

We conclude our study of the character and benefits of God's Word by focusing on the benefit that ties all the others together—training in righteousness. Everything the Word accomplishes in you through teaching, reproof, and correction is aimed at increasing your righteousness, so you'll "be thoroughly equipped for every good work" (2 Tim. 3:17, NIV).

"Training" refers to training or educating a child. The New Testament also uses that term to speak of chastening, which is another important element in both child-rearing and spiritual growth (Heb. 12:5-11). The idea is that from spiritual infancy to maturity, Scripture trains and educates believers in godly living.

Scripture is your spiritual nourishment. Jesus said, "Man shall not live on bread alone, but on every word that proceeds out of the mouth of God" (Matt. 4:4). Peter exhorted us to be like "newborn babes [who] long for the pure milk of the word, that by it [we] may grow in respect to salvation" (1 Peter 2:2).

You should crave the Word just like a baby craves milk. But Peter prefaced that statement with an exhortation to put aside "all malice and all guile and hypocrisy and envy and all slander" (v. 1). That's the prerequisite. James taught the same principle: "Putting aside all filthiness and all that remains of wickedness, in humility receive the word" (James 1:21). Attempting to feast on Scripture without confessing your sin is like attempting to eat a meal while wearing a muzzle.

Either the Word will keep you from sin, or sin will keep you from the Word. Deal with sin immediately, so it doesn't spoil your appetite for God's Word. And even if you know the Bible well, be regularly refreshed by its power and reminded of its truths. That's the key to enjoying spiritual health and victory.

❖❖❖

Suggestions for Prayer: Thank God for the nourishment His Word provides. ❖ Seek His wisdom and grace in dealing with personal sin. Don't ignore it, for it will diminish your desire for Biblical truth.

For Further Study: Read Philippians 3:1 and 2 Peter 1:12-15. ❖ What did Paul and Peter say about the importance of being reminded of Biblical truths you've already learned? ❖ Do you follow that advice?

"Faith is the assurance of things hoped for, the conviction of things not seen. For by it the men of old gained approval" *(Heb. 11:1-2).*

❖❖❖

Christian faith produces righteous deeds.

Hebrews 11 has been called "The Heroes of Faith," "The Faith Chapter," "The Saints' Hall of Fame," "The Honor Roll of the Old Testament Saints," and "The Westminster Abbey of Scripture." Those are appropriate titles because this chapter highlights the virtues of faith as demonstrated in the lives of great Old Testament saints. It also reminds us that without faith, it is impossible to please God.

Such a reminder was necessary for the first-century Hebrew people because Judaism had abandoned true faith in God for a legalistic system of works-righteousness. Its message is also valid today because our devotion to Christ can easily degenerate into a religion of rules and regulations.

While affirming the primacy of faith, the writer of Hebrews doesn't undermine the importance of righteous works. Quite the contrary. He exhorts us "to stimulate one another to love and good deeds" (10:24) and to pursue holiness so others will see Christ in us and be drawn to Him (12:14).

Yet, righteous works are the by-product of true salvation, not its means. As the Apostle Paul wrote, "We are His workmanship, created in Christ Jesus for good works, which God prepared beforehand, that we should walk in them" (Eph. 2:10). Apart from faith, all attempts to please God through good works alone are as useless and offensive to Him as filthy rags (Isa. 64:6). That's why Paul gladly set all his Jewish legalistic practices aside, counting them as "rubbish." He wanted only "the righteousness which comes from God on the basis of faith" (Phil. 3:8-9).

This month we'll study the heroes of faith listed in Hebrews 11. As we do, remember that they weren't perfect people. But their faith was exemplary, and by it they gained God's approval. I pray that's true of you as well.

❖❖❖

Suggestions for Prayer: Thank God for the gift of faith. ❖ Undoubtedly you know people who are trying to please God by their own efforts. Pray for them, and take every opportunity to tell them about true salvation through faith in Christ.

For Further Study: Select one of the individuals mentioned in Hebrews 11, and read the Old Testament account of his or her life.

"Faith is the assurance of things hoped for" (Heb. 11:1).

❖❖❖

**Faith is the solid ground on which we stand
as we await the fulfillment of God's promises.**

An elderly man, on his seventy-fifth birthday, received an invitation to fly over the little West Virginia town in which he had spent his entire life. Although he had never before flown, the man accepted the gracious offer.

After circling the town for about twenty minutes, the pilot safely returned his passenger to the ground. The man's grandson greeted him excitedly, asking, "Were you scared, Grandpa?" "No," he replied sheepishly, "but I never did put my full weight down."

Unlike that hesitant grandfather, true faith trusts fully in its object. For the Christian, that means resting in God and His promises. That's the primary characteristic of each faithful individual listed in Hebrews 11. They all believed God and responded accordingly.

People often confuse faith with a wistful longing that something, however unlikely, will come to pass in the future. But "assurance" in Hebrews 11:1 speaks of essence and reality—the real thing as opposed to mere appearance. Faith, then, involves absolute certainty.

For example, the Old Testament saints had the promise of a coming Messiah who would take away sin. They believed God, even though their understanding of Messiah was incomplete and somewhat vague. They knew their hopes would be fulfilled, and that assurance dominated their lives.

It's the same for New Testament believers. Peter said, "Though you have not seen [Christ], you love Him, and though you do not see Him now, but believe in Him, you greatly rejoice with joy inexpressible and full of glory, obtaining as the outcome of your faith the salvation of your souls" (1 Peter 1:8-9).

Man's natural tendency is to trust only in the things he can see, hear, touch, or taste. But our physical senses may lie, whereas God cannot (Titus 1:2). It is far better to believe God and to trust in His promises.

❖❖❖

Suggestions for Prayer: Which promises of God are especially meaningful to you today? Thank Him for them, and reaffirm your commitment to living on the basis of His Word.

For Further Study: Skim Hebrews 11, and note all the divine promises you find there. To gain a fuller understanding of each one, find other Scripture references that mention the same promises.

"Faith is . . . the conviction of things not seen" (Heb. 11:1).

✧✧✧

True faith goes beyond assurance to action.

When the writer said, "Faith is the assurance of things hoped for, the conviction of things not seen," he used two parallel and almost identical phrases to define faith.

We've seen that faith is the assurance that all God's promises will come to pass in His time. "The conviction of things not seen" takes the same truth a step further by implying a response to what we believe and are assured of.

James addressed the issue this way: "Someone may well say, 'You have faith, and I have works; show me your faith without the works, and I will show you my faith by my works.' . . . But are you willing to recognize . . . that faith without works is useless? . . . For just as the body without the spirit is dead, so also faith without works is dead" (James 2:18, 20, 26). In other words, a non-responsive faith is no faith at all.

Noah had a responsive faith. He had never seen rain because rain didn't exist prior to the Flood. Perhaps he knew nothing about building a ship. Still, he followed God's instructions and endured 120 years of hard work and ridicule because he believed God was telling the truth. His work was a testimony to that belief.

Moses considered "the reproach of Christ [Messiah] greater riches than the treasures of Egypt; for he was looking to the reward" (Heb. 11:26). Messiah wouldn't come to earth for another 1,400 years, but Moses forsook the wealth and benefits of Egypt in order to pursue the messianic hope.

Shadrach, Meshach, and Abednego, when faced with a life-threatening choice, chose to act on their faith in God, whom they couldn't see, rather than bow to Nebuchadnezzar, whom they could see all too well (Dan. 3). Even if it meant physical death, they wouldn't compromise their beliefs.

I pray that the choices you make today will show that you are a person of strong faith and convictions.

✧✧✧

Suggestions for Prayer: Ask God to increase and strengthen your faith through the events of this day. ✧ Look for specific opportunities to trust Him more fully.

For Further Study: Read Daniel 3:1-30. How was the faith of Shadrach, Meshach, and Abednego tested?

"By [faith] the men of old gained approval" (Heb. 11:2).

❖❖❖

God makes His approval known to those who trust in Him.

The book *Catch-22* tells of a squadron of World War II fliers stationed on the fictitious island of Pianos in the Mediterranean. Before a flier could transfer off the island, he had to complete twenty-five extremely dangerous missions over southern Europe.

One flier, Yosarian, was especially anxious to leave. After completing his twenty-fifth mission, his commanding officer began raising the number of qualifying missions. Insanity became the only justification for a transfer. But the commander decided that whoever feigned insanity to obtain a transfer proved his sanity by that sane act!

Realizing it was all a cruel game with no way out, Yosarian devised a plan to build a raft and float to Sweden. Even though there was a whole continent between him and Sweden and the ocean currents would take him in the opposite direction, he couldn't be dissuaded. He took a leap into the absurd with a hopeless and impossible plan to escape a hopeless and impossible situation.

In their relentless quest for meaning in life, many people become spiritual Yosarians. Rejecting God, who is the only sure and rational answer to life, they jump headlong into alcohol, drugs, witchcraft, astrology, reincarnation, or countless other absurdities.

Many acknowledge God but try to gain His approval through self-righteous deeds apart from true faith. In either case the results are the same: no faith, no salvation, no hope, no peace, and no assurance.

But those who take God at His word and approach Him in true faith receive His approval and enjoy His blessings. Theirs isn't a blind leap into the absurd but a living hope in the God who made man and who alone can fulfill man's deepest longings. They know the joy and satisfaction of a life spent in service to Christ and have the peace and assurance that all is well—both now and for eternity.

❖❖❖

Suggestions for Prayer: Pray for those you know who have rejected God or are trying to gain His approval on their own. Explain to them the meaning and purpose Christ alone can bring to their lives.

For Further Study: According to 2 Timothy 2:24-26, what is the spiritual state of those who oppose the gospel, and how are we to approach them?

"By faith we understand that the worlds were prepared by the word of God, so that what is seen was not made out of things which are visible" (Heb. 11:3).

❖❖❖

God's greatest truths are discovered by simple faith.

As a man or woman of faith, you have insights into life that unbelievers can't know. You know how the physical universe began, where it is heading, and how it will end. You know Who governs the universe and how you fit into the total scheme of things. You know why you exist and how to invest your life in matters of eternal consequence.

Unbelievers can't possibly appreciate those things because "a natural man does not accept the things of the Spirit of God; for they are foolishness to him, and he cannot understand them, because they are spiritually appraised" (1 Cor. 2:14).

Some of the most basic issues of life remain a mystery to most people because they refuse God's counsel. For example, the most brilliant thinkers have never agreed on the origin of the universe. Theirs is a futile attempt to explain what is beyond the realm of scientific investigation.

But such things aren't beyond the realm of knowing—if a person is willing to be taught by God's Word. The Bible clearly states that God spoke the physical universe into existence, creating visible matter from what was non-physical or invisible (Rom. 4:17). No humans observed that event. It cannot be measured or repeated. It must be taken by faith.

Any attempt to explain the origin of the universe or the nature of man apart from God's Word is foolhardy. The unregenerate mind, no matter how brilliant it might be, cannot fathom such things.

So never feel you have to apologize for trusting God's Word. Let the confidence of the psalmist be yours: "I have more insight than all my teachers, for Thy testimonies are my meditation. I understand more than the aged, because I have observed Thy precepts" (Ps. 119:99-100).

❖❖❖

Suggestions for Prayer: Read Genesis 1–2 as a reminder of the power and wisdom of God in creating the universe. From those chapters select specific things for which you can praise Him.

For Further Study: Memorize Psalm 19:1. Can you think of ways that the natural creation brings glory to God? (See also Romans 1:18-20.)

"By faith Abel offered to God a better sacrifice than Cain, through which he obtained the testimony that he was righteous, God testifying about his gifts, and through faith, though he is dead, he still speaks" (Heb. 11:4).

❖❖❖

The character of your life will determine the legacy you leave to others.

B ible scholar James Moffatt wrote: "Death is never the last word in the life of a . . . man. When a man leaves this world, be he righteous or unrighteous, he leaves something in the world. He may leave something that will grow and spread like a cancer or a poison, or he may leave something like the fragrance of perfume or a blossom of beauty that permeates the atmosphere with blessing."

That's illustrated in the lives of Adam and Eve's first sons—Cain and Abel. Cain was an unrighteous man who sought to please God by his own efforts. God rejected him (Gen. 4:5). Abel was a righteous man who worshiped God in true faith. God accepted him (v. 4).

In a jealous rage, Cain murdered Abel, becoming the first human being to take the life of another. He forever stands as a testimony to the utter tragedy of attempting to please God apart from true faith. For "without faith," Hebrews 11:6 says, "it is impossible to please Him." Cain tried and failed—as have millions who have followed in his footsteps.

Abel, on the other hand, was the first man of faith. Prior to the Fall, Adam and Eve had no need of faith in the same way as their descendants. They lived in the paradise of Eden and had direct contact with God. Their children were the first to have need of faith in its fullest sense.

Cain's legacy is rebellion, heartache, and judgment. Abel's is righteousness, justice, and saving faith. His life proclaims the central message of redemption: righteousness is by faith alone.

What legacy will you leave to those who follow? I pray they will see in you a pattern of righteousness and faithfulness that inspires them to follow suit.

❖❖❖

Suggestions for Prayer: Praise God for righteous Abel and all who have followed his example. ❖ Ask Him to guard you from ever rebelling against His Word.

For Further Study: Read Genesis 4:1-16 and 1 John 3:11-12. ❖ What was God's counsel to Cain after rejecting his offering? ❖ Why did Cain kill Abel? ❖ How did God punish Cain?

*"By faith Abel offered to God a better sacrifice than Cain"
(Heb. 11:4).*

❖❖❖

True worship requires coming to God on His terms.

At the heart of every false religion is the notion that man can come to God by any means he chooses—by meditating, doing good deeds, and so on. But Scripture says, "There is no other name under heaven that has been given among men, by which we must be saved" (Acts 4:12). That name is Jesus Christ, and we come to Him by confessing and repenting of our sin, trusting in His atoning death on the cross, and affirming His bodily resurrection from the grave (cf. Rom. 10:9-10). There is no other way to God.

Centuries before Christ's death, God provided a means of worship and sacrifice. Genesis 4:3-5 says, "It came about in the course of time that Cain brought an offering to the Lord of the fruit of the ground. And Abel, on his part also brought of the firstlings of his flock and of their fat portions. And the Lord had regard for Abel and for his offering; but for Cain and for his offering He had no regard."

Apparently God had designated a special time for sacrificing because "in the course of time" (v. 3) literally means, "at the end of days"—at the end of a certain period of time. Additionally, He initiated a particular pattern for worship and sacrifices. Otherwise Cain and Abel would have known nothing about how it was to be done.

God required a blood offering for sin. Abel came in faith, acknowledged his sin, and made the appropriate sacrifice. His offering was better than Cain's because Cain neglected the prescribed sacrifice, thereby demonstrating his unwillingness to submit to God and deal with his sin.

There was nothing intrinsically wrong with Cain's offering. Grain, fruit, or vegetable offerings were included in the Mosaic Covenant. But the sin offering had to come first. Like so many today, Cain wrongly assumed he could approach God on his own terms. In doing so, he became the father of all false religions, and his name became synonymous with rebellion and apostasy (cf. Jude 11).

❖❖❖

Suggestions for Prayer: Thank God for graciously providing salvation through faith in Jesus Christ. ❖ Be careful never to approach Him irreverently or presumptuously.

For Further Study: Read Jude 11. How did Jude describe the false teachers of his day?

"Cain brought an offering to the Lord of the fruit of the ground. And Abel . . . brought of the firstlings of his flock and of their fat portions. And the Lord had regard for Abel and for his offering; but for Cain and for his offering He had no regard" (Gen. 4:3-5).

❖❖❖

True discipleship is characterized by obedience to God's Word.

In John 8:31 Jesus issued an important statement to a group of people who were showing an interest in Him: "If you abide in My word, then you are truly disciples of Mine." Sadly, they rejected His words, proving themselves to be less than true disciples. Jesus went on to explain why: "He who is of God hears the words of God; for this reason you do not hear them, because you are not of God" (v. 47). They listened but didn't really hear. They were interested but not truly committed. They were hearers of the Word but not doers (James 1:22).

In contrast, Abel did what God told him to do. He was, in effect, the first disciple. He was probably a better person than Cain—more friendly, moral, and dependable. But that's not why God accepted his sacrifice and rejected Cain's. Abel trusted God, and his faith was counted as righteousness. Like Abraham, whose faith was evidenced by his willingness to obey God and to sacrifice his son Isaac (James 2:21-22), Abel's faith was evidenced in his obedient offering. He didn't rely on his own goodness but acknowledged his sin and made the prescribed sacrifice.

Perhaps God indicated His acceptance of Abel's sacrifice by consuming it with fire, as He did on other occasions in Scripture (Judg. 6:21; 1 Kings 18:38). But whatever means He used, God made his pleasure known to Abel.

Abel's brief life conveys a simple three-point message: we must come to God by faith; we must receive and obey God's Word; and, sin brings serious consequences. If you hear and heed that message, you'll walk the path of true discipleship and will be assured of God's pleasure.

❖❖❖

Suggestions for Prayer: Make it your goal to please the Lord in everything you do today. Seek His wisdom and grace to do so faithfully.

For Further Study: Read the following verses, noting what they say about pleasing God: 2 Corinthians 5:9; Ephesians 5:6-10; Philippians 2:12-13; Hebrews 11:6; and Hebrews 13:15-16, 20-21.

"By faith Enoch was taken up so that he should not see death; and he was not found because God took him up; for he obtained the witness that before his being taken up he was pleasing to God" (Heb. 11:5).

✧✧✧

When you walk by faith, you enjoy intimacy with God.

Our second hero of faith is Enoch. Genesis 5:21-24 records that "Enoch lived sixty-five years, and became the father of Methuselah. Then Enoch walked with God three hundred years after he became the father of Methuselah, and he had other sons and daughters. So all the days of Enoch were three hundred and sixty-five years. And Enoch walked with God; and he was not, for God took him."

What a wonderful epitaph: "Enoch walked with God." His life exemplifies the walk of faith. Adam and Eve had walked with God in the Garden of Eden, but their sin separated them from such intimacy. Enoch experienced the fellowship with God they had forfeited.

Enoch's faithful walk pleased God greatly. And after more than three hundred years on earth, Enoch was translated to Heaven without ever experiencing death. It's as if God simply said, "Enoch, I enjoy your company so much, I want you to join Me up here right now."

Like Enoch, there is coming a generation of Christians who will never see death. Someday—perhaps soon—Jesus will return for His church, and "then we who are alive and remain shall be caught up . . . in the clouds to meet the Lord in the air, and thus we shall always be with the Lord" (1 Thess. 4:17). Enoch is a beautiful picture of that great future event, which we call the Rapture of the church.

As you walk with God, He delights in you. You're His child, and your praises and fellowship bring Him joy. Psalm 116:15 says, "Precious in the sight of the Lord is the death of His godly ones." Death simply ushers you into His presence for all eternity.

Let the joy of intimacy with God, and the anticipation of seeing Christ face to face—either by Rapture or by death—motivate you to please Him more and more each day of your life.

✧✧✧

Suggestions for Prayer: Thank God for the promise of Christ's return.

For Further Study: Read 1 Thessalonians 4:13-18. ✧ What events surround the Rapture of the church? ✧ How were the Thessalonians to respond to Paul's teaching about the Rapture? ✧ How should you respond?

"Enoch walked with God" (Gen. 5:24).

❖❖❖

**Walking with God includes reconciliation,
obedience from the heart, and ongoing faith.**

When Scripture speaks of walking with God, it's referring to one's manner of life. For example, Paul prayed that the Colossian believers (and us) would be "filled with the knowledge of [God's] will in all spiritual wisdom and understanding," so they could "walk [live] in a manner worthy of the Lord" (Col. 1:9-10). To the Ephesians he said, "Walk no longer just as the Gentiles also walk, in the futility of their mind . . . [but] be imitators of God, as beloved children; and walk in love, just as Christ also loved you" (Eph. 4:17; 5:1-2).

The Old Testament describes Enoch as a man who walked with God. Though relatively little is said about this special man, we can derive implications from his life that will help us better understand what it means to walk with God.

First, Enoch's walk with God implies reconciliation. Amos 3:3 says, "Do two walk together unless they have agreed to do so?" (NIV). Two people can't have intimate fellowship unless they agree. Obviously Enoch wasn't rebellious toward God but had been reconciled with Him through faith.

Second, walking with God implies loving service. Second John 6 says, "This is love, that we walk according to His commandments." We obey Christ, but our obedience is motivated by love, not by legalism or fear of punishment.

Third, a godly walk implies continuing faith, "for we walk by faith, not by sight" (2 Cor. 5:7). Colossians 2:6-7 adds, "As you therefore have received Christ Jesus the Lord, so walk in Him, having been firmly rooted and now being built up in Him and established in your faith." By grace Enoch believed God and pleased Him all his life.

Do those who know you best see you as one who walks with God? I trust so. After all, that's the distinguishing mark of a true believer: "The one who says he abides in Him ought himself to walk in the same manner as He walked" (1 John 2:6).

❖❖❖

Suggestions for Prayer: Praise God for granting the reconciliation, faith, and love that enables you to walk with Him day by day.

For Further Study: What do the following verses teach about your Christian walk? Romans 8:4; Galatians 5:16; Ephesians 2:10; 1 Thessalonians 2:12; 1 John 1:7.

"Without faith it is impossible to please Him, for he who comes to God must believe that He is" (Heb. 11:6).

❖❖❖

Nothing you do can please God apart from faith.

Throughout history, people have tried everything imaginable to gain favor with God. Most turn to religion, but religion apart from Christ is merely a Satanic counterfeit of the truth.

Many trust in their own good works, not realizing that even their best efforts are offensive to God (Isa. 64:6; Phil. 3:8). And the more we try to justify ourselves, the more we offend God, because "by the works of the Law no flesh will be justified in His sight" (Rom. 3:20).

Some trust in their family heritage or nationality. The Jewish people thought they were pleasing to God simply because they were descendants of Abraham. But John the Baptist warned them, saying, "You brood of vipers, who warned you to flee from the wrath to come? Therefore bring forth fruit in keeping with your repentance; and do not suppose that you can say to yourselves, 'We have Abraham for our father'; for I say to you, that God is able from these stones to raise up children to Abraham" (Matt. 3:7-9).

Apart from faith, man cannot please God. And the first step of faith is simply believing God exists. That isn't enough to save a person—even the demons have that level of faith (James 2:19)—but it's a start, and by God's grace it can blossom into full saving faith.

God has given ample evidence of His existence. Romans 1:20 says, "Since the creation of the world [God's] invisible attributes, His eternal power and divine nature, have been clearly seen, being understood through what has been made." David said, "The heavens are telling of the glory of God; and the firmament is declaring the work of His hands" (Ps. 19:1).

Creation itself proclaims the existence, power, and glory of God, and yet most people "suppress the truth in unrighteousness" (Rom. 1:18) by rejecting the Creator and by denying their accountability to Him. Rather than bowing to the true God, they pay homage to "Mother Nature" or evolution. How foolish!

❖❖❖

Suggestions for Prayer: Praise God for the beauty of His creation. ❖ Worship Him as the giver of every good gift (James 1:17).

For Further Study: Read Romans 1:18-32. Is there a connection between denying God, practicing idolatry, and committing gross immoralities? Explain.

"He who comes to God must believe that He is, and that He is a rewarder of those who seek Him" (Heb. 11:6).

❖❖❖

All who come to God in faith will receive the reward of eternal life.

We've seen that without faith it's impossible to please God. And the first step in faith is believing that God exists. In addition, we must also believe that He answers our prayers—more specifically, that He redeems those who come to Him in faith.

Scripture repeatedly tells us that God not only *can* be found but also *desires* to be found. David said to his son Solomon, "If you seek Him, He will let you find Him; but if you forsake Him, He will reject you forever" (1 Chron. 28:9). The Lord says in Jeremiah 29:13, "You will seek Me and find Me, when you search for Me with all your heart." Jesus said, "Everyone who asks receives; and he who seeks finds; and to him who knocks it shall be opened" (Luke 11:10).

At first glance those verses may seem to contradict Paul's teaching that "there is none who seeks for God; all have turned aside" (Rom. 3:11-12) and Jesus' statement that no one can come to Him unless the Father "draws" him (John 6:44). But really they're two sides of the same theological coin.

On one side you see man believing God and receiving Christ for salvation. On the other you see God enabling man to do so. Prior to salvation, a person is spiritually dead and utterly incapable of responding to the gospel. God must grant him or her saving faith. That's why the Bible contains statements like, "To you it has been granted for Christ's sake . . . to believe in Him" (Phil. 1:29); "As many as had been appointed to eternal life believed" (Acts 13:48); and "The Lord opened [Lydia's] heart to respond to the things spoken by Paul" (Acts 16:14).

God is the Great Rewarder, extending His love and grace to all who call upon Him. "Whoever believes in Him will not be disappointed" (Rom. 10:11).

❖❖❖

Suggestions for Prayer: If you've been praying for someone's salvation, don't become discouraged. Only God can grant saving faith, but He gives us the privilege of participating in His redemptive work through faithful prayer and evangelism (Rom 10:1).

For Further Study: Memorize Ephesians 2:8-9.

"By faith Noah, being warned by God about things not yet seen, in reverence prepared an ark for the salvation of his household, by which he condemned the world, and became an heir of the righteousness which is according to faith" (Heb. 11:7).

✧✧✧

True faith works.

W hen James said, "Faith without works is dead" (James 2:26), he stated a principle that's consistent throughout Scripture: True faith always produces righteous works.

The people described in Hebrews 11 made their genuine faith known in the things they did. The same applies to us today. Paul said, "The grace of God has appeared, bringing salvation to all men, instructing us to deny ungodliness and worldly desires and to live sensibly, righteously and godly in the present age" (Titus 2:11-12).

Perhaps better than anyone else in history, Noah illustrates the obedience of faith. Scripture characterizes him as "a righteous man, blameless in his time . . . [who] walked with God" (Gen. 6:9).

I remember a sportscaster interviewing a professional football player and asking him what he thought of his team's chances of winning the Super Bowl. The player replied, "We believe that if we just do what the coach says, we'll win." The team had absolute confidence in their coach, but they realized they had to do their part as well.

That illustrates the quality of faith Noah had in God, whom he trusted absolutely as he pursued a task that seemed utterly foolish and useless from a human perspective. Imagine instantly surrendering all your time and effort to devote 120 years to building something you'd never seen (a vessel the size of an ocean liner or battleship) to protect you from something you'd never experienced (rain and flooding). Yet Noah did it without question.

Noah's faith is unique in the sheer magnitude and time span of the task God gave him to do. He didn't argue with God or deviate from his assignment. Is that true of you? Are you pursuing your ministry as faithfully and persistently as Noah did his? Is your faith a faith that works?

✧✧✧

Suggestions for Prayer: Thank God for the ministry to which He has called you. If you sense there's more you could be doing, ask Him for guidance. ✧ Pray for added faithfulness and tenacity in serving Him.

For Further Study: Read the account of Noah in Genesis 6:1–9:17.

"By faith Noah, being warned by God about things not yet seen, in reverence prepared an ark for the salvation of his household" *(Heb. 11:7).*

✧✧✧

The ark is a beautiful picture of salvation by grace through faith.

God called Noah to a gargantuan task. Conservative figures estimate that the ark was about 438 feet long, seventy-three feet wide, and forty-four feet high. That makes it almost one and a half times the length of a football field and more than four stories high. Its three decks totaled almost 96,000 square feet, with a total volume of about 1.3 million cubic feet. Naval engineers concur that its shape and dimensions constitute an incredibly stable ship design.

But beyond the enormity of its size and the precision of its measurements, the ark is a wonderful illustration of salvation through faith in Jesus Christ. For example, Noah was instructed to cover the ark inside and out with pitch (Gen. 6:14). The Hebrew word for *pitch* has the same root as the word for *atonement.* The pitch kept the waters of judgment from entering the ark, just as Christ's atoning blood keeps judgment from the repentant sinner.

The ark was large enough to hold two of each species of animals plus every person who turned to God for safety. Only eight persons chose to be saved on God's terms, but had more come, surely God would have accommodated them. It is His desire that none perish, but that all "come to repentance" (2 Peter 3:9). Those who perished in the Flood did so because they rejected God's means of salvation.

Similarly, Jesus' blood is sufficient to atone for every sinner and every sin since man's fall in the Garden of Eden. No one who comes to Him will be cast out (John 6:37), and yet so few avail themselves of His gracious provision (Matt. 7:14).

Noah was a man who "walked with God" (Gen. 6:9), and yet he wasn't without sin. That's obvious from his drunken and immodest behavior after the Flood (9:20-21). But Noah, like every true believer, was justified by God's grace, his faith being counted as righteousness. That has always been the basis of salvation (Gen. 15:6; Rom. 4:5).

✧✧✧

Suggestions for Prayer: Thank God for His amazing grace, by which He saved you and continues to cleanse you from every sin.

For Further Study: Read Romans 4:1-8. ✧ What is the main point of that passage? ✧ Who is the primary example?

"By faith Noah . . . condemned the world, and became an heir of the righteousness which is according to faith" (Heb. 11:7).

❖❖❖

Your actions and words should rebuke our godless society.

Genesis 6:5 says, "The Lord saw that the wickedness of man was great on the earth, and that every intent of the thoughts of his heart was only evil continually." Before moving in judgment against the most evil and corrupt society in history, God appointed Noah to build an ark, which became a symbol of life and salvation to all who believed God. For those who disbelieved, it represented impending death and judgment.

Concurrent with constructing the ark, Noah preached about coming judgment. Peter called him "a preacher of righteousness" (2 Peter 2:5), and every board he cut and every nail he drove in was a living illustration of the urgency of his message.

God's warning was stern and His message horrifying, but His patience and mercy prevailed for 120 years. As Peter said, "The patience of God kept waiting in the days of Noah, during the construction of the ark" (1 Peter 3:20). The people had ample warning of judgment, but they chose to disregard Noah's message.

As sad as the account of Noah's day is, perhaps the greatest tragedy is that man's attitude toward God hasn't changed since then. Jesus said, "The coming of the Son of Man will be just like the days of Noah. For as in those days which were before the flood they were eating and drinking, they were marrying and giving in marriage, until the day that Noah entered the ark, and they did not understand until the flood came and took them all away, so shall the coming of the Son of Man be" (Matt. 24:37-39).

Like Noah, you are to proclaim righteousness to an evil and perverse generation by your works and by your life. Be faithful to do so even if people don't want to listen. After 120 years of diligent work and faithful preaching by Noah, only eight people entered the ark. But God's purposes were accomplished, and the human race was preserved.

❖❖❖

Suggestions for Prayer: Sometimes you'll encounter people who scoff at God's judgment and mock your testimony. Don't be discouraged. Pray for them, and be available to minister to them whenever possible.

For Further Study: Read 2 Peter 3. What effect should the prospect of future judgment have on your present behavior?

"By faith Abraham, when he was called, obeyed by going out to a place which he was to receive for an inheritance; and he went out, not knowing where he was going" (Heb. 11:8).

❖❖❖

The life of faith begins with a willingness to forsake everything that displeases God.

Abraham is the classic example of the life of faith. As the father of the Jewish nation, he was the most strategic example of faith available to the writer of the book of Hebrews. But the people to whom Hebrews was written needed to understand that Abraham was more than the father of their race; he also was, by example, the father of everyone who lives by faith in God (Rom. 4:11).

Contrary to popular first-century Jewish thought, God didn't choose Abraham because he was righteous in himself. When called by God, Abraham was a sinful man living in an idolatrous society. His home was in the Chaldean city of Ur, which was located in ancient Mesopotamia between the Tigris and Euphrates Rivers.

God's call to Abraham is recorded in Genesis 12:1-3: "Go forth from your country, and from your relatives and from your father's house, to the land which I will show you; and I will make you a great nation, and I will bless you, and make your name great; and so you shall be a blessing; and I will bless those who bless you, and the one who curses you I will curse. And in you all the families of the earth shall be blessed."

Note Abraham's response: "So Abram went forth as the Lord had spoken to him" (v. 4). He listened, trusted, and obeyed. His pilgrimage of faith began when he separated himself from the pleasures of a pagan land to pursue God's plan for his life.

So it is with you if you're a man or woman of true faith. You've forsaken sinful pleasures to follow Christ. And as your love for Christ increases, there's a corresponding decrease in worldly desires.

I pray that your focus will continually be on fulfilling God's will for your life and that you'll always know the joy and assurance that come from following Him.

❖❖❖

Suggestions for Prayer: Ask God for the grace and spiritual fortitude to walk by faith today.

For Further Study: Memorize 1 John 2:15 as a reminder to remain separate from the world.

> *"By faith [Abraham] lived as an alien in the land of promise, as in a foreign land, dwelling in tents with Isaac and Jacob, fellow-heirs of the same promise; for he was looking for the city which has foundations, whose architect and builder is God"* *(Heb. 11:9-10).*

❖❖❖

Focusing on Heaven is the best way to endure difficulties on earth.

Following God's call isn't always easy. He expects us to trust Him explicitly, and yet He doesn't ask our advice on decisions that may impact us dramatically. He doesn't tell us His specific plans at any given point in our lives. He doesn't always shelter us from adversity. He tests our faith to produce endurance and spiritual maturity—tests that are sometimes painful. He makes some promises that we'll never see fulfilled in this life.

If following God's call is a challenge for us, imagine how it was for Abraham, who had no Bible, no pastor, no sermons, no commentaries, and no Christian encouragement or accountability. But what he did have was the promise of a nation, a land, and a blessing (Gen. 12:1-3). That was good enough for him.

Abraham never settled in the land of promise. Neither did his son Isaac or his grandson Jacob. They were aliens, dwelling in tents like nomads. Abraham never built houses or cities. The only way he would possess the land was by faith. Yet Abraham patiently waited for God's promises to be fulfilled.

As important as the earthly land was to him, Abraham was patient because his sight was on his heavenly home, "the city . . . whose architect and builder is God" (Heb. 11:10). He knew beyond any doubt that he would inherit that city, whether or not he ever saw his earthly home in his lifetime.

Similarly, being heavenly minded gives you the patience to continue working for the Lord when things get tough. It's the best cure I know for discouragement or spiritual fatigue. That's why Paul says to "set your mind on the things above, not on the things that are on earth" (Col. 3:2). If your mind is set on Heaven, you can endure whatever happens here.

❖❖❖

Suggestions for Prayer: Praise God for your heavenly home. ❖ Seek His grace to help you keep a proper perspective amid the difficulties of this life.

For Further Study: Read the portion of Abraham's life recorded in Genesis 12–17.

"By faith even Sarah herself received ability to conceive, even beyond the proper time of life, since she considered Him faithful who had promised; therefore also there was born of one man, and him as good as dead at that, as many descendants as the stars of heaven in number, and innumerable as the sand which is by the seashore" (Heb. 11:11-12).

❖❖❖

Your faith in Christ will influence future generations.

I've been blessed with a wonderful Christian heritage. In fact, I'm the fifth generation of preachers in our family. The faith of my predecessors has had an enormous impact on my life—either directly or indirectly. I have the same responsibility they did to influence others for good, as do you.

Hebrews 11:11-12 gives a very personal example of how one man's faith influenced an entire nation. Verse 11 is better rendered: "By faith Abraham, even though he was past age—and Sarah herself was barren—was enabled to become a father because he considered him faithful who had made the promise" (NIV).

God had promised Abraham that he would become the father of a great nation (Gen. 12:2). But Sarah, Abraham's wife, had always been barren, and both of them were advanced in years. At one point Sarah became impatient and decided to take things into her own hands. She persuaded Abraham to have a son by her maid, Hagar (16:1-4). That act of disobedience proved to be costly because Ishmael, the child of that union, became the progenitor of the Arab people, who have been constant antagonists of the Jewish nation.

Despite his times of disobedience, Abraham believed that God would keep His promise. God honored Abraham's faith by giving him not only Isaac, the child of promise, but descendants too numerous to count. One man's faith literally changed the world!

Similarly, the faith you exercise today will influence others tomorrow. So, be faithful and remember that despite your failures, God "is able to do exceeding abundantly beyond all that we ask or think, according to the power that works within us" (Eph. 3:20).

❖❖❖

Suggestions for Prayer: Thank God for those who have had a righteous influence on you. ❖ Pray for greater opportunities to influence others for Christ.

For Further Study: Read the account of Abraham and Sarah in Genesis 18–21 and 23.

"All these died in faith, without receiving the promises, but having seen them and having welcomed them from a distance, and having confessed that they were strangers and exiles on the earth. For those who say such things make it clear that they are seeking a country of their own. And indeed if they had been thinking of that country from which they went out, they would have had opportunity to return. But as it is, they desire a better country, that is a heavenly one. Therefore God is not ashamed to be called their God; for He has prepared a city for them" (Heb. 11:13-16).

❖❖❖

Resting in God's promises brings true satisfaction.

I remember watching in horror and disgust as angry mobs swept through Los Angeles, killing people and setting thousands of buildings on fire. Under the cover of chaos, countless people ransacked and looted every store in sight. I saw entire families—moms, dads, and little children—loading their cars and trucks with anything they could steal.

That was the most graphic demonstration of lawlessness I've ever seen. It was as if they were saying, "I'm not satisfied with the way life's treating me, so I'm entitled to grab everything I can—no matter who gets hurt in the process."

Perhaps we don't realize how selfish and restless the human heart can be until the restraints of law and order are lifted and people can do whatever they want without apparent consequences. Then suddenly the results of our godless "me first" society are seen for what they are. Instant gratification at any cost has become the motto of the day.

That's in stark contrast to people of faith like Abraham, Isaac, and Jacob, who trusted in God even when their circumstances were less than they might have expected. God promised them a magnificent land, but they never possessed it. They were, in fact, strangers and refugees in their own land. But that didn't bother them because they looked forward to a better place—a heavenly city.

Their faith pleased God, and He was not ashamed to be called their God. What a wonderful testimonial! I pray that's true of you. Don't let earthbound hopes and dreams make you dissatisfied. Trust in God's promises, and set your sights on your heavenly home.

❖❖❖

Suggestions for Prayer: Thank God for the blessing of a satisfied heart.

For Further Study: Memorize Psalm 27:4.

"By faith Abraham, when he was tested, offered up Isaac; and he who had received the promises was offering up his only begotten son; it was he to whom it was said, 'In Isaac your seed shall be called.' He considered that God is able to raise men even from the dead" (Heb. 11:17-19).

❖❖❖

**A willingness to sacrifice something precious to you
is proof of genuine faith.**

John Bunyan had a little blind daughter, for whom he had a special love. When he was imprisoned for preaching the gospel, he was deeply concerned about his family, especially that little girl. He wrote: "I saw in this condition I was a man who was pulling down his house upon the head of his wife and children. Yet, thought I, I must do it; I must do it. The dearest idol I have known, what ere that idol be, help me to tear it from Thy throne and worship only Thee."

Despite his personal grief, Bunyan was willing to sacrifice the most precious thing he had, if God so willed. So it was with Abraham. Every promise God had made to him was bound up in his son Isaac.

Abraham believed God's promises, and his faith was reckoned to him as righteousness (Gen. 15:6). But the moment of truth came when God instructed him to offer his son as a sacrifice. Abraham realized that to kill Isaac was to put to death God's covenant. So he reasoned that surely God would raise Isaac from the dead. He believed in resurrection before the doctrine was revealed in clear terms.

God tested Abraham, and Abraham passed the test: he was willing to make the sacrifice. And that's always the final standard of faith. Jesus said, "If any one wishes to come after Me, let him deny himself, and take up his cross, and follow Me" (Matt. 16:24). Romans 12:1 says, "I urge you therefore, brethren, by the mercies of God, to present your bodies a living and holy sacrifice, acceptable to God, which is your spiritual service of worship."

I pray that you are willing to sacrifice whatever is necessary to minister most effectively for Christ.

❖❖❖

Suggestions for Prayer: Thank God for those you know who are passing the test of a sacrificial faith. ❖ Pray for the courage and grace to follow their example.

For Further Study: Read the account of Abraham's test in Genesis 22.

"By faith Isaac blessed Jacob and Esau, even regarding things to come. By faith Jacob, as he was dying, blessed each of the sons of Joseph, and worshiped, leaning on the top of his staff. By faith Joseph, when he was dying, made mention of the exodus of the sons of Israel, and gave orders concerning his bones" (Heb. 11:20-22).

❖❖❖

Faith triumphs over death.

Commentator Matthew Henry said, "Though the grace of faith is of universal use throughout the Christian's life, yet it is especially so when we come to die. Faith has its great work to do at the very last, to help believers to finish well, to die to the Lord so as to honor Him, by patience, hope and joy so as to leave a witness behind them of the truth of God's Word and the excellency of His ways."

God is honored when His people die triumphantly. When we've lived a life to His glory, and have joyfully left the world behind to enter into His presence for all eternity, He is pleased, for "precious in the sight of the Lord is the death of His godly ones" (Ps. 116:15).

Many believers who have dreaded facing death have experienced a special measure of God's grace that made their final hours the sweetest and most precious of their lives.

Isaac, Jacob, and Joseph are examples of men who faced death with great faith and confidence. Each "died in faith, without receiving the promises, but having seen them and having welcomed them from a distance, and having confessed that they were strangers and exiles on the earth" (Heb. 11:13). They hadn't seen all God's promises fulfilled, but by faith they passed them on to their children.

These men didn't have perfect faith. Joseph was exemplary, but Isaac and Jacob often vacillated in their walk with God. Yet, each ended his life triumphantly. That's the reward of all who trust God and cling to His promises.

Like every believer before you, you haven't seen the fulfillment of all God's promises. But certainly you've seen far more than Isaac, Jacob, or Joseph did. How much more, then, should you trust God and encourage those who follow you to do the same!

❖❖❖

Suggestions for Prayer: Thank God for His marvelous grace, which triumphs over sin and death.

For Further Study: Read the final words of Jacob and Joseph in Genesis 48:1–49:33 and 50:22-26.

"By faith Isaac blessed Jacob and Esau, even regarding things to come" (Heb. 11:20).

❖❖❖

When you disobey God, you forfeit joy and blessing.

Isaac is a fascinating Old Testament character. He was Abraham's long-awaited son, the covenant child, the child of promise. Yet aside from that, he was rather ordinary, passive, and quiet. Just over two chapters of Genesis center on him, whereas the other patriarchs (Abraham, Jacob, and Joseph) command about twelve chapters each.

In the final analysis, Isaac believed God and submitted to His will. But overall, his spiritual character seems more reluctant than resolute.

After a famine prompted Isaac to move his family to Gerar (a Philistine city on the border between Palestine and Egypt), he received a vision from the Lord. In it God passed on to Isaac the covenant promises He had made to Abraham: "Sojourn in this land and I will be with you and bless you, for to you and to your descendants I will give all these lands, and I will establish the oath which I swore to your father Abraham. And I will multiply your descendants as the stars of heaven, and will give your descendants all these lands; and by your descendants all the nations of the earth shall be blessed" (Gen. 26:3-4).

You would think such promises would infuse Isaac with boldness and confidence; yet no sooner had he received them when he lied to the men of Gerar about his wife, Rebekah, because he feared they might kill him to have her (v. 7).

It was only with great difficulty and prodding that the Lord finally brought Isaac into the Promised Land, where He once again repeated the covenant promises (vv. 23-24).

Later in his life Isaac even sought to bless his son Esau after Esau had sold his birthright to Jacob (27:4; 25:33). Only after he realized that God's choice of Jacob was irreversible did Isaac acquiesce.

Isaac is a vivid reminder of how believers can forfeit joy and blessing by disobeying God. But he's also a reminder of God's faithfulness—even toward reluctant saints.

Is your obedience reluctant or resolute?

❖❖❖

Suggestions for Prayer: Thank God for His unwavering faithfulness to you. ❖ Seek His forgiveness when your obedience is reluctant or withheld altogether. ❖ Ask Him to teach you to love Him in the same unwavering, resolute way He loves you.

For Further Study: Read about Isaac in Genesis 25:19–26:33.

"By faith Jacob, as he was dying, blessed each of the sons of Joseph, and worshiped" (Heb. 11:21).

✧✧✧

Jacob's life typifies the spiritual pilgrimage from selfishness to submission.

Jacob's life can be outlined in three phases: a stolen blessing, a conditional commitment, and a sincere supplication.

From the very beginning it was God's intention to bless Jacob in a special way. But Jacob, whose name means "trickster," "supplanter," or "usurper," tricked his father into blessing him instead of his older brother, Esau (Gen. 27:1-29). As a result, Jacob had to flee from Esau and spend fourteen years herding flocks for his Uncle Laban.

As Jacob traveled toward Laban's house, God appeared to him in a dream (Gen. 28:10-22) and made him the recipient of the covenant promises first made to his grandfather, Abraham, and then to his father, Isaac.

Jacob's response is revealing, for he "made a vow, saying, '*If* God will be with me and will keep me on this journey that I take, and will give me food to eat and garments to wear, and I return to my father's house in safety, *then* the Lord will be my God'" (vv. 20-21, emphasis added). Jacob's conditional vow said in effect, "God, if You'll give me what I want, I'll be Your man."

Despite Jacob's selfish motives, God did bless him, but He humbled him too. By the time he left Laban's house, Jacob was ready to yield to God's will unreservedly. Note his change of heart in Genesis 32:10: "I am unworthy of all the lovingkindness and of all the faithfulness which Thou hast shown to [me]."

Then the Lord appeared in the form of a man and wrestled with Jacob all night (v. 24). Jacob refused to let Him go until he received a blessing. That wasn't a selfish request, but one that came from a heart devoted to being all God wanted him to be. That's when the Lord changed Jacob's name to "Israel," which means "he fights or persists with God."

Like Abraham and Isaac before him, Jacob never saw the fulfillment of God's covenant promises. Yet on his spiritual journey from Jacob to Israel, from selfishness to submission, he learned to trust God and to await His perfect timing.

✧✧✧

Suggestions for Prayer: Pray for grace to consistently pursue God's will and for patience to wait on His timing.

For Further Study: Read Jacob's story in Genesis 27–35.

"By faith Joseph, when he was dying, made mention of the exodus of the sons of Israel, and gave orders concerning his bones" (Heb. 11:22).

❖❖❖

God uses your present circumstances to accomplish His future purposes.

Like Abraham, Isaac, and Jacob, Joseph was an heir to the covenant promises of God. His hope was firmly fixed on God, and he knew that someday his people would be at home in the Promised Land.

Although he spent all his adult life in Egypt, never seeing the Promised Land for himself, Joseph's faith never wavered. At the end of his life, he instructed his brothers to remove his bones from Egypt and bury them in their future homeland (Gen. 50:25). That request was fulfilled in the Exodus (Ex. 13:19).

But Joseph's faith wasn't in the promises of future events only, for his life was marked by exceptional trust in God and personal integrity. His understanding of God's sovereignty was unique among the patriarchs. Even though he suffered greatly at the hands of evildoers (including his own brothers, who sold him into slavery), Joseph recognized God's hand in every event of his life and submitted to His will.

Joseph said to his brothers, "Do not be grieved or angry with yourselves, because you sold me here; for God sent me before you to preserve life . . . and to keep you alive by a great deliverance. Now, therefore, it was not you who sent me here, but God" (Gen. 45:5, 7-8). Later, after their father's death, he reassured them again: "Do not be afraid, for am I in God's place? And as for you, you meant evil against me, but God meant it for good in order to . . . preserve many people alive" (Gen. 50:19-20).

The genius of Joseph's faith was his understanding the role that present circumstances play in fulfilling future promises. He accepted blessing and adversity alike because he knew God would use both to accomplish greater things in the future.

Joseph is the classic Old Testament example of the truth that God works all things together for good to those who love Him (Rom. 8:28). That's a promise you can rely on too.

❖❖❖

Suggestions for Prayer: Reaffirm your trust in God's sovereign work in your life.

For Further Study: Read about Joseph's life in Genesis 37–50.

*"By faith Moses, when he was born, was hidden for three months
by his parents, because they saw he was a beautiful child; and they
were not afraid of the king's edict" (Heb. 11:23).*

❖❖❖

**God makes His plans; you walk in them by faith. He doesn't need your
help or counsel—just your obedience and trust.**

It has been wisely said that trying to improve on God's plan is more pre-
tentious than trying to improve the *Mona Lisa* with an ink pen. All you'd
do is ruin the masterpiece.

The story of Amram and Jochebed, the parents of Moses, is about two people who refused to ruin the masterpiece. They trusted God implicitly and did
everything possible to see His plan for their son come to fruition.

Because of the number and might of the Hebrew people in Egypt, Pharaoh
enslaved them and ordered that all male Hebrew babies be put to death. In
direct defiance of that wicked edict, Moses' parents hid their baby for three
months, then placed him in a waterproofed basket along the banks of the Nile
River near the place where Pharaoh's daughter bathed. One can only imagine the faith it took for them to risk their own lives, as well as the life of their
baby, by placing him in that basket and introducing him into the very household of the one who wanted all male Hebrew babies slain.

By God's providence, Pharaoh's daughter found the baby, took pity on him,
and adopted him into her family. More than that, the Lord used Moses' quick-
thinking sister, Miriam, to arrange for Jochebed to nurse and care for her own
son! That gave Moses' family the opportunity to teach him about God's
promises for Israel to inherit the Promised Land, become a mighty nation, and
be a blessing to all nations. They helped instill within Moses the faith in God
that would later characterize his life.

You may never be called on to make the kind of sacrifice that Moses' parents made, but no matter what the risks, remember that God always honors
your obedience.

❖❖❖

Suggestions for Prayer: Thank God for His plan for your life. Seek wisdom
and grace to live accordingly.

For Further Study: Read about Israel's oppression and Moses' birth in
Exodus 1:1–2:10.

> *"By faith Moses, when he had grown up, refused to be called the son of Pharaoh's daughter; choosing rather to endure ill-treatment with the people of God, than to enjoy the passing pleasures of sin" (Heb. 11:24-25).*

❖❖❖

The world has little to offer compared to the riches of Christ.

For forty years Moses enjoyed the best of everything Egypt had to offer—formidable wealth, culture, education, and prestige (Acts 7:22). Yet he never forgot God's promises toward his own people, Israel.

Then, "when he was approaching the age of forty, it entered his mind to visit his brethren, the sons of Israel. And when he saw one of them being treated unjustly, he defended him and took vengeance for the oppressed by striking down the Egyptian. And he supposed that his brethren understood that God was granting them deliverance through him; but they did not understand" (vv. 23-25).

Somehow Moses knew he was to deliver his people from Egyptian oppression. Although it would be another forty years before he was fully prepared for the task, by faith he forsook the pleasures and prestige of Egypt and endured ill-treatment with God's chosen people.

Humanly speaking, Moses made a costly choice. He seemed to be sacrificing everything for nothing. But the opposite was much more the case since Moses considered "the reproach of Christ greater riches than the treasures of Egypt; for he was looking to the [greater] reward" (Heb. 11:26).

Sometimes obedience to Christ seems very costly, especially when evil people prosper while many who faithfully serve God suffer poverty and affliction. Asaph the psalmist struggled with the same issue: "Behold, these are the wicked; and always at ease, they have increased in wealth. Surely in vain I have kept my heart pure" (Ps. 73:12-13).

But be assured that the eternal rewards of Christ far outweigh the passing pleasures of sin. The wicked have only judgment and Hell to look forward to; you have glory and Heaven. So always choose obedience, and trust God to guide your choices, just as He did with Moses.

❖❖❖

Suggestions for Prayer: Praise God that the righteous will one day be fully rewarded. ❖ Seek God's grace to be obedient when you're faced with difficult choices.

For Further Study: Read Stephen's account of Moses in Acts 7:20-39.

> *Moses considered "the reproach of Christ greater riches than the treasures of Egypt; for he was looking to the reward. By faith he left Egypt, not fearing the wrath of the king; for he endured, as seeing Him who is unseen" (Heb. 11:26-27).*

❖❖❖

When you suffer for Christ, you bear His reproach.

How could Moses, who lived 1,500 years before Christ, bear His reproach? *Christ* is the Greek form of the Hebrew title *Messiah*, meaning "the Anointed One." Many Old Testament personalities were spoken of as being anointed for special service to the Lord. Some have suggested that Moses was thinking of himself as a type of messiah, for he delivered his people from the Egyptian bondage. They would translate verse 26 as, "Considering the reproach of his own messiahship as God's deliverer."

However, it seems best to see this verse as a reference to Jesus Himself, the future great Deliverer. We don't know how much knowledge Moses had of Jesus, but certainly it was more than that of Abraham, of whom Jesus said, "Abraham rejoiced to see My day; and he saw it, and was glad" (John 8:56).

The Messiah has always been identified with His people. When they suffer for righteousness' sake, they suffer in His place. That's why David said, "The reproaches of those who reproach Thee have fallen on me" (Ps. 69:9). Speaking from a New Testament perspective, Paul made a similar statement: "I bear on my body the brand-marks of Jesus" (Gal. 6:17).

There's also a sense in which Christ suffers with His people. When Jesus confronted Paul, who was heavily persecuting the church, He said, "Saul, Saul, why are you persecuting Me? . . . I am Jesus whom you are persecuting" (Acts 9:4-5).

Moses chose to turn his back on Pharaoh's household and to identify with God's people because he knew that suffering for Christ was far better than enjoying the riches of Egypt. At some point in time you too will be persecuted for Christ's sake (2 Tim. 3:12), so be prepared. When that time comes, follow Moses' example of faith and courage, knowing that God will be your shield and your reward (cf. Gen. 15:1).

❖❖❖

Suggestions for Prayer: Follow the examples of the apostles by thanking God for the privilege of bearing a small portion of the reproach that the world aims at Christ (Acts 5:27-41).

For Further Study: Memorize Psalm 27:1 as a source of encouragement when facing difficulty.

"By faith [Moses] kept the Passover and the sprinkling of the blood, so that he who destroyed the first-born might not touch them. By faith they passed through the Red Sea as though they were passing through dry land; and the Egyptians, when they attempted it, were drowned" (Heb. 11:28-29).

❖❖❖

The man or woman of faith gratefully accepts all God's provisions, no matter how pointless some of them may seem.

When the time came for Moses to lead the Israelites out of Egypt, everything on the human level said it couldn't be done. Pharaoh wasn't about to let two or three million slaves just pack up and leave. His formidable army was ready to ensure that no such exodus occurred.

But when God devises a plan, He always makes the necessary provisions for carrying it out. On this occasion, His provision came in the form of ten terrifying plagues designed to change Pharaoh's mind.

The tenth and worst plague was the death of all the first-born (Ex. 11:5). To protect themselves from this plague, the Israelites sprinkled the blood of a lamb on the doorposts and lintels of their homes. When the angel of death saw the blood, he passed over that house. Thus the Passover was instituted.

The blood from those first Passover lambs had no intrinsic power to stave off the death angel, but its presence demonstrated faith and obedience, thus symbolizing the future sacrifice of Christ (cf. John 1:29).

Pharaoh got the message and allowed the Israelites to leave. But soon afterwards he changed his mind and commanded his army to pursue them. Again God intervened by parting the Red Sea, allowing His people to walk across on dry land. He then drowned the entire Egyptian army when it followed the Israelites into the sea.

That was a graphic demonstration of a lesson every believer must learn: God's provisions are always best. They may sometimes seem foolish to the human intellect—just as "the word of the cross is to those who are perishing foolishness" (1 Cor. 1:18)—but the man or woman of faith trusts God and receives His provisions gratefully.

❖❖❖

Suggestions for Prayer: Thank God for the wise and gracious provisions He has made for your salvation and ongoing Christian walk.

For Further Study: Read the account of the Passover and the parting of the Red Sea in Exodus 11–14.

"By faith the walls of Jericho fell down, after they had been encircled for seven days" (Heb. 11:30).

❖❖❖

Faith is the key to spiritual conquest.

Forty years had elapsed since the Israelites refused to enter the Promised Land. That unbelieving generation had perished in the wilderness. Now Joshua was leading a new generation into the land. The first obstacle they faced was Jericho—a well-fortified city that was near the mouth of the Jordan River.

Some city walls of that day were wide enough at the top to allow two chariots to ride side by side. That was probably true of Jericho because of its strategic location. That, coupled with the caliber of its army, made the city virtually impregnable—especially to unsophisticated Israelites, who lacked military training.

But what is impossible for man is easy for God. And the stage was set for Him to demonstrate His power and for the Israelites to demonstrate their faith and humility.

One can only imagine how embarrassed the Hebrew people felt as they marched around Jericho once a day for six days. That certainly is not your typical military strategy. But on the seventh day, after marching around the city seven times, with the priests blowing their rams' horns, the priests gave one final blast, the people all shouted out loud, and the walls of the city collapsed (Josh. 6:20). Faith had reduced a formidable obstacle to a crumbled ruin.

Can you identify some spiritual obstacles you've faced recently? How did you handle them? You'll always have them to deal with in your Christian walk, but don't fret. See them as opportunities to exercise faith and to see God's power on display in your life. Continue to trust the Lord and to demonstrate your faith by courageously doing what He has called you to do.

❖❖❖

Suggestions for Prayer: Ask God to help you humbly trust in God's power when you face spiritual conflicts.

For Further Study: Read about the conquest of Jericho in Joshua 6:1-21. Note each occasion where the people obeyed one of Joshua's commands without hesitation.

"By faith Rahab the harlot did not perish along with those who were disobedient, after she had welcomed the spies in peace" (Heb. 11:31).

❖❖❖

Rahab illustrates the depth and breadth of God's amazing grace.

Our final Old Testament hero of faith is an unlikely addition to the list. Not only was she a prostitute, she also was a Gentile—and a Canaanite at that.

The Canaanites were an idolatrous, barbaric, debauched people, infamous even among pagans for their immorality and cruelty. Yet in the midst of that exceedingly wicked society, Rahab came to faith in the God of Israel.

Joshua 2:9-11 records her confession of faith to the two men Joshua had sent into Jericho as spies: "I know that the Lord has given you the land, and that the terror of you has fallen on us, and that all the inhabitants of the land have melted away before you. For we have heard how the Lord dried up the water of the Red Sea before you when you came out of Egypt, and what you did to the two kings of the Amorites who were beyond the Jordan, to Sihon and Og, whom you utterly destroyed. And when we heard it, our hearts melted and no courage remained in any man any longer because of you; for *the Lord your God, He is God in heaven above and on earth beneath*" (emphasis added).

Rahab demonstrated the genuineness of her profession of faith by risking her life to hide the spies from the king of Jericho, who sought to capture them.

Because Rahab lied to protect the spies (vv. 4-5), some people question the validity of her faith. Surely genuine believers wouldn't lie like that—or would they? Abraham did. Sarah did. Isaac did. Jacob did. But the important thing to understand is that God honored their faith, not their deception.

As with all the heroes of faith before her, Rahab's faith wasn't perfect, nor was her knowledge of God's moral law. But because she trusted God, she was spared during Jericho's conquest, and then was given an even greater honor. She became the mother of Boaz, who married Ruth, the great-great-grandmother of David, thereby becoming an ancestor of the Lord Jesus Christ (Matt. 1:5).

❖❖❖

Suggestions for Prayer: Praise God for receiving even the vilest sinner who turns to Him in faith.

For Further Study: Read all about Rahab in Joshua 2:1-24, 6:22-25, and James 2:25.

"God . . . has spoken to us in His Son, whom He appointed heir of all things, through whom also He made the world. And He is the radiance of His glory and the exact representation of His nature, and upholds all things by the word of His power. When He had made purification of sins, He sat down at the right hand of the Majesty on high" (Heb. 1:1-3).

❖❖❖

Christ is superior to everyone and everything.

The book of Hebrews was addressed to an audience composed of Jewish Christians, Jewish non-Christians who were intellectually convinced about Jesus but hadn't yet committed themselves to Him, and Jewish non-Christians who didn't believe the gospel at all.

The author's goal was to demonstrate Christ's superiority over everyone and everything that had preceded Him, whether Old Testament persons, institutions, rituals, or sacrifices. He specifically contrasted Christ with angels, Moses, Joshua, Aaron and his priesthood, the Old Covenant, and the sacrificial system.

The Jewish believers needed this focus on Christ's superiority because most of them were suffering some form of persecution because of their Christian testimony. Some were in danger of confusing the gospel with Jewish ceremonies and legalism and of drifting back into their former practices.

Those who were intellectually convinced but spiritually uncommitted needed to be warned not to stop at that point but to go all the way to saving faith. They were in danger of committing the greatest sin any person can commit: rejecting Jesus Christ as Savior and Lord.

Those who didn't believe in Christ at all needed to see that Jesus was in fact who He claimed to be. To such people the author explains the unique priesthood of Christ and the urgency of turning to Him in faith.

Within your circle of friends and associates, you probably have Christians who are weak in faith and need your encouragement and instruction. Be available to minister to them whenever possible.

Undoubtedly you also know people who are intellectually convinced that Jesus is who He claimed to be but aren't willing to embrace Him as their Lord. Don't be shy about urging them to move on to salvation.

To those who reject Christ outright, boldly proclaim the gospel, and trust the Holy Spirit to convict their hearts.

❖❖❖

Suggestions for Prayer: Praise Christ for His preeminence and surpassing grace.

For Further Study: Read Hebrews 1–2. To whom does the writer compare Christ? Be specific.

> *"The main point in what has been said is this: we have such a high priest, who has taken His seat at the right hand of the throne of the Majesty in the heavens" (Heb. 8:1).*

❖❖❖

Since Jesus serves as our High Priest, we have access to God.

Access to God was always a problem for the Jewish people. Exodus 33:20 declares that no man can see God and live. Once each year, on the great Day of Atonement (Yom Kippur), the Jewish high priest entered into the Holy of Holies, where God's presence dwelt in a unique sense, to approach God on behalf of the people.

God's covenant with Israel was the basis for their communion with Him. And the sacrificial system that accompanied the Old Covenant gave the people an outward act to represent their inner repentance. But their sacrifices were incessant because their sin was incessant. They needed a perfect priest and sacrifice to provide access to God permanently. That's exactly what Jesus was and did.

Hebrews 10 says that Jesus offered His body as a sacrifice for mankind's sins once for all, then sat down at the right hand of the Father (vv. 10, 12). That was a revolutionary concept to Jewish thinking. A priest on duty could never sit down because his work was never done. But Jesus introduced a new and wonderful element into the sacrificial system: one sacrifice, offered once, sufficient for all time. That was the basis of the New Covenant.

Our Lord's priesthood is permanent and perpetual: "Because He abides forever, [He] holds His priesthood permanently. Hence also He is able to save forever those who draw near to God through Him, since He always lives to make intercession for them" (Heb. 7:24-25). That's the central message of the book of Hebrews.

It wasn't easy for the Jewish people to accept the need for a new covenant. Most rejected Christ outright. Similarly, many people today reject His priesthood, supposing they can gain access to God on their own terms. But they're tragically mistaken. Jesus Himself said, "No one comes to the Father, but through Me" (John 14:6).

❖❖❖

Suggestions for Prayer: Praise God for receiving you into His presence through His Son, Jesus Christ.

For Further Study: Read Hebrews 10:19-25, noting how God wants you to respond to Christ's priesthood.

> *"God, after He spoke long ago to the fathers in the prophets in many portions and in many ways, in these last days has spoken to us in His Son" (Heb. 1:1-2).*

❖❖❖

Man can't discover God on his own; God must reveal Himself to man.

Since the beginning of time, man has deceived himself by thinking he can discover God through various religions. But in reality, man lives in a box enclosed within the walls of time and space. God is outside the box, and man senses He's there but can't get to Him. Each new religion is but another futile attempt to penetrate the walls of the box and catch a glimpse of God.

Man's only hope is for God to enter the box, which Hebrews 1:1-2 declares He did—first by letter (the Old Testament), then in person (in Jesus Christ). Regarding God's Word David said, "The Spirit of the Lord spoke by me, and His word was on my tongue" (2 Sam. 23:2). Jeremiah added, "The Lord stretched out His hand and touched my mouth, and the Lord said to me, 'Behold, I have put My words in your mouth'" (Jer. 1:9). Of Christ, the Apostle John said, "The Word became flesh, and dwelt among us, and we beheld His glory, glory as of the only begotten from the Father, full of grace and truth. . . . No man has seen God at any time; the only begotten God, who is in the bosom of the Father, He has explained Him" (John 1:14, 18).

The irony of people thinking they can discover God on their own is that apart from the Holy Spirit's leading, no one really *wants* to find Him. They merely want to add a cosmic good luck charm to their lives or to satiate their guilty consciences. Paul said, "There is *none* righteous, not even one; there is *none* who understands, there is *none* who seeks for God" (Rom. 3:10-11, emphasis added).

God could have left us in our sin and ignorance, but He penetrated the box and revealed everything we need to know in order to have redemption and fellowship with Him. What a privilege we have to study His Word and live by its principles! Be diligent to do so each day.

❖❖❖

Suggestions for Prayer: Praise God for granting you the ability to appreciate His Word.

For Further Study: Read 1 Corinthians 2:6-16, noting how natural (unregenerate) people respond to divine revelation.

"God, after He spoke long ago to the fathers in the prophets in many portions and in many ways, in these last days has spoken to us in His Son" (Heb. 1:1-2).

❖❖❖

The Old Testament is but a sample of what is revealed in the New Testament.

When Jesus said, "Do not think that I came to abolish the Law or the Prophets [the Old Testament]; I did not come to abolish, but to fulfill" (Matt. 5:17), He was affirming that Scripture progressed from promise to fulfillment, from partial to complete. We call that progressive revelation.

For example, the Old Testament anticipated Christ's coming; the New Testament records His coming. The Old Testament writers didn't understand everything they wrote because it didn't always apply to their day. That's why Peter said, "As to this salvation, the prophets who prophesied of the grace that would come to you made careful search and inquiry, seeking to know what person or time the Spirit of Christ within them was indicating as He predicted the sufferings of Christ and the glories to follow. It was revealed to them that they were not serving themselves but you in these things which now have been announced to you through those who preached the gospel to you by the Holy Spirit" (1 Peter 1:10-12).

Progressive revelation doesn't at all imply that the Old Testament is inaccurate. The distinction isn't in the rightness or wrongness of the revelation but in its completeness. Just as a child progresses from letters to words to sentences, so God's revelation progressed from types, ceremonies, and prophecies to final completion in Jesus Christ and the New Testament.

Thought incomplete by New Testament standards, the Old Testament is nonetheless fully inspired by God. That's affirmed often in the New Testament. Peter tells us that no human writer of the Old Testament wrote of his own will but only as he was directed by the Holy Spirit (2 Peter 1:21). Paul added that "*all* Scripture is inspired by God and profitable for teaching, for reproof, for correction, [and] for training in righteousness" (2 Tim. 3:16, emphasis added).

The Old Testament isn't all of God's truth, but all of it is true. And as you progress from the Old to the New, you see God's character and redemptive plan unfolding in greater detail.

❖❖❖

Suggestions for Prayer: Praise God for the fullness of revelation you enjoy in Scripture.

For Further Study: Memorize 2 Timothy 3:16-17.

"God, after He spoke long ago to the fathers in the prophets in many portions and in many ways, in these last days has spoken to us in His Son" (Heb. 1:1-2).

❖❖❖

Jesus not only brought but in fact* was *God's full and final revelation.

A Samaritan woman declared, "I know that Messiah is coming (He who is called Christ); when that One comes, He will declare all things to us" (John 4:25). The expectation of that day, even among the Samaritans, was that Messiah would unfold the full and final revelation of God. The Holy Spirit, through the writer of Hebrews, affirms that to be true: "God . . . in these last days has spoken to us in His Son" (Heb. 1:1-2).

The Old Testament had given divine revelation in bits and pieces. Every piece was true, yet incomplete. But when Jesus came, the whole picture became clear; and though rejected by His own people, He was, in fact, the fulfillment of the messianic hope they had cherished for so many centuries.

The Old Testament age of promise ended when Jesus arrived. He is God's final word: "As many as may be the promises of God, in Him they are yes; wherefore also by Him is our Amen to the glory of God through us" (2 Cor. 1:20).

God fully expressed Himself in His Son. That's why John said, "The Word became flesh, and dwelt among us, and we beheld His glory, glory as of the only begotten from the Father, full of grace and truth. . . . No man has seen God at any time; the only begotten God, who is in the bosom of the Father, He has explained Him" (John 1:14, 18). Paul added that in Christ "all the fulness of Deity dwells in bodily form" (Col. 2:9).

The practical implications of that truth are staggering. Since Christ is the fullness of divine revelation, you need nothing more. In Him you have been made "complete" (Col. 2:10) and have been granted "everything pertaining to life and godliness" (2 Peter 1:3). His Word is sufficient, needing no additions or amendments.

❖❖❖

Suggestions for Prayer: Ask God to teach you how to rely more fully on your resources in Christ.

For Further Study: Read John 1:1-18 as a reminder of the fullness of God's revelation in His Son.

"In these last days [God] has spoken to us in His Son, whom He appointed heir of all things" (Heb. 1:2).

✧✧✧

Since Jesus is the Son of God, He is the heir of all that God possesses.

W hen Christ first came to earth He became poor for our sakes, that we, through His poverty, might be made rich (2 Cor. 8:9). He had nothing for Himself; He had "nowhere to lay His head" (Luke 9:58). Even His clothes were taken from Him when He died, and He was buried in a tomb that belonged to someone else.

It is beyond human understanding to imagine that the Galilean carpenter who was crucified like a common criminal, naked and bleeding on a cross outside the city of Jerusalem, is the King of kings and Lord of lords. But He is!

As the Son of God, Jesus is the heir of all that God possesses. The Apostle Paul explains that all things not only were created *by* Christ but also *for* Him (Col. 1:16). Everything that exists will find its true meaning only when it comes under the final control of Christ.

The book of Psalms predicted that Christ would one day be the heir to all that God possesses. The Father, speaking to the Son, says, "Ask of Me, and I will surely give the nations as Thine inheritance, and the very ends of the earth as Thy possession" (Ps. 2:8). God also declared, "I also shall make Him My first-born, the highest of the kings of the earth" (Ps. 89:27; cf. Col. 1:15). "First-born" refers to legal rights—especially those of inheritance and authority.

When Christ comes to earth again, He will completely and eternally inherit all things (Rev. 11:15). And because we have trusted in Him, we are to be "fellow-heirs with Christ" (Rom. 8:16-17). When we enter into His eternal Kingdom, we will jointly possess all that He possesses. We will not be joint Christs or joint Lords, but we will be joint-heirs. His marvelous inheritance will be ours as well.

✧✧✧

Suggestions for Prayer: Thank God for making you a joint-heir with Christ. Thank your Lord for allowing that to happen through His death on the cross.

For Further Study: Read Revelation 5:1-14 and 11:15-18, noting how the inhabitants of Heaven respond to Christ.

"In these last days [God] has spoken to us in His Son . . . through whom also He made the world" (Heb. 1:2).

❖❖❖

Christ is the agent through whom God created the world.

John 1:3 testifies, "All things came into being through Him; and apart from Him nothing came into being that has come into being." Jesus has the ability to create something out of nothing (cf. Rom. 4:17), and that sets Him apart from mere creatures. Only God can create like that; we can't. If you could create, you'd live in a different house, drive a different car, and probably have a different job—if you had any job at all. You could just sit in your backyard and make money. Fortunately, God didn't give depraved men and women the right to be creators.

The ability to create *ex nihilo* (out of nothing) belongs to God alone, and the fact that Jesus creates like that indicates He is God and establishes His absolute superiority over everything. He created everything material and spiritual. Though man has stained His work with sin, Christ originally made it good, and the very creation itself longs to be restored to what it was in the beginning (Rom. 8:19-21).

The common Greek word for "world" is *kosmos*, but that's not the one used in Hebrews 1:2. The word here is *aionas*, which does not refer to the material world but to "the ages," as it is often translated. Jesus Christ is responsible for creating not only the physical earth, but also time, space, energy, and matter. The writer of Hebrews does not restrict Christ's creation to this earth; he shows us that Christ is the Creator of the entire universe and of existence itself. And He made it all without effort.

What about you? If you don't recognize God as the Creator, you'll have difficulty explaining how this universe came into being. Where did it all come from? Who conceived it? Who made it? It cannot be an accident. Someone made it, and the Bible tells us who He is: Jesus Christ.

❖❖❖

Suggestions for Prayer: Praise God for the wonder of His creation, which we can so easily take for granted.

For Further Study: Read Colossians 1:16-23 to discover the relationship between the creation and your salvation.

December 8 CHRIST'S RADIANCE AND REPRESENTATION

"He is the radiance of [God's] glory and the exact representation of His nature" (Heb. 1:3).

❖❖❖

Jesus is both God manifest and God in substance.

Just as the rays of the sun give light, warmth, life, and growth to the earth, so Jesus Christ is the glorious light of God shining into the hearts of men and women. As "the radiance of God's glory," Jesus expresses God to us. No one can see God in His full glory; no one ever will. The radiance of that glory that reaches us from God appears in the Person of Jesus Christ.

Just as the sun was never without and can never be separated from its brightness, so God was never without and cannot be separated from the glory of Christ. Never was God without Him or He without God, and never in any way can He be separated from God. Yet the brightness of the sun is not the sun, and neither is Jesus' incarnation glory exactly the same as God in that sense. He is fully and absolutely God, and yet a distinct Person within the Triune Godhead.

Jesus said, "I am the light of the world; he who follows Me shall not walk in the darkness, but shall have the light of life" (John 8:12). As the radiance of God's glory, Christ can transmit that light into your life and mine, so we can radiate the glory of God to a dark world.

In using the term "exact representation" to describe Christ's relationship to God's nature, the writer employs terminology usually associated with an impression reproduced on a seal by a die or a stamp. Jesus Christ is the reproduction of God—the perfect, personal imprint of God in time and space.

How wonderful to realize that Jesus Christ, who is both the full expression of God and the exact reproduction of God's nature in human history, can come into our lives and give us light to see and to know God! His light is the source of our spiritual life. And His light gives us purpose, meaning, happiness, peace, joy, fellowship, *everything*—for all eternity.

❖❖❖

Suggestions for Prayer: Thank God that He determined to become a man so we could know what He is like.

For Further Study: Read 2 Corinthians 4:3-6 and note who allows people to see or not see spiritually.

"[Christ] upholds all things by the word of His power" (Heb. 1:3).

❖❖❖

Christ, by His almighty power, holds together all creation.

We base our entire lives on the constancy of physical laws. When something like an earthquake disrupts the normal condition or operation of things even a little, the consequences are often disastrous. Can you imagine what would happen if Jesus Christ relinquished His sustaining power over the laws of the universe, for it is He in whom "all things hold together" (Col. 1:17)? We would go out of existence, our atoms scattering throughout the galaxy.

If He suspended the laws of gravity only for a brief moment, we would lose all points of reference. If any of the physical laws varied slightly, we could not exist. Our food could turn to poison; we ourselves could drift out into space or get flooded by the ocean tides. Countless other horrible things could happen.

But the universe remains in balance because Jesus Christ sustains and monitors all its movements and interworkings. He maintains cohesion. He is not the deists' "watchmaker" creator, who made the world, set it in motion, and has not bothered with it since. The reason the universe is a cosmos instead of chaos—an ordered and reliable system instead of an erratic and unpredictable muddle—is the upholding power of Jesus Christ.

The entire universe hangs on the arm of Jesus. His unsearchable wisdom and boundless power are manifested in governing the universe. And He upholds it all by "the word of His power." The key to the Genesis creation is seen in two words: "God said." God spoke, and it happened.

When I contemplate Christ's power to uphold the universe, I'm drawn to the wonderful promise of Philippians 1:6—"I am confident of this very thing, that He who began a good work in you will perfect it until the day of Christ Jesus." When Christ begins a work in your heart, He doesn't end there. He continually sustains it until the day He will take you into God's very presence. A life, like a universe, that is not sustained by Christ is chaos.

❖❖❖

Suggestions for Prayer: Ask God to remind you of Christ's sustaining power when you endure your next trial.

For Further Study: Read Job 38-39 for a greater appreciation of what Christ does to uphold the universe.

*"When He had made purification of sins, He sat down at the right
hand of the Majesty on high" (Heb. 1:3).*

✧✧✧

**Jesus Christ offered one sacrifice for all the sins of mankind, then sat
down with the Father once He had accomplished it.**

The Bible makes it perfectly clear that "the wages of sin is death" (Rom.
6:23). Jesus Christ went to the cross, died the death we deserved, and
consequently freed us from the penalty of sin by our faith in Him.

The writer of Hebrews goes on to say that Christ "does not need daily, like
those [Old Covenant] high priests, to offer up sacrifices, first for His own sins,
and then for the sins of the people, because this He did once for all when He
offered up Himself" (Heb. 7:27). In the Old Testament, the priests had to
make continual sacrifices, but Jesus made only one. And not only was He the
priest, but also the sacrifice! He made a tremendously potent sacrifice, for He
forever purged our sins—something the Old Testament sacrifices could
never do.

When His sacrifice was complete, "He *sat down* at the right hand of the
Majesty on high" (Heb. 1:3, emphasis added). That is significant, because the
Old Testament priests never sat down; there were no seats in the sanctuary
because they offered sacrifices day in and day out. But Jesus offered one sac-
rifice, finished it, and then went to the Father and sat down. What the Old
Testament sacrifices couldn't accomplish, Christ's did for all time.

As a result, God exalted Him to His right hand, the seat of honor and rule
and rest. But perhaps most important, it is the place where Christ intercedes
to the Father on our behalf (Rom 8:34).

Don't ever forget what Jesus accomplished for us—and what He still does
for us: "If anyone sins, we have an Advocate with the Father, Jesus Christ the
righteous" (1 John 2:1).

✧✧✧

Suggestions for Prayer: Thank Jesus for His sacrifice on your behalf. Also
thank Him for the salvation He has given you and the access you now have
to God.

For Further Study: Read Hebrews 9:1–10:18 to gain a deeper understanding
of Christ's ultimate fulfillment of the Old Testament priestly system. In what
specific ways did He fulfill it?

". . . having become . . . much better than the angels" (Heb. 1:4).

❖❖❖

***Through a deft use of the Old Testament, the writer proves
that Christ is the mediator of a greater covenant.***

Man is a wonderful and amazing creation—higher than plants, animals, and any other material creation in this world. But there are created beings even higher than man—angels.

Hebrews 2:9 shows this to be the case because when Jesus became a man, He was "made for a little while lower than the angels." After the fall of the rebellious angels under Lucifer, the angels in Heaven were no longer able to choose sin. These angels are holy, powerful, and wise. They are special beings created by God before He created man.

The Jewish people understood the exalted position of angels because they knew that the Old Covenant was brought to men and maintained by angelic mediation. Galatians 3:19 says, "Why the Law then? It was added because of transgressions, having been ordained through angels by the agency of a mediator, until the seed should come to whom the promise had been made."

Because of this high regard for angels by his readers, the writer of Hebrews was faced with a problem. If he was to show that Christ was the mediator of a better covenant, he would have to prove that Christ is better than angels. To do so, he used seven Old Testament passages to verify his claim.

If he had tried to prove from Christian writings that Christ is a better mediator, his unbelieving Jewish readers would have said, "We don't accept these writings as being from God." So in effect he wisely replies, "Open up your own Scriptures, and I'll prove my claim from them." This results in a powerful and irresistible argument.

For the next several days, we'll see in what ways Christ is superior to angels and how He could mediate a better covenant for us.

❖❖❖

Suggestions for Prayer: Because much of our understanding of the New Testament is based on the writings of the Old Testament, thank God for how He has brought His complete Word to us intact throughout the centuries.

For Further Study: Read Galatians 3:8, Romans 9:15, and Matthew 4:4. What Old Testament verses do those passages quote? What truth does each of them verify?

"He has inherited a more excellent name than they. For to which of the angels did [God] ever say, 'Thou art My Son, today I have begotten Thee'? And again, 'I will be a Father to Him, and He shall be a Son to Me'?" (Heb. 1:4-5).

✧✧✧

Jesus is better than the angels because Christ was more than a messenger—He was a Son.

In our culture, the names we pick for our children don't have much connection with the child's character. But in the Bible, God chose specific names that related to some character quality of the individuals who bore them.

The writer of Hebrews was well aware of that when He asked this rhetorical question: "To which of the angels did [God] ever say, 'Thou art My Son, today I have begotten Thee'? And again, 'I will be a Father to Him, and He shall be a Son to Me'?"—quoting Psalm 2:7 and 2 Samuel 7:14. Of course, the answer is, no angel.

The title *Son* refers to Jesus Christ in His incarnation. Though His sonship was anticipated in the Old Testament (Prov. 30:4), He did not become a Son until He was begotten into time. Prior to that, He was eternal God with God. Presenting Jesus as the Son is God's analogy to help us understand the relationship between the First and Second Persons of the Trinity.

Christ became a Son in two different ways. First, He was not a Son until He came into the world through the virgin birth (Luke 1:35; 3:22). But second, His Sonship came to full bloom in His resurrection (Rom. 1:3-4).

The Old Testament prophesied that Christ would come as a Son. In the New Testament He came as a Son in His virgin birth and was declared to be the Son by His resurrection from the dead. Don't ever get trapped into the heresy of those who claim that Jesus Christ is eternally subservient to God. For a temporary period of time, He set aside what was rightfully His and humbled Himself to become a Son for our sakes.

✧✧✧

Suggestions for Prayer: Thank God for His amazing plan to redeem man through the incarnation of the Second Person of the Trinity. Praise Him that He became man to redeem you.

For Further Study: Read Acts 13:33 and Romans 1:3-4, noting the reason Christ can be considered God's Son.

"When He again brings the first-born into the world, He says, 'And let all the angels of God worship Him'" (Heb. 1:6).

❖❖❖

Jesus Christ is greater than angels because He is worshiped.

E ven though Jesus Christ humbled Himself and was made lower than the angels for a time, angels are still to worship Him. Since angels are to worship Him, Christ must be greater than them.

Angels have always worshiped Christ—as God. It wasn't until His incarnation that angels were commanded to worship Him as God's Son. It is a sin to worship anyone or anything but God. In fact, note how sternly the Apostle John was rebuked for worshiping angels (Rev. 19:10; 22:8-9). The very fact that angels are to worship Christ verifies that Christ is indeed God.

At present, the angels don't fully understand the entire picture of God's redemptive plan. Peter tells us that the prophets didn't understand all that they wrote, "seeking to know what person or time the Spirit of Christ within them was indicating as He predicted the sufferings of Christ and the glories to follow" (1 Peter 1:11). Then he added, ". . . things into which angels long to look" (v. 12). They are still trying to figure out things they don't understand.

But that won't always be the case. Notice that Hebrews 1:6 says, "When He *again* brings the first-born into the world . . ." (emphasis added). God already brought Christ into the world once; at the Second Coming He will bring Him into the world in blazing glory. Then the fullness of the prophecy of Psalm 97:7, quoted in Hebrews 1:6, will come to pass: "Let all the angels of God worship Him."

In His Second Coming Christ will be revealed in full glory as the Son. More than ever we will have reason to join the heavenly chorus in declaring, "Worthy is the Lamb that was slain to receive power and riches and wisdom and might and honor and glory and blessing" (Rev. 5:12).

❖❖❖

Suggestions for Prayer: Thank God for His wonderful plan of salvation. Ask Him to make it more real to you every day.

For Further Study: Read Revelation 5:1-12, and note the reactions of the angels to the Lamb of God. What specific event motivated their response?

"Of the angels He says, 'Who makes His angels winds, and His ministers a flame of fire.' But of the Son He says, 'Thy throne, O God, is forever and ever'" (Heb. 1:7-8).

❖❖❖

Jesus Christ is God, and He created the angels.

People today who claim that Jesus was just a man, an angel, a prophet, or some inferior god are in error and bring upon themselves the curse of God. The Bible, and especially the writer of Hebrews, are clear about who Christ is.

First, the writer deals with the nature of angels when he says, "Who makes His angels winds, and His ministers a flame of fire." "Makes" simply means "to create." The antecedent of "who" is Christ. Therefore, it is obvious that Christ created the angels.

They are also His possession—"His angels." They are His created servants who do not operate on their own initiative but at the direction of Christ.

But the greatest difference between the nature of angels and of Christ is that He is the eternal God. The Father says to the Son, "Thy throne, O God, is forever and ever" (v. 8). That is one of the most powerful, clear, emphatic, and irrefutable proofs of the deity of Christ in Scripture.

Jesus throughout His ministry claimed equality with God. He said, "I and the Father are one" (John 10:30). The Apostle John closed his first epistle by saying, "We know that the Son of God has come, and has given us understanding, in order that we might know Him who is true, and we are in Him who is true, in His Son Jesus Christ. This is the true God and eternal life" (1 John 5:20).

God the Son came to help us understand that God is truth and that Christ Himself is the true God. Our faith is based on the deity of our Lord Jesus Christ.

❖❖❖

Suggestions for Prayer: Ask God to give you a greater understanding of the reality that Jesus is, in fact, God.

For Further Study: Read John 1:1-18, and mark the verses that define Christ's relationship to God. If an unbeliever were to ask you what that passage means, how would you answer him or her?

"'Thy throne, O God, is forever and ever, and the righteous scepter is the scepter of His Kingdom. Thou hast loved righteousness and hated lawlessness; therefore God, Thy God, hath anointed Thee with the oil of gladness above Thy companions'" (Heb. 1:8-9).

❖❖❖

As the eternal God and King, Christ loves righteousness and hates lawlessness.

In these days it's difficult for us as Christians to be totally supportive of our governmental leaders when we see so much of what God calls righteousness compromised or ridiculed. But the King of kings—Christ Himself—is the only leader who has a perfectly right attitude toward righteousness.

Christ rules from an eternal throne, and He rules eternally as God and King. The scepter He holds is symbolic of His rule, particularly as a rule of righteousness.

But there's more to it than that. He not only acts righteously—He loves righteousness itself. How often have we obeyed without joy, expressing an attitude of willing condescension? But Jesus gives us a different model.

James 1:17 says, "Every good thing bestowed and every perfect gift is from above, coming down from the Father of lights, with whom there is no variation, or shifting shadow." True righteousness never varies from what is true, just, and good. And 1 John 1:5 says, "God is light, and in Him there is no darkness at all." God is total light and total righteousness. Everything Jesus did resulted from His love of righteousness.

Because Christ loves righteousness, He hates lawlessness. Since He loves what is right, He must hate what is wrong. The two are inseparable; one cannot exist without the other. You cannot truly love righteousness and also love sin. When there is true love for God, there will also be true love for righteousness and total hatred of sin.

The more you and I become conformed to Jesus Christ, the more we will love righteousness. Our attitudes toward righteousness and sin will ultimately reveal how closely we are conformed to Christ. Check out your attitudes and actions. How are you doing?

❖❖❖

Suggestions for Prayer: Like the psalmist, ask God to show you "any hurtful way" in you (Ps. 139:24).

For Further Study: Read Psalm 119, and note how many times the psalmist makes reference to either his love for God's law or righteousness.

"Thou, Lord, in the beginning didst lay the foundation of the earth, and the heavens are the works of Thy hands; they will perish, but Thou remainest; and they all will become old as a garment, and as a mantle Thou wilt roll them up; as a garment they will also be changed. But Thou art the same, and Thy years will not come to an end" (Heb. 1:10-12).

❖❖❖

Christ existed before the beginning of the world; thus He is without beginning.

Jesus Christ is no creature. To be able to lay the foundation of the earth and create the heavens in the beginning implies that He must have existed before the beginning. The Apostle John testified to this when he said, "In the beginning was the Word" (John 1:1). Christ is eternal.

Jesus is also immutable, which means He never changes. Hebrews 13:8 says, "Jesus Christ is the same yesterday and today, yes and forever." We need to hang on to this truth as we approach a day when much of what we know will change drastically.

One day what looks so permanent will fold up. Like the people Peter warned, we are tempted to think that "all continues just as it was from the beginning of creation" (2 Peter 3:4). But Hebrews 1:11 tells us that one day Jesus will discard the heavens and the earth, just as we would a useless garment.

Even more amazing, verse 12 specifies that Christ will roll up the heavens. Revelation 6:14 says, "The sky was split apart like a scroll when it is rolled up; and every mountain and island were moved out of their places." During the time of the Tribulation period, the heavens, as if stretched to all corners, will roll up like a scroll.

But we can be confident that although creation will perish, Jesus will not, and He will create a new heaven and a new earth. Living creatures, worlds, and stars are subject to decay, but not Christ. He never changes and is never subject to change. What confidence that should give us for the daily issues of life we face each day!

❖❖❖

Suggestions for Prayer: Thank the Lord for His unchanging plan for your life and for His ability to keep it.

For Future Study: Read 2 Peter 3, and develop an approach to answering charges unbelievers make about Biblical prophecies regarding the end times.

"To which of the angels has He ever said, 'Sit at My right hand, until I make Thine enemies a footstool for Thy feet'? Are they not all ministering spirits, sent out to render service for the sake of those who will inherit salvation?" (Heb. 1:13-14).

❖❖❖

The destiny of Jesus Christ is that ultimately everything in the universe will be subject to Him.

A t the name of Jesus every knee [will] bow, of those who are in heaven, and on earth, and under the earth" (Phil. 2:10). This great promise confirms that Jesus Christ is destined to be the ruler of the universe.

Yet notice this about Christ's rule: "When all things are subjected to Him, then the Son Himself also will be subjected to the one who subjected all things to Him, that God may be all in all" (1 Cor. 15:28). Christ is subordinate to His Father, but only in His role as the Son. While the eternal Son is equally divine, He is officially in subjection to God.

Eventually God will put all kingdoms, authorities, and powers of the world in subjection under Christ when He comes in glory at His Second Coming. "He will rule [the nations] with a rod of iron; and He treads the wine press of the fierce wrath of God, the Almighty. And on His robe and on His thigh He has a name written, 'KING OF KINGS, AND LORD OF LORDS'" (Rev. 19:15-16). Christ's eternal destiny is to reign over the new heavens and the new earth.

But what about the angels? While Christ has the greater destiny, it is their destiny to serve forever those who will inherit salvation (Heb. 1:14)—and that's us!

Angels protect and deliver believers from temporal danger. They rescued Lot and his family from the destruction of Sodom. They went into the lions' den with Daniel and protected him. In addition to being forever in God's presence, our destiny is to be served by angels forever—service that begins at the moment of our salvation.

❖❖❖

Suggestions for Prayer: Thank God for the many ways He takes care of you— by saving you, having Christ intercede for you, giving you the Holy Spirit to teach you, and sending His angels to serve you.

For Further Study: Read 2 Kings 6:8-23, and note the amazing way that angels served the prophet Elisha.

"I urge you, brethren, bear with this word of exhortation"
(Heb. 13:22).

❖❖❖

Invitations to salvation must provide both exhortation and warning.

Hell is undoubtedly full of people who did not actively oppose Jesus Christ but simply drifted into damnation by neglecting to respond to the gospel. These are the kinds of people the writer challenges in Hebrews 2:1-4. They were aware of the good news of salvation in Jesus Christ, but they weren't willing to commit their lives to Him. As a result, they were drifting past the call of God into eternal disaster.

The Word of God always demands a response. Any effective teacher of it must do more than just dispense facts; he must warn, exhort, and extend an invitation. He may have impressive knowledge of the truth, but if he doesn't have a passionate concern for how people react to it, he is not a worthy representative of Jesus Christ.

Jesus had that kind of compassion. Despite the rejection of His own people, He ached for their salvation: "O Jerusalem, Jerusalem, who kills the prophets and stones those who are sent to her! How often I wanted to gather your children together, the way a hen gathers her chicks under her wings, and you were unwilling" (Matt. 23:37). You can feel His heart go out to the people.

Paul had similar compassion: "I have great sorrow and unceasing grief in my heart. For I could wish that I myself were accursed, separated from Christ for the sake of My brethren, my kinsmen according to the flesh" (Rom. 9:2-3). A true teacher is interested in more than just academics; he is concerned that people respond rightly to what is taught.

Just as the writer of Hebrews had to warn and exhort his readers, at times it becomes necessary for us to warn those to whom we are witnessing. If you want to see unbelieving friends, relatives, or associates come to Christ, warn them. Let them see the passion in your heart and your love for them. Please don't allow anyone to slip into eternal destruction without being warned sufficiently.

❖❖❖

Suggestions for Prayer: Ask God to give you wisdom regarding when to warn the people to whom you are witnessing.

For Further Study: Read Hebrews 3:7–4:13, 6:4-8, 10:26-31, and 12:25-29, noting the pattern the writer followed in presenting these other warnings.

December 19   A WARNING TO THE INTELLECTUALLY CONVINCED

"How shall we escape if we neglect so great a salvation? After it was at first spoken through the Lord, it was confirmed to us by those who heard" (Heb. 2:3).

❖❖❖

Many people know the facts of the gospel but won't make a commitment to it.

I will never forget a lady who came to my office, confessing that she was a prostitute and was desperate for help. I presented the claims of Christ to her and asked if she wanted to confess Christ as Lord of her life. She said yes and prayed, seemingly inviting Christ into her life.

Then I suggested that we burn her book of contacts. She looked at me incredulously and said, "What do you mean?" "If you want to live for Jesus Christ," I explained, "and you've truly accepted His forgiveness and embraced Him as Lord, then you need to prove it." "But that book is worth a lot of money," she said. "I don't want to burn it." After putting it back in her purse, she looked me right in the eye and said, "I guess I don't really want Jesus, do I?"

When it came to counting the cost, she wasn't ready. I don't know whatever became of her, but my heart aches for her and others like her.

I'm sure you know people like her. They know and believe that Christ is the Savior, they know they need Him, but they are unwilling to make a commitment to Him. Perhaps they even go to church and hear the Word of God. They are like the proverbial man who says he believes a boat will keep him afloat but never sets foot in one.

Those people are the most tragic of all. They need to be warned—to be given a powerful shove toward Christ. May the Lord use you as His instrument for that purpose in the lives of many who are on the edge of a decision for Christ.

❖❖❖

Suggestions for Prayer: Ask God to soften the hearts of people you know who understand the facts of the gospel but haven't yet made a commitment to it.

For Further Study: Read Matthew 19:16-22. What kinds of questions should you ask of someone who appears eager to become a Christian?

"For this reason we must pay much closer attention to what we have heard, lest we drift away from it" (Heb. 2:1).

❖❖❖

**God's Word is the anchor that will prevent people
from drifting past the harbor of salvation.**

When English explorer William Edward Parry and his crew were exploring the Arctic Ocean, they needed to go further north to continue their chartings. So they calculated their location by the stars and began a treacherous march.

After many hours they stopped, exhausted. After taking their bearings, they discovered they were now further south than when they'd started! They had been walking on an ice floe that was traveling faster south than they were walking north.

That is similar to the situation that people who continue rejecting Christ find themselves in. Therefore Hebrews 2:1 says, "We must pay closer attention to what we have heard, lest we drift away from it."

Why would anyone knowingly reject Christ? He came into the world as God incarnate, died on a cross to bring us forgiveness for our sins, paid our penalty, showed us divine love, and gives us blessing and joy beyond imagination.

The Greek words translated "pay much closer attention to" and "drift away from" both have a nautical usage. The first means "to tie up a ship," and the second can be used of a ship that has been carelessly allowed to drift past the harbor because the sailor forgot to attend to the steerage or to chart the wind, tides, and current. Hebrews 2:1 could be translated: "We must diligently anchor our lives to the things we have been taught, lest the ship of life drift past the harbor of salvation and be lost forever."

Most people don't deliberately turn their backs on God; they almost imperceptibly slip past the harbor of salvation and are broken on the rocks of destruction. Be sure you warn those you know who might be slipping past that harbor.

❖❖❖

Suggestions for Prayer: Ask God to strengthen your resolve when you know you need to confront someone regarding his or her relationship with the Lord.

For Further Study: Memorize Proverbs 4:20-22 as your own reminder of how important it is to hold on to God's Word.

"If the word spoken through angels proved unalterable, and every transgression and disobedience received a just recompense, how shall we escape if we neglect so great a salvation?" (Heb. 2:2-3).

❖❖❖

There is certain judgment for everyone who does not receive Christ as Savior and Lord.

Today the majority believes that God is a God of love and grace but not of justice. One brief look at Hebrews 2:2-3 ought to convince anyone otherwise. The writer's point is this: Since the Old Testament makes it clear that transgression and disobedience met with severe and just punishment, how much more so will equal or greater punishment be rendered under the New Testament, which was revealed by the Lord Jesus Christ Himself!

Both the Old and New Testaments confirm that angels were instrumental in bringing the law (Deut. 33:2; Acts 7:38). The law the angels spoke, primarily the Ten Commandments, was steadfast. That meant that if someone broke the law, the law would break the lawbreaker. The law was inviolable; punishment for breaking it was certain.

"Every transgression and disobedience received a just recompense" (v. 2). "Transgression" refers to stepping across a line—a willful, purposeful sin. "Disobedience," however, refers to imperfect hearing—the sin of shutting one's ears to the commands, warnings, and invitations of God. It is a sin of neglect or omission—doing nothing when something should be done.

Hebrews 2:2 also puts to rest the notion that God is not fair. The writer says every sin received "a just recompense." God, by His very nature, is just. Every punishment He meted out to those who defied Him was a deterrent to the sin He wanted to stop.

God severely punished the nation of Israel because they knew better. That leads to the important principle that punishment is always related to how much truth one knows but rejects. The person who knows the gospel, who has intellectually understood it and believed it, yet drifts away will experience the severest punishment of all.

❖❖❖

Suggestions for Prayer: Ask God to give you an even greater appreciation of the punishment He has saved you from in order to motivate you to pursue the lost more vigorously.

For Further Study: Read Matthew 11:20-24, 12:38-42, and Luke 12:47-48 to discover Christ's attitude toward those who know the truth and yet rebel against it.

"How shall we escape if we neglect so great a salvation? After it was at the first spoken through the Lord, it was confirmed to us by those who heard, God also bearing witness with them, both by signs and wonders and by various miracles and by gifts of the Holy Spirit according to His own will" (Heb. 2:3-4).

✧✧✧

God confirmed the truth of the gospel preached through Christ with many miracles.

When Jesus preached the gospel, He performed miracles that made what He said believable. He said, "Though you do not believe Me, believe the works" (John 10:38). Jesus claimed to be from God, then made it obvious He really was from God.

Nicodemus came to Jesus by night and said to Him, "No one can do these signs that You do unless God is with him" (John 3:2). Jesus confirmed His ministry by His own miracles. Peter reiterated that fact on the day of Pentecost: "Jesus the Nazarene [was] a man attested to you by God with miracles and wonders and signs" (Acts 2:22).

God also gave these same confirming signs to His second generation of preachers—the apostles, so no one could dispute the validity of their message. What the apostles said was not their own opinion; it was divine truth substantiated by signs, wonders, and miracles.

Signs, wonders, and miracles are synonyms referring to all the supernatural things the apostles did. But the apostles also confirmed the Word with "gifts of the Holy Spirit." That's a reference to the temporary sign gifts described in Scripture, such as tongues and healings, not to the permanent edifying gifts given to the church for all time.

Today God attests to the gospel with the miracle of His written Word. Let it not be said that you neglected Jesus Christ. History confirms that hours of neglect cost Napoleon Waterloo. Neglecting Christ's salvation will cost you eternal blessing and joy and will bring you damnation. Don't allow yourself to drift past God's grace.

✧✧✧

Suggestions for Prayer: Thank God for His Word and that through it you have all the truth you need to communicate the gospel.

For Further Study: Read Acts 5–19, and list all the miracles performed by the apostles to confirm the gospel.

"He did not subject to angels the world to come, concerning which we are speaking. But one has testified somewhere, saying, 'What is man, that Thou rememberest him? Or the son of man, that Thou art concerned about him? Thou hast made him for a little while lower than the angels; Thou hast crowned him with glory and honor, and hast appointed him over the works of Thy hands; Thou hast put all things in subjection under his feet.' For in subjecting all things to him, He left nothing that is not subject to him" (Heb. 2:5-8).

❖❖❖

Man's original intended destiny was to be king of the earth.

When we look at the vast, seemingly endless universe and then think about the little dot we call Earth in the middle of it all, we cannot help but wonder, "What is man? What right do we have to be on God's mind so much?"

David had an answer: "Thou hast made him for a little while lower than the angels; Thou hast crowned him with glory and honor, and . . . appointed him over the works of Thy hands; Thou hast put all things in subjection under his feet" (Heb. 2:6-8). The writer of Hebrews was quoting one of the Psalms (8:4-6) to show that God made man to be king.

David undoubtedly penned his psalm based on what God said in the beginning: "Let us make man in our image, according to our likeness; and let them rule over the fish of the sea and over the birds of the sky and over the cattle and over all the earth, and over every creeping thing that creeps on the earth" (Gen. 1:26). God's original design for man in his innocence was to be king over an undefiled earth.

When God made Adam, who was pure and innocent, He gave him honor and glory. God crowned man king of the earth: "Thou hast put all things in subjection under his feet" (Heb. 2:8). One day we again will be given the right to rule the earth, and all God's creation will be put under our feet.

❖❖❖

Suggestions for Prayer: Read Psalm 8, and offer it as your own praise to God.

For Further Study: Read Daniel 7:18, 27, and note the extent of the saints' ultimate rule.

"But now we do not yet see all things subjected to him" (Heb. 2:8).

❖❖❖

God's original destiny for man was restricted by man's sin.

God gave man dominion over all the earth, and the earth supplied his every need. All he had to do was accept and enjoy the earth as provided for him. But Adam sinned, and Satan usurped the crown. A new chain of command was born; the earth now rules man.

To know how true that is, all you need to do is look at the amount of effort expended on restoring the ecological balance of the earth. Environmentalism is a popular watchword of our day. Yet with all our modern technology, we are still unable to gain control over the earth.

Look what happened once Adam sinned. No longer could man easily harvest what the earth provided; now he had to toil by the sweat of his brow (Gen. 3:18). Women would experience pain in childbirth (3:16). Murder soon followed in Adam's family. God had to destroy virtually all mankind in the Flood because they had become so debauched.

Much of the animal kingdom now lives in fear of man and cannot be tamed. Where once the earth produced good things naturally and abundantly, now it produces thorns, weeds, and other harmful things. Extremes of heat and cold, poisonous plants and reptiles, earthquakes, typhoons, floods, hurricanes, and disease were all products of the Fall. Man was no longer a king but a slave—a dying creature fighting a losing battle with a dying earth.

Amazingly, the earth is aware of its condition: "For the creation was subjected to futility, not of its own will, but because of Him who subjected it" (Rom. 8:20). Now it eagerly awaits the day when the sons of God—believers—will be manifest in the Kingdom, for then it will be liberated from the bondage of corruption (vv. 19, 21-22).

There is coming a day, in the wonderful plan of God, when man will receive once again the dominion that he lost. May our Lord hasten its coming!

❖❖❖

Suggestions for Prayer: Thank God that He will one day redeem the earth from its subjection to the curse.

For Further Study: Read Isaiah 60:21, 65:25, 2 Peter 3:13, and Revelation 21:27. What will characterize the new earth?

"We . . . see Him who has been made for a little while lower than the angels, namely, Jesus, because of the suffering of death crowned with glory and honor, that by the grace of God He might taste death for every one" (Heb. 2:9).

❖❖❖

Jesus Christ is the only One who could recover man's destiny.

The ultimate curse of our lost destiny is death. God warned Adam that if he ate from the tree of the knowledge of good and evil, he would die (Gen. 2:17). In the restored Kingdom we will be elevated again over a redeemed earth. But the only way we could ever reign again as kings was to have the curse of sin removed, and the only way to remove it was to pay the penalty of sin, which is death (Rom. 6:23).

There's just one problem: how can we reign if we are dead? We need to be raised from the dead, but we certainly can't do that ourselves. That's why God sent Jesus Christ.

To accomplish this great work for us, Jesus had to become a man. He Himself had to be made "for a little while lower than the angels." To regain man's dominion, He had to taste death for every man. Christ came to die for us because in His dying He could conquer death.

But He was also raised from the dead: "Christ, having been raised from the dead, is never to die again; death no longer is master over Him" (Rom. 6:9). How does that help us? "If we have become united with Him in the likeness of His death, certainly we shall be also in the likeness of His resurrection" (v. 5).

The moment you put your faith in Christ, you were identified with Him. You died with Him on the cross, you were resurrected, and you began to walk in newness of life. You now are a joint-heir with Christ in His eternal Kingdom.

Christ tasted death for you and me so we could recover our lost destiny. Celebrate that glorious truth as you celebrate His birth today.

❖❖❖

Suggestions for Prayer: Before you do another thing today, praise your Heavenly Father for His wonderful plan of salvation.

For Further Study: Read Isaiah 2:2-4 and 11:6-9, noting the character of our future Kingdom.

"We ... see Him who has been made for a little while lower than the angels, namely, Jesus, because of the suffering of death crowned with glory and honor, that by the grace of God He might taste death for every one" (Heb. 2:9).

❖❖❖

Jesus Christ was born to die as our substitute.

A t this time of year, it is difficult for us to see Jesus other than as a little baby. We, of course, know why He came, but we usually focus on His death on the cross at another time of year. But we must never forget that He came to die.

Those soft baby hands fashioned by the Holy Spirit in Mary's womb were made to have two great nails hammered through them. Those little chubby feet were made to walk up a hill and be nailed to a cross. That sacred head was made to wear a crown of thorns. His tender body wrapped in swaddling clothes would be pierced by a spear to reveal a broken heart. The death of Christ was no accident; He was born to die.

Jesus died to remove the curse so we could regain our dominion. But to do that, He had to come as a man. Even though in doing so He temporarily became lower than the angels, He accomplished something no angel could: our restoration.

The first and foremost reason for the Incarnation is that Christ might taste death on behalf of every man and woman. He came to die in our place—to be our substitute. God had two options: Either let us die and pay for our own sins, or allow a substitute to take our punishment and die in our place. He mercifully chose the latter.

It is vital that we affirm the fact of Christ's substitutionary death because modern liberal theology claims Jesus died merely as an example, like a martyr dying for some cause. But in reality He died as a substitute for you and me. As a result He freed us to live for and with God. Rejoice that the Creator of angels, the Lord of hosts, was willing to become lower than His creation for our sakes.

❖❖❖

Suggestions for Prayer: Thank the Lord for His willingness to humble Himself to become a man in order to save you.

For Further Study: Read Psalm 22, and note which verses prophesy Jesus' suffering on the cross.

"We . . . see Him who has been made for a little while lower than the angels, namely, Jesus, because of the suffering of death crowned with glory and honor, that by the grace of God He might taste death for every one" (Heb. 2:9).

❖❖❖

In serving as our substitute, Christ humbled Himself supremely.

J esus' death on the cross was not easy or costless; it was a horrific death. It was not calm and peaceful; it was accompanied by outward torture and inward agony. The death He tasted was the curse of sin. In a few hours on that cross, He suffered the total agony of every soul for all eternity. He was guilty of no sin, and yet He chose to suffer the weight of all sins committed for all time.

God sent His Son, and His Son willingly came to die to redeem mankind. Paul writes, "When the fulness of the time came, God sent forth His Son, born of a woman, born under the Law, in order that He might redeem those who were under the Law" (Gal. 4:4-5).

Only by tasting death as a man could He free mankind from death. Historically, kings have had someone taste their food and drink before they consumed it. Christ drained to the dregs the cup of poison rightfully meant for us before it could ever touch our lips. He substituted His death for ours, releasing us from the deadness of sin and bringing us into life with God.

What moved Jesus to suffer for us? Grace. What we did not deserve (salvation) we received, and what we did deserve (death) we did not receive. Unbounded love prompted Christ's gracious work on our behalf: "In this is love, not that we loved God, but that He loved us and sent His Son to be the propitiation for our sins" (1 John 4:10).

After He accomplished the work of His substitutionary death, He was "crowned with glory and honor" and was exalted to the right hand of the Father, where He will reign forever and ever. He is our great substitute, whom we can thank and praise throughout all eternity.

❖❖❖

Suggestions for Prayer: Ask God to give you opportunities to communicate the gospel to people you haven't shared Christ with before, even if you might suffer in the process.

For Further Study: Read Isaiah 52:13–53:12 to understand what the God of the universe had to endure at the hands of men.

"It was fitting for Him, for whom are all things, and through whom are all things, in bringing many sons to glory, to perfect the author of their salvation through sufferings" (Heb. 2:10).

✧✧✧

Through His death, Christ became the perfect leader for His people.

As we look at what Christ has done, we must never forget that He was fulfilling the sovereign plan of God. The writer of Hebrews tells us it was "fitting" in God's sight for Christ to bring "many sons to glory." That means that everything God did through Christ was consistent with His character.

The cross was a masterpiece of God's wisdom. It displayed His holiness in His hatred of sin. It was consistent with His power—Christ endured in a few hours what it would take an eternity to expend on sinners (and even then, sinners couldn't atone for their own evil). The cross also displayed God's love for mankind. And Christ's death on the cross agreed with God's grace because it was substitutionary.

To bring "many sons to glory," God had "to perfect the author of their salvation through sufferings." The Greek word translated "author" (*archēgos*) means "pioneer" or "leader." It was commonly used of a pioneer who blazed a trail for others to follow. The *archēgos* never stood at the rear giving orders; he was always out front blazing the trail. As the supreme *archēgos*, Christ has gone before us—He is our trailblazer.

Life seems most anxious and dreadful when death is near. That's a trail we cannot travel by ourselves. But the author of our salvation says, "Because I live, you shall live also" (John 14:19). Only the perfect pioneer could lead us out of the domain of death and into the presence of the Father. All you have to do is put your hand in His nail-scarred hand and He will lead you from one side of death to the other. Then you can say with the Apostle Paul, "O death, where is your victory? O death, where is your sting?" (1 Cor. 15:55).

✧✧✧

Suggestions for Prayer: Praise God for all His attributes—specifically for each one displayed in Christ's death for you.

For Further Study: Read Hebrews 5:8-9 and 1 Peter 2:19-25. How do those verses expand on Hebrews 2:10?

> *"Both He who sanctifies and those who are sanctified are all from one Father; for which reason He is not ashamed to call them brethren, saying, 'I will proclaim Thy name to My brethren, in the midst of the congregation I will sing Thy praise.' And again, 'I will put My trust in Him.' And again, 'Behold, I and the children whom God has given Me'" (Heb. 2:11-13).*

❖❖❖

Our holy Christ has made us holy; thus He can now call us His brothers.

From our own perspective and experience, it is difficult to think of ourselves as holy. Sin simply is too much a part of us in this fallen world. In thought and practice we are far from holy, but in Christ we are perfectly "sanctified" or holy.

We may not always act holy, but because of our faith in Christ we are perfectly holy in God's sight. Though a child does not always act like his father, he is still his son. We are holy in the sense that before God, the righteousness of Christ has been applied and imputed on our behalf through faith. We were made holy through His sacrifice and have become "those who are sanctified."

"By one offering He has perfected for all time those who are sanctified" (Heb. 10:14). We are as pure as God is pure, as righteous as Christ is righteous, and are therefore entitled to be called His brothers because we now share in His righteousness.

The Sanctifier and the sanctified now have "one Father," and the Sanctifier "is not ashamed" to call the sanctified His brothers. What an overwhelming truth!

The practical experience of a Christian's life in this world includes sin, but the positional reality of his or her new nature is holiness. "In Him [we] have been made complete" (Col. 2:10). Yet practically, we have a long way to go. So the overriding purpose of our lives is to become in practice what we are in position. Now that we are Christ's brothers and God's children, let that be all the motivation we need to live like it.

❖❖❖

Suggestions for Prayer: Thank the Lord for His sanctifying work on the cross, which enables you to be holy.

For Further Study: Read Romans 1:16. Based on what God has done for you through Christ, can you wholeheartedly echo Paul's statement?

*"Since . . . the children share in flesh and blood, He Himself like-
wise also partook of the same, that through death He might render powerless him who had the power of death, that is, the devil;
and might deliver those who through fear of death were subject to
slavery all their lives" (Heb. 2:14-15).*

❖❖❖

**Christ came to break the power of Satan
which He did by conquering death.**

To be free to live with God and share in all His blessings, someone had
to shatter Satan's death grip on us. Sin is what gives Satan his powerful
hold on us, but the power itself is death.

Satan knew that God required death for us because of sin. He knew that all
died in Adam—that death became a certain fact of life. And he knew that
men, if they remained as they were, would die and go out of God's presence
into Hell forever. So the Devil wants to hang on to men until they die because
once they are dead, the opportunity for salvation is gone forever.

To wrest the power of death from Satan's hand, God sent Christ into the
world. If you have a greater weapon than your enemy, his weapon is useless.
You can't fight a machine gun with a bow and arrow. Satan's weapon is death,
but eternal life is God's weapon, and with it Jesus destroyed death.

How was He able to do it? He rose again, proving He had conquered death.
That's why He said, "Because I live, you shall live also" (John 14:19). His resurrection provides the believer with eternal life.

Nothing terrifies people more than the fear of death. But when we receive
Christ, death in reality holds no more fear for us since it simply releases us
into the presence of our Lord. We can say with Paul, "To me, to live is Christ,
and to die is gain" (Phil. 1:21). Rejoice that you have placed your hand in the
hand of the conqueror of death, who will lead you through death and out the
other side.

❖❖❖

Suggestions for Prayer: Ask God to give you a greater realization that He has
conquered death and is thus able to help you live life more fully to His glory.

For Further Study: Read 1 Corinthians 15:50-58. How are we to live our lives,
based on what we know about death?

"Assuredly He does not give help to angels, but He gives help to the seed of Abraham. Therefore, He had to be made like His brethren in all things, that He might become a merciful and faithful high priest in things pertaining to God, to make propitiation for the sins of the people. For since He Himself was tempted in that which He has suffered, He is able to come to the aid of those who are tempted" (Heb. 2:16-18).

✧✧✧

**Jesus came to sympathize with us,
so He could be our merciful and faithful High Priest.**

In his letters to Timothy, Paul counseled and encouraged his young associate about many things—his health, his critics, his moral and spiritual warfare, and so on. His counsel is well summed up in these words: "Remember Jesus Christ, risen from the dead, descendant of David" (2 Tim. 2:8).

Like Timothy, we need to be reminded of Christ's humanity, especially when life becomes particularly tough. Then we can pray, "Lord, You know what You endured while You were here. I'm going through it now." We can be sure that He knows and will encourage us.

Jesus came not only to save us but also to sympathize with us. He experienced what we experience, so He could be a "merciful and faithful high priest." After all, "we do not have a high priest who cannot sympathize with our weaknesses, but one who has been tempted in all things as we are, yet without sin" (Heb. 4:15).

Jesus felt everything we will ever feel—and more. Most of us will never know the full degree of any given temptation because we usually succumb long before we reach it. But since Jesus never sinned, He took the full measure of every temptation.

Ours is not a cosmic God who is powerful and holy but indifferent. He knows when we hurt, where we are weak, and how we are tempted. Jesus is not only our Savior, but our loving Lord who sympathizes with us. Rejoice in the greatness of His love for us.

✧✧✧

Suggestions for Prayer: Ask God to remind you of your need of Him at all times, not just when times are tough.

For Future Study: Memorize 1 Corinthians 10:13 for quick recall whenever you are faced with any trial.

Through the Bible

Daily Readings
Covering the Entire Bible in a Year

Publisher's Note: This reading schedule has been adapted from a publication of the National Association of Evangelicals. Copies may be ordered in quantities of 25, 50, and 100 or more. Write to: National Association of Evangelicals, P.O. Box 28, Wheaton, IL 60189.

JANUARY

Day	Book and Chapter
☐ 1	John 1:1-18
☐ 2	Gen. 1-4
☐ 3	Gen. 5-8
☐ 4	Gen. 9-12
☐ 5	Gen. 13-16
☐ 6	Psalms 1-3
☐ 7	Gen. 17-19
☐ 8	Gen. 20-22
☐ 9	Job 1-4
☐ 10	Job 5-8
☐ 11	Job 9-12
☐ 12	Job 13-16
☐ 13	Psalms 4-7
☐ 14	Job 17-20
☐ 15	Job 21-24
☐ 16	Job 25-28
☐ 17	Job 29-32
☐ 18	Job 33-36
☐ 19	Job 37-39
☐ 20	Psalms 8-11
☐ 21	Job 40-42
☐ 22	Gen. 23-26
☐ 23	Gen. 27-30
☐ 24	Gen. 31-34
☐ 25	Gen. 35-38
☐ 26	Gen. 39-42
☐ 27	Psalms 12-14
☐ 28	Gen. 43-46
☐ 29	Gen. 47-50
☐ 30	Ex. 1-3
☐ 31	Ex. 4-6

FEBRUARY

Day	Book and Chapter
☐ 1	Ex. 7-9
☐ 2	Ex. 10-12

☐	3	Psalms 15-17
☐	4	Ex. 13-15
☐	5	Ex. 16-18
☐	6	Ex. 19-21
☐	7	Ex. 22-24
☐	8	Ex. 25-27
☐	9	Ex. 28-30
☐	10	Psalms 18-20
☐	11	Ex. 31-33
☐	12	Ex. 34-37
☐	13	Ex. 38-40
☐	14	Lev. 1-3
☐	15	Lev. 4-6
☐	16	Lev. 7-9
☐	17	Psalms 21-23
☐	18	Lev. 10-12
☐	19	Lev. 13-15
☐	20	Lev. 16-18
☐	21	Lev. 19-21
☐	22	Lev. 22-24
☐	23	Lev. 25-27
☐	24	Psalms 24-26
☐	25	Num. 1-3
☐	26	Num. 4-6
☐	27	Num. 7-10
☐	28	Num. 11-12

MARCH

Day		Book and Chapter
☐	1	Num. 13-15
☐	2	Num. 16-18
☐	3	Psalms 27-29
☐	4	Num. 19-21
☐	5	Num. 22-24
☐	6	Num. 25-27
☐	7	Num. 28-30
☐	8	Num. 31-33
☐	9	Num. 34-36
☐	10	Psalms 30-32
☐	11	Deut. 1-3
☐	12	Deut. 4-6
☐	13	Deut. 7-9
☐	14	Deut. 10-12
☐	15	Deut. 13-15
☐	16	Deut. 16-18
☐	17	Psalms 33-35
☐	18	Deut. 19-21
☐	19	Deut. 22-24

☐	20	Deut. 25-27
☐	21	Deut. 28-30
☐	22	Deut. 31-34
☐	23	Joshua 1-3
☐	24	Psalms 36-38
☐	25	Joshua 4-6
☐	26	Joshua 7-9
☐	27	Joshua 10-12
☐	28	Joshua 13-15
☐	29	Joshua 16-18
☐	30	Joshua 19-21
☐	31	Psalms 39-41

APRIL

Day		Book and Chapter
☐	1	Joshua 22-24
☐	2	Judges 1-3
☐	3	Judges 4-6
☐	4	Judges 7-9
☐	5	Judges 10-12
☐	6	Judges 13-15
☐	7	Psalms 42-44
☐	8	Judges 16-18
☐	9	Judges 19-21
☐	10	Ruth 1-4
☐	11	1 Sam. 1-3
☐	12	1 Sam. 4-6
☐	13	1 Sam. 7-9
☐	14	Psalms 45-47
☐	15	1 Sam. 10-13
☐	16	1 Sam. 14-16
☐	17	1 Sam. 17-19
☐	18	1 Sam. 20-22
☐	19	1 Sam. 23-25
☐	20	1 Sam. 26-28
☐	21	Psalms 48-50
☐	22	1 Sam. 29-31
☐	23	2 Sam. 1-3
☐	24	2 Sam. 4-6
☐	25	2 Sam. 7-9
☐	26	2 Sam. 10-12
☐	27	2 Sam. 13-15
☐	28	Psalms 51-53
☐	29	2 Sam. 16-18
☐	30	2 Sam. 19-21

MAY

Day	Book and Chapter
☐ 1	2 Sam. 22-24
☐ 2	1 Kings 1-4
☐ 3	Prov. 1-3
☐ 4	Prov. 4-6
☐ 5	Psalms 54-56
☐ 6	Prov. 7-9
☐ 7	Prov. 10-12
☐ 8	Prov. 13-15
☐ 9	Prov. 16-18
☐ 10	Prov. 19-21
☐ 11	Prov. 22-24
☐ 12	Psalms 57-59
☐ 13	Prov. 25-27
☐ 14	Prov. 28-31
☐ 15	S. of Sol. 1-4
☐ 16	S. of Sol. 5-8
☐ 17	1 Kings 5-7
☐ 18	1 Kings 8-11
☐ 19	Psalms 60-62
☐ 20	Eccl. 1-4
☐ 21	Eccl. 5-8
☐ 22	Eccl. 9-12
☐ 23	1 Kings 12-14
☐ 24	1 Kings 15-17
☐ 25	1 Kings 18-20
☐ 26	Psalms 63-65
☐ 27	1 Kings 21-22; 2 Kings 1
☐ 28	2 Kings 2-4
☐ 29	2 Kings 5-7
☐ 30	2 Kings 8-10
☐ 31	2 Kings 11:1-14:25

JUNE

Day	Book and Chapter
☐ 1	Jonah
☐ 2	Psalms 66-68
☐ 3	2 Kings 14:26-29; Amos 1-3
☐ 4	Amos 4-6
☐ 5	Amos 7-9
☐ 6	2 Kings 15-17
☐ 7	2 Kings 18-21
☐ 8	2 Kings 22-25
☐ 9	Psalms 69-71
☐ 10	1 Chron. 1-3
☐ 11	1 Chron. 4-6
☐ 12	1 Chron. 7-9
☐ 13	1 Chron. 10-12
☐ 14	1 Chron. 13-16
☐ 15	1 Chron. 17-19
☐ 16	Psalms 72-74
☐ 17	1 Chron. 20-22
☐ 18	1 Chron. 23-25
☐ 19	1 Chron. 26-29
☐ 20	2 Chron. 1-3
☐ 21	2 Chron. 4-6
☐ 22	2 Chron. 7-9
☐ 23	Psalms 75-77
☐ 24	2 Chron. 10-12
☐ 25	2 Chron. 13-15
☐ 26	2 Chron. 16-18
☐ 27	2 Chron. 19-22
☐ 28	Joel 1-3; Obadiah
☐ 29	2 Chron. 23:1-26:8
☐ 30	Psalms 78-80

JULY

Day	Book and Chapter
☐ 1	Isaiah 1-3
☐ 2	Isaiah 4-6; 2 Chron. 26:9-23
☐ 3	2 Chron. 27-29
☐ 4	2 Chron. 30-32
☐ 5	Isaiah 7-9
☐ 6	Isaiah 10-12
☐ 7	Psalms 81-83
☐ 8	Isaiah 13-15
☐ 9	Isaiah 16-18
☐ 10	Isaiah 19-21
☐ 11	Isaiah 22-24
☐ 12	Isaiah 25-27
☐ 13	Isaiah 28-30
☐ 14	Psalms 84-86
☐ 15	Isaiah 31-33
☐ 16	Isaiah 34-36
☐ 17	Isaiah 37-39
☐ 18	Isaiah 40-42
☐ 19	Isaiah 43-45
☐ 20	Isaiah 46-48
☐ 21	Psalms 87-90
☐ 22	Isaiah 49-51
☐ 23	Isaiah 52-54
☐ 24	Isaiah 55-57
☐ 25	Isaiah 58-60
☐ 26	Isaiah 61-63

☐	27	Isaiah 64-66
☐	28	Psalms 91-93
☐	29	Hosea 1-3
☐	30	Hosea 4-6
☐	31	Hosea 7-9

AUGUST

Day		Book and Chapter
☐	1	Hosea 10-12
☐	2	Hosea 13, 14; Micah 1
☐	3	Micah 2-4
☐	4	Psalms 94-96
☐	5	Micah 5-7
☐	6	Nahum 1-3
☐	7	2 Chron. 33-34; Zeph. 1
☐	8	Zeph. 2-3; 2 Chron. 35
☐	9	Hab. 1-3
☐	10	Jer. 1-3
☐	11	Psalms 97-99
☐	12	Jer. 4-6
☐	13	Jer. 11, 12, 26
☐	14	Jer. 7-9
☐	15	Jer. 10, 14, 15
☐	16	Jer. 16-18
☐	17	Jer. 19, 20, 35
☐	18	Psalms 100-102
☐	19	Jer. 25, 36, 45
☐	20	Jer. 46-49
☐	21	Jer. 13, 22, 23
☐	22	Jer. 24, 27, 28
☐	23	Jer. 29, 50-51
☐	24	Jer. 30-33
☐	25	Psalms 103-105
☐	26	Jer. 21, 34, 37
☐	27	Jer. 38, 39, 52
☐	28	Jer. 40-42
☐	29	Jer. 43-44; Lam. 1
☐	30	Lam. 2-5
☐	31	2 Chron. 36:1-8; Daniel 1-3

SEPTEMBER

Day		Book and Chapter
☐	1	Psalms 106-108
☐	2	Daniel 4-6
☐	3	Daniel 7-9

☐	4	Daniel 10-12
☐	5	2 Chron. 36:9-21; Ezekiel 1-3
☐	6	Ezekiel 4-6
☐	7	Ezekiel 7-9
☐	8	Psalms 109-111
☐	9	Ezekiel 10-12
☐	10	Ezekiel 13-16
☐	11	Ezekiel 17-20
☐	12	Ezekiel 21-24
☐	13	Ezekiel 25-28
☐	14	Ezekiel 29-32
☐	15	Psalms 112-114
☐	16	Ezekiel 33-36
☐	17	Ezekiel 37-40
☐	18	Ezekiel 41-44
☐	19	Ezekiel 45-48
☐	20	2 Chron. 36:22-23; Ezra 1-3
☐	21	Ezra 4; Haggai 1-2
☐	22	Psalms 115-117
☐	23	Zech. 1-3
☐	24	Zech. 4-6
☐	25	Zech. 7-9
☐	26	Zech. 10-12
☐	27	Zech. 13, 14
☐	28	Ezra 5-7
☐	29	Psalms 118:1–119:16
☐	30	Ezra 8-10

OCTOBER

Day		Book and Chapter
☐	1	Esther 1-3
☐	2	Esther 4-6
☐	3	Esther 7-10
☐	4	Neh. 1-3
☐	5	Neh. 4-6
☐	6	Psalms 119:17-72
☐	7	Neh. 7-9
☐	8	Neh. 10-13
☐	9	Malachi
☐	10	Matthew 1-3
☐	11	Matthew 4-7
☐	12	Matthew 8-10
☐	13	Psalms 119:73-120
☐	14	Matthew 11-13
☐	15	Matthew 14-16
☐	16	Matthew 17-19
☐	17	Matthew 20-22

☐	18	Matthew 23-25
☐	19	Matthew 26-28
☐	20	Psalms 119:121-176
☐	21	Mark 1-4
☐	22	Mark 5-8
☐	23	Mark 9-12
☐	24	Mark 13-16
☐	25	Luke 1-4
☐	26	Luke 5-8
☐	27	Psalms 120-122
☐	28	Luke 9-12
☐	29	Luke 13-16
☐	30	Luke 17-20
☐	31	Luke 21-24

NOVEMBER

Day		Book and Chapter
☐	1	John 1-3
☐	2	John 4-6
☐	3	Psalms 123-125
☐	4	John 7-9
☐	5	John 10-12
☐	6	John 13-15
☐	7	John 16-18
☐	8	John 19-21
☐	9	Acts 1-4
☐	10	Psalms 126-128
☐	11	Acts 5:1-8:3
☐	12	Acts 8:4-11:18
☐	13	Acts 11:19-14:28
☐	14	James
☐	15	Galatians
☐	16	Acts 15-17:10
☐	17	Psalms 129-131
☐	18	Philippians
☐	19	1 Thess.
☐	20	2 Thess.; Acts 17:11; 18:11
☐	21	1 Cor. 1-3
☐	22	1 Cor. 4-7
☐	23	1 Cor. 8:1-11:1
☐	24	Psalms 131-134

☐	25	1 Cor. 11:2-14:40
☐	26	1 Cor. 15-16
☐	27	2 Cor. 1-5
☐	28	2 Cor. 6-9
☐	29	2 Cor. 10-13
☐	30	Acts 18:12-19:41; Eph. 1, 2

DECEMBER

Day		Book and Chapter
☐	1	Psalms 135-137
☐	2	Eph. 3-6
☐	3	Romans 1-3
☐	4	Romans 4-6
☐	5	Romans 7-9
☐	6	Romans 10-12
☐	7	Romans 13-16
☐	8	Psalms 138-140
☐	9	Acts 20-22
☐	10	Acts 23-25
☐	11	Acts 26-28
☐	12	Colossians
☐	13	Heb. 1-4
☐	14	Heb. 5-8
☐	15	Psalms 141-144
☐	16	Heb. 9-11
☐	17	Heb. 12-13; Titus
☐	18	Philemon
☐	19	1 Tim.; 2 Tim.
☐	20	1 Peter
☐	21	1 John
☐	22	Psalms 145-147
☐	23	2 Peter; 2, 3 John; Jude
☐	24	Rev. 1-3
☐	25	Rev. 4-7
☐	26	Rev. 8-10
☐	27	Rev. 11-13
☐	28	Rev. 14-17
☐	29	Psalms 148-150
☐	30	Rev. 18-20
☐	31	Rev. 21-22